THE UNCITRAL MODEL LAW AND A͡
ARBITRATION LA͡

In the Asia-Pacific, 38 jurisdictions have adop.   ͜CITRAL Model
Law on International Commercial Arbitration. This book looks at how
the text and the principles of the Model Law have been implemented
(or not) in key Asian jurisdictions. Most of the jurisdictions covered in
this book have declared that they have adopted the Model Law but often
with significant modifications. Even when jurisdictions adopt some provisions of the Model Law verbatim, their courts may have interpreted
these provisions in a manner inconsistent with their goals and with
how they are interpreted internationally. When a jurisdiction has not
adopted the Model Law, the chapter compares its legislation to the Model
Law to determine whether it is consistent with its principles. Each chapter
follows the structure of the Model Law allowing the reader easily to
compare the arbitration laws of different jurisdictions on each topic.

GARY F. BELL is an associate professor at the National University of
Singapore (NUS) where he teaches arbitration, Indonesian law, Inter-
national and comparative sale of goods and legal systems of Asia and is
Director of the LL.M in arbitration. He is also Director of the Asian Law
Institute. He co-edited *Law and Legal Institutions of Asia: Traditions,
Adaptations and Innovations* (Cambridge University Press, 2011) with
E. Ann Black. He acts frequently as arbitrator.

THE UNCITRAL MODEL LAW AND ASIAN ARBITRATION LAWS

Implementation and Comparisons

Edited by

GARY F. BELL

National University of Singapore

CAMBRIDGE
UNIVERSITY PRESS

University Printing House, Cambridge CB2 8BS, United Kingdom

One Liberty Plaza, 20th Floor, New York, NY 10006, USA

477 Williamstown Road, Port Melbourne, VIC 3207, Australia

314–321, 3rd Floor, Plot 3, Splendor Forum, Jasola District Centre, New Delhi – 110025, India

79 Anson Road, #06–04/06, Singapore 079906

Cambridge University Press is part of the University of Cambridge.

It furthers the University's mission by disseminating knowledge in the pursuit
of education, learning, and research at the highest international levels of excellence.

www.cambridge.org
Information on this title: www.cambridge.org/9781107183971
DOI: 10.1017/9781316875070

© Cambridge University Press 2018

First published 2018

Printed and bound in Great Britain by Clays Ltd, Elcograf S.p.A.

A catalogue record for this publication is available from the British Library.

Library of Congress Cataloging-in-Publication Data
Names: Bell, Gary F., editor.
Title: The UNCITRAL model law and Asian arbitration laws / edited by Gary F. Bell,
National University of Singapore.
Description: New York : Cambridge University Press, 2018. | Includes bibliographical
references and index.
Identifiers: LCCN 2018013762 | ISBN 9781107183971 (hardback : alk. paper) |
ISBN 9781316635315 (pbk. : alk. paper)
Subjects: LCSH: Arbitration and award–Asia. | International commercial arbitration. |
United Nations Commission on International Trade Law. | Law–International unification.
Classification: LCC K2400 .U525 2018 | DDC 341.5/22095–dc23
LC record available at https://lccn.loc.gov/2018013762

ISBN 978-1-107-18397-1 Hardback
ISBN 978-1-316-63531-5 Paperback

À ma sœur, Kathleen.

CONTENTS

CONTRIBUTORS

SHAHLA ALI's research and practice centre on questions of governance, development and the resolution of cross-border disputes in the Asia Pacific region. She is an associate professor and associate dean (International) and Deputy Director of the LL.M in arbitration and dispute resolution in the Faculty of Law at the University of Hong Kong. Dr Ali is the author of *Court Mediation Reform: Efficiency, Confidence and Perceptions of Justice* (2018), *Governing Disasters: Engaging Local Populations in Humanitarian Relief* (Cambridge University Press, 2016), *Consumer Financial Dispute Resolution in a Comparative Context* (Cambridge University Press, 2013) and *Resolving Disputes in the Asia Pacific Region* (2010) and writes for law journals in the area of comparative ADR. She received her JD and PhD in jurisprudence and social policy from the University of California Berkeley, an MA in conflict resolution from Landegg University and a BA in international relations and Chinese language from Stanford University. She has consulted with USAID, IFC/World Bank and the United Nations on issues pertaining to access to justice, peace process negotiation training and land use conflict resolution. She serves as a bilingual arbitrator (English/Chinese) with CIETAC, HKIAC (ADNDRC), SIAC and is a member of the IBA Drafting Committee for Investor–State Mediation Rules, the DOJ Mediation Regulatory Framework Sub-Committee, the UN Mediation Roster and the FDRC Appointments Committee.

GARY F. BELL is an associate professor at the National University of Singapore (NUS) where he teaches arbitration, Indonesian law, international and comparative sale of goods and legal systems of Asia and is Director of the LL.M in arbitration. He acts regularly as an arbitrator, is on the panels of the SIAC and Korean Commercial Arbitration Board and has been appointed to many ICC arbitrations. He trained in both common law and civil law at McGill and has an LL.M from Columbia University. He is the Director of the Asian Law Institute (ASLI) – a

network of some 100 law schools in Asia. He has published on Indonesian law, the UN Convention on Contracts for the International Sale of
Goods (CISG), on arbitration and on comparative law. He co-edited *Law
and Legal Institutions of Asia: Traditions, Adaptations and Innovations*
(Cambridge University Press, 2011) with E. Ann Black, is one of the
editors of the *Asian Journal of Comparative Law* and is on the Executive
Editorial Board of the *American Journal of Comparative Law*.

CHOONG YEOW CHOY is a professor and former Dean at the Faculty of
Law, University of Malaya, Malaysia. He is currently a member of the
Judicial Appointments Commission of Malaysia. His primary areas of
research include transnational civil litigation, international commercial
arbitration and the administration of the civil justice system. Yeow Choy
travels extensively and collaborates with scholars and academics from
around the globe. He has taught courses in similar areas in the Duke Law
School Summer Program, Chulalongkorn University, Kyushu University,
the University of Hong Kong, the National University of Singapore and
the University of Tokyo. He obtained his LL.B from the University of
Malaya, his LL.M from Harvard Law School and his PhD from the
University of Melbourne. Yeow Choy is also an advocate and solicitor
(non-practising) of the High Court of Malaya.

DANG XUAN HOP is a full time arbitrator based in Hanoi, Vietnam. Before
setting up Hop Dang's Chambers in Hanoi, he was a partner at an international law firm for many years with a strong practice in cross-border
infrastructure projects and international commercial arbitration. He has
been a Visiting Senior Fellow at the Law Faculty, National University of
Singapore and a Senior Fellow at the Law Faculty, University of Melbourne.
He advised the Vietnamese government in drafting the Law on Commercial
Arbitration 2010 and has acted as arbitrator in many disputes at the
Singapore International Arbitration Centre, the Swedish Chamber of Commerce, the Vietnam International Arbitration Centre, the ICC, the Finland
Arbitration Institute and elsewhere. He has taught in law schools in Viet-
nam, Singapore, Japan, Australia and China. He holds law degrees from
both Vietnam and Australia and wrote his doctoral thesis at the University
of Oxford on the choice of international law in state contracts.

GUO YU is an associate professor and the Director of the Maritime Law
Research Centre of the Law School, Beijing University. She obtained her
master's degree from Shanghai Maritime University, her PhD from

Beijing University and her LL.M from the University of Cambridge. She is a faculty member at the Law School of Beijing University, where she has been teaching since 1996. Her main research interests are in the fields of maritime law and international commercial law. She works as arbitrator for several prestigious arbitration organizations both at home and abroad. Her publications include: *A Study on the Bill of Lading* (1997), *The Law of International Sale of Goods* (1999), *The Law of International Economic Organization* (1999), *Carriage of Goods by Sea* (2000) and *The Spirit of Maritime Law: Theory and Practice in China* (2006).

HISASHI HARATA is Professor of Law at the University of Tokyo, Faculty of Law, where he teaches private international law, including international civil procedure and international commercial arbitration. His specializes in private international law and comparative law, especially between the Western and Asian systems. His current research focuses on reconstructing a framework for transnational law. He has conducted research on the historical background of the 1923 Geneva Protocol and the 1927 Geneva Convention, focusing on the ICC and the New York Chamber of Commerce. He has been a visiting scholar at Università di Napoli Federico II Dipartimento di Diritto Romano (2005–2007), National University of Singapore (2013), a distinguished visiting scholar at Cornell University (2014) and has delivered lectures at several foreign universities, including Università di Salento, Università di Napoli, Michigan University, Chicago Kent College of Law, Cornell University and Columbia University. His publications include: 'Interpretation and Application of the New York Convention in Japan', in George A. Bermann (ed.), *Recognition and Enforcement of Foreign Arbitral Awards: The Interpretation and Application of the New York Convention by National Courts* (2017) [in English], 'Characteristics and Background of the Understanding of Private International Law in the Last Decades of the Nineteenth Century (1)–(4)' 133 *Hogaku kyokai zassi* (2016) [in Japanese], and 'L'exterritorialité, la juridiction consulaire et le droit international privé : une réflexion sur le droit international privé à la fin de XIXème siècle', in Luigi Nuzzo and Miloš Vec (eds.), *Constructing International Law: The Birth of a Discipline* (2012) [in French].

AAKANKSHA KUMAR is a doctoral candidate at the National Law University, Jodhpur, India (NLU). Until May 2017, she was an assistant professor of law at NLU, where she taught courses in international commercial arbitration, ADR and the law of IPR in international trade.

During this time, she was the head of the Centre for Advanced Research and Training in Arbitration Law as its Executive Director and also served as the faculty advisor on the editorial board of *Indian Journal of Arbitration Law*. Prior to this she was a full-time research associate at the School of Law, ITM University, Gurgaon, where she taught courses in ADR, comparative competition law and private international law. She is an alumnus of the Hidayatullah National Law University, Raipur, India, where she won fifteen gold medals for exemplary academic performance. She graduated from the Faculty of Law, National University of Singapore, in June 2013 with a specialized master's degree in international and comparative law, and completed a directed research dissertation entitled, 'The Taking of Evidence in International Arbitration: A New Legal Regime', supervised by Gary F. Bell. Currently she is pursuing her doctoral studies at the National Law University, Jodhpur in the area of celebrity personality rights.

CHANG-FA LO has been Justice of the Constitutional Court since October 2011. He was Chair Professor and Lifetime Distinguished Professor at the National Taiwan University (NTU). He was Dean of NTU College of Law; the founding director of Asian WTO and International Health Law and Policy (ACWH) of NTU; Commissioner of the Fair Trade Commission (in charge of competition law); Commissioner of International Trade Commission (in charge of the safeguard measures and the injury determination for anti-dumping and countervailing measures); and legal advisor for Taiwan's GATT/WTO accession negotiations. In his capacity as the Director of ACWH, he launched two English-language law journals: the *Asian Journal of WTO and International Health Law and Policy* (SSCI listed) and *Contemporary Asia Arbitration Journal*, in 2006 and 2008 respectively. He served as panellist for two WTO disputes and member of the Permanent Group of Experts (PGE) under the ASCM of WTO. He was a practising lawyer before he went to Harvard Law School, where he received his LL.M (1987) and SJD (1989). He has authored more than 100 publications, including journal papers, books and book chapters.

JOHN LUMBANTOBING is an associate lecturer in international law and arbitration at the Faculty of Law, Universitas Katolik Parahyangan, having practised commercial litigation and international arbitration in Jakarta. His main research interests and publications are in the fields of arbitration, international investment law and the domestic application of international law. He obtained his LL.B from Universitas Katolik Parahyangan and an LL.M in international law from the University of Cambridge. He is also the current Chartered Institute of Arbitrators' YMG Ambassador for Indonesia and is admitted to the bar in Indonesia.

MINN NAING OO is Managing Director, Allen & Gledhill (Myanmar) Co. Ltd and Partner, Allen & Gledhill Singapore LLP. He was previously the CEO and Registrar of the Singapore International Arbitration Centre and before that a Director at the Ministry of Trade and Industry Singapore, with oversight for Singapore's trade agreements and World Trade Organization (WTO) related matters, including policy review, formulation and negotiations. He is also a member of the expert panel of the Singapore Management University Centre for Cross-Border Commercial Law in Asia and a former member of the Singapore Academy of Law Promotion of the Singapore Law Committee. Minn has been appointed a WTO dispute panellist for disputes between WTO member states. He is also a fellow of the Chartered Institute of Arbitrators and the Singapore Institute of Arbitrators.

SUNDRA RAJOO is the Director of the Asian International Arbitration Centre (AIAC), formerly known as the Kuala Lumpur Regional Centre for Arbitration and was the President of the Chartered Institute of Arbitrators (CIArb) in 2016. Sundra is a chartered arbitrator with extensive arbitration experience that includes over 200 appointments locally and internationally. He serves on the panel of numerous international arbitral institutions and organizations. He is the chairman of the Asian Domain Name Dispute Resolution Centre and deputy chairman of the Adjudicatory Chamber of FIFA Ethics Committee. Sundra is also an advocate and solicitor of the High Court of Malaya (non-practising), a professional architect and a registered town planner. He is a visiting professor at the Faculty of Built Environment, University of Technology Malaysia. He is an adjunct professor with the Faculty of Law, University of Malaysia. He has authored and co-authored a number of books on construction law and arbitration. In July 2015, Sundra was conferred an honorary doctorate in laws from the Leeds Beckett University in England.

RENA M. RICO-PAMFILO is Professor of International Commercial Arbitration at the Ateneo de Manila University Law School. She lectures on mandatory continuing legal education in the Philippines and in the

USA. She was a member of the working group of the Supreme Court Committee on the Special ADR Rules, which was promulgated by the Supreme Court and became effective on October 2009. She is also chief legal counsel of Seawood Resources, Inc., a Philippines-based investment company. She was admitted to the Philippine Bar (2001) and the New York Bar (2009). She gained her JD from the Ateneo de Manila University Law School in 2000 and her LL.M from the National University of Singapore in 2004. She was a Sheridan Fellow at NUS and was awarded the ASEAN Scholarship. She has authored various publications on international commercial arbitration in the Philippines.

HARISANKAR K. SATHYAPALAN is a doctoral candidate at the Faculty of Law of the National University of Singapore. Prior to joining NUS, he was an assistant professor at the National Law University Jodhpur, India, where he served as the founding Executive Director of the Centre for Advanced Research and Training in Arbitration Law. In this capacity, he established the *Indian Journal of Arbitration Law* and served as its founding faculty advisor. Before that, he was an assistant lecturer at the Hidayatullah National Law University, Raipur, India. Harisankar holds an LL.M degree from the Indian Law Institute, New Delhi and has attended The Hague Academy of International Law on a full scholarship. He completed a BSc in Science and an LL.B from Mahatma Gandhi University, Kerala and has been a visiting research scholar at the International Institute for the Unification of Private Law (UNIDROIT), Rome. He has published articles in *Arbitration International, Journal of International Arbitration* and *International Arbitration Law Review.*

HI-TAEK SHIN retired as a professor at Seoul National University (SNU) School of Law in August 2017. Prior to joining the law faculty at SNU in 2007, he was a partner at Kim & Chang, the leading Korean law firm, where he specialized in cross-border investment projects and resolution of disputes arising therefrom. He sits regularly as an arbitrator both in investment treaty arbitrations and international commercial arbitrations. He is on the panel of arbitrators of ICSID, HKIAC, ICDR, SIAC and Korean Commercial Arbitration Board. He is currently serving as the Chairman of KCAB INTERNATIONAL, an independent division of the Korea Commercial Arbitration Board. He was a member of the task force of the Ministry of Justice of Korea which recommended the 2016 amendment to the Korean Arbitration Act. He received LL.M and JSD degrees from Yale Law School, and LL.B and LL.M degrees from SNU.

GATOT SOEMARTONO holds a senior lectureship in law at Tarumana-gara University (Untar) in Jakarta, Indonesia and serves as the Vice-Rector of the university. He obtained a BSc in economics from Dipone-goro University, an LL.B and an MSc in management from Gadjah Mada University, an LL.M from Harvard Law School, and a PhD in law from the National University of Singapore (NUS), where he was awarded a graduate research scholarship and the President's graduate fellowship. He teaches investment law, international business transactions, arbitra-tion and alternative dispute resolution and environmental law. He is the author of 'Interpretation and Application of the New York Convention in Indonesia', in George A. Bermann (ed.), *Recognition and Implementation of Foreign Arbitral Awards: Application of the New York Convention by National Courts* (2017).

FOREWORD

The use of arbitration to resolve international commercial disputes is as ancient as it is universal. Businesses, as well as states and individuals, have resorted to arbitration to resolve their disagreements since the dawn of recorded history. They have done so for everything from border disputes to criminal cases to commercial controversies to domestic feuds. In many respects, arbitration has been the handmaiden of the rule of law throughout human history – particularly in cross-border and other international disputes.

In recent decades, the use of international arbitration has become ever more prevalent and essential to the rule of law in international matters. Central to this development have been the United Nations Convention on the Recognition of Enforcement of Foreign Arbitration Awards ('New York Convention' or 'Convention') and the UNCITRAL Model Law on International Commercial Arbitration ('Model Law'). Taken together, these two instruments have provided the legal framework for the dramatic growth in international arbitration over the past three decades. Asian states have been at the forefront of adoption of both the New York Convention and the Model Law – with most Asian states having ratified the Convention and nearly forty states having adopted the Model Law.

Although the Convention and Model Law have been central to the development of international arbitration, both globally and in Asia, the actual application of both instruments by national courts is at least equally important. Unless the Convention and the Model Law are faithfully interpreted as applied by national courts, they will not and cannot fulfil their purposes. This book, thoughtfully edited by Professor Gary Bell of the National University of Singapore, provides a detailed and comprehensive examination of the treatment of international arbitration and the Model Law in a dozen leading Asian jurisdictions, including India, mainland China, Hong Kong, Singapore and Malaysia.

Each chapter of the book explores the law and practice of international arbitration in one of these jurisdictions.

The chapters of this book provide countless valuable insights. The challenges of interpreting the Model Law and the instrument's benefits are illustrated by, for example, studies of Indian and Singaporean judicial decisions. The difficulties encountered by jurisdictions that have not adopted the Model Law are explored in chapters examining, for example, mainland Chinese and Taiwanese judicial decisions.

More than anything else, this book confirms the critical importance of international law to international arbitration – and vice versa. The uniform international standards prescribed by the Convention and the Model Law have been essential to the success of international arbitration. Conversely, the efficacy of the arbitral process has been essential to the rule of law. Arbitration has continued its historic role as handmaiden to the rule of law – providing a stable and predictable, but flexible and nuanced, means of international dispute resolution that has enabled international trade and investment to flourish over the past thirty years. This book helps facilitate that continued efficacy and growth of international arbitration by focusing attention on both past achievements and topics for future improvement.

Gary Born
Singapore

ABBREVIATIONS

ADR	alternative dispute resolution
ADR Act	Republic Act No. 9285; Alternative Dispute Resolution Act of 2004 (Philippines)
AO	Arbitration Ordinance Cap. 609 (Hong Kong)
BAC	Beijing Arbitration Commission
CAL	Arbitration Law of the People's Republic of China
CIETAC	The China International Economic and Trade Arbitration Commission
CMAC	China Maritime Arbitration Commission
CPC	Code of Civil Procedure (India)
CPI	Cargill Philippines, Inc.
FTZ	free trade zone
HKIAC	Hong Kong International Arbitration Centre
JAA	Japan Arbitration Act
KAA	Korea Arbitration Act
KCAB	Korean Commercial Arbitration Board
LCA	Law on Commercial Arbitration 2010 (Vietnam)
ML	UNCITRAL Model Law on International Commercial Arbitration 1985, amended 2006
ML 1985	UNCITRAL Model Law on International Commercial Arbitration 1985, UN General Assembly Resolution 40/72 (11 December 1985)
MOJ	Ministry of Justice (Korea)
NYC	Convention on the Recognition and Enforcement of Foreign Arbitral Awards, New York, 10 June 1958, in force 7 June 1959, 330 UNTS 4739
OCA	Ordinance on Commercial Arbitration 2003 (Vietnam)
PDRCI	Philippine Dispute Resolution Center, Inc.
PDRCI Rules	Arbitration Rules of the PDRCI
PGSMC	Pacific General Steel Manufacturing Corp.
SHIAC	Shanghai International Arbitration Center
Special ADR Rules	Special Rules of Court on Alternative Dispute Resolution (Philippines)

~

Introduction

The Model Law and its Importance in Asia

The United Nations Commission on International Trade Law (UNCI-TRAL) adopted the UNCITRAL Model Law on International Commercial Arbitration in 1985 and amended it in 2006 ('ML').[1] As of 30 November 2017, legislation based on the ML has been adopted in seventy-six states in a total of 107 jurisdictions.[2]

There are thirty-eight states or jurisdictions in the Asia-Pacific[3] which claim that their law governing international commercial arbitration is based on a version of the ML (including Australian states or territories). Among these, one can find seven of the ten ASEAN countries.[4] The ML is therefore very important in Asia.

In fact, none of the most popular seats for international commercial arbitration in Europe and the Americas has adopted the ML: London, Paris, New York and Geneva are all in jurisdictions that have not adopted

Gary F. Bell is an associate professor at the National University of Singapore. Special thanks to the EW Barker Centre for Law & Business at the Faculty of Law of the National University of Singapore for financing my participation in the conference entitled, 'The UNCITRAL Model Law on International Commercial Arbitration in Asia', which led to this book.

[1] UNCITRAL Model Law on International Commercial Arbitration 1985, amended 2006, UN Documents A/40/17, annex I and A/61/17, annex I, available at www.uncitral.org/pdf/ english/texts/arbitration/ml-arb/07-86998_Ebook.pdf. The original 1985 version is available at www.uncitral.org/pdf/english/texts/arbitration/ml-arb/06-54671_Ebook.pdf.

[2] See www.uncitral.org/uncitral/en/uncitral_texts/arbitration/1985Model_arbitration_status .html (accessed 30 November 2017).

[3] Armenia, Australia (Australian Capital Territory, New South Wales, Northern Territory, Queensland, South Australia, Tasmania, Victoria, Western Australia), Azerbaijan, Bahrain, Bangladesh, Brunei Darussalam, Cambodia, Egypt*, Fiji, Georgia, Hong Kong (China), India, Iran, Japan, Jordan, Korea (Republic of), Macao (China), Malaysia, Mongolia, Myanmar, New Zealand, Oman, Philippines, Qatar, Russia*, Singapore, Sri Lanka, Thailand, Turkey* and Turkmenistan. The countries with an asterisk cross two continents, including Asia.

[4] Brunei Darussalam, Cambodia, Malaysia, Myanmar, Philippines, Singapore and Thailand.

the ML.[5] The only two top international arbitration seats that have their law based on the ML are in Asia: Singapore and Hong Kong are two very successful international arbitration seats which have adopted the ML.

The second largest jurisdiction in the world, India, is a ML jurisdiction. However, the largest and fourth largest jurisdictions in the world, the People's Republic of China and Indonesia, are not ML jurisdictions.

However, not all ML jurisdictions are equal. On its website, the UNCITRAL posts the following disclaimer:

> Disclaimer: A model law is created as a suggested pattern for law-makers to consider adopting as part of their domestic legislation. Since States enacting legislation based upon a model law have the flexibility to depart from the text, the above list is only indicative of the enactments that were made known to the UNCITRAL Secretariat. The legislation of each State should be considered in order to identify the exact nature of any possible deviation from the model in the legislative text that was adopted. [. . .][6]

It is therefore impossible to know merely by looking at the list of jurisdictions that claim they have legislation based on the ML whether they have actually adopted the text of the ML in full, only in part or, in some cases, not at all. Hong Kong and Singapore, for example, have substantially adopted the text and structure of the ML with, however, some significant modifications. There are also jurisdictions that say they have adopted the ML but in fact have not adopted its text at all, but rather claim to have adopted the principles of the ML.[7]

There are also many jurisdictions in Asia that have not claimed to have adopted the text or the principles of the ML, including, for example, the People's Republic of China[8] and Indonesia. One may still wish to know the extent to which their arbitration laws are similar to or different from the ML and this is why such jurisdictions are included in this book.

The book is the result of a thorough examination of the extent to which the text and/or the principles of the ML have been adopted in

---

[5] 'London, Paris, New York and Geneva are the seats that were used most frequently by respondents over the past five years.' *2010 International Arbitration Survey: Choices in International Arbitration*, www.arbitration.qmul.ac.uk/media/arbitration/docs/2010_InternationalArbitrationSurveyReport.pdf at 17.
[6] See www.uncitral.org/uncitral/en/uncitral_texts/arbitration/1985Model_arbitration_status.html.
[7] Outside Asia, Quebec is the prime example of this – it claims to have been the first jurisdiction to adopt the ML, but its Code of Civil Procedure does not in fact adopt any of the wording of the ML in either French or English.
[8] Hong Kong and Macao are ML jurisdictions.

twelve jurisdictions from East, Southeast and South Asia. More specifically, it will investigate the following issues:

1. When a jurisdiction claims to have adopted the ML, the chapter on that country will check whether and to what extent it has adopted the text of the ML, with or without modification, and whether modifications are generally consistent with the principles of the ML. There are eight jurisdictions in this category in this book, all eight of which are found in Part 1 of the book.
2. If a jurisdiction makes no claim to have adopted the ML, the chapter will nonetheless compare the national/internal law with the principles and provisions of the ML to find similarities and differences. There are four jurisdictions in this category in this book, all four of which are found in Part 2 of the book.
3. Beyond the text of the law compared with the text of the ML, each chapter will also analyse whether the jurisprudence or case law interpreted the law in a way that is consistent with how the ML has been interpreted internationally.

This book is the result of a research project financed by the EW Barker Centre for Law & Business at the Faculty of Law of the National University of Singapore. Early drafts of the chapters were first presented at a conference held at the National University of Singapore on 28 and 29 May 2015 and financed by the EW Barker Centre for Law & Business.

Choice of the Jurisdictions and Authors

This book could not realistically cover all the jurisdictions of Asia. I therefore had to pick some. Of course, the three largest jurisdictions in Asia (the People's Republic of China, India and Indonesia) had to be included. Japan, because of its economic importance, also had to be included. The 'four Asian tigers' (Hong Kong, Singapore, Republic of Korea, i.e., South Korea, and Taiwan) were also included and in the case of Singapore and Hong Kong this could also have been justified by the fact that they are very popular seats for international arbitrations. The Philippines is a large Southeast Asian country that has adopted the ML and Vietnam is one that has not. Malaysia is also a ML country and has the Kuala Lumpur Regional Centre for Arbitration (KLRCA) recently renamed the Asian International Arbitration Centre (AIAC). Myanmar was included as an example of a country that recently became a party to the New York Convention and adopted a new law based on the ML.

There could have been many other chapters and I regret that I could not include more jurisdictions in this exercise, but I see this as a good start.

The authors of the chapters were chosen carefully. They are a mix of academics and top arbitration practitioners. Some are very experienced, others are bright young stars. Most of them I have come to know over the years either because they studied at or visited the Faculty of Law at the National University of Singapore where I teach. Others I knew because they were associated with the Asian Law Institute of which I am the Director. In other cases, I have met colleagues through my arbitration practice. They have all produced very impressive accounts of how the ML was implemented in their jurisdiction or how their jurisdiction's law compares to the ML.

How to Read this Book: The Contents of Each Chapter

Each and every chapter has the exact same structure which follows the structure of the ML. This makes comparisons between the ML and the law of a given jurisdiction easier and, in addition, makes comparisons between the different jurisdictions much easier. The ML is the measurement against which every arbitration law is compared in this book. The outline of each and every chapter, taken from the ML, is as follows:

Introduction
    Part I General Provisions of the Model Law (Articles 1 to 6)
    Part II Arbitration Agreement (Articles 7 to 9)
    Part III Composition of Arbitral Tribunal (Articles 10 to 15)
    Part IV Jurisdiction of Arbitral Tribunal (Article 16)
Part IV-A Interim Measures and Preliminary Orders (Articles 17 to 17J)
        Sub-Part I Measures and Orders by the Tribunal (Articles 17 to 17G)
        Sub-Part II Recognition and Enforcement of Interim Measures (Articles 17H to 17I)
        Sub-Part III Court-Ordered Interim Measures (Article 17J)[9]
    Part V Conduct of Arbitral Proceedings (Articles 18 to 27)

[9] These sub-parts are not stated as such in the ML, but the editor thought they were useful categories for the purpose of comparison. When a jurisdiction did not implement the provisions of the 2006 version of the ML on interim measures, the relevant chapter may have omitted the sub-parts under Part IV-A.

Part VI Making of Award and Termination of Proceedings (Articles 28 to 33)

Part VII Recourse against Award (Article 34)

Part VIII Recognition and Enforcement of Awards (Articles 35 to 36)

Conclusion

There are therefore many ways to read this book. If you are interested only in the law of a particular jurisdiction, you may of course read the relevant chapter. However, if you are interested in, for example, interim measures in Asia, you could read Part IV-A of each chapter and quickly get an overview of interim measures in twelve Asian jurisdictions.

The fact that each chapter has the same structure allows for comparisons to be drawn between them. This is the case even for the four jurisdictions that have not adopted the ML – the authors have compared their law to the ML.

It would be too sensitive a task for me to comment on which jurisdictions better implement the ML and I therefore leave it to the reader to pass judgement on this, but, as you will see, the authors candidly describe the law of their jurisdiction, including its shortcomings, therefore allowing for an honest evaluation of the implementation of the ML or its principles by both the legislator and the courts.

I hope that this book will contribute to knowledge of the ML and of its implementation in Asia.

PART I

Jurisdictions That Have Adopted the Model Law:
Implementation and Comparisons

Hong Kong Special Administrative Region, China

The Adoption of the UNCITRAL Model Law on International Commercial Arbitration in Hong Kong

SHAHLA ALI

Introduction

In 1985, the Hong Kong Law Reform Commission was asked to consider whether the UNCITRAL Model Law on International Commercial Arbitration ('ML') should be adopted as part of the law in Hong Kong, and to make recommendations on modifications to the Arbitration Ordinance accordingly.[1] The Commission held the opinion that the adoption of the ML as part of Hong Kong law, subject to a few minor changes (including merely one deletion and four additions to the ML), would bring Hong Kong a great benefit.[2] Their proposal was fully implemented by Arbitration (Amendment) (No. 2) Ordinance in 1989.[3]

Coming into effect in June 2011, the new Arbitration Ordinance Cap. 609 ('AO') established in Hong Kong a unified legal regime for both domestic and international arbitration based on the international principles of the ML.

Shahla Ali is an associate professor and associate dean (International) and Deputy Director of the LL.M in arbitration and dispute resolution in the Faculty of Law at the University of Hong Kong. The author thanks the EW Barker Centre for Law & Business at the Faculty of Law of the National University of Singapore for financing her participation in the conference entitled, 'The UNCITRAL Model Law on International Commercial Arbitration in Asia', which led to this book. Special thanks also to GRF Grant (HKU 17603215) and the HKU University grants committee (HKU 201409176036) and for the research assistance of William Yang and Florence Tse.

[1] The Law Reform Commission of Hong Kong, Report on the Adoption of the UNCITRAL Model Law of Arbitration 1 (1987).
[2] *Ibid.* at 5, 12, 18–26.
[3] See Law Reform Commission of Hong Kong, *Implementation* (last revised 12 May 2015), www.hkreform.gov.hk/en/implementation/#a.

Whilst the AO gives legal effect to a majority of expressly stated provisions of the ML,[4] this is subject to the application of certain interpretational limitations and amendments tailoring the procedure to existing arbitration mechanisms and procedures in Hong Kong. Some of these jurisdictional characteristics are reflected in previous local cases interpreting various ML provisions, which continue to provide guidance as to the proper application of the new Ordinance. Whilst the bulk of the ML provisions were reproduced verbatim or near-verbatim to the AO, provisions relating to the recognition and enforcement of arbitral awards were not included in the Ordinance. These and other minor omissions have, however, been alternatively provided for.

The ML is largely integrated into the new Arbitration Ordinance, in the hope of '[facilitating] the "fair and speedy" resolution of disputes, providing for maximum party autonomy and minimal court intervention'.[5] The new Ordinance has distinguished features, including: (1) abolishing the distinction between 'domestic' and 'international' arbitration; (2) availing interim measures (by both the court and the arbitral tribunal); (3) codifying the new obligation of confidentiality; (4) promoting alternative dispute resolution; and (5) including provisions in regard of the enforcement of arbitral awards.[6]

Prior to the enactment of the new Arbitration Ordinance, under the old dual regime in Hong Kong, there was a distinction between international and domestic arbitration. Legal practitioners had first to analyse within which category the case fell in order to apply the correct provisions to the arbitration. The new Ordinance abolishes such a distinction, and places all arbitration in Hong Kong under the single unified regime on the basis of the ML.[7]

However, under pressure mainly from the construction industry, Schedule 2 to the new Arbitration Ordinance allows parties to opt into some old arbitration provisions of the domestic regime. Section 2 of Schedule 2 allows the court to consolidate arbitral proceedings and hearings. Section 3 of Schedule 2 states the court may decide any

---

[4] Typically, a section of the AO which adopts an article of the ML without modification would simply state: 'Article X of the UNCITRAL Model Law, the text of which is set out below, has effect: [. . .]', followed by the text of the article of the ML.
[5] Justin D'Agostino, Simon Chapman and Ula Cartwright-Finch for Herbert Smith Freehills, *New Hong Kong Arbitration Ordinance Comes Into Effect*, Kluwer Arbitration Blog (1 June 2011), http://kluwerarbitrationblog.com/blog/2011/06/01/new-hong-kong-arbitration-ordinance-comes-into-effect/.
[6] *Ibid.*   [7] *Ibid.*

preliminary question of law. Section 4 of Schedule 2 permits a party to apply to the court challenging an award in the arbitral proceedings on the ground of serious irregularity. Section 5 of Schedule 2 allows a party to appeal to the court on a question of law arising from arbitral awards. However, this greater extent of court intervention would only apply if it is expressly stated in the arbitration agreement, or under an agreement of 'domestic arbitration' entered into before or within six years of the new Ordinance coming into effect.[8]

Part I   General Provisions of the Model Law (Articles 1 to 6)

Article 1   Scope of Application

Article 1, concerning the application of the ML and the definition of 'international' arbitration, was not adopted by the jurisdiction of Hong Kong. However, section 7 of the Arbitration Ordinance Cap. 609 does make reference to section 5 as a viable substitute for article 1.[9] Specifically, section 5 only covers the applicabilities of arbitration agreements entered into outside and inside Hong Kong,[10] and appears much less extensive than article 1, which also discusses different interpretations of international arbitration. It seems that the new Arbitration Ordinance did not adopt ML articles 1(3) and (4) which define when an arbitration is 'international' since any such definition is not useful in light of the abolishment of the distinction between 'domestic' and 'international' arbitration under the new arbitration regime.[11]

Article 2   Definitions and Rules of Interpretation

Article 2, concerning the definitions of 'arbitration' and the related interpretation rules, was not adopted verbatim. Section 8(1) of the

---

[8] *Ibid.*

[9] Section 7 AO:

> Section 5 has effect in substitution for article 1 of the UNCITRAL Model Law.

[10] Section 5(1) AO:

> Subject to subsection (2), this Ordinance applies to an arbitration under an arbitration agreement, whether or not the agreement is entered into in Hong Kong, if the place of arbitration is in Hong Kong.

[11] See Department of Justice, Consultation Paper on the Reform of the Law of Arbitration in Hong Kong and Draft Arbitration Bill 11 (December 2007), www.gov.hk/en/residents/government/publication/consultation/docs/2008/arbitration.pdf.

Arbitration Ordinance Cap. 609 does mention that section 2 has effect in substitution of article 2.[12] In turn, section 2 makes minor adjustments to the original substance of the UNCITRAL definition, such as adding that an arbitral tribunal is defined as 'includ[ing] an umpire' and applying the meaning of 'court' to only mean the Court of First Instance (CFI) rather than the entire judicial system.[13]

However, section 2 mostly does not discuss article 2(d), (e) and (f) of the ML, which deal with authorizing any third party to determine a certain issue as well as granting the same legal provisions to 'claims' and 'counter-claims' the same way.

Notwithstanding the differences between article 2 and section 2, section 8(2) does state that 'a reference to this Ordinance in section 2 is to be construed as including the UNCITRAL Model Law.'[14] Thus it can be said that section 2 is essentially consistent with the intention of article 2.

Section 5(1) states that the Ordinance applies to an arbitration in Hong Kong, whether or not the arbitration agreement is entered into in Hong Kong.[15] There is no other part in this Ordinance regarding the distinction between an agreement entered into in Hong Kong and that entered outside Hong Kong. Hence, the same rules under this Ordinance apply to an arbitration agreement regardless of the place in which it was entered.

Article 2A   *International Origin and General Principles*

This article was adopted verbatim.[16]

Article 3   *Receipt of Written Communications*

Article 3, dealing with the interpretation of 'received' written communication, was adopted verbatim, but there are several amendments in the form of section 10 of the AO.[17] Most significantly, section 10(2) adds that

---

[12] Section 8(1) AO:

> Section 2 has effect in substitution for article 2 of the UNCITRAL Model Law.

[13] Section 2(1) AO:

> 'arbitral tribunal' (仲裁庭) means a sole arbitrator or a panel of arbitrators, and includes an umpire; [...] 'Court' (原訟法庭) means the Court of First Instance of the High Court.

[14] See section 8(2) AO.   [15] See note 9.   [16] Section 9 AO.   [17] Section 10 AO.

'if a written communication [...] is sent by any means by which information can be recorded and transmitted to the addressee, the communication is deemed to have been received on the day it is so sent.'[18]

Article 4   Waiver of Right to Object

This article was adopted verbatim.[19]

Article 5   Extent of Court Intervention

This article was adopted verbatim.[20]

As reflected by section 3(2)(b) of the AO,[21] an objective of this new Ordinance is to minimize court intervention and to give a greater degree of deference to arbitral tribunals in Hong Kong.[22]

Article 6   Court or other Authority for Certain Functions of Arbitration Assistance and Supervision

Article 6, which delegates the functions of arbitration to specific named courts or authorities, was not adopted verbatim. However, this is necessary because the ML asks member states to amend the article to include the courts and bodies of their jurisdiction. Section 13 of the AO stipulates that section 13(2) to section 13(6) have effect in substitution of the ML, which in turn delegate functions to the Hong Kong International Arbitration Centre (HKIAC) and the CFI.[23]

---

[18] See section 10(2) AO.   [19] Section 11 AO.   [20] Section 12 AO.

[21] Section 3(2)(b) AO:

> This Ordinance is based on the principles –
>> (b) that the court should interfere in the arbitration of a dispute only as expressly provided for in this Ordinance.

[22] See D'Agostino, Chapman and Cartwright-Finch, note 5.

[23] Section 13 AO:

> (1) Subsections (2) to (6) have effect in substitution for article 6 of the UNCITRAL Model Law [...]
> (2) The functions of the court or other authority referred to in article 11(3) or (4) of the UNCITRAL Model Law, given effect to by section 24, are to be performed by the HKIAC.
> (3) The HKIAC may, with the approval of the Chief Justice, make rules to facilitate the performance of its functions under section 23(3), 24 or 32(1).
> (4) The functions of the court or other authority referred to in –

Part II   Arbitration Agreement (Articles 7 to 9)

Article 7   Definition and Form of Arbitration Agreement

Option I of Article 7, which defines and creates requirements for an arbitration agreement, was adopted but amended slightly in the form of section 19(2) of the AO.[24] This section defines an arbitration agreement as having been 'in writing' if the agreement is in a document regardless of signature, or the agreement is recorded by one of the parties or a third party.

Tommy CP Sze & Co. v. *Li & Fung (Trading) Ltd & Ors* [2003] 1 HKC 418 attempted to interpret this section. It ruled that for an agreement to be an arbitration agreement, 'there must be its element of compulsion in the agreement between the parties that any disputes or differences must be arbitration [*sic*]', meaning that an agreement giving an *option* for arbitration but leaving litigation in play is not an arbitration agreement.

> (a) article 13(3) of the UNCITRAL Model Law, given effect to by section 26; or
> (b) article 14(1) of the UNCITRAL Model Law, given effect to by section 27,
> are to be performed by the Court.
> (5) The functions of the court referred to in –
> (a) article 16(3) of the UNCITRAL Model Law, given effect to by section 34; or
> (b) article 34(2) of the UNCITRAL Model Law, given effect to by section 81,
> are to be performed by the Court.
> (6) The functions of the competent court referred to in article 27 of the UNCITRAL Model Law, given effect to by section 55, are to be performed by the Court.

[24] Section 19 AO:

> (1) Option I of Article 7 of the UNCITRAL Model Law, the text of which is set out below, has effect –
> [follows the text of Option I of article 7 of the ML]
> (2) Without affecting subsection (1), an arbitration agreement is in writing if –
> (a) the agreement is in a document, whether or not the document is signed by the parties to the agreement; or
> (b) the agreement, although made otherwise than in writing, is recorded by one of the parties to the agreement, or by a third party, with the authority of each of the parties to the agreement.

Article 8   Arbitration Agreement and Substantive Claim before Court

This article was adopted verbatim.[25] In addition, *Hoo Cheong Building Construction Co. Ltd* v. *Jade Union Investment Ltd* [2004] HKCFI 21 ruled that an 'action' under article 8 does not include an action seeking liquidation of a company. Even where the parties have agreed to refer their disputes to arbitration, the court handling winding up actions would first have to be satisfied that the debt relied upon is bona fide disputed on substantial grounds before leaving the disputes to an arbitrator.[26] The existence of an arbitration clause is neither here nor there in determining whether there is any dispute of substance so as to warrant the court to make a winding up order and refer the parties to arbitration in the first place.[27]

Liu Man Wai and Anor v. *Chevalier (Hong Kong) Ltd* [2002] HKEC 803 ruled that the plaintiff's claim fell outside the scope of the arbitration agreement under clauses 4(a) and (b) thereof; and that the arbitrator did not have the jurisdiction to decide whether there had been an agreement as to quantum.

Article 9   Arbitration Agreement and Interim Measures by Court

This article was adopted verbatim.[28] Furthermore, *'Lady Muriel'* v. *Transorient Shipping Ltd* [1995] HKCA 615 ruled that there is nothing to preclude courts from offering an interim measure of protection. More recently, in *Muginoho Co. Ltd* v. *Vimiu HK Co. Ltd* [2012] HKEC 420, interim measures were requested by a party, granted and affirmed by the court despite the fact that arbitration proceedings had commenced outside Hong Kong.

Part III   Composition of Arbitral Tribunal (Articles 10 to 15)

Article 10   Number of Arbitrators

Article 10, dealing with the freedom to choose the number of arbitrators, was not adopted verbatim.[29] There were two significant amendments in

---

[25] Section 20 AO.

[26] *Hoo Cheong Building Construction Co. Ltd* v. *Jade Union Investment Ltd* [2004] HKCFI 21

[27] *Ibid.*   [28] Section 21 AO.

[29] Section 23 AO:

> (1) Article 10(1) of the UNCITRAL Model Law, the text of which is set out below, has effect –

the form of section 23(2) and section 23(3) of the AO.[30] These amendments afforded freedom for the parties to authorize a third party to determine the number of arbitrators, as well as to let the HKIAC decide the number of arbitrators (either 1 or 3) if the parties fail to agree on the number.

Article 11   Appointment of Arbitrators

Article 11, which deals with the procedure of appointing an arbitrator, was adopted but amended.[31] Section 24(2)(a) of the AO adds that, 'In an arbitration with an even number of arbitrators, if the parties have not agreed on a procedure for appointing the arbitrators under article 11(2) of the UNCITRAL Model Law, each party is to appoint the same number of arbitrators.'[32]

Article 12   Grounds for Challenge

This article, dealing with the ability to challenge an arbitrator should there be a factor of impartiality, was adopted verbatim.[33] The article also concerned the arbitrator's duty to disclose any factor of impartiality.

Jung Science Information Technology Co. Ltd v. *ZTE Corporation* [2008] HKCFI 606 ruled that there was a difference between the circumstances on the basis of which an arbitrator may be challenged and the circumstances which fall within the arbitrators' duty of disclosure. An arbitrator's failure to comply with the disclosure requirement may, in

---

'*Article 10. Number of arbitrators*
(1) The parties are free to determine the number of arbitrators.
(2) [*Not applicable*]'.

[30] Section 23 AO:

   (2) For the purposes of subsection (1), the freedom of the parties to determine the number of arbitrators includes the right of the parties to authorize a third party, including an institution, to make that determination.
   (3) Subject to section 1 of Schedule 2 (if applicable), if the parties fail to agree on the number of arbitrators, the number of arbitrators is to be either 1 or 3 as decided by the HKIAC in the particular case.

[31] Section 24 AO:

   (1) Article 11 of the UNCITRAL Model Law, the text of which is set out below, has effect subject to section 13(2) and (3) –
   [follows the text of article 11 of the ML].

[32] Section 24(2)(a) AO.   [33] Section 25 AO.

itself, give rise to justifiable doubts as to that arbitrator's impartiality and independence.

Article 13   Challenge Procedure

This article, dealing with the procedure to challenge an arbitrator, was not adopted verbatim.[34] Section 26(4) of the AO states that: 'The mandate of a challenged arbitrator terminates under article 13 of the UNCITRAL Model Law [. . .] if (a) the arbitrator withdraws from office; (b) the parties agree to a challenge; (c) the arbitral tribunal upholds the challenge and no request is made for the Court to decide on the challenge; or (d) the Court, upon request to decide on the challenge, upholds the challenge.'[35]

Article 14   Failure or Impossibility to Act

This article was adopted verbatim.[36] In interpreting this article, *Noble Resources Pte Ltd* v. *China Sea Grains and Oils Industry Co. Ltd* [2006] HKCFI 334 held that an arbitrator having been detained and arrested in a foreign jurisdiction would have his mandate terminated. This is one example of a circumstance giving rise to 'impossibility to act' where a mandate is terminated.

Article 15   Appointment of Substitute Arbitrator

This article was adopted verbatim.[37]

Part IV   Jurisdiction of Arbitral Tribunal (Article 16)

Article 16   Competence of Arbitral Tribunal to Rule on its Jurisdiction

Article 16, which deals with the authority of a tribunal to rule on its own jurisdiction as well as the procedure to raise a plea otherwise, was not

---

[34] Section 26 AO.

> (1) Article 13 of the UNCITRAL Model Law, the text of which is set out below, has effect subject to section 13(4) –
> [Follows the text of article 13 ML].

[35] Section 26(4) AO.   [36] Section 27 AO.   [37] Section 28 AO.

adopted verbatim.[38] Section 34(5) of the AO adds that, 'if the arbitral tribunal rules that it does not have jurisdiction to decide a dispute, the court must, if it has jurisdiction, decide that dispute.'[39]

Part IV-A   Interim Measures and Preliminary Orders (Articles 17 to 17J)

Sub-Part I   Measures and Orders by the Tribunal (Articles 17 to 17G)

Article 17   Power of Arbitral Tribunal to Order Interim Measures

This article was adopted verbatim.[40]

The new Ordinance emphasizes minimal court intervention. The arbitral tribunal is empowered to order interim measures in prescribed circumstances, such as 'to preserve assets or evidence, or to maintain or restore the status quo'.[41]

Article 17A   Conditions for Granting Interim Measures   This article was adopted verbatim.[42]

Article 17B   Applications for Preliminary Orders and Conditions for Granting Preliminary Orders   This article was adopted verbatim.[43]

Article 17C   Specific Regime for Preliminary Orders   This article was adopted verbatim.[44]

Article 17D   Modification, Suspension, Termination   This article was adopted verbatim.[45]

Article 17E   Provision of Security   This article was adopted verbatim.[46]

---

[38] Section 34(1) AO:

> Article 16 of the UNCITRAL Model Law, the text of which is set out below, has effect subject to section 13(5) –
> [Follows the text of article 16 ML].

[39] Section 34(5) AO.   [40] Section 35 AO.
[41] See D'Agostino, Chapman and Cartwright-Finch, note 5.   [42] Section 36 AO.
[43] Section 37 AO.   [44] Section 38 AO.   [45] Section 39 AO.   [46] Section 40 AO.

Article 17F   Disclosure   This article was adopted verbatim.[47]

Article 17G   Costs and Damages   This article was adopted verbatim.[48]

Sub-Part II   Recognition and Enforcement of Interim Measures (Articles 17H and 17I)

Article 17H   Recognition and Enforcement   Article 17H ML, which deals with the enforcement of interim measures, was not adopted. Instead, section 61 of the AO has effect in substitute of it.[49] Most significantly, section 61 gives enforceability to any order made, whether inside or outside Hong Kong, in the same manner as an order of the court that has the same effect.[50] It also bars the granting of leave to enforce an order made outside Hong Kong, 'unless the party seeking to enforce it can demonstrate that it belongs to a type or description of order or direction that may be made in Hong Kong in relation to arbitral proceedings by an arbitral tribunal'.[51]

Once again, this reflects the purpose of this Ordinance to minimize court supervision, as the court could no longer refuse to enforce the interim measure awarded by an arbitral tribunal.

Article 17I   Grounds for Refusing Recognition or Enforcement   The entirety of article 17I does not have effect.[52] This article deals with the refusal of the recognition of interim measures.

---

[47] Section 41 AO.   [48] Section 42 AO.

[49] Section 43 AO: 'Section 61 has effect in substitution for article 17H of the UNCITRAL Model Law.'

[50] Section 61 AO:
> (1) An order or direction made, whether in or outside Hong Kong, in relation to arbitral proceedings by an arbitral tribunal is enforceable in the same manner as an order or direction of the Court that has the same effect, but only with the leave of the Court.

[51] Section 61 AO:
> (2) Leave to enforce an order or direction made outside Hong Kong is not to be granted, unless the party seeking to enforce it can demonstrate that it belongs to a type or description of order or direction that may be made in Hong Kong in relation to arbitral proceedings by an arbitral tribunal.

[52] Section 44 AO:
> Article 17I of the UNCITRAL Model Law does not have effect.

Sub-Part III   Court-Ordered Interim Measures (Article 17J)

Article 17J   Court-Ordered Interim Measures   The entirety of article 17J does not have effect.[53] This article deals with the authority for the court to issue an interim measure regardless of the territory where the place of arbitration is, cautioning that the court must consider the features of international arbitration.

Under section 45(2), the court may grant an interim measure, in relation to arbitral proceedings in or outside Hong Kong.[54] However, section 45(4) sets out circumstances where the court may refuse to grant the interim measure.[55]

The court in *Muginoho Co. Ltd* v. *Vimiu HK Co. Ltd* [2012] HKEC 420 ruled that 'the court may grant an interim measure in relation to any arbitral proceedings which have been or are to be commenced outside Hong Kong, if the proceedings are capable of giving rise to an arbitration award that may be enforced in Hong Kong.' Hence, it could be granted regarding the arbitration proceedings commenced in Japan.

In *Ever Judger Holding Co. Ltd* v. *Kroman Celik Sanayii Anonim Sirketi* [2015] HKEC 605, the court granted an anti-suit injunction under section 45 of the AO, restraining foreign proceedings brought in breach of an arbitration clause. Yet, the court was hesitant to draw the conclusion that such an anti-suit injunction was an 'interim measure' that was 'in relation to' actual or contemplated arbitral proceedings, which was provided in section 45(2).[56]

---

[53] Section 45 AO:

      (1) Article 17J of the UNCITRAL Model Law does not have effect.

[54] Section 45(2) AO:

      On the application of any party, the Court may, in relation to any arbitral proceedings which have been or are to be commenced in or outside Hong Kong, grant an interim measure.

[55] Section 45(4) AO:

      The Court may decline to grant an interim measure under subsection (2) on the ground that –

        (a) the interim measure sought is currently the subject of arbitral proceedings; and

        (b) the Court considers it more appropriate for the interim measure sought to be dealt with by the arbitral tribunal.

[56] *Ever Judger Holding Co. Ltd* v. *Kroman Celik Sanayii Anonim Sirketi* [2015] HKEC 605, paras 30–33.

Part V   Conduct of Arbitral Proceedings (Articles 18 to 27)

Article 18   Equal Treatment of Parties

Article 18, concerning the equality of each party in presenting their cases, was not adopted verbatim.[57] Section 46 of the AO has effect in substitution of article 18. The main difference lies in that the Hong Kong legislation specifically provides that the parties be given a 'reasonable' opportunity to present their case as opposed to the ML provision providing for a 'full' opportunity for case presentation.[58] Here the rationale seems to be to provide the arbitral tribunal with the power to help prevent parties from deploying excessive delay tactics such as unhelpful discovery requests or excessive number of witnesses under the guise of exercising the right to a 'full' opportunity for case presentation.

In *Grand Pacific Holdings Ltd* v. *Pacific China Holdings Ltd (in liq.) (No. 1)* [2012] 4 HKLRD 1, it was stated 'only a sufficiently serious error could be regarded as a violation of article 18' and as long as a party had a 'reasonable opportunity' to present its case, it could hardly establish it had been denied due process. Hence, the 'full opportunity' test is not applicable in Hong Kong cases.

Article 19   Determination of Rules of Procedure

Only article 19(1) has effect, while article 19(2) does not.[59] Article 19(1) concerns the fact that the parties are free to agree on the procedure to be followed by the tribunal in conducting the proceedings. Article 19(2)

---

[57] Section 46 AO:

> (1) Subsections (2) and (3) have effect in substitution for article 18 of the UNCITRAL Model Law.

[58] Section 46 AO:

> (3) When conducting arbitral proceedings or exercising any of the powers conferred on an arbitral tribunal by this Ordinance or by the parties to any of those arbitral proceedings, the arbitral tribunal is required –
> [...]
> [...] *(b)* to act fairly and impartially as between the parties, giving them a reasonable opportunity to present their cases and to deal with the cases of their opponents.

[59] Section 47 AO.

concerns the event of failure to agree on the procedure. Section 47 AO replaces article 19(2) with slightly different wording.[60]

Article 20   Place of Arbitration

This article was adopted verbatim.[61]

Article 21   Commencement of Arbitral Proceedings

This article was adopted verbatim.[62] In interpreting this article, *Fung Sang Trading Ltd* v. *Kai Sun Sea Products & Food Co. Ltd* [1991] HKCFI 190 ruled that a letter, or request for arbitration, is taken to be a sufficient commencement under this article.

Article 22   Language

This article was adopted verbatim.[63]

Article 23   Statements of Claim and Defence

This article was adopted verbatim.[64]

Article 24   Hearings and Written Proceedings

This article was adopted verbatim.[65]

Article 25   Default of a Party

This article was adopted verbatim.[66]

---

[60] Section 47 AO:

   [...]
   (2) If or to the extent that there is no such agreement of the parties, the arbitral tribunal may, subject to the provisions of this Ordinance, conduct the arbitration in the manner that it considers appropriate.
   (3) When conducting arbitral proceedings, an arbitral tribunal is not bound by the rules of evidence and may receive any evidence that it considers relevant to the arbitral proceedings, but it must give the weight that it considers appropriate to the evidence adduced in the arbitral proceedings.

[61] Section 48 AO.   [62] Section 49 AO.   [63] Section 50 AO.
[64] Section 51 AO.   [65] Section 52 AO.   [66] Section 53 AO.

Article 26   Expert Appointed by Arbitral Tribunal

This article was adopted verbatim.[67]

Article 27   Court Assistance in Taking Evidence

This article was adopted verbatim.[68] In *Vibroflotation A.G.* v. *Express Builders Co. Ltd* [1994] HKCFI 205, the court ruled that should a party wish to seek a subpoena, the party must obtain express written approval from the arbitrator.

Part VI   Making of Award and Termination of Proceedings
(Articles 28 to 33)

Article 28   Rules Applicable to Substance of Dispute

This article was adopted verbatim.[69]

Article 29   Decision-Making by Panel of Arbitrators

This article was adopted verbatim.[70]

Article 30   Settlement

This article was adopted verbatim.[71]

Article 31   Form and Contents of Award

This article was adopted verbatim.[72]

Article 32   Termination of Proceedings

This article was adopted verbatim.[73]

Article 33   Correction and Interpretation of Award; Additional Award

This article was adopted verbatim.[74]

---

[67] Section 54 AO.   [68] Section 55 AO.   [69] Section 64 AO.   [70] Section 65 AO.
[71] Section 66 AO.   [72] Section 67 AO.   [73] Section 68 AO.   [74] Section 69 AO.

Part VII   Recourse against Award (Article 34)

Article 34   Application for Setting Aside as Exclusive Recourse against Arbitral Award

Article 34, concerning the procedure to set aside an arbitral award, was not adopted verbatim.[75] A modification in the form of section 81(2) of the AO provides that: article 34(1) does not affect the right of a court to set aside a tribunal award.[76]

In addition, if parties opt into Schedule 2, section 81(2) expressly states that article 34 would not affect the abovementioned rights. Hence, if parties opt into Schedule 2, a party could: (1) challenge the arbitral award on ground of serious irregularity under Section 4 of Schedule 2, or (2) appeal against the arbitral award on question of law under Section 5 of Schedule 2.[77]

Part VIII   Recognition and Enforcement of Awards (Articles 35 and 36)

Article 35   Recognition and Enforcement

This article was not adopted at all.[78]

Regarding enforcement of awards, most of the previous regime is adopted. Section 84 gives an arbitral award (with leave of the court) the

[75] Section 81 AO:

> (1) Article 34 of the UNCITRAL Model Law, the text of which is set out below, has effect subject to section 13(5) –
> [Follows the text of article 34 ML]
> Section 13(5) AO simply states that the CFI is the court which has jurisdiction to exercise the power described in article 34.

[76] Section 81(2) AO:

> (2) Subsection (1) does not affect –
> (a) the power of the Court to set aside an arbitral award under section 26(5);
> (b) the right to challenge an arbitral award under section 4 of Schedule 2 (if applicable); or
> (c) the right to appeal against an arbitral award on a question of law under section 5 of Schedule 2 (if applicable).

[77] Ibid.

[78] Section 82 AO: 'Article 35 of the UNCITRAL Model Law does not have effect.'

same status as a judgment of the court.[79] According to section 85, the duly authenticated original award or a duly certified copy of it; and the original arbitration agreement or a duly certified copy of it, are required for the enforcement.[80] Different rules apply for the enforcement of Convention awards, of Mainland awards, and of other awards. Note that an outstanding award in the mainland is not enforceable as a Mainland award.[81]

In 樓外樓房地產咨詢有限公司 對 何志蘭 [2015] HKCFI 664, the court applied section 95(2)(c)(i) and suspended two injunctions for the enforcement of the Mainland awards, on the basis that the defendant was not given proper notice of the arbitral proceedings.

Article 36   Grounds for Refusing Recognition or Enforcement

This article was not adopted at all.[82]

---

[79] Section 84 AO:
> (1) Subject to section 26(2), an award, whether made in or outside Hong Kong, in arbitral proceedings by an arbitral tribunal is enforceable in the same manner as a judgment of the Court that has the same effect, but only with the leave of the Court.

[80] Section 85 AO:
> The party seeking to enforce an arbitral award, whether made in or outside Hong Kong, which is not a Convention award, Mainland award or Macao award, must produce – (Amended 7 of 2013 s. 9)
> (a) the duly authenticated original award or a duly certified copy of it;
> (b) the original arbitration agreement or a duly certified copy of it; and
> (c) if the award or agreement is not in either or both of the official languages, a translation of it in either official language certified by an official or sworn translator or by a diplomatic or consular agent.

[81] Section 93(1) AO:
> A Mainland award is not, subject to subsection (2), enforceable under this Division if an application has been made on the Mainland for enforcement of the award.

[82] Section 83 AO: 'Article 36 of the UNCITRAL Model Law does not have effect.' The AO has its own rules for refusing enforcement of, for example, convention awards, see section 89 AO.

Part IX   Additional Provisions in the New Arbitration Ordinance supplemental to the Model Law

Confidentiality

Confidentiality of arbitral proceedings is deemed in the new Arbitration Ordinance. Section 18(1) states that publication, disclosure or communication of any information relating to the arbitral proceedings under the arbitration agreement or an award made in those arbitral proceedings is not allowed, unless it is agreed by the parties.[83]

Mediation-Arbitration/Arbitration-Mediation

The new AO expressly provides for mediation-arbitration or arbitration-mediation proceedings. Section 32 of this Ordinance allows HKIAC to appoint a mediator on application of any party if the mediator appointed in the arbitration agreement is unavailable.[84] Moreover, a mediator could further be appointed as an arbitrator where it is provided in the arbitration agreement under section 32(3)(a).[85] Furthermore, section 33 allows

---

[83] Section 18(1) AO:
>   Unless otherwise agreed by the parties, no party may publish, disclose or communicate any information relating to –
>   (a) the arbitral proceedings under the arbitration agreement; or
>   (b) an award made in those arbitral proceedings.

[84] Section 32(1) AO:
>   If –
>   (a) any arbitration agreement provides for the appointment of a mediator by a person who is not one of the parties; and
>   (b) that person –
>   (i) refuses to make the appointment; or
>   (ii) does not make the appointment within the time specified in the arbitration agreement or, if no time is so specified, within a reasonable time after being requested by any party to make the appointment,
>   the HKIAC may, on the application of any party, appoint a mediator.

[85] Section 32(3)(a) AO:
>   If any arbitration agreement provides for the appointment of a mediator and further provides that the person so appointed is to act as an arbitrator in the event that no settlement acceptable to the parties can be reached in the mediation proceedings –
>   (a) no objection may be made against the person's acting as an arbitrator, or against the person's conduct of the arbitral proceedings, solely on the ground that the person had acted previously as a mediator in

an arbitrator to act as a mediator after the arbitral proceedings have commenced, as long as all parties consent in writing.[86] However, the fact that confidential information obtained by an arbitrator during the mediation proceedings must be disclosed to all other parties if the arbitrator considers it as material to the arbitral proceedings[87] might be a hindrance to effective mediation.[88]

The court in *Chok Yick Interior Design & Engineering Co. Ltd v. Fortune World Enterprises Ltd* [2010] HKEC 146 ruled that the court had the inherent jurisdiction to stay the proceedings where necessary. One of the court's powers of case management is to encourage parties to use an alternative dispute resolution procedure where appropriate.[89] This includes the power to stay a case such that it could proceed to arbitration, as in this case.

In *Gao Haiyan* v. *Keeneye Holdings Ltd* [2012] 1 HKLRD 627, the court affirmed that an award pursuant to a mediation-arbitration procedure conducted in mainland China was enforceable in Hong Kong, albeit there was an alleged irregularity. Hong Kong courts would avoid overturning the decision of the supervisory court, unless a case of apparent bias had been established, or the enforcement was contrary to the fundamental conceptions of morality and justice of Hong Kong.[90]

---

connection with some or all of the matters relating to the dispute submitted to arbitration.

[86] Section 33(1) AO:

If all parties consent in writing, and for so long as no party withdraws the party's consent in writing, an arbitrator may act as a mediator after the arbitral proceedings have commenced.

[87] Section 33(4)(a) AO:

If –

(a) confidential information is obtained by an arbitrator from a party during the mediation proceedings conducted by the arbitrator as a mediator [...]

the arbitrator must, before resuming the arbitral proceedings, disclose to all other parties as much of that information as the arbitrator considers is material to the arbitral proceedings.

[88] See D'Agostino, Chapman and Cartwright-Finch, note 5.

[89] *Chok Yick Interior Design & Engineering Co. Ltd* v. *Fortune World Enterprises Ltd* [2010] HKEC 146.

[90] *Gao Haiyan* v. *Keeneye Holdings Ltd* [2012] 1 HKLRD 627.

Conclusion

The new AO adopts verbatim a large number of provisions in the ML on International Commercial Arbitration, concerning both substantive and procedural matters. Whilst the ambit of the procedure in the AO may appear narrower compared to the ML – for instance, the requirement that arbitration agreements must be in writing (s. 19(2)) – other discrepancies between the AO and the ML point to jurisdiction-specific norms, instituted in the light of the existing procedure in Hong Kong. As such, section 13 of the AO is a substitution of article 6 ML, referring specifically to the HKIAC and the Court (of First Instance) in relation to authorities for arbitration supervision. This is consistent with the purpose of the new AO, which was to incorporate the ML into local legislation having regard to Hong Kong's specific circumstances.

In conformity with ML article 2A(1), Hong Kong courts in interpreting the ML have generally acted with regard to its international origin and the need for uniformity in its application. Whilst such cases were largely heard before the Arbitration Ordinance Cap. 609 came into effect in June 2011, they have been instrumental in shedding light upon the proper interpretation of the ML, as well as fleshing out the arbitration rules with respect to the specific situation in Hong Kong. Finally, it is noted that the lack of inclusion of certain ML provisions – namely relating to the recognition and enforcement of arbitral awards (articles 35–36) – does not mark lacunae in the AO, but instead such provisions have been substituted by the inclusion of related provisions from the old Arbitration Ordinance (Cap. 341) and Hong Kong's adoption of the Convention on the Recognition and Enforcement of Foreign Arbitral Awards, New York, 10 June 1958, in force 7 June 1959, 330 UNTS 4739. Whilst these are not inconsistent with the ML, the applicability of the excluded provisions to the local situation may be reconsidered in order to further the need to promote uniformity.

India

The 1985 Model Law and the 1996 Act: A Survey of the Indian Arbitration Landscape

HARISANKAR K. SATHYAPALAN AND
AAKANKSHA KUMAR

Introduction

While arbitration as a dispute resolution mechanism was not unknown in India since ancient times, the first Indian legislation on arbitration dates back to 1899, followed by a few provisions under the Code of Civil Procedure, 1908. India ratified the Geneva Protocol, 1923 and the Geneva Convention, 1927 under the Arbitration (Protocol and Convention) Act 1937. Thereafter, the Arbitration Act of 1940 was enacted to consolidate and amend the law relating to domestic arbitration. Later, the country became a contracting party to the New York Convention on the Recognition and Enforcement of Foreign Arbitral Awards, 1958[1] ('NYC') and

Harisankar K. Sathyapalan is a doctoral candidate at the Faculty of Law of the National University of Singapore. Email: harisankar@u.nus.edu. Aakanksha Kumar is a doctoral candidate at the National Law University, Jodhpur, India. kumar.aakanksha@gmail.com. The authors gratefully acknowledge the excellent research assistance provided by Mr Rohan Tigadi, Ms Sparsha Janardhan and Mr Sandeep Suresh (all of them graduated from National Law University, Jodhpur, India) during the course of this research. We thank our colleagues from different Model Law jurisdictions for sharing their insights during the conference held at NUS Law school in Singapore on 28–29 May 2015. Finally, we are immensely grateful to our editor Professor Gary F. Bell of NUS Faculty of Law for masterminding a great symposium and reviewing the manuscript for the publication of this edited volume. We also thank the EW Barker Centre for Law & Business at the Faculty of Law of the National University of Singapore for financing our participation in the conference entitled, 'The UNCITRAL Model Law on International Commercial Arbitration in Asia', which led to this book. Errors (if any) are the sole responsibility of the authors. This chapter is up to date as of 1 November 2017.

[1] Convention on the Recognition and Enforcement of Foreign Arbitral Awards, New York, 10 June 1958, in force 7 June 1959, 330 UNTS 4739 ('NYC').

enacted its corresponding legislation, namely, the Foreign Awards (Recognition and Enforcement) Act 1961 ('FARE Act 1961').

The history of the drafting of the present-day Arbitration and Conciliation Act 1996 ('A&C Act,1996') is fairly controversial. Following three re-promulgated ordinances,[2] the Arbitration and Conciliation Bill, 1995 was passed by parliament in August 1996 and this received Presidential assent on 16 August 1996, becoming the A&C Act 1996 that India follows today.[3] This Act repeals, amends and consolidates the provisions of the 1937, 1940 and 1961 legislations. With some significant deviations, this Act adopts the original 1985 text of the UNCITRAL Model Law on International Commercial Arbitration[4] ('ML 1985'). The A&C Act 1996 has been divided into four parts. Part I of the Act is entitled 'arbitration' and Part II concerns itself with 'enforcement of certain foreign awards'. Part III and Part IV deal with 'conciliation' and 'miscellaneous provisions' respectively but are outside the scope of this chapter.

While the Statement of Objects and Reasons of the Act clearly highlights the aim of the ML 1985 in 'ensuring uniformity of the law of arbitral procedures and the specific needs of international commercial arbitration practice', the Indian law in its letter, and the interpretations thereof, was far from internationally accepted interpretations and practice. It has been opined that due to the lack of parliamentary debate on the provisions of the Act, and the absence of public consultation, the law has inherent weaknesses and shortcomings and thus the judiciary has had a hard time in revealing lacunae and filling the gaps in the law.[5]

The Supreme Court decision in *Bharat Aluminium Co.* v. *Kaiser Aluminium Technical Service Inc.* marked a turning point for arbitration jurisprudence in India.[6] By undoing the earlier controversial and severely

---

[2] Arbitration and Conciliation Ordinance (8 of 1996) on 16 January 1996; Arbitration and Conciliation (Second) Ordinance (11 of 1996) on 26 March 1996 and Arbitration and Conciliation (Third) Ordinance (27 of 1996) on 21 June 1996.

[3] Ministry of Law and Justice, The Arbitration and Conciliation Act 1996, No. 26 of 1996. This law was brought into force retrospectively from 26 January 1996. Certain provisions have been amended through the Arbitration & Conciliation (Amendment) Act 2015 with effect from 23 October 2015.

[4] UNCITRAL Model Law on International Commercial Arbitration 1985, UN General Assembly Resolution 40/72 (11 December 1985) ('ML 1985'). It is important to note that amendments to articles 1(2), 7, and 35(2), a new chapter IVA to replace art. 17 and a new art. 2 A were adopted by UNCITRAL on 7 July 2006.

[5] Indu Malhotra, *O. P. Malhotra on the Law and Practice of Arbitration and Conciliation*, 3rd edn (Thomson Reuters, 2014) at 41.

[6] (2012) 9 SCC 552 ('*BALCO*').

criticized interpretations, the court finally laid down the law with respect to the differences in Part I and Part II of the Act, such that, in its wake, several subsequent judgments have furthered the attempt of bringing India's law and legal interpretation in line with the underlying philosophy and ethos of the NYC and the ML 1985.

After a few failed endeavours to modernize arbitration law,[7] the Government of India, based on the 246th Report of the Law Commission, promulgated the Arbitration & Conciliation Ordinance 2015 ('Ordinance') bringing about large-scale changes to the A&C Act 1996.[8] The Ordinance, dated 23 October 2015, was later enacted into law in parliament on 31 December 2015 as the Arbitration & Conciliation (Amendment) Act 2015 ('2015 amendment') which is in force retrospectively from the date of promulgation of the Ordinance.[9]

Part I   General Provisions of the Model Law (Articles 1 to 6)

Part I of the A&C Act 1996 contains provisions for the regulation of both domestic and international commercial arbitration taking place in India. This includes reference to arbitration by courts, interim measures of protection, appointment and challenge of arbitral tribunal, decision-making process and post-award remedies, among other things. International commercial arbitration as defined under the Act relates to disputes that arise from a legal relationship which is considered as 'commercial'[10] under Indian law.[11] Nevertheless, according to the Supreme Court, non-commercial civil disputes are also arbitrable.[12]

---

[7] For a chronicle of the attempts to amend the law, see Ministry of Law and Justice, Government of India, Amendments to the Arbitration & Conciliation Act 1996 – A Consultation Paper (April 2010), available at http://lawmin.nic.in/la/consultationpaper .pdf (accessed 30 October 2017).

[8] Law Commission of India, Amendments to the Arbitration and Conciliation Act 1996, 246th Report (August 2014), available at http://lawcommissionofindia.nic.in/reports/ Report246.pdf ('Report 246, 2014') (accessed 30 October 2017).

[9] Ministry of Law and Justice, The Arbitration and Conciliation (Amendment) Act 2015, No. 3 of 2016, available at www.indiacode.nic.in/acts-in-pdf/2016/201603.pdf (accessed 30 October 2017).

[10] Supreme Court has given a wider meaning to the term 'commercial' to include all kinds of commercial transactions as provided under art. 1 of the ML 1985 (see footnote to art. 1). See *R.M. Investments & Trading Co. Pvt Ltd* v. *Boeing Corporation*, AIR 1994 SC 1136.

[11] A&C Act 1996 section 2(1)(f).

[12] *H. Srinivas Pai and Anr* v. *H.V. Pai* (2010) 12 SCC 521 (court opined that 'reference to arbitration and arbitrability depends upon the existence of an arbitration agreement, and not upon the question whether it is a civil dispute or commercial dispute').

Further, foreign nationality of at least one of the parties determines the international nature of arbitration in Indian law.[13] In the case of *TDM Infrastructure Pvt Ltd* v. *UE Development India Pvt Ltd*, the Supreme Court held that a body corporate registered under the Indian Companies Act would be an Indian national irrespective of its foreign control and management.[14] The 2015 amendment has espoused this interpretation based on the 'place of incorporation' as opposed to the place of 'central management' for a body corporate, and has restricted the central management test to only an association or body of individuals.

Strictly speaking, arbitration between Indian parties, even if it is seated outside India, is not an international arbitration.[15] A minor deviation – rather a significant one from the ML 1985 – was the absence of the word 'only' and the accompanying exceptions in section 2(2) of the A&C Act 1996.[16] This created much confusion in the initial years of the enactment and led to a creative and controversial decision by the Supreme Court in 2002.[17] In *Bhatia International* v. *Bulk Trading SA*,[18] the parties agreed to have their dispute arbitrated in Paris under the ICC rules. However, one of the parties approached an Indian court to get an interim measure under section 9 of the Act. On final appeal, the Supreme Court held that Part I of the Act would apply to all arbitrations, including an international commercial arbitration seated abroad, unless the parties have expressly or impliedly excluded its application. Thus, Indian courts were

[13] See note 11. One party could be (i) an individual who is habitually resident abroad, (ii) a body corporate incorporated outside India, (iii) a company having its place of business in a foreign country or (iv) a foreign government.

[14] 2008(2) ArbLR439 (SC) ('*TDM Infrastructure*').

[15] Seat of arbitration is not a determining factor to define 'internationality' of arbitration under the Act. Part II of the Act applies if the seat is outside India, provided that country is a member state to either the NYC or Geneva Convention.

[16] Prior to the 2015 amendment, section 2(2) stated, 'This Part (Part 1) shall apply where the place of arbitration is in India.' Whereas, the corresponding provision in ML 1985 (art. 1(2)) says: 'The provisions of this law, except article 8, 9, 35 and 36 is applicable *only* if the place of arbitration is in the territory of this state.'

[17] Some of the inconsistent interpretations include the following: *Dominant Offset Pvt Ltd* v. *Adamovske Strojirny AS* (1997) 68 DLT 157 (Delhi High Court opined that the provision does not exclude the applicability of Part I to those arbitrations which are not being held in India); also, in *East Coast Shipping* v. *M.J. Scrap* (1997) 1 Cal HN 444, Calcutta High Court held that Part I of the Act would apply only to arbitrations held in India. Later, High Court of Delhi in *Olex Focas Pvt Ltd* v. *Skodaexport Co. Ltd*, AIR 2000 Del. 161 rejected the stand taken by Calcutta High Court, and afterwards endorsed the view that 'Part I of the Act would apply only to arbitrations where the place of arbitration is in India', in *Marriott International Inc.* v. *Ansal Hotels Ltd*, AIR 2000 Del. 377 (DB).

[18] AIR 2002 SC 1432 ('Bhatia').

deemed authorized to extend its supervisory jurisdiction to foreign arbitrations through a bizarre notion of 'implied exclusion'.

Principle of Implied Exclusion

The position of law enunciated by the Supreme Court in *Bhatia* ruled the scope and applicability of Part I of the A&C Act 1996 for a decade. The case of *Venture Global Engineering* v. *Satyam Computer Services*[19] was the most troublesome decision of the court that followed the *Bhatia* principle. In this case, the court set aside a foreign arbitral award under section 34 of the Act (Part I), which was essentially meant for challenging domestic awards. Subsequent decisions from Indian courts continued the trend of this judicial innovation and extended the concept of implied exclusion to other provisions of Part I. In *Indtel Technical Services* v. *W.S. Atkin PLC*,[20] English law governed both the main contract and the arbitration agreement. Despite such a provision in the contract the court did not accept the argument that Part I of the Act is impliedly excluded. Similarly, in a dispute involving a contract governed by the law of California, it was held that the Supreme Court can appoint an arbitrator under section 11 of the Act.[21] However, the High Court of Gujarat in an earlier judgment decided that Part I is impliedly excluded where the place of arbitration has been expressly agreed to be as London and the law governing arbitration as English law.[22] In a similar situation involving Singapore as the place of arbitration and its law the governing law, the High Court of Delhi declined to exercise its supervisory jurisdiction.[23] In an almost identical factual context, the Delhi High Court again declined to grant an injunction under the Act.[24] The logic applied by the high courts was upheld by the Supreme Court in its later decisions. For example, in *Dozco India Pvt Ltd* v. *Doosan*,[25] where the governing law was Korean law and the place of arbitration located abroad (Seoul), the court held that the agreement expressly excluded Part I. Similarly, in *Videocon Industries Ltd* v. *Union of India*,[26] the court held that Indian courts would not have jurisdiction under Part I, despite the fact that

---

[19] AIR 2008 SC 1061 ('*Venture Global*').   [20] AIR 2009 SC 1132.
[21] *Citation Infowares Ltd* v. *Equinox Corporation* (2009) 7 SCC 220.
[22] *Hardy Oil and Gas Ltd* v. *Hindustan Oil Exploration Co.* (2006) 1 GLR 658.
[23] *Max India Ltd* v. *General Binding Corp.* (2009) 3 Arb LR 162 (Delhi).
[24] *Bhushan Steel Ltd* v. *Singapore International Arbitration Centre*, 2010 (3) Arb LR 70 (Delhi).
[25] (2011) 6 SCC 179.   [26] (2011) 6 SCC 161.

Indian law governed the contract. Here, the Supreme Court also clarified the distinction between 'seat' and 'venue' of arbitration.[27] The court confirmed its position with respect to the principle of implied exclusion in *Yograj Infrastructure Ltd* v. *Ssang Yong Engineering Construction Co. Ltd*,[28] by observing that the parties' agreement to follow the rules of a foreign arbitral institution makes Part I of the Act excluded.

BALCO Judgment

The Supreme Court decided to revisit its infamous decisions in *Bhatia* and *Venture Global* at the start of 2012. In *BALCO*, a five-judge bench of the court overruled the then existing legal position and held that Part I of the Act shall not apply to foreign seated arbitrations, and, therefore, supervisory jurisdiction of Indian courts shall not extend to those arbitrations.[29] While doing so, the court approved the 'territoriality' principle of the Act in conformity with the ML 1985. Moreover, it endorsed the importance of seat in international arbitration and declared it as the 'centre of gravity' of an arbitral process. Notwithstanding the welcoming stand of the court, some concerns were raised due to the prospective effect of the judgment.[30] The new legal position applied only to arbitration agreements concluded on or after 6 September 2012, which was the date of pronouncement of the judgment. However, the anxiety was put to rest by the court in *Reliance Industries Ltd* v. *Union of India*[31] by declining to exercise jurisdiction over a London-seated arbitration despite the fact that the dispute was in connection with an arbitration agreement concluded in the pre-*BALCO* period. Since then courts have continued their pro-arbitration stance and turned down several requests to extend their jurisdiction to foreign-seated arbitrations.[32] Furthermore,

---

[27] *Ibid*. Kuala Lumpur was the designated seat of arbitration. However, due to the outbreak of an epidemic, the arbitration proceedings were held in Amsterdam and later in London. The court decided that a mere agreement to shift the venue (place of hearings) does not change the juridical seat of arbitration.

[28] AIR 2011 SC 3517.   [29] *BALCO*, note 6.

[30] Harisankar K. Sathyapalan, 'Supervisory Jurisdiction of Indian Courts in Foreign Seated Arbitration: The Beginning of a New Era or the End of Bhatia Doctrine?' (2013) 3 *The Arbitration Brief* 56–64 at 63.

[31] AIR 2014 SC 3218.

[32] Recently in the case of *Eitzen Bulk A/S* v. *Ashapura Minechem Ltd and Anr*, AIR 2016 SC 2438, the Supreme Court held that the mere choosing of the seat of arbitration attracts the law of the seat, and it would apply *ipso jure* excluding Part I of the Act. The case dealt with a pre-*BALCO* arbitration agreement.

the 2015 amendment, while ensuring that supervisory powers of the Indian courts are limited to arbitrations with its seat in India, made certain exceptions to section 9 (interim measures), section 27 (court assistance in taking evidence) and section 37 (1)(a) and (3) (appealable orders) of the Act.[33] Most recently, the Supreme Court has further fortified its stance of not applying Part I of the Act to arbitrations held outside India. In *Roger Shashoua & Others* v. *Mukesh Sharma & Others*,[34] the court upheld a 2009 finding of the Commercial Court of London that the courts in London had supervisory jurisdiction. Also, in *I-Max Corporation* v. *M/S E-City Entertainment (I) Pvt Ltd*,[35] the court found that in a pre-*BALCO* contract where the ICC rules had been made applicable to the proceedings by the agreement of the parties, the consequent choice of seat by the arbitral institution operated as exclusion of Part I of the Act, thereby ousting the jurisdiction of Indian courts to maintain and entertain a challenge to the foreign award.

Extent of Judicial Intervention

Section 5, which is based on article 5 of the ML 1985, restricts the intervention of courts to matters for which the law has made an express provision. However, contrary to the spirit of this provision, ever since the existence of the Act, courts were uncomfortable with the limited judicial interference.[36] Conversely, in their attempt to make India an arbitration-friendly jurisdiction, the courts have toned down their interventionist attitude in recent times. For instance, in *Enercon (India) Ltd* v. *Enercon GMBH*,[37] the Supreme Court remarked about the role of courts in supporting arbitration rather than undermining it and observed that minimum judicial intervention is a recognized principle in all jurisdictions that follow ML 1985. In this context, it is also important to note that section 5 uses the expression 'judicial authority' instead of 'court'. So, the principle of minimum judicial intervention is applicable even to special tribunals like the consumer forum[38] and the Board for Industrial and Financial Reconstruction.[39] In *BALCO*, the court observed that the

---

[33] A&C Act 1996, proviso to section 2(2) (added by 2015 amendment).
[34] AIR 2017 SC 3166.   [35] AIR 2017 SC 1372.
[36] Promod Nair, 'Surveying a Decade of the "New" Law of Arbitration in India' (2007) 23 *Arbitration International* 4, 699.
[37] AIR 2014 SC 3152 ('Enercon').   [38] *Fair Air Engineers* v. *N.K. Modi* (1996) 6 SCC 385.
[39] *Morgan Securities and Credit Pvt Ltd* v. *Modi Rubber Ltd* (2006) 12 SCC 642.

use of the term 'judicial authority' is in recognition of the phenomenon that the judicial control of commercial disputes is no longer in the exclusive jurisdiction of courts. Nonetheless, 'the use of the term judicial authority in no manner has any reference to arbitrations not held in India.'[40] Furthermore, the 2015 amendment has brought in an important change in the definition of supervisory court under section 2(1)(e) of the Act by precluding the civil courts in district levels from exercising jurisdiction in matters related to international commercial arbitration. Therefore, only High Courts can grant reliefs in the context of an international commercial arbitration seated in India. Certainly, this amendment is expected to minimize the scope of judicial intervention, which is a fundamental principle of the ML 1985.

Part II   Arbitration Agreement (Articles 7 to 9)

An arbitration is founded on an agreement to arbitrate between the parties, and it is also the source of the arbitral tribunal's jurisdiction. Section 7 of the Act, a verbatim adoption of article 7 of the ML 1985, defines an arbitration agreement and prescribes its form.[41] It may be in the form of an arbitration clause in a contract or in the form of a separate agreement, as long as it is in writing.[42] The writing requirement has been given a wide-ranging meaning by providing various means for conclud- ing an agreement.[43] Moreover, in the context of a charter party agree- ment, the Supreme Court has even held that the agreement need not be in writing and it can be inferred from the acts of the parties.[44]

---

[40]   *BALCO*, note 6 at ¶130.

[41]   A&C Act 1996 section 7(1) – 'arbitration agreement means an agreement by the parties to submit to arbitration all or certain disputes which have arisen or which may arise between them in respect of a defined legal relationship, whether contractual or not.'

[42]   A&C Act 1996 section 7(3).

[43]   A&C Act 1996 section 7(4) – an arbitration agreement is in writing if it is contained in: (a) a document signed by the parties; (b) an exchange of letters, telex, telegrams or other means of telecommunication which provide a record of the agreement; or (c) an exchange of statements of claim and defence in which the existence of the agreement is alleged by one party and not denied by the other.
(5) The reference in a contract to a document containing an arbitration clause constitutes an arbitration agreement if the contract is in writing and the reference is such as to make that arbitration clause part of the contract.

[44]   *Shakti Bhog Food Ltd* v. *Kola Shipping Ltd* (2009) 2 SCC 134.

Mere technicalities such as seal and signatures need not be insisted upon while enforcing an arbitration agreement.[45] In the advent of electronic communication and online commercial transactions, identification of the parties and their record of agreement would be sufficient to construe an arbitration agreement.[46]

The 2015 amendment brings the Act in conformity with the ML and clarifies that an arbitration agreement can be concluded by way of electronic communication as well.[47] It is sufficient for the clause to be incorporated by reference either to a standard form clause or to a set of trade terms which themselves include provisions requiring disputes to be submitted to arbitration.[48] The arbitration agreement may also be incorporated by reference from an earlier contract that contains an arbitration clause, provided, however, it is not repugnant to or inconsistent with the terms of the contract in which it is incorporated.[49]

The Supreme Court is of the opinion that courts must play a supportive role and adopt a pragmatic and reasonable approach while interpreting arbitration agreements.[50] The intention to arbitrate a dispute is the most necessary component of any arbitration agreement, and this can be gathered from the terms of the agreement.[51] Thus, important attributes that must be present in an arbitration agreement include consent of the parties, impartial and judicial determination, a binding decision of the tribunal and enforceability.[52] The words used in an arbitration agreement should disclose a determination and obligation to go to arbitration and not merely the contemplation of a possibility of going to arbitration.[53] In addition, an arbitration clause has an independent life even if the

[45] *Great Offshore Ltd* v. *Iranian Offsore Engineering & Construction Co.* (2008) 14 SCC 240.
[46] *Govind Rubber Ltd* v. *Louis Dreyfus Commodities Asia Pvt Ltd*, 2014 (14) SCALE 92 (signing an agreement is not an essential requirement).
[47] A&C Act 1996 section 7(4)(b) (added via 2015 amendment).
[48] *J.K. Jain* v. *Delhi Development Authority*, AIR 1996 SC 318.
[49] *Alimenta SA* v. *National Agriculture Co-op Marketing Federation of India Ltd*, AIR 1987 SC 643.
[50] *Enercon*, note 37 ('courts must strive to make a seemingly unworkable arbitration agreement workable').
[51] *Jagdish Chander* v. *Ramesh Chander & Ors*, 2007 3 AWC 2402 SC ('where there is merely a possibility of the parties agreeing to arbitration in future, as contrasted from an obligation to refer disputes to arbitration, there is no valid and binding arbitration agreement').
[52] *K.K. Modi* v. *K.N. Modi*, AIR 1998 SC 1297.
[53] *Sara International Ltd* v. *Golden Agri International Pte Ltd* (2010) ILR 6 Delhi 318; recently, the Karnataka High Court has upheld the requirement of an express intention in the agreement in *Karnataka Power Transmission Corporation Ltd* v. *Deepak Cables*

underlying contract is held to be invalid.[54] Under the Act, in the event of death of a party, an arbitration agreement can be enforced against the legal representative as it shall not be discharged.[55]

Arbitrability under Indian Law

The power of a state to reserve certain categories of disputes exclusively for the determination of national courts is spelled out in section 2(3) of the Act.[56] However, the type of non-arbitrable disputes is not listed under the Act. As defined earlier, the Act allows parties to conclude an arbitration agreement in respect of a 'defined legal relationship, whether contractual or not'.[57] Although additions proposed by the Law Commission made it clear that a dispute must be arbitrable in the first place, the 2015 amendment failed to include those wordings.[58] In *Booz Allen and Hamilton Inc.* v. *SBI Home Finance Ltd*,[59] the Supreme Court observed that arbitrability has three conceptions in different contexts: (a) disputes capable of being adjudicated through arbitration, (b) disputes covered by the arbitration agreement, and (c) disputes that parties have referred to arbitration. While dealing with this question the court held that disputes that involve a determination of rights or obligations *in rem* are not arbitrable, while rights or obligations *in personam* are generally considered to be suitable for arbitration.[60] Further, certain legislations preclude arbitration by mandating exclusive jurisdiction to special courts and tribunals to adjudicate disputes relating to the matters contained therein.[61]

(India) Ltd, AIR 2014 SC 1626 ('there has to be intention, expressing the consensual acceptance to refer the disputes to an arbitrator').

[54] A&C Act 1996 section 16(1). See *Firm Ashok Traders and Anr* v. *Gurumukh Das Saluja and Others*, AIR 2004 SC 1433.

[55] A&C Act 1996 section 40.

[56] A&C Act 1996, section 2(3) – 'This Part shall not affect any other law for the time being in force by virtue of which certain disputes may not be submitted to arbitration.'

[57] A&C Act 1996 section 7(1); see note 41.

[58] Report 246, 2014, note 8 at 42 – amendment of section 7(1) – 'concerning a subject matter capable of settlement by arbitration'.

[59] (2011) 5 SCC 532.   [60] *Ibid*.

[61] These legislations include matters pertaining to the validity and revocation of patents under the Patents Act 1970; matters regarding infringement and rectification of trade marks under the Trademarks Act 1999; infringement of copyright under the Copyright Act 1957; matters relating to the amalgamation and takeover of companies and so on. See Nair, 'Surveying a Decade', note 36 at 706.

Arbitrability of corporate related disputes are considered a grey area in this context. The Supreme Court in *Haryana Telecom* v. *Sterlite Industries*[62] decided that an arbitral tribunal has no jurisdiction to order the winding up of a company, as this power has been vested on High Courts under the Companies Act. Similarly, arbitrability of shareholders' rights against the oppression and mismanagement by a company remained a contentious issue for a long time. Clarifying this issue, the High Court of Bombay held that issues relating to oppression and mismanagement are not arbitrable under the Act as the power to adjudicate these matters are given to a specially empowered Company Law Board (now the National Company Law Tribunal).[63]

Another delicate issue of arbitrability in the Indian context is regarding subject matters involving fraud. The Supreme Court was of the opinion that where allegations of fraud and serious malpractices are involved an arbitral tribunal is not empowered to adjudicate the matter.[64] However, later, in the context of a foreign-seated arbitration, the court clarified that there is no bar to arbitrate a dispute even if it involved allegations of fraud.[65] The court meanwhile revisited its earlier legal position and ruled that issues of fraud are arbitrable in India-seated international arbitrations.[66] Despite the Law Commission's proposal, the 2015 amendment, however, did not make issues of fraud expressly arbitrable under the Act.[67] But, recently, the Supreme Court, bolstering its pro-arbitration stance, held that matters involving fraud can be arbitrated upon unless the allegations of fraud are 'serious and complex' in nature.[68] Thus, the current legal position with respect to the arbitrability of fraud is different for foreign-seated and India-seated arbitrations. While matters involving fraud are arbitrable, unconditionally, for arbitrations seated outside India, it could be made 'inarbitrable' for an arbitration seated in India if the issues involve serious charges of fraud.

---

[62] (1999) 5 SCC 688.
[63] *Rakesh Malhotra* v. *Rajinder Kumar Malhotra* [2015]192 CompCas 516 (Bombay) (the court laid down some exceptions, holding that if the petition is malicious and one that is 'dressed up' to avoid an arbitration clause, then it could be referred to arbitration).
[64] *N. Radhakrishnan* v. *M/S Maestro Engineers*, 2010 (1) SCC 72 ('Radhakrishnan').
[65] *World Sport Group (Mauritius) Ltd* v. *MSM Satellite (Singapore) Pte Ltd*, AIR 2014 SC 968.
[66] *Swiss Timing Ltd* v. *Organising Committee, Commonwealth Games 2010*, AIR 2014 SC 3723 (however, it did not overrule the decision in *Radhakrishnan*, as the petition was filed under a different provision of the Act).
[67] Report 246, 2014, note 8 at 28, ¶52.
[68] *A. Ayyasamy* v. *A. Paramaṣivam & Ors*, AIR 2016 SC 4675.

Enforcement of an Arbitration Agreement

The Act contains two provisions that confer power to a judicial authority to refer disputes to arbitration if the parties have concluded an agreement to arbitrate. In the case of a domestic arbitration (where Part I applies), section 8 mandates a judicial authority to enforce an arbitration agreement by referring the parties to arbitration.[69] Similarly, section 45 empowers a judicial authority to refer a matter to international arbitration to which an arbitration agreement under NYC applies.[70] Courts have issued a series of judgments with respect to the mandatory power specified in section 8. According to the Supreme Court, the language of section 8 of the Act is pre-emptory, and it is obligatory on the part of the court to refer the matter to arbitration if there exists an arbitration agreement.[71] Further, it clarified that once the matter has been referred to the arbitral tribunal 'the suit stands disposed of and nothing remains to be decided by the court'.[72] The court upheld its legal position when it ruled that a judicial authority is statutorily mandated to refer the matters to arbitration when the conditions under section 8 are met.[73] Nevertheless, in *Sukanya Holdings (P) Ltd* v. *Jayesh H. Pandya*, the court decided that bifurcation of the subject matter of a suit, one to be decided by the arbitral tribunal and the other to be decided by the court, is not permissible as it would result in parallel proceedings and would give rise to conflicting judgments from two different forums.[74]

There is an ongoing debate as to the scope of enquiry by a judicial authority, which considers an application either under section 8 or section 45. The controversy is due to a linguistic difference that lies in the last sentence of section 45, which states, 'unless it (judicial authority) finds that the said agreement is null and void, inoperative or incapable of being performed'.[75] Thus, the question is about the nature of judicial enquiry as to the existence and validity of an arbitration clause before referring it to arbitration. A literal interpretation of section 8 will not allow

---

[69] See A&C Act 1996 section 8 (1).   [70] See A&C Act 1996 section 45.

[71] *Hindustan Petroleum Co. Ltd* v. *Pinkcity Midway Petroleums* (2003) 6 SCC 503; *Sundaram Finance Ltd and Ors* v. *T. Thankam*, AIR 2015 SC 1303 (held that the approach of a court faced with an application under section 8 should be not to see whether the court has jurisdiction but to see whether its jurisdiction has been ousted).

[72] *P. Anand Gajapati Raju* v. *P.V.G. Raju* (2000) 4 SCC 539.

[73] *Rashtriya Ispat Nigam Ltd* v. *Verma Transport Co.* (2006) 7 SCC 275.

[74] (2003) 5 SCC 531 ('Sukanya Holdings') ('enforcing the agreement to arbitrate in such a circumstance would also lead to a delay and increasing the cost of litigation').

[75] Section 8 does not contain similar words, unlike art. 8 of the ML 1985.

the court to go into the material validity of the arbitration agreement. Even in the context of section 45 the standards to be followed by the court may not involve a fully fledged trial about the existence and validity of the clause; rather, the court should contend itself with a prima facie enquiry. This liberal approach was considered by the Supreme Court in *Shin Etsu Chemical Co.* v. *Aksh Optifibre Ltd*,[76] and confirmed by a majority, holding that the provision did not require the court to make a final and conclusive determination on this issue. The 2015 amendment settles the controversy by substituting a sub-clause to section 8 that mandates a judicial authority to refer the parties to arbitration unless it finds on a prima facie basis that no arbitration agreement exists between them. Further, in the case of *Chloro Controls (I) Pvt Ltd* v. *Severn Trent Water Purification Inc.*,[77] the Supreme Court decided in favour of binding non-signatories to an arbitration agreement. Even though the 2015 amendment did not change the definition of 'party' under section 2(h) to include 'any person claiming through or under such party',[78] this has been amended through section 8(1). Additionally, the role of the judicial authority has been restricted to a prima facie finding of the existence of an arbitration agreement.[79]

Interim Measures by the Court

Section 9 of the Act provides for grant of interim measures of protection by the court. This provision, modelled on article 9 of the ML 1985, seeks to clarify that merely because a party requests the court for an interim measure, before or during arbitration proceedings, such recourse would not be regarded as incompatible with an arbitration agreement.[80] Arbitration may commence and continue notwithstanding a party having approached the court for interim protection.

In the case of *Sundaram Finance Ltd* v. *NEPC India Ltd*,[81] the Supreme Court discussed the similarities between section 9 and article

[76] AIR 2005 SC 3766.
[77] 2013 (1) SCC 641 (person claiming 'through or under' as provided under section 45 of the Act, i.e., in arbitrations with their seat outside India, would mean and take within its ambit multi-party agreements and therefore even non-signatory parties to some of the agreements can make an application and be referred to arbitration).
[78] Report 246, 2014, note 8 at 33, ¶64.
[79] A&C Act 1996 section 8(1) (substituted via 2015 amendment). This amended provision has come to be increasingly relied on by High Courts; most recently by the Delhi High Court in *Ameet Lalchand Shah and Ors* v. *Rishabh Enterprises and Ors*, 2017 (4) Arb LR 1 (Delhi).
[80] See ML 1985 art. 9.   [81] AIR 1999 SC 565 ('Sundaram Finance').

9. It was held that when a party makes an application under section 9 it is implicit that they accept the existence of a binding arbitration agreement. When this application is made before the commencement of arbitration proceedings, a manifest intention on the part of the applicant to take recourse to arbitral proceedings is required. To ensure timely initiation of arbitration proceedings by a party who has been granted an interim measure of protection, the 2015 amendment to section 9 stipulates a time period of ninety days from the date of the order or within such further time as the court may determine.[82]

In *Firm Ashok Traders and Anr* v. *Gurumukh Das Saluja*,[83] the court observed that during the period of arbitration the power conferred on the arbitral tribunal under section 17 and the power of the court under section 9 might overlap to some extent. But, so far as the time period before and after the arbitral proceedings (before the award is enforced) are concerned, a party seeking an interim measure of protection has only one option, which is the court. The 2015 amendment restricts the power of a civil court to entertain applications to grant an interim measure once the arbitral tribunal has been constituted, 'unless the court finds that circumstances exist which may not render the remedy provided under s. 17 efficacious'.[84] The powers vested in the arbitral tribunal to grant interim measures under section 17(2) of the Act are discussed below.[85]

Another important matter for consideration is the possibility of interim measures by an Indian court when the arbitration is seated abroad. As discussed earlier, in *BALCO*, the Supreme Court clarified that Part I of the Act shall not be applicable in a foreign-seated arbitration by upholding the territoriality principle of the ML 1985.[86] Therefore according to this legal position, Indian courts were not allowed to entertain an application under section 9. Conversely, ML 1985 makes an exception to the territoriality rule by conferring the power to national courts in granting interim measures even when the arbitration is seated outside the country.[87] To eliminate the uncertainty, 2015 amendment to section 2(2) makes section 9 an exception, and thus brings it in conformity with the ML 1985.[88]

---

[82] A&C Act 1996 section 9(2) (added via 2015 amendment).

[83] AIR 2004 SC 1433 (note 54).

[84] A&C Act 1996 section 9(3) (added via 2015 amendment); see *Pradeep K N* v. *The Station House Officer, Perumbavoor Police Station*, 2017(1) Arb LR 57 (Kerala).

[85] See Part IV.   [86] See 'BALCO judgment' (see note 29 and the accompanying text).

[87] ML 1985 art. 1(2).   [88] See note 33.

Part III   Composition of Arbitral Tribunal (Articles 10 to 15)

Constitution of an arbitral tribunal is a contentious gateway issue in international arbitration, especially in India. Based on article 10 of the ML 1985, section 10 respects the autonomy of parties in constituting their tribunal with a condition that the number of arbitrators shall not be an even number.[89] It is obvious that parliament intended to avoid any potential deadlock in final decisions if a tribunal consisted of an even number of members. However, the Supreme Court clarified that this requirement of an odd number is not a mandatory requirement.[90] In addition, the Act provides for a sole arbitrator as the default number as opposed to a three-member tribunal in ML 1985.[91]

Appointment of Arbitrators by the Court

In India, the most frequent root for judicial intervention in arbitration is through section 11 of the Act, where the court is supposed to act as a last resort in appointing an arbitral tribunal. The appointment procedure under ML 1985, as well, mentions the national court as the default mechanism when all other procedures fail.[92] On the other hand, under section 11 of the Act prior to the 2015 amendment the chief justice of a High Court (in the case of a domestic arbitration) or the Chief Justice of India (in the case of an international commercial arbitration) could get involved when the parties fail to appoint or when two arbitrators fail to choose the presiding arbitrator, or if the designated appointment mechanism fails.[93] A major controversy with respect to this provision was the nature of authority exercised by the chief justice.[94] In the case of *SBP & Co.* v. *Patel Engineering*,[95] the Supreme Court held that the power exercised by a chief justice while making an appointment of an arbitrator is a judicial power.[96] As a corollary, all the threshold questions relating to

[89] A&C Act 1996, section 10(1).
[90] *Narayan Prasad Lohia* v. *Nikunj Kumar Lohia*, AIR 2002 SC 1139 ('Lohia') (however, there is no such condition under ML 1985).
[91] A&C Act 1996, section 10(2).   [92] ML 1985 art. 11(4).
[93] A&C Act 1996, section 11(6).
[94] *Konkan Railways* v. *Rani Construction* (2002) 2 SCC 388 ('the power exercised by the chief justice is an administrative function').
[95] (2005) 8 SCC 618 ('SBP').
[96] Report 246, 2014, note 8 at 45 (explanation 2 clarifies that the reference by the High Court to any person or institution designated by it shall not be regarded as a delegation of judicial power).

the jurisdiction of a tribunal, including the existence and validity of an arbitration agreement, shall stand curtailed to the extent the chief justice has made a decision on this issue. Subsequently, the court identified and segregated the preliminary issues that may arise for consideration in an application under section 11 into three categories, that is: (i) issues which the chief justice or her designate is bound to decide; (ii) issues which the chief justice may choose to decide on her discretion; and (iii) issues which should be left to the arbitral tribunal to decide.[97] Recently, the Supreme Court in its attempt to resolve the jurisdictional tussle between a judge and an arbitrator decided that a question whether a claim falls under an arbitration agreement shall be left to the tribunal to decide with the merits of the case.[98]

The 2015 amendment has made wide-ranging modifications with respect to the appointment procedure. Accordingly, the final authority in the appointment shall be the Supreme Court or the High Court, as the case may be, instead of the Chief Justice of India or the Chief Justice of the High Court. Furthermore, it added two important sub-sections. First, it mandates that while considering an application under section 11 the courts must confine the scope of examination to the existence of the arbitration agreement.[99] Further, it adds that 'the designation of any person or institution by the Supreme Court or, as the case may be, the High Court, for the purposes of section 11 shall not be regarded as a delegation of judicial power' and thereby removes the anomalies created by the court in the *SBP* decision.[100] The changes made by parliament have already begun to enable applications under section 11 to be dealt with in a timely manner[101] and, further, to attempt to fix limits on the fee payable to the arbitrators.[102]

---

[97] *National Insurance Co. v. Boghara Polyfab*, AIR 2009 SC 170.
[98] *Arasmeta Captive Power Company Pvt Ltd v. Lafarge India Pvt Ltd*, AIR 2014 SC 525.
[99] A&C Act 1996 section 11(6-A) (added via 2015 amendment).
[100] A&C Act 1996 section 11(6-B) (added via 2015 amendment).
[101] A&C Act 1996 section 11(13) (added via 2015 amendment) (warrants that 'an application made under this section [...] shall be disposed of [...] as expeditiously as possible and an endeavour shall be made to dispose of the matter within a period of sixty days from the date of service of notice on the opposite party'). High Courts have begun to dispose of section 11 applications without engaging arguments on validity of the arbitration agreement and have proceeded to appoint arbitrators, as has been seen in the Karnataka High Court decision in *Techno Aircon Industries Pvt Ltd v. AAB Ltd*, MANU/KA/0805/2016, and the Delhi High Court decision in *Picasso Digital Media Pvt Ltd v. Pick-A-Cent Consultancy Service Pvt Ltd*, MANU/DE/2841/2016.
[102] A&C Act 1996 section 11(14) (added via 2015 amendment).

Challenge and Removal of Arbitrator

Both ML 1985 and the A&C Act 1996 require an arbitrator to disclose any circumstance which gives rise to justifiable doubts as to her independence or impartiality before the appointment as well as during the proceedings.[103] However, it is not possible to codify all situations which would give rise to justifiable doubts as to the impartiality and independence of a person.[104] The test of a real likelihood of bias is whether a reasonable person, in possession of relevant information, would have thought that bias was likely.[105] In order to remedy the absence of possible bias situations, and to make the declaration on the part of the arbitrator more onerous, the 2015 amendment has inserted the fifth schedule to the Act, indicating the circumstances which would give rise to justifiable doubts as to the independence or impartiality of an arbitrator.[106] Additionally, a provision in the newly added seventh schedule states that: 'notwithstanding any prior agreement of the parties, if the arbitrator's relationship with the parties or the counsel or the subject matter of dispute falls in any of the categories mentioned in the seventh schedule' it would make the arbitrator ineligible.[107]

Parties have the freedom to agree on a procedure to challenge an arbitrator failing which the party who alleges a bias can send a written statement of the reasons for the challenge to the arbitral tribunal. The recourse available to the parties when a challenge before the arbitral tribunal fails differs in the Act and the ML 1985. According to the ML

---

[103] A&C Act 1996, section 12 and ML 1985 art. 12.

[104] *Chintakayala Sivaramakrishna* v. *Nadimpalli Venkata Rama Raju and Others*, 2013 (1) Arb LR 384 (AP).

[105] *Ranjit Thakur* v. *Union of India and Ors*, AIR 1987 SC 2386.

[106] A&C Act 1996 section 12(1) Explanation 1 (added via 2015 amendment). Fifth Schedule is drawn on the basis of the 2014 International Bar Association (IBA) Guidelines on conflict of interests in international arbitration. India is, apparently, the only jurisdiction to have incorporated an adapted version of the IBA guidelines in its national law.

[107] A&C Act 1996, section 12(5) (added via 2015 amendment). The employees of public sector undertakings and statutory corporations are ineligible to sit as arbitrators unless both the parties expressly agree in writing. Two recent rulings of the Supreme Court have further clarified the amendments in section 12(5). In *TRF Ltd* v. *Energo Engineering Projects*, AIR 2017 SC 3889, the court opined that the power to nominate an arbitrator extinguishes if the appointing authority was also a named arbitrator disqualified under section 12. Also, in *HRD Corporation* v. *GAIL India Ltd*, 2017 (5) Arb LR 1 (SC), the court held that, for any infraction of section 12(5) read with the seventh schedule, recourse to section 14 of the Act would be available and the court would have the power to terminate the mandate of the arbitrator.

1985, a party can request a court to decide on the challenge of an arbitrator if the agreed procedure or the challenge made before the tribunal is not successful[108] whereas the Act does not allow the parties to get the court involved in a challenge procedure immediately: they have to wait until the award is made by the tribunal.[109] This is a significant and sufficient indicator of parliament's resolve not to brook any interference by the court until the publication of the award.[110]

The mandate of an arbitrator terminates, if she becomes *de jure* or *de facto* unable to perform the functions or for other reasons fails to act without undue delay.[111] In such situations, either the arbitrator may withdraw from the office or the parties by agreement may make a termination.[112] Further, a party may request the court to decide on the termination of the mandate if the controversy remains unsettled.[113] Both ML 1985 and the Act require a replacement of an arbitrator if the challenge is successful or if the mandate is terminated.[114] The procedure agreed upon by the parties for the appointment of the original arbitrator is equally applicable to the appointment of a substitute arbitrator, even if the arbitration agreement does not specifically say so.[115]

Part IV   Jurisdiction of Arbitral Tribunal (Article 16)

The jurisdictional tension between arbitral tribunals and national courts is one of the major controversies in international arbitration with a seat in India. The law as adopted from ML 1985, confers power on the arbitral tribunal to rule on its own jurisdiction, including ruling on any objection with respect to the existence or validity of the arbitration agreement.[116] As mentioned earlier, a seminal case on this issue is *SBP*, where the Supreme Court in contrast to the spirit of this provision ruled that 's. 16 cannot be held to empower the arbitral tribunal to ignore the decision

---

[108] ML 1985 art. 12(3).
[109] A&C Act 1996 section 15(5) – 'the party challenging the arbitrator may make an application for setting aside such an arbitral award in accordance with section 34.'
[110] *Progressive Career Academy Pvt Ltd* v. *FIITJEE Ltd*, 2011 (2) Arb LR 323(Delhi).
[111] A&C Act 1996, section 14(1) and ML 1985 art. 14(1).
[112] *Ibid*. See *M/S B.M.G. Construction* v. *National Small Industries Corporation Ltd*, 2013 (2) Arb LR 567 (All).
[113] A&C Act 1996 section 14(2).   [114] ML 1985 art. 15 and A&C Act section 15.
[115] *ACC Ltd* v. *Global Cements Ltd* (2012) 7 SCC 71.   [116] A&C Act 1996 section 16(1).

given by a judicial authority before the reference to it was made.'[117] However, parliament's intention to make the Act more arbitration friendly is clear from the language of this provision when it states that 'the Tribunal shall [...], where the arbitral tribunal takes a decision rejecting the plea [that it has no jurisdiction],[118] continue with the arbitral proceedings and make an arbitral award.'[119] The ML 1985 allows the party to make a request to the court to reconsider the rejection of this plea whereas under the Act a party has to wait until the award is rendered.[120] The object of the said provision is that an aggrieved party is not without remedy but the stage of remedy is when the final award is made.[121] On the other hand, if the arbitral tribunal decides to accept the plea that it has no jurisdiction such an order is appealable under section 37(2) of the Act.[122]

Compétence-Compétence and Separability

Section 16 of the Act recognizes two important principles of international arbitration law, namely, *kompetenz-kompetenz/compétence-compétence* and separability of the arbitration agreement. While the principle of *kompetenz-kompetenz/compétence-compétence* empowers the tribunal to rule on its own jurisdiction, the separability doctrine asserts that the arbitration clause in a contract can be treated independently of the main contract[123] of which it forms part and, as such, survives the invalidity of the underlying contract.[124] It is important to note that the Law Commission report suggested the extension of the power to arbitral tribunals to make an award or give a ruling 'notwithstanding that the dispute before it involves a serious question of law, complicated questions of fact or allegations of fraud, corruption etc.'.[125] Nonetheless, the 2015 amendment omitted this proposal.

---

[117] See note 95 (court went on to observe that 'the competence to decide does not enable the tribunal to get over the finality conferred to an order passed prior to its entering upon the reference by the very statute that creates it').

[118] A&C Act 1996 section 16(2).   [119] A&C Act 1996 section 16(5).

[120] A&C Act 1996 section 16(3) & (6).

[121] *Triad India* v. *Tribal Cooperative Marketing and Development Federation of India Ltd and Anr*, 2007 (1) Arb LR 327 (Delhi).

[122] *Pharmaceutical Products of India Ltd* v. *Tata Finance Ltd* (2002) 4 AllMR 412.

[123] A&C Act 1996 section 16(1)(a).   [124] A&C Act 1996 section 16(1)(b).

[125] Report 246, 2014, note 8 at 50, ¶10.

The Supreme Court is of the opinion that an arbitration clause continues to be enforceable notwithstanding a declaration of the contract being null and void,[126] but the question would be different where the entire contract containing the arbitration clause stands vitiated by reason of fraud.[127] The concept of the separability of an arbitration clause from the underlying contract is 'a necessity to ensure that the intention of the parties to resolve the disputes by arbitration does not evaporate into thin air with every challenge to the legality, validity, finality or breach of the underlying contract'.[128] Recently, the Supreme Court considered this question in the context of novation of a contract and decided that when a contract is superseded by a new contract the arbitration clause which was part of the first contract falls with it[129] by reversing its earlier stand on this issue.[130]

Part IV-A   Interim Measures and Preliminary Orders (Articles 17 to 17J)

Sub-Part I   Measures and Orders by the Tribunal (Articles 17 to 17G)

Sub-Part II   Recognition and Enforcement of Interim Measures (Articles 17H and 17I)

Sub-Part III   Court-Ordered Interim Measures (Article 17J)

Article 17 was adopted at section 17 as it stood before the 2015 amendment. While the default power given to the tribunal to order interim measures was widely worded, the orders of protection so issued had been made restricted in their direction to the parties before the tribunal itself, and cannot influence third parties,[131] which was clear from the wording of the provision itself.[132] The Supreme Court had also clarified on

---

[126] *Reva Electric Car Co. Pvt Ltd* v. *Green Mobil*, AIR 2012 SC 739.

[127] *India Household and Healthcare Ltd* v. *LG Household and Healthcare Ltd*, AIR 2007 SC 1376.

[128] *Enercon*, note 37, ¶80.   [129] *Young Achievers* v. *IMS Learning* (2013) 10 SCC 535.

[130] *Chatterjee Petrochem* v. *Haldia Petrochemicals Ltd*, 2013 (4) Arb LR 456 (SC) (the court held that the second contract did not amount to a novation of the original one and therefore the arbitration clause in the original contract was valid and binding on the parties).

[131] *SPA Agencies [India] Pvt Ltd rep. by its Managing Director* v. *Harish Rawtani S/o late Ramachand Rawtani*, 2010 (2) Arb LR 221 (AP)(DB) at ¶8.

[132] Stavros Brekoulakis and Laurence Shore, 'UNCITRAL Model Law on International Commercial Arbitration, 1985/2006', in Loukas A. Mistelis (ed.), *Concise International Arbitration* (Kluwer Law International, 2010) at 581.

multiple occasions that though section 17 gives the arbitral tribunal the power to pass orders, the same cannot be enforced as orders of a court.[133] Nonetheless, the High Court of Delhi made the case for enforcing the orders of an arbitral tribunal, contrary to these findings. According to the court, any person failing to comply with a section 17 order would be deemed to be 'making any other default' or 'guilty of any contempt to the arbitral tribunal during the conduct of the proceedings' under section 27(5) of Act, such that the aggrieved party can seek a representation to the court. Upon receipt of this representation, the court would be competent to deal with such party in default as if it is in contempt of an order of the court.[134] This decision prompted the Law Commission to suggest that section 17 orders of the arbitral tribunal be given more teeth and be statutorily enforceable in the same manner as the orders of a court, in line with the 2006 ML amendment.[135] The 2015 amendment now has not only expanded the powers of the arbitral tribunal with respect to the range of measures available at its disposal but has also made these orders enforceable via a deeming provision at section 17(2). The arbitral tribunal has now been vested with the same powers as those of the court under section 9(1)(ii) of the amended Act, keeping in line with the fact that the availability of a recourse to section 9 during continuation of arbitral proceedings has now been curtailed, thus furthering the 'minimum judicial intervention' aims of the 2015 amendment.

Part V   Conduct of Arbitral Proceedings (Articles 18 to 27)

Natural Justice in Arbitration and Applicability of Central Procedural Laws

The Indian legislation, like ML 1985, imposes a mandatory duty[136] on the arbitral tribunal to treat the parties equally and to give each party the full opportunity to present her case.[137] This mandatory duty includes an inviolable obligation to conduct a fair trial during arbitration

[133] Sundaram Finance, note 81 at ¶12; M.D., Army Welfare Housing v. Sumangal Services Pvt Ltd, AIR 2004 SC 1344 at ¶59.
[134] Sri Krishan v. Anand (2009) 3 Arb LR 447 (Delhi) at ¶11, followed in Indiabulls Financial Services v. Jubilee Plots, MANU/DE/1829/2009.
[135] Report 246, 2014, note 8 at ¶49.
[136] Brekoulakis and Shore, note 132 at 624. Further, a failure to do so would render the award open to challenge under section 34(2)(iii).
[137] Article 18 ML adopted at section 18, A&C Act 1996.

proceedings. Thus, for example, a party to the proceedings must know what is the evidence that has been given, and she must also be given an opportunity to show why it is not to be used against her.[138] However, failure of a party to send over written submissions to the counter party in advance is not a fault on the part of the arbitrator.[139]

Section 19(1) makes a specific reference to the central laws on evidence and civil procedure by clarifying that the arbitral proceedings are not bound by these laws. Further, article 19(2) has been split into two separate sub-sections in section 19; but the language has been retained. Under section 19(2), if the parties do not agree to a procedure to be followed by the arbitral tribunal in conducting its proceedings by virtue of sub-section 19(3), it is open to the tribunal to conduct the proceedings in the manner it considers appropriate. It is, therefore, falling within the jurisdiction of the arbitral tribunal to lay down the just and proper procedure.[140] However, it has been opined[141] that not every aspect of the Code of Civil Procedure (CPC) is excluded, especially in the context of sections 9, 27 and 36 of the A&C Act 1996. The interesting aspect is that some features of the procedural law are available to the court while dealing with issues arising in arbitral proceedings before, during and after passing of the award and also at the stage of execution of the award. Therefore, the attempt, it seems, in the legislation, is to lend greater efficiency to the arbitral process, by allowing the scope for recourse to the procedural law, while also expressly making the conduct of the proceedings themselves free from the 'entanglement' of the complexities of the CPC.[142]

The 'Place', 'Seat' and 'Venue' Conundrum

Section 20 in the Act has the first paragraph of article 20 ML 1985 split into two subsections while retaining the language and intent of the provision. Like elsewhere in the world,[143] the differences between 'place',

---

[138] *Union of India v. Bharath Builders & Contractors*, 2012 (4) Arb LR 448 (Kerala) at ¶10.

[139] *Viraj Holdings v. Motilal Oswal Securities Pvt Ltd and Others* [2003] 115 CompCas 102 (Bombay) at ¶16.

[140] *Vimal Madhukar Wasnik (Dr.) v. Sole Arbitrator, the Honourable Shri Justice M.S. Deshpande and Others*, 2006 (1) Arb LR 255 (Bombay, DB) at ¶5.

[141] *National Highway Authority of India v. Oriental Structure Engineers Ltd - Gammon India Ltd (JV)*, AIR 2013 Delhi 67 at ¶9.1.

[142] *Ibid.* at ¶9.5.

[143] Brekoulakis and Shore, note 132 at 627; Phillip Capper, 'When is the "Venue" of an Arbitration its "Seat"?' Kluwer Arbitration Blog, 25 November 2009.

'seat' and 'venue' of arbitration have given rise to ample litigation in India. The *BALCO* decision[144] is definitive as it has brought the interpretation in line with international practice.[145] While the seat has been identified as being the juridical seat that would determine the applicable *lex arbitri* and confer supervisory jurisdiction on local courts,[146] it has also been observed that the arbitral hearings may take place at a location other than the seat of arbitration. The court further observed that it was clear from the language of section 20 itself that a most convenient venue may be fixed, irrespective of the 'seat' of arbitration in India, considering that section 20 has to be read in the context of section 2(2) that provides for the applicability of Part I, only where the arbitration is seated in India. This 'territorial principle' inherent in the ML 1985[147] has been taken on in Indian law such that section 20 does not support the extra-territorial applicability of Part I, so far as purely domestic arbitration is concerned.[148] Further, in an international commercial arbitration, while it may be required that hearings and proceedings be held outside India for convenience, this location change does not in any way influence the 'seat' in India that enables supervisory jurisdiction of Indian courts over such arbitrations.[149]

This idea of the 'seat' being the territorial link between the arbitration and the applicable *lex arbitri*[150] was further concretized by the Supreme Court in *Enercon*.[151] Therefore, where an Indian party and a German party had made an express agreement to be bound by the A&C Act 1996 in an arbitration with its 'venue' in London, it was held that 'by making such a choice, the parties have made the curial law provisions contained in chapters III, IV, V and VI of the Indian Arbitration Act 1996 applicable [...] by choosing that Part I of the Indian Arbitration Act 1996 would apply, the parties have made a choice that the seat of arbitration would be in India' and that 'London would only be the "venue" to hold the proceedings of arbitration'.[152]

Report 246, 2014 went a step further in its suggestions for amendment to section 20 in that it advocated doing away with the usage of the term 'place' altogether and instead provided for insertion of the words 'seat

---

[144] *BALCO*, note 6.   [145] Report 246, 2014, note 8 at 23, ¶40.
[146] *BALCO*, note 6 at ¶¶72, 95 citing *Naviera Amazonica Peruana S.A. v. Compania Internacionale De Seguros Del Peru*, 1988 (1) Lloyd's Law Reports 116.
[147] *Ibid.* at ¶¶66, 88–89; see also ML 1985 art. 1(2); Brekoulakis and Shore, note 132 at 588.
[148] *BALCO*, note 6 at ¶99.   [149] *Ibid.* at ¶100.   [150] *Ibid.* at ¶74.
[151] *Enercon*, note 37.   [152] *Ibid.* at ¶90.

and venue'. This was being done to make the wording of the Act more consistent with the international usage of the concept of a 'seat' of arbitration, while also legislatively distinguishing between the concepts of 'seat' and 'venue'.[153] The suggestion was touted as a major step in the right direction in furtherance of India's aims towards projecting itself as a pro-arbitration venue,[154] along with amendments in section 2 with respect to remedies at the seat as well as some degree of extra-territoriality to the legislation.[155] While section 2 was partially amended as mentioned earlier, the 2015 Amendment did not take this into account and section 20 has been left as is, without clarifying the 'place', 'seat' and 'venue' conundrum.

Limitation, Commencement and the Arbitral Proceedings

Section 21 of the Act has retained the language of article 21. The language of section 21 is fairly clear in that arbitration proceedings will commence from the date when a request is received by the respondent for referring the dispute to arbitration, unless the parties have agreed to the contrary.[156] Further, the Supreme Court has also clarified that since section 9 enables the filing of a request for interim measures before the commencement of arbitration proceedings a court is not debarred from dealing with an application under section 9 merely because no notice has been issued under section 21 of the Act.[157]

The interplay between section 21 and section 43 of the Act has led to interesting litigation[158] and academic opinion[159] in India. Section 43(1) provides that the Limitation Act 1963 shall apply to arbitrations as it applies to proceedings in courts. Section 43(2) provides that for the purposes of section 43 and the Limitation Act 1963 an arbitration shall be deemed to have commenced on the date referred to in section 21 of the Act. Having

[153] Report 246, 2014, note 8 at 52 (amendment of section 20).
[154] Badrinath Srinivasan, 'Part II of the Comments on the Law Commission's 246th Report: "Amendment to Arbitration and Conciliation Act 1996"' (11 August 2014), http://practicalacademic.blogspot.in/2014/08/part-ii-of-comments-on-law-commissions.html (accessed 30 October 2017).
[155] Report 246, 2014, note 8 at ¶41 at 39.
[156] Sundaram Finance, note 81 at ¶12; *Milkfood Ltd* v. *GMC Ice Cream (P) Ltd* (2004) 7 SCC 288 at ¶109.
[157] Sundaram Finance, note 81 at ¶20.
[158] *State of Goa* v. *Praveen Enterprises*, AIR 2011 SC 3814 ('Praveen Enterprises'); *Voltas Ltd* v. *Rolta India Ltd*, AIR 2014 SC 1772 ('Voltas').
[159] Badrinath Srinivasan, 'Reference, Counter-Claims and Limitation in Arbitration: SCI Clarifies' (9 October 2011), http://practicalacademic.blogspot.in/2011/10/reference-counter-claims-and-limitation.html (accessed 30 October 2017).

regard to section 43 of the Act, any claim made beyond the period of limitation prescribed by the Limitation Act 1963 will be barred by limitation and the arbitral tribunal will have to reject such claims as barred by limitation.[160] Section 3 of the Limitation Act 1963 does not specify the date of institution for arbitration proceedings, an omission which is remedied by section 21.[161] However, with respect to counter-claims, since section 3 of the Limitation Act does provide guidance with respect to counter-claims in courts, it has been further held that the date on which the counter-claim is made before the arbitrator will be the date of 'institution' in so far as the counter-claim is concerned, thus not requiring the application of section 21 for counter-claims.[162] To this general rule, an exception was carved out that where the respondent against whom a claim is made had previously served a notice of arbitration to the claimant through a statement of claim, and later in a subsequent arbitration submits the same as a 'counter-claim' instead, the limitation for such counter-claim should be computed as on the date of service of notice of such claim on the claimant and not on the date of filing of the counter-claim.[163]

The first paragraph of article 22 has been split in section 22 into three further sub-sections, such that section 22 has four sub-sections. Nonetheless, the language remains unaltered. Retaining the international practice on party autonomy over the language for conduct of arbitral proceedings,[164] it gives the arbitrator only default powers of determination of the language of arbitration.[165] Party autonomy over language extends not only to the conduct of proceedings but also to written statements and any hearing and any arbitral award, decision or other communication by the arbitral tribunal.[166] Further, in any case, the tribunal can seek a translation of any documentary evidence before it.[167]

Section 23 provides for the manner of conducting the arbitral proceedings, by stating the rules to be applied to the pleadings of the parties. The prescription under section 23 is not to be confused with the provisions under section 21, which talk of the request of a party for commencement of arbitration.[168] Under section 23, the claimant need not restrict her claims to those made in the notice submitted under section 21, and may also amend or add to the same, thus modifying the scope of the arbitration,[169] unless

[160] Praveen Enterprises, note 158 at ¶13. [161] Ibid. at ¶15. [162] Ibid. at ¶17.
[163] Ibid. upheld in Voltas, note 158 at ¶24. [164] A&C Act 1996 section 22(1).
[165] A&C Act 1996 section 22(2). [166] A&C Act 1996 section 22(3).
[167] A&C Act 1996 section 22(4).
[168] Malhotra, Law and Practice of Arbitration, note 5 at 953; see also preceding discussion under section 21.
[169] Ganesh Benzoplast Ltd v. Saf Yeast Company Ltd, 2007 (4) Arb LR 385 (Bombay) at ¶8.

there is an agreement to the contrary. Further, the respondent too can submit a counter-claim and further add to or amend the same, on a joint reading of section 23(1), (3) and section 2(9).[170] Upon receipt of the claims and counter-claims, it is for the arbitrator to determine whether they fall within the scope of the arbitration agreement and whether she has jurisdiction to adjudicate on those disputes.[171] The Law Commission has called for an addition to the present section 23 by inserting a new explanation which provides for the inclusion of a claim for set-off in the counter-claim by the respondent without affecting the initial submission to arbitration. The same thus would enable the arbitrator to adjudicate upon claims for set-off, without having to seek a separate or new reference from the parties.[172] The 2015 amendment inserts a new provision as sub-section (2A) to include the option of a respondent to plead a set-off which shall be adjudicated upon by the arbitral tribunal.

Section 24 provides that whether the arbitrator should hold an oral hearing for the presentation of evidence, or for oral argument, or whether the proceedings shall be conducted on the basis of documents and other materials, depends primarily upon the agreement of the parties. Further, there is a statutory mandate binding upon the arbitrator to conduct the arbitration proceedings fairly, under section 24(2) and (3), apart from under section 18.[173] Therefore, where no notice was sent upon submission of claim after the party was declared *ex parte* it has been held to amount to a violation of sections 18 and 24.[174] Such a violation can render the award capable of being set aside as 'patently illegal' under section 34 of the Act.[175] To expedite arbitration proceedings, the Law Commission had suggested an amendment to section 24(1) by insertion of a further proviso that prevents the arbitrator from granting adjournments unless 'sufficient cause is made out', and empowers the tribunal to impose costs on the party seeking the adjournment.[176] This suggestion has been included as a further proviso to section 24(1) vide the 2015 amendment.

Section 25 adopts article 25 of the ML 1985 in full, with 'negligible verbal variations'.[177] Section 25 is concerned with three types of default:

[170] Praveen Enterprises, note 158 at ¶22.   [171] *Ibid.* at ¶24.

[172] Report 246, 2014, note 8 at 52.

[173] *Union of India* v. *Bharath Builders & Contractors*, 2012 (4) Arb LR 448 (Kerala) at ¶12.

[174] *Impex Corporation and Ors* v. *Elenjikal Aquamarine Exports Ltd*, AIR 2008 Ker 119 at ¶¶5–8; *Sulaikha Clay Mines* v. *M/S Alpha Clays & Another*, AIR 2005 Ker 3 at ¶3.

[175] *Oil & Natural Gas Corporation Ltd* v. *SAW Pipes Ltd*, AIR 2003 SC 2629 at ¶21 ('SAW Pipes').

[176] Report 246, 2014, note 8 at 52.

[177] Malhotra, *Law and Practice of Arbitration*, note 5 at 995.

claimant's with respect to her claim statement, defendant's with respect to her defence statement, and default of any party with respect to appearance or evidence submission.[178] A joint reading of sections 23(1) and 25(a) makes it clear that if the claimant fails to communicate the statement of claim within the period of time agreed upon by the party or within the period of time determined by the arbitral tribunal the proceedings have to be terminated. Nonetheless, section 25(a) is not a mandatory provision.[179] Further, if the arbitral tribunal terminates the proceedings pursuant to section 25(a), the mandate of the tribunal shall also terminate co-extensively.[180] Section 25(c) enables the taking of evidence, on account of failure of a party to appear at an oral hearing, from the party itself, or from any 'third person.' This phrase 'any person' also appears in section 27(2)(c), and covers not only witnesses, but also parties to the proceedings, such that the arbitral tribunal can proceed *ex parte* under section 25(c) for default.[181] Moreover, since the arbitral tribunal is to make its award on merits, evidence collection is enabled even in circumstances of default by virtue of section 25(c).[182] The Law Commission recommended the insertion of an elucidatory phrase to section 25(b) in that if the respondent defaults on communication of her statement of defence she also forfeits her right subsequently to file the same,[183] which now finds mention on the statute books pursuant to the 2015 amendment.

While paragraphs (1) and (2) have been retained in section 26 of the Act, a sub-section (3) has been inserted that enables parties to request that the expert make available for examination all documents she relied on. Since the provision is non-mandatory, the parties may exclude such a power, and the arbitrator cannot then seek external expert opinion.[184] Further, it has been held that since section 26(2) empowers parties to summon and examine the expert, an averment by the arbitrator that a subsequent request for examination of the expert cannot stand unless specified in the initial request for appointment, and in fact amounts to repudiation of the statutory mandate.[185]

---

[178] *Ibid.* at 996–97.

[179] *N. Jayalaxmi* v. *R. Veeraswamy and Anr*, 2004 (1) Arb LR 31(AP) ¶¶19, 20, 30.

[180] *Indian Oil Corporation Ltd* v. *ATV Projects India Ltd and Anr*, 2004 (2) Arb LR 432 (Delhi) at ¶¶11, 15.

[181] *Delta Distilleries Ltd* v. *United Spirits Ltd* (2013) 4 Arb LR 47 (SC) at ¶19.   [182] *Ibid.*

[183] Report 246, 2014, note 8 at 53.

[184] Malhotra, *Law and Practice of Arbitration*, note 5 at 1017.

[185] *Union of India* v. *Bharath Builders & Contractors*, 2012 (4) Arb LR 448 (Kerala) at ¶11.

Court Interference During the Proceedings: Evidence Taking

Section 27 of the Act differs considerably from the ML 1985 in that the section also provides for a detailed procedure for requesting for assistance in taking evidence. Under section 27, the requirement is that the party should apply to the court specifying:[186]

i. the names and addresses of the parties and the arbitrators;
ii. the general nature of the claim and the relief sought;
iii. the evidence to be obtained in particular, referring to the names and addresses of any person to be heard as witness or expert witness;
iv. a statement of the subject matter of the testimony required; and
v. a description of the documents to be produced or property to be inspected.

Further, it has been held that, under section 27, where either the arbitral tribunal or the party before the arbitral tribunal, with its approval, applies to the court for assistance in taking evidence, recourse can be taken to the provisions of the CPC.[187] Upon failure of persons to attend in accordance with such processes being issued to them or committing a default or refusing to give evidence or even being guilty of contempt of the arbitral tribunal, they would be subject to such disadvantages, penalties and punishments which the court may impose by its order on a representation of the arbitral tribunal as it can do in suits being tried before it.[188]

Part VI   Making of Award and Termination of Proceedings (Articles 28 to 33)

Identifying the Proper Law Applicable to the Merits

The Act, contrary to the express intent of the ML 1985, adopts its text for both purely domestic as well as domestic international arbitrations[189] [seated in India]. Therefore, section 28 provides for substantive law rules applicable to the merits in both types of arbitration.

---

[186] *Rasiklal Ratilal* v. *Fancy Corporation Ltd and Anr*, 2007 (4) Arb LR 173 (Bom) at ¶4.
[187] *NHAI* v. *Oriental Structural Engineers Ltd Gammon India Ltd* (2013) 1 Arb LR 362 (Delhi) at ¶10.2.
[188] A&C Act 1996 section 27(5).   [189] *BALCO*, note 6 at ¶88.

For purely domestic arbitrations in India, the parties do not have autonomy over choice of substantive law applicable, and the arbitrator is bound to apply the law for the time being in force in India.[190] It has been held that to permit otherwise would be against the public policy of India,[191] and that a contravention of the substantive law of India would result 'in the death knell of an arbitral award'.[192] Further, it has been clarified that a contravention of section 28(3) is also covered as 'patent illegality', such that when the arbitrator construes the contract in such a way that it could be said to be something that no fair minded or reasonable person could do, it would become liable to be set aside under section 34(2)(b)(ii).[193] The effect of the *SAW Pipes* decision that leaves awards open to being set aside for violation of public policy of India if contracts are contrary to section 28 was sought to be negated by the proposed amendment to the law in Report 246, 2014.[194]

Also, while the ML 1985 allows the tribunal to use the conflict of laws rules it deems appropriate in the absence of an express choice of law by parties to an international arbitration, section 28(1)(b)(iii) of the Act provides for a direct route in selecting the substantive law, as it is under the laws of France, Canada, Kenya and the Netherlands.[195] According to this, a tribunal has the authority not only directly to choose a system of substantive law without recourse to a nation's private international law rules, it also is not obliged to choose a national system of law as the substantive law and instead it may choose such other rules of law as it considers appropriate for the resolution of the dispute.[196] It has been elsewhere argued by the authors that though this seems logical considering the argument that an international arbitral tribunal has no specific *lex fori*, however, by requiring the tribunal to apply the appropriate rules of law considering the surrounding circumstances of the case the Indian legislation creates a degree of

---

[190] A&C Act 1996 section 28(1)(a).
[191] *TDM Infrastructure*, note 14 at ¶20; see also, *BALCO*, note 6 at ¶123.
[192] SAW Pipes, note 175 at ¶¶12, 21; clarified further in *Associate Builders* v. *Delhi Development Authority*, AIR 2015 SC 620 ('Associate Builders') at ¶12 – 'a contravention of s. 28(1)(a) of the Act would render the award capable of being set aside under s.34(2)(b)(ii) as an award against the public policy of India'.
[193] *Ibid.*   [194] Report 246, 2014, note 8 at 53.
[195] Alan Redfern, J. Martin Hunter et al., *Redfern and Hunter on International Arbitration*, 5th edn (Oxford University Press, 2009) at 234–35.
[196] *Ibid.*

uncertainty.[197] The 2015 amendment has also tweaked s. 28(3) and has added that the arbitral tribunal shall take into account the terms of the contract and the trade usages 'while deciding and making an award'.

The Decision of the Arbitral Tribunal and Award Making

The mandate of section 29 is that a majority award prevails. However, for the award to be valid, all the arbitrators must sit together and apply their mind to the dispute before taking the final decision and should have taken part in the proceedings and deliberations.[198] Further, if sections 29 and 31 are read together, it is also obligatory on the part of each of the members of the arbitral tribunal to sign the award to make it a valid one, as the signature requirement is not a mere formality under the Indian regime.[199] The newly inserted sections 29A and 29B are a departure from the ML 1985 in that they have been inserted to ensure that arbitral proceedings are completed in a timely manner. Under these articles, the award must be rendered within a year from the date the arbitral tribunal enters upon the reference (within six months under the fast-track procedure).

A&C Act 1996 further adopts article 30 of the ML 1985 at section 30. Sub-section (1) is an additional provision which explicitly states that the arbitral tribunal can encourage any methods to settle the dispute at any time during the arbitral proceedings. The settlement agreement shall have the same effect as the arbitral award on agreed terms on the substance of the dispute rendered by the arbitral tribunal.[200] Further, the Supreme Court has also held that if both the parties to an arbitration agreement agree for conciliation, and the matter is settled through conciliation, the settlement agreement is enforceable as if it were a decree of the court.[201]

Article 31 on the form and contents of awards has been adopted but with additional sub-sections. The arbitral tribunal has been further

---

[197] See Harisankar K. Sathyapalan, 'International Commercial Arbitration in Asia and the Choice of Law Determination' (2013) 30 (6) *Journal of International Arbitration* 621–36 at 635.

[198] *Subhash Chugh and Co. v. Girnar Fibres Ltd* (2000) 3 RAJ 461 (Punjab & Haryana).

[199] *Transmission Corporation of Andhra Pradesh Ltd v. Galada Power and Telecommunication Ltd*, 2007 (1) ALT 515.

[200] *Visa International Ltd v. Continental Resources Ltd* (2009) 2 SCC 55 at ¶29; *Mysore Cement Ltd v. Svedala Barmac Ltd* (2003) 10 SCC 375 at ¶16.

[201] *Afcons Infrastructure Ltd v. Cherian Varkey Construction Co.* (2010) 8 SCC 24 at ¶¶27, 28.

empowered to: make interim awards,[202] award interest in awards for payment of money,[203] and fix costs.[204] Under section 31(1), the award is complete and final only after it is signed by the arbitrators,[205] and such an award must carry reasons unless otherwise agreed by the parties.[206] It has been explained by the Supreme Court that the delivery of an arbitral award under sub-section (5) of section 31 is not a matter of mere formality. It is a matter of substance, as this delivery by the arbitral tribunal and receipt by the party of the award sets in motion several periods of limitation, constituting an important stage in the arbitral proceedings.[207]

Further, a two-judge bench of the Supreme Court has held that since section 31(7) makes no reference to payment of compound interest or payment of interest upon interest, the same cannot be done.[208] This is against two earlier opinions of the court,[209] such that in *Hyder Consulting (U.K.)* v. *Governor of Orissa*,[210] this issue has been referred to a three-judge bench. In light of these conflicting opinions, several amendments had been suggested to section 31 in Report 246, 2014.[211] The proposed amendment sought legislatively to undo the decision in the *Arora* matter by empowering the arbitral tribunal to award compound interest, and also amending the current rate, and instead sought to provide for interest payable at current market rates.[212] Thus, section 31(7)(b) now stands amended, with a further explanation.[213] Section 31(8) further makes a reference to the newly inserted section 31A which provides for a 'regime for costs', empowering the court or the arbitral tribunal to determine the costs of arbitral proceedings or of any proceedings under the A&C Act 1996.

---

[202] A&C Act 1996 section 31(6).   [203] A&C Act 1996 section 31(7)(a).

[204] A&C Act 1996 section 31(8).

[205] *State of Maharashtra and Others* v. *Ark Builders Pvt Ltd* (2011) 4 SCC 616.

[206] A&C Act 1996 section 31(3), *State of Uttar Pradesh* v. *Combined Chemicals Pvt Ltd* (2011) 2 SCC 151, *Som Datt Builders Ltd* v. *State of Kerala* (2009) 10 SCC 259.

[207] *Union of India* v. *Tecco Trichy Engineers and Contractors* (2005) 4 SCC 239 at ¶8.

[208] *State of Haryana* v. *L. Arora & Co.* (2010) 3 SCC 690 [Arora].

[209] *ONGC* v. *M.C. Clelland Engineers S.A.* (1999) (4) SCC 327, *UP Cooperative Federation Ltd* v. *Three Circles* (2009) 10 SCC 374.

[210] (2013) 2 SCC 719.   [211] Report 246, 2014, note 8 at ¶¶65–69.

[212] Report 246, 2014, note 8 at 5.

[213] A&C Act 1996 s. 31(7)(b) (added via 2015 amendment) reads: '(b) A sum directed to be paid by an arbitral award shall, unless the award otherwise directs, carry interest at the rate of two per cent higher than the current rate of interest prevalent on the date of award, from the date of award to the date of payment. Explanation. – The expression "current rate of interest" shall have the same meaning as assigned to it under clause (b) of section 2 of the Interest Act 1978.'

Termination of Proceedings and Functus Officio Exceptions

Section 32 provides for the automatic termination of the mandate of the tribunal upon the expiry of the agreed period of time for making the award, unless such period be extended.[214] Once the final arbitral award is passed, it has the effect, *ipso jure*, of terminating the arbitral proceeding.[215] Section 33 extends the mandate of the tribunal, enabling correction of clerical errors, or for offering interpretation of a specific part of the award, or for making an additional award on claims not addressed in the earlier final award.[216] However, an arbitral tribunal cannot review its own award under the garb of correcting clerical or typographical errors.[217] Further, an application for interpretation of a specific point or a part of the award can only be made if both parties agree for the same,[218] unlike the power to correct clerical, typographical or computation errors, which can be exercised *suo motu* by the tribunal.[219] Section 33 also enables an arbitrator to make an additional award on claims not covered in an earlier partial award, and a challenge to such an additional award has been held to not stand for the mere allegation of the additional award being on claims that were unaddressed in the earlier award.[220] The court cannot correct errors of the arbitrators. It can only quash the award leaving the parties free to begin the arbitration again if it is desired.[221]

Part VII   Recourse against Award (Article 34)

While the side-heading of section 34 excludes the 'exclusivity' of setting aside as a remedy against the award as is present in ML 1985, section 34(1) provides that setting aside is the '*only*' recourse against an arbitral award. Further explanation has been inserted to section 34(2)(b)(ii),

---

[214] *NBCC Ltd v. JG Engineering Pvt Ltd*, AIR 2010 SC 640 at ¶5.
[215] *Futuristics Offshore Services and Chemicals Ltd v. ONGC*, MANU/MH/1625/2012 at ¶12.
[216] Malhotra, *Law and Practice of Arbitration*, note 5 at 1215; see also *McDermott International Inc. v. Burn Standard Co. Ltd and Ors* (2006) 11 SCC 181 at ¶47 ('*McDermott International*'); *Gujarat State Fertilizers Co. Ltd v. Tata Motors Ltd*, MANU/MH/0008/2015 at ¶75.
[217] *State of Arunachal Pradesh v. Damani Construction Co.* (2007) 10 SCC 742 at ¶8.
[218] *Sushi Pandit v. Adsert Web Solutions Pvt Ltd* (2011) 4 Arb LR 43 at ¶3.
[219] A&C Act 1996 section 33(3).   [220] McDermott International, note 216.   [221] *Ibid.*

where an award is in conflict with the public policy of India if the making of the award was induced or affected by fraud or corruption. Sub-section (3) also has a proviso that extends the time period for filing an application under section 34 by a further thirty days if 'sufficient' cause for the delay is shown. It is interesting to note that while section 34 is applicable only to awards covered by Part I of the Act, where Part I applies only where the seat of arbitration is in India, according to the language of the law, two views still prevail. For agreements entered into prior to 6 September 2012, the *Bhatia* decision still holds good, which would mean that the recourse under section 34 is also available to awards made outside India. However, for agreements entered into after 6 September 2012, the decision in *BALCO* applies, such that recourse under section 34 is available only where the seat is in India.[222]

A civil court hearing a section 34 matter exercises supervisory and not appellate jurisdiction over the awards of an arbitral tribunal, such that where an award is modified, allowing or granting a claim, contrary to any provision of the contract, it would violate section 34(2)(b)(ii) read with section 28(3) of the Act.[223] A significant departure from the ML jurisprudence elsewhere in the world relates to the number of arbitrators and a request seeking setting aside for improper tribunal composition. The Supreme Court has held that the parties get a right to challenge the award only where the composition is contrary to agreement of the parties. However, where the parties themselves agreed to a two-member panel then there can be no challenge under section 34(2)(a)(v), even if the panel that made the award had two members, contrary to section 10.[224] It is

---

[222] This dichotomy, amongst other issues, is a topic of debate, given section 26 of the 2015 amendment on prospective application. While the section makes clear that the 2015 amendment does not apply to arbitral proceedings commenced before 23 October 2015, the question that remains is whether it also does not apply to related court proceedings commenced before this date. Several conflicting High Court opinions exist on this point. For instance, while a single judge of the High Court of Calcutta in *M/S Reliance Capital Ltd* v. *Chandana Creations* (GA 1406 of 2016, dated 17 May 2016) held that the 2015 Amendment did not apply to arbitral proceedings commenced prior to the said date, a single Judge of the Gujarat High Court in *M/S Manibhai and Brothers.* v. *General Manager* (O/IAAP/11/2016 dated 29 April 2016) applied the amendments to section 12 to proceedings for termination of the mandate of an arbitrator, commenced before 23 October 2015.

[223] *M/S J.G. Engineers Pvt Ltd* v. *Union of India and Anr*, Civil Appeal No. 3349 of 2005 dated 28 April 2011 at ¶7.

[224] Lohia, note 90 at ¶¶19–20.

submitted that this finding of the derogable nature of section 10 is errone-ous.[225] Further, if a plea of jurisdiction is not taken before the arbitrator, such a plea cannot be permitted to be raised in proceedings under section 34.[226]

A lot of litigation, in the recent past, has been on the interpretation of the 'public policy of India' exception under section 34(2)(b)(ii). It has been held that the phrase in the section 34 context is required to be given a wider meaning, such that the award could be set aside if it is contrary to:[227]

(a) fundamental policy of Indian law;
(b) the interest of India;
(c) justice or morality, or
(d) in addition, if it is patently illegal.

While Report 246, 2014 tried to remedy the situation and suggested an express inclusion of the 'patent illegality' ground for purely domestic arbitrations only, in a proposed explanation to section 34(2)(b)(ii),[228] after this report, the Supreme Court made two very important pro-nouncements.[229] These decisions clarified the meanings of the four phrases used in the *SAW Pipes* matter, such that the Law Commission was compelled to issue a supplement to its Report 246, 2014 on 'public policy'.[230] The Law Commission expressed concerns over the expansive meaning attributed to the phrase 'fundamental policy of India' by the *Western Geco* decision that incorporated the test of the Wednesbury principles of reasonableness,[231] as it enables a substantive review of an arbitral award, contrary to the language and intent of the ML 1985 as well as the Act. Therefore, in an attempt to ensure the aim of India to

---

[225] Refer discussion under s. 10; see also Malhotra, *Law and Practice of Arbitration*, note 5 at 1309.

[226] *Gas Authority of India Ltd and Anr* v. *Keti Construction (I) Ltd and Others* (2007) 5 SCC38 at ¶¶18–19.

[227] SAW Pipes, note 175 at ¶¶15, 21, 30. The decision was also, albeit erroneously, used to set aside a foreign award in the aftermath of the *Bhatia* ruling in the case of *Venture Global* wherein this finding was cited with approval at ¶¶13, 19.

[228] Report 246, 2014 at 55.

[229] *ONGC Ltd* v. *Western Geco International Ltd* (2014) 9 SCC 263 ('Western Geco'); Associate Builders, note 192.

[230] Law Commission of India, Supplementary to Report number 246 on Arbitration and Conciliation Act 1996 – 'Public Policy' Developments Post Report No. 246 (February 2015), http://lawcommissionofindia.nic.in/reports/Supplementary_to_Report_No._246.pdf ('Supp. Report 246, 2015').

[231] Western Geco, note 229 at ¶¶39–40; Supp. Report 246, 2014, note 8 at ¶10.4–10.6.

project itself as an arbitration facilitative nation with minimal judicial intervention,[232] it was further suggested by the Law Commission that explanation 2 be inserted to section 34(2)(b)(ii) that would clarify that the application of the tests for public policy violation does not entail a substantive review of the award.[233]

The 2015 amendment keeps the suggested scheme the same, having inserted two explanations to section 34(2)(b)(ii). Explanation 1 clarifies what is meant by an 'award in conflict with the public policy of India', by providing an exhaustive, 'only' list, and explanation 2 further incorporates the caveat that the test for contravention of the fundamental policy of India does not entail a merits-based review of the award. Further, sub-section 2(A) as inserted provides that the patent illegality ground is available only for the setting aside of awards arising from arbitration other than international commercial arbitrations under Part I of the A&C Act 1996, a proviso which clarifies that a mere erroneous application of the law does not amount to a patent illegality.

More recently, in further magnification of the Indian judiciary's disposition towards upholding party autonomy, a two-tiered arbitration clause has been upheld as not violative of the public policy of India by the Supreme Court in *M/S Centrotrade Minerals & Metal Inc. v. Hindustan Copper Ltd.*[234] The agreement of the parties provided that the 'arbitration result' be subject to a further arbitration on appeal – a form of non-statutory appeal process. The court held that there is nothing in the law that prohibits the contracting parties from agreeing upon a second instance or appellate arbitration, either explicitly or implicitly. No such prohibition or mandate can be read into the A&C Act 1996 except by an unreasonable and awkward misconstruction and by straining its language to a vanishing point.[235] It is submitted that this judgment seems erroneous in that it distorts the mandatory nature of the language of section 34(1) where the setting aside remedy has been made the exclusive recourse against an award, lending a 'non-derogable' nature to the provision. It further undoes the provision in section 35 that renders finality and binding value to the arbitral award based on expiration of timelines under section 34.[236]

---

[232] Supp. Report 246, 2015, ¶10.6.   [233] *Ibid.*
[234] 2016 (12) SCALE 1015 ('Centrotrade').   [235] *Ibid.* at ¶44.
[236] For a contrary view, see Nakul Dewan and Vinayak Panikkar, 'The Legality of Two-Tier Arbitrations' (2017) 4 *NLUD Student Law Journal* 47.

Part VIII   Recognition and Enforcement of Awards
(Articles 35 and 36)

Enforcement and Finality

Paragraph 1 of article 35 of the ML 1985 has been adopted in two different sections. Section 35 lends finality to arbitral awards[237] and section 36 provides for enforcement. Paragraph 2 of article 35 has been adopted at section 47 [evidence] that figures in Part II of the Act, and this provides for the power of the court to call for evidence in an enforcement proceeding for a foreign award. Section 36 of the Act is a deeming provision which provides for the enforcement of award as if it is a decree of a civil court under the CPC.[238] Thus, a legal fiction has been created that on expiry of the period prescribed for setting aside an award it becomes capable of being executed and enforced.[239] Further, the party seeking to enforce a foreign award has to make an application under section 47 of the Act enclosing therewith the evidence as mentioned therein. However, none of the seven grounds under section 48 envisages a situation where a prayer for enforcement could be refused when it is not accompanied by any of the evidence/documents as mentioned in section 47 of the Act.[240]

Refusal of Enforcement for Foreign Awards

Article 36 has been adopted by the Act in section 48 in Part II with minor modifications in the language. In addition, it has appended an explanation to the term public policy of India: 'that an award is in conflict with the public policy of India if the making of the award was induced or affected by fraud or corruption'. The conditions set out in section 48 are exhaustive. The court may exercise its discretion to refuse enforcement of a foreign award on any of the first five conditions set forth in this section, only if the party objecting to enforcement makes a request and furnishes the necessary proof. However, with respect to the last two conditions in section 48(2) the court may *suo motu* refuse enforcement.

If a foreign award has not become binding on the parties under the corresponding law of the country where it was made, the courts in

---

[237] See *Ravi Prakash Goel* v. *Chandra Prakash Goel and Anr*, AIR 2007 SC 1517 at ¶19.
[238] *Thyssen Stahlunion Gmbh* v. *Steel Authority of India Ltd*, AIR 1999 SC 3923 at ¶8.
[239] *Centrotrade Minerals and Metal Inc.* v. *Hindustan Copper Ltd* (2006) 11 SCC 245 at ¶14.
[240] *Austbulk Shipping SDN BHD* v. *P.E.C. Ltd*, 2005 (2) Arb LR 6 (Delhi).

India under this sub-section may refuse enforcement. The words 'suspended or set aside', in clause (e) of section 48(1), cannot be interpreted to mean that, by necessary implication, the foreign award sought to be enforced in India can also be challenged in Indian courts. So far as India is concerned, the Act does not confer any such jurisdiction on its courts to annul an international commercial award made outside India.[241]

The interpretation of 'public policy' under section 7(1)(b)(ii) of the FARE Act 1961 came in question before the Supreme Court in *Renusagar*.[242] It laid down that a foreign award can be challenged on the grounds of public policy if it was against: first, fundamental policy of Indian law; secondly, the interests of India; or, thirdly, justice or morality. Therefore, it was safely said that this move made by the courts maintained the enforceability of the foreign awards on Indian soil.[243]

The *SAW Pipes*[244] decision has provoked considerable adverse comments[245] considering that it triggered the slew of decisions that followed it that used the same grounds for refusing recognition to foreign awards. As mentioned earlier,[246] in *Venture Global*, following the judgment in *Bhatia*, the Supreme Court held that foreign awards can be set aside by Indian courts under section 34 of the 1996 Act, i.e., for violating Indian statutory provisions and being contrary to Indian public policy.

However, the entire damage done by these opinions was sought to be remedied in a significant decision, where the Supreme Court stated:

> A distinction in the rule of public policy between a matter governed by the domestic law and a matter involving conflict of laws has been noticed in *Renusagar*. For all this there is no reason why *Renusagar* should not apply as regards the scope of inquiry under Section 48(2)(b). Following *Renusagar*, we think that for the purposes of Section 48(2)(b), the expression a 'public policy of India' must be given narrow meaning and the enforcement of foreign award

---

[241] *BALCO*, note 6 at ¶138.
[242] *Renusagar Power Co., Ltd* v. *General Electric Co.*, 1994 Supp (1) SCC 644.
[243] See Aakanksha Kumar, 'Foreign Arbitral Awards Enforcement and the Public Policy Exception: India's Move Towards Becoming an Arbitration-Friendly Jurisdiction' (2014) 17(3) *International Arbitration Law Review* 76.
[244] See note 175.
[245] See Harisankar K. Sathyapalan, 'Public Policy vis-à-vis Enforcement of Foreign Arbitral Awards: Some Reflections on the Indian Approach', in Surya Prakash (ed.), *Critical Issues in International Commercial Arbitration* (National Law Institute University, India, 2012) at 63; see also, McDermott International, note 216 at ¶42.
[246] Refer earlier discussion for section 34(2)(b)(ii).

would be refused on the ground that it is contrary to public policy of India if it is covered by one of the three categories enumerated in *Renusagar*.[247]

This decision was welcomed and was widely hailed to be consistent with the recent trend of judgments rendered by the Supreme Court which consciously sought to reduce judicial intervention in enforcement of foreign awards and endeavoured to make the process less time consuming.[248] The decision in *SAW Pipes* now is only of some little relevance to pre-*BALCO* arbitrations, seated outside India, given the 2015 amendment and its part-prospective, part-retrospective application.[249]

Conclusion

There is no doubt that the landscape of international commercial arbitration in India has changed with the adoption of the ML 1985 in the year 1996. The Act has incorporated modern notions of an arbitration friendly legal regime, and sometimes it traverses even beyond the principle of minimum judicial intervention, as shown in the preceding discussions.[250] However, the statistics of the first fifteen years of the Act demonstrate that India has only paid lip service to the ethos of the ML 1985, and the actual working relationship between the courts and the arbitral process has not been satisfactory. We believe that the discomfort in extending a laissez-faire regime to international arbitration was a common phenomenon in the developing world and was deep rooted in Asian society. There used to be a widely held view that western solutions to the problems of dispute resolution are of little relevance to the east.[251] The reluctance of the Indian judicial system to accommodate the needs of private international arbitration played a major role in creating a fragile architecture of international commercial arbitration in the country.

---

[247] *Shri Lal Mahal Ltd* v. *Progetto Grano Spa* (2014) 2 SCC 433 at ¶25.

[248] Harisankar K. Sathyapalan, 'Second Look at the Foreign Award Forbidden on Enforcement – Indian Supreme Court', Kluwer Arbitration Blog, 1 August 2013, available at www.kluwerarbitrationblog.com (accessed 30 October 2017); Kumar, 'Foreign Arbitral Awards Enforcement', note 243 at 83, 86.

[249] Kumar, 'Foreign Arbitral Awards Enforcement', at 83; see also note 222.

[250] For instance, the Act does not provide an immediate judicial remedy against the acceptance of jurisdiction by an arbitral tribunal, as opposed to ML 1985.

[251] Fali Nariman, 'East Meets West: Tradition, Globalization and the Future of Arbitration: The Clayton Utz International Arbitration Lecture' (2004) 20 *Arbitration International* 123.

The distrust (or nescience?) towards international commercial arbitration had been evinced by some of the infamous decisions from Indian courts. At the cost of repetition, it is to be noted that the judiciary erred mainly in three areas and thus deviated from the spirit of the ML 1985. First, by extending its supervisory arm to overseas arbitrations and allowing courts to annul foreign awards, the regime has disrespected the seat theory of international commercial arbitration.[252] Secondly, taking away 'gateway questions' from the realm of arbitrators indicated a departure from the established principle of *kompetenz-kompetenz/compétence-compétence*. Thirdly, the ways in which Indian courts have dealt with the enforcement of foreign awards through a topsy-turvy construction of 'public policy' of India have labelled India as a legal system hostile to international commercial arbitration. But, judges alone cannot be blamed. A transnational outlook on the part of the lawyers in dealing with the idiosyncrasies of private international arbitration is equally important for any jurisdiction effectively to implement a progressive legal framework like that of the A&C Act 1996.

India, unlike some of its Asian counterparts, took its own good time to adapt to the realities of modern international arbitration. With the start of a new decade in the twenty-first century, the Indian judiciary seems to have learned from their past mistakes and started contributing to the mission of making the country an attractive destination for international arbitration. It is heartening to see that with some admirable decisions the judiciary has come to terms with the preamble of the present Act, which has been drafted in line with the ML 1985. We think it is important to reiterate a few welcoming developments: first, by emphasizing the territoriality principle of the ML, the Supreme Court said extra-territorial jurisdiction in international commercial arbitration is no longer permissible; second, merits review is unacceptable in the context of a foreign award and the defence of public policy is limited in scope; and, finally, threshold issues, including the question of arbitrability, are left to the arbitrator to decide.

The greener side of the story does not end here. As mentioned earlier, the Indian parliament has made extensive amendments aiming to plug many loopholes in the law that surfaced during the working of the Act

---

[252] However, the *BALCO* decision has set right the legal position, and brought it in conformity with the ML 1985.

over a period of almost two decades. No doubt, things are changing and there are visible efforts in maintaining a right balance between judicial control and arbitral autonomy. To conclude, in the past thirty years or so, if the Model Law has served as a model for many parliaments in the region, we hope that India will become a role model for many other Model Law jurisdictions in the next thirty years.

Japan

Japanese Arbitration Law and UNCITRAL Model Law

HISASHI HARATA

Introduction

Arbitration law in a recognizably modern form has a long history in Japan that began in 1890 with the enactment of the nation's first Code of Civil Procedure.[1] Little legislative change took place until 2003, when Japan enacted the new – and still current – Arbitration Act ('JAA').[2] Later that year, the Japanese government informed UNCITRAL of Japan's adoption of the Model Law[3] (the original 1985 version) ('ML 1985').[4]

There is some basis for Japan's claim to have adopted the ML 1985: during the JAA's drafting process, the drafters took into consideration

Hisashi Harata is Professor of Law at the University of Tokyo, Faculty of Law. The author thanks the EW Barker Centre for Law & Business at the Faculty of Law of the National University of Singapore for financing his participation in the conference entitled, 'The UNCITRAL Model Law on International Commercial Arbitration in Asia', which led to this book; to Gary Bell for his exceptional kindness and efforts as the conference organizer and editor of this book and for his incisive feedback on earlier drafts; and to the Centre for Asian Legal Studies at NUS Law, and in particular, Alan K. Koh, for their editorial and administrative support. The usual caveats apply.

[1] Legislative provisions on arbitration were first enacted in Japan as part of the Code of Civil Procedure: Minji Soshō Hō (Law No. 29 of 1890), Book VIII (arts. 786–805). With the enactment of the current Code of Civil Procedure in 1996, the old Code – stripped of all but the original arbitration provisions – was renamed Kōji Saikoku Tetsuduki oyobi Chūsai Tetsuduki ni kansuru Hōritsu (Law No. 29 of 1890, as amended by Law No. 109 of 1996) ('Old Arbitration Statute'). The final version of this statute (as amended by Law No. 151, 1999) continued to serve as Japan's arbitration legislation until 29 February 2004.

[2] Chūsai Hō (Law No. 138 of 2003). This statute entered into force on 1 March 2004.

[3] UNCITRAL Model Law on International Commercial Arbitration 1985, UN General Assembly Resolution 40/72 (11 December 1985) ('ML 1985').

[4] For a brief historical overview of Japanese arbitration legislation, see H. Harata, 'Interpretation and Application of the New York Convention in Japan', in G. Bermann (ed.), *Recognition and Enforcement of Foreign Arbitral Awards: The Interpretation and Application of the New York Convention by National Courts* (Springer, 2017) at 585.

the English text of the ML 1985 almost exclusively, except article 26(3) JAA (corresponding to article 19 ML), for which the French text was also referred to. However, as this Chapter will show, Japan's claim to have adopted the ML is, at the very least, subject to qualifications. First, the JAA departs from the ML on several critical issues. As such, it is better to consider Japan's purported adoption of the ML as partial at best. It is also doubtful if Japan truly adopted the general principles underlying the ML together with specific wording used by the ML.

The challenges of writing about Japanese law – a jurisdiction with a highly challenging vernacular and impenetrable legal language – in English are amplified by the lack of authoritative, high-quality translations of core legal sources, including but not limited to important statutes. Arbitration law is no exception. This is further compounded by a general dearth of in-depth legal literature on crucial areas of law adjacent to arbitration law, including civil procedure.[5] For the JAA, the most accessible and popular English version of the statute is the unofficial English translation offered by the Ministry of Justice, which this Chapter will generally use for the convenience of readers.[6] However, readers ought to bear in mind that this translation is presented as 'tentative', and is in any event incomplete as it does not include the supplementary provisions of the same Act containing important exceptions applying to consumer contracts and labour disputes.[7] Even more importantly, parts of this translation are not completely congruent with the original Japanese provisions, a critical issue which this Chapter will address in detail. This is due to the translators' intentional use of English terminology from the ML 1985 that did not find their way into the JAA as it was officially enacted in Japanese. As exclusive reliance on the JAA's English translation might obscure substantive differences between the JAA and the ML, readers are advised to treat the JAA translation with a degree of scepticism and circumspection.

In illuminating the challenges and pitfalls in the implementation, or failure thereof, of non-binding, 'model' international instruments in

---

[5] This Chapter will endeavour to provide adequate explanation, in jurisdiction-neutral terminology, of concepts that are likely to be unfamiliar to a reader schooled in the common law tradition – or even in other branches of the civil law family.

[6] In this Chapter, the English translation of the JAA is taken from the website of the Ministry of Justice (www.japaneselawtranslation.go.jp) (accessed 30 October 2017). Note that the translations of Japanese statutes on this website are unofficial and often revised.

[7] Translations of supplementary provisions in this Chapter are sourced from M. Kondo, T. Goto, K. Uchibori, H. Maeda and T. Kataoka, *Arbitration Law of Japan* (Shojihomu, 2004).

otherwise well-governed, economically developed jurisdictions with sophisticated legal cultures, the story of the ML in Japan is an instructive case study not only for jurists and scholars interested in arbitration law in Asia but also anyone interested in model laws and legal harmonization. Model laws are generally perceived as easier to amend than international treaties – it is for this reason that there are those who would prefer to amend international treaties that have been ratified (and implemented) and become domestic law via the model law method, instead of undergoing a formal treaty revision. However, even if the model law itself is easy to amend, that is not necessarily the case for the domestic law that has been enacted based on the model law. Even two jurisdictions that have 'adopted' the same model law may exhibit substantial differences if one has adopted an older version of the model law and the other a newer version. A further complication arises where the model law incorporates the substantive content of an existing treaty, but part of that incorporated content is subsequently amended in a revision of the model law. In this case, differences arise not only as between different versions of the model law, but also as between the model law and the treaty. As I will show in this chapter, to achieve international harmonization in arbitration law, not only was the ML used in tandem with (rather than in lieu of) the treaty (the New York Convention ('NYC')[8]), an attempt was made to change international standards not by revising the treaty but rather by amending the ML and leaving the issue of its adoption to domestic laws. As we will see, this hybrid phenomenon not only fails to promote harmonization but has rather become a key obstacle to it.

Part I General Provisions of the Model Law (Articles 1 to 6)

General Observation

The JAA's general provisions differ from the ML in three major aspects. First, although the JAA has adopted the same concept of *locus arbitri* in defining the territorial scope of its own application, it did not adopt the ML's limitations based on concepts of 'international' and 'commercial' arbitration. Instead, the JAA is broader, covering arbitrations of 'civil' disputes.

Second, the JAA does not define some of the main concepts addressed in article 2 ML; it does, however, define arbitration agreement, arbitral tribunal

---

[8] Convention on the Recognition and Enforcement of Foreign Arbitral Awards, New York, 10 June 1958, in force 7 June 1959, 330 UNTS 4739 ('NYC').

and the writing requirement.[9] The JAA does not clarify the practical boundary between arbitration and other dispute resolution mechanisms.[10]

Third, the JAA's provisions on judicial intervention differ from the prevailing interpretation of the ML[11] by permitting judicial intervention even prior to the determination of the *locus arbitri* (article 8 JAA).

Article 1   Scope of Application

Following article 1 ML, the JAA's scope of application is territorially defined and based on the *locus arbitri* (article 3 JAA). However, the JAA adopts neither the international/non-international nor commercial/non-commercial distinctions.[12] Subject-matter restrictions on arbitrability (as contemplated by article 1(5) ML and reserved in article 13(1) JAA) apply to consumer contracts and labour disputes; special rules governing these classes of cases are found in the Arbitration Act's supplementary provisions.[13]

Article 2   Definitions and Rules of Interpretation

The JAA does not contain any equivalent to article 2(a), (c), (d), (e) and (f) of the ML. The exception is article 2(2) JAA, which corresponds to article 2(b) ML and provides a definition of 'arbitral tribunal'.

The concept of 'arbitral award' has not raised any serious issues of interpretation in Japan.[14] The arbitral award is generally considered to be a final and binding decision by a third-party arbitrator with respect to the defined

---

[9] A. Takakuwa, 'Chūsai-hō no Tekiyō', in T. Kojima and A. Takakuwa (eds.), *Chūshaku to Ronten Chūsaihō* (Seirinshoin, 2007) at 23.

[10] UNCITRAL 2012 Digest of Case Law on the Model Law on International Commercial Arbitration (New York, 2012) ('Digest') at 12–13, nos. 2 and 3 and 26–27, nos. 6 to 8. See also nn. 43–44 on arbitration agreement.

[11] See Digest, note 10 at 68 no. 3; 71 no. 4; 73 no. 2.

[12] The former Japanese arbitration statute, note 1, made no distinction between international versus domestic matters, or commercial/non-commercial cases. If the JAA had, following the ML, adopted such distinctions, there would have been issues of interpretation on the JAA's scope of application in relation to the former arbitration statute. Within Japan, there are concerns that limiting the JAA's application to disputes of an international and commercial character would undermine certainty for parties: K. Miki and K. Yamamoto (eds.), *Shin Chūsaihō no Riron to Jitsumu* (Yūhikaku, 2006), N. Idei at 18 ('JAA Symposium' followed by the name of the speaker (if applicable) and page number). Limiting the JAA's application to 'international' disputes (art. 1(3) ML) also raises concerns that disputes between foreign companies carrying on business in Japan and Japanese companies would fall outside the JAA's scope: JAA Symposium (*ibid.*), T. Nakamura at 18.

[13] On these supplementary provisions of the JAA, see note 47 and text thereto.

[14] Cf. N. Koyama, *Chūsaihō*, 2nd edn (Yūhikaku, 1983) at 24, 174.

legal relationship pursuant to the parties' agreement.[15] Although article 2(1) JAA addresses the concept of an arbitral award, it is not a definition.

The Tokyo District Court in 1993[16] granted enforcement, as an arbitral award under the NYC, of a decision made by the China International Economic and Trade Arbitration Commission that contained the terms of the parties' settlement.[17] More recently, in 2015, the Tokyo District Court[18] held that a decision rendered by the Shanghai Labour Dispute Arbitration Commission pursuant to Chinese labour law[19] is not an 'arbitral award' because proceedings did not require any bilateral agreement of the parties, but may be commenced by a party unilaterally.[20]

Critically, the JAA has no equivalent to article 2A ML on interpretative principles based on the instrument's international origin and its underlying general principles. As mentioned above, even though the JAA adopted, by and large, the provisions of the ML 1985 which focused on international commercial disputes,[21] the JAA generalized and extended the rules' scope of application to civil disputes, regardless of their international or commercial nature or lack thereof. This is why any principle of interpretation based on the ML's international origin is not correspondingly adopted in the JAA. As a matter of practice, Japanese courts do not regularly refer to international or foreign arbitration practice when interpreting the JAA. Hence, the JAA has not implemented the international spirit of the ML, but rather nationalized it as just another part of domestic law.

---

[15] A. Takakuwa, 'Gaikoku Chūsai Handan no Shōnin oyobi Shikkō ni kansuru Jōyaku, Dai-1-jō', in T. Kojima and A. Takakuwa (eds.), *Chukai Chūsaihō* (Seirinshoin, 1988) at 362–63.

[16] Tokyo District Court Judgment, 20 July 1993, 1494 *Hanrei Jihō* 128.

[17] The decision is in line with scholarly opinion in Japan. See H. Kobayashi and M. Murakami, *Kokusai Minji Soshōho* (Kōbundō, 2009) at 216–17; JAA Symposium, note 12, Y. Taniguchi at 368; T. Kojima, 'Wakai Chūsai Handan (Wakai ni motoduku Chūsai Handan)', in Kojima and Takakuwa, note 9 at 220–22.

[18] Tokyo District Court Judgment, 27 February 2015, *Westlaw* 2015 WLJP CA02278003.

[19] Laodong Fa (People's Republic of China), art. 77.

[20] However, according to the defendant's case, both contracting parties had signed the labour contract that included a clause referring to the Chinese Labour Law. This point also concerns the characterization of the arbitration agreement.

[21] Kōichi Miki argues (but without citing any authority) that there was no acknowledgment during the drafting process of the ML of any particular necessity to create provisions for domestic arbitration that are separate and distinct from those for international arbitration. He goes on to say that the ML itself has expected a country adopting it to extend the scope of application to include domestic arbitration: JAA Symposium, note 12, K. Miki at 18.

Article 10 JAA applies the Code of Civil Procedure with necessary modifications to court proceedings under the JAA. Cf. art. 26(2) JAA (corresponding to art. 19(2) ML 1985).

Article 3   Receipt of Written Communications

Article 3(1)(a) ML was adopted in article 12(1) and (5) JAA, with additional options of domicile and office. Article 3(2) ML was adopted as article 12(6) JAA. In addition, other provisions of the article of the ML were added in article 12(2)–(4) JAA. These provisions are considered also to cover the proceedings before the arbitral tribunal's composition.[22]

In addition, the JAA provides court support for written communication (court serving notices in support of arbitration) (art. 12(2),[23] and see also (3), (4) and (6)).[24] Chapter 1 JAA including this article is put out of the territorial limitation of the scope of application based on *locus arbitri*. Therefore, court support for written communication (art. 12(2) JAA) is also generally available.[25]

Article 4   Waiver of Right to Object

The corresponding provision is not placed under the general provisions of the JAA, but rather adopted as article 27, in the chapter on arbitral proceedings. Although article 27 JAA appears to be concerned only with the waiver of right to object in an arbitration procedure, this provision is generally considered to cover other aspects in arbitration procedure, e.g., including procedures for the appointment, challenge and removal of an arbitrator.[26] Article 27 JAA does not include the condition that a

---

[22] JAA Symposium, note 12, M. Kondo at 38. For facsimile as 'written communication', JAA Symposium note 12 at 43. Miki argues that there is insufficient discussion on the ML regarding this point: JAA Symposium, note 12, K. Miki at 44–45. For e-communication (email), see JAA Symposium, note 12 at 48.

[23] Article 12(2):

> With regard to the notice to be given by means of documents in an arbitration procedure, if it is possible to deliver the document to the addressee's domicile, habitual residence, business office, office, or place of delivery of the addressee, but it is difficult for the sender to obtain the materials that prove the fact of delivery, and the court finds it necessary, it may decide that it will serve the document by itself, upon the petition of the sender. With respect to the service in this case, the provisions of Article 104, and Articles 110 to 113 of the Code of Civil Procedure shall not apply.

[24] For the procedure on judicial proceedings on arbitration, see art. 11 JAA and Chūsai Kankei Jiken Tetsuduki Kisoku [Rules of Procedure on Arbitration-Related Matters] (Rules of the Supreme Court No. 27 of 26 November 2003).

[25] However, there are issues on the scope of application of art. 12(1) and (5), and choice of law in relation thereto.

On the how the court's failure to serve notice impacts the waiver of objections, see JAA Symposium, note 12 at 223.

[26] Kondo et al., note 7 at 148. See also art. 25 JAA.

party 'yet proceeds with the arbitration' (art. 4 ML). Neither article 27 JAA nor article 4 ML directly addresses the issue of waiver of right to object where rules laid down by the arbitral tribunal are infringed.[27] In any event, mandatory rules in institutional procedural rules chosen by the parties should provide clarification on the possibility of waiver.

Article 5   Extent of Court Intervention

Article 4 JAA is slightly different from article 5 ML.[28] With the ML, there is still the possibility of a court intervention on matters left out of scope of application of the ML (cf. article 1(1) and (5) ML).[29] As the JAA covers broadly arbitrations on civil disputes and in principle on the basis of *locus arbitri*, regardless of internationality, article 4 JAA explicitly limits the power of courts as for arbitral proceedings in all arbitration cases.[30] There is considerable debate within Japan on whether it is possible to invite the court to intervene in ways other than as provided for in the JAA.[31]

---

[27] JAA Symposium, note 12, M. Kondo at 222.

[28] Article 4 'With respect to an arbitration procedure, the court may exercise its authority only in the case provided for in this Act' (emphasis added).

[29] Digest, note 10 at 21, no. 4.

[30] In Japan, whether 'intervention' (art. 5 ML) also includes the court's support for arbitration remains debated (cf. art. 6 ML): H. Sakai, 'Chūsai to Shihō Saibansho no Kanyo', in Kojima and Takakuwa, note 9 at 28. Cf. Digest, note 10 at 21, no. 5. The JAA restricts the extent to which the parties may, by agreement, empower the court to intervene and provide support to the arbitration; conversely, parties also cannot by agreement impose further limits on the court's power except to the extent explicitly permitted by the JAA: see Kondo et al., note 7 at 13–14.

[31] On the possibility of court intervention in situations for which there is no express authorization in the JAA, some scholars discuss the possibility of filing suit against either the other party or the members of the arbitral tribunal, and to claim damages allegedly caused by and through arbitral proceedings; if a court were to hear such a claim, it might imply indirect intervention in the arbitration. For instance, on the issue of loss caused by interim measures ordered by the arbitral tribunal (cf. art. 17 ML), some scholars take the position that it is not possible to pursue such a claim in court, arguing that the tribunal has exclusive competence over such a claim according to the spirit of art. 5 ML and art. 4 JAA. It is also argued that damages claims against arbitrators do not fall within the meaning of 'arbitration procedure' and thus are beyond the scope of the court's powers as prescribed under art. 4 JAA: JAA Symposium, note 12 at 21. Cf. *Zivilprozessordnung* [Civil Procedure Code] (Federal Republic of Germany), §1041(4) (under German law, if the imposition of an interim measure is unjustified, the party who obtained that measure is liable to compensate the other party for loss suffered by the latter party due to the measure or from the latter party's provision of security).

Further, scholars are divided on whether it is possible to seek a court declaration of validity or invalidity of the arbitration agreement. Scholars denying this possibility rely on

Article 6   Court or other Authority for Certain Functions of Arbitration Assistance and Supervision

Article 5 JAA lays down rules on which the court shall have jurisdiction to intervene in the dispute at issue.[32] Parties may by agreement specify a particular court (art. 5(1)(i) JAA), but there is disagreement over whether the jurisdiction agreement needs to be in writing,[33] because article 5(1)(i) JAA does not prescribe form requirements for the agreement.[34]

When judicial intervention occurs, the court may render a final decision (*kettei*) without oral argument (art. 6 JAA).[35] The provisions of the current Code of Civil Procedure shall, except as otherwise provided, apply *mutatis mutandis* to court proceedings under the JAA (art. 10 JAA).

Article 7 JAA stipulates that an appeal (*kōkoku*) against a judicial decision must be made within a strict, non-extendable period of two weeks; this differs from the general rule in the Code of Civil Procedure, which prescribes a one-week period.[36] This divergence is

---

art. 23(1) JAA (cf. art. 16(1) ML) and also refer to a particular interpretation of German arbitration law: JAA Symposium, note 12, K. Miki and T. Nakamura at 23–26; *Zivilprozessordnung*, §1026. Contra JAA Symposium, note 12, M. Kondo and Y. Aoyama at 24–25.

[32] Cf. Digest, note 10 at 20–21, nos. 3–6.

[33] Minji Soshō Hō (Law No. 109 of 1996) ('Code of Civil Procedure'), art. 11(2) (requiring choice of court agreements to be in writing).

[34] JAA Symposium, note 12 at 29.

[35] Under Japanese civil procedure, court proceedings are broadly classified into two tracks. The first track, which is typical of most contentious matters by which the court is bound by the parties' pleadings, leads to a final disposition in the form of a *hanketsu* court ruling (often translated as 'judgment'). Under the second track, which is adopted in a variety of 'non-contentious' matters such as valuation disputes and in family law matters, the court is not bound by the parties' contentions, and is decided as it sees fit within the boundaries of the law. Oral argument is not necessary, and the matter is disposed of by a court ruling called *kettei* ('decision'). See, generally, in English, A. K. Koh, 'Appraising Japan's Appraisal Remedy' (2014) 62 *American Journal of Comparative Law* 417 at 428–29. (A further type of disposition is *meirei* ('order'), which typically applies only for interlocutory matters and thus need not concern us here.) This is a distinction inherited from German civil procedure (cf. *Urteil* and *Beschluss*).

[36] Code of Civil Procedure, art. 332. For a brief explanation in English of the different appellate procedures applying to different types of judicial proceedings, see Koh, note 35 at 429 n. 92.

explained as taking into account the possibility that some parties may reside abroad.[37]

Article 9 JAA establishes special provisions for the inspection of a case record pertaining to a procedure conducted by a court under the JAA.[38] Article 11 JAA states that necessary particulars on proceedings under the JAA may be specified by rules made by the Supreme Court.

The most remarkable divergence from the ML is article 8 JAA, which governs the court's intervention in the situation where the *locus arbitri* is yet to be determined.[39] Due to this provision, which differs from the prevailing view on the ML, Japanese courts may actively intervene in the arbitration under one condition: 'the place of arbitration is likely to be in Japan'. There is no case law on this provision as yet, but the more loosely this condition is interpreted the more room there will be for the court to intervene even if the *locus arbitri* is yet to be determined as somewhere within the country.

Part II   Arbitration Agreement (Articles 7 to 9)

General Observation

The corresponding provisions of the JAA are by and large congruent with articles 7 to 9 ML 1985. However, when a party raises an arbitration agreement as an objection to a court action, the JAA only allows the court to dismiss the claim (not to 'refer the parties to arbitration'), which is different not only from the ML but also the NYC.

The provisions on arbitration agreements in the JAA are concerned only with cases where the *locus arbitri* is Japan. However, to rule on the validity of an arbitration agreement, a Japanese court must first address the problem of choice of law. The choice of law issue is important not only in the context of having the court action summarily dismissed,[40] but also as the basis for setting aside, recognizing or enforcing an arbitral

---

[37] Kondo et al., note 7 at 21. See also the similar two-week period in Gaikoku Tōsan Shori Tetsuduki no Shōnin Enjo ni kansuru Hōritsu [Act on Recognition of and Assistance for Foreign Insolvency Proceedings] (Act No. 129 of 29 November 2000), art. 7.

[38] Cf. art. 10 JAA with art. 122 Code of Civil Procedure.

[39] Article 8(1) The Petitions set forth in the following items may be filed with a court, even if the place of arbitration has yet to be determined and the place of arbitration is likely to be in Japan, and the location of the general venue of the petitioner or respondent (excluding general venues which shall be determined by the last domicile) is in Japan [. . .].

[40] This is equivalent to the concept of motions to dismiss in American federal and state law, and applications to strike out in Anglo-Commonwealth law.

award (or refusal thereof). The way in which the choice of law issue is dealt with is not necessarily the same in the two situations above. At present, this point has not been adequately addressed in the literature not only in the context of the JAA (and the ML), but for the NYC as well.[41]

The choice of applicable law on formalities should also be clarified. Before the enactment of the JAA in 2003, no formalities seem to have been required according to Japanese case law.[42] The relation between the new JAA and the previous Japanese jurisprudence but also the current treatment of formalities in the case of recognition/enforcement are yet to be clarified.

Due to article 8 JAA, the Japanese court's intervention is also admitted under some conditions prior to the determination of *locus arbitri*.

Article 7   Definition and Form of Arbitration Agreement

The provisions corresponding to article 7 ML are set forth in article 13 JAA.[43] Article 7(1) ML was adopted in article 2(1) JAA with

[41] On choice of law issues arising from the arbitration agreement, see, generally, Harata, note 4 at 597–99.

[42] For agreements on the court's jurisdiction, see Supreme Court Judgment 28 November 1975, 29-10 *Minshū* 1554 (in view of the need for speed in international transactions, a jurisdiction clause in a bill of lading need not meet the strict requirement of an agreement in writing to be valid). For choice of court agreements under the current Japanese law of civil procedure, see Code of Civil Procedure, art. 3-7.

[43] Article 13(1) 'Except as otherwise provided for in laws and regulations, an Arbitration Agreement shall be effective only when the subject thereof is a civil dispute (excluding disputes of divorce or dissolution of adoptive relation) which can be settled between the parties.'

There is precedent suggesting that the ouster of jurisdiction of the court must be clear in the arbitration agreement itself in order for a party successfully to resist a claim in court: Sapporo District Court Judgment 16 May 2003, 1174 *Kinyū Shōji Hanrei* 33. Cf. Digest, note 10 at 27–28, no. 9 and 31–32, nos. 21–22. See also the supplementary provision (art. 3) on the arbitration agreement of consumer contract.

For the definition of an arbitration agreement, see the judgment of the Tokyo District Court 31 January 2012, which featured a contract of sale by way of internet auction on a web page which included provisions on dispute resolution, including an arbitration clause. The court held that the parties that participated in the auction had agreed to arbitration, and that the dispute resolution provisions on the auction site are deemed to be incorporated into the contract of sale: Tokyo District Court Judgment 31 January 2012, *Westlaw* 2012 WLJP CA01318016. Cf. Digest, note 10 at 13, no. 3. For a similar situation arising in the context of a labour dispute, see Tokyo District Court Judgment 27 February 2015, note 18.

an amendment to limit the scope of application to 'civil disputes' (cf. article 1(5) ML).[44]

It is necessary to note that although the JAA (art. 13(1)) deals with arbitrability as an issue of the arbitration agreement's validity, there still remains a choice of law issue. It is also important to remember that the issue of arbitrability itself needs to be addressed not only in terms of the validity of the agreement, but also in terms of the types of the disputes that the public policy of the forum considers to be arbitrable (art. 1(5) ML).[45] In any event, the Japanese courts have had the opportunity to address a variety of issues concerning the arbitration agreement over the course of several reported decisions.[46]

An example of how the court interprets an arbitration agreement is found in Tokyo District Court Judgment 23 August 2013, 1417 *Hanrei Taimuzu* 243. There, the court held that the agreement to submit the dispute to arbitration at the 'International Commercial Arbitration Court' did not mean submission to ICC arbitration given that such a court can be found in Russia, Belgium or the Ukraine, even though none of these countries has any relevant connection to the parties or the transaction. See also Intellectual Property High Court Judgment 28 February 2006, *Westlaw* 2006 WLJP CA02280016.

For an implied revocation of an arbitration agreement, see Tokyo District Court Judgment 25 March 2009, 1309 *Hanrei Taimuzu* 220 (rejecting the argument on the facts).

For the difference between an arbitration agreement and an agreement to call for an expert's opinion, see JAA Symposium, note 12 at 69–71. Cf. Digest, note 10 at 126, no. 3.

[44] For the few cases addressing the characteristics of 'civil disputes' (or arbitrability thereof) post-enactment of the JAA, see Tokyo District Court Judgment 21 October 2005, 1926 *Hanrei Jihō* 127; Tokyo District Court Judgment 10 March 2011, 1358 *Hanrei Taimuzu* 236 (referring to the law of Monaco in characterizing the dispute); Tokyo District Court Judgment 28 August 2007, 1991 *Hanrei Jihō* 89 (on the provisional remedy of an injunction under article 24 of the Japanese Anti-Monopoly Act [Dokusen Kinshi Hō]). For a scholarly discussion, see T. Kojima and T. Inomata, *Chusai Hō* (Nihonhyōronsha, 2014) at 67–83.

[45] For a detailed analysis, see Harata, note 4 at 606–08.

[46] For details on the treatment of arbitration agreements in Japanese courts, see Harata, note 4 at 598 n. 64. Cf. Supreme Court Judgment 4 September 1997, 51-8 *Minshū* 3657 and the discussion thereof in Harata, note 4 at 598–99.

As for the formation (existence) and validity (effect) of arbitration agreements, see Tokyo High Court Judgment 21 December 2010, 2112 *Hanrei Jihō* 36; Tokyo District Court Judgment 10 March 2011, note 44; Tokyo District Court Judgment 28 August 2007, note 44; Tokyo District Court Judgment 25 March 2009, note 43.

For labour contract disputes, see Tokyo District Court Judgment 15 February 2011, 1350 *Hanrei Taimuzu* 189.

As for abusive applications for summary dismissal by defendants based on arbitration agreements against plaintiffs' claims in court, see Tokyo District Court Judgment 10 March 2011, note 44 and Tokyo District Court Judgment 16 January 2004, 1847 *Hanrei Jihō* 123.

Special provisions – articles 3 and 4 of the Supplementary Provisions of the JAA[47] – govern labour and consumer contract disputes. Arbitration agreements in consumer contracts can be avoided by the consumer (art. 3 (2)) and those purporting to govern labour-related disputes are null and void (art. 4) 'for the time being until otherwise enacted'. Most remarkably, the special provisions do not expressly state how long such exceptional treatment will be maintained.[48] A further question concerns the scope of the special provisions. These provisions apply, prima facie, when the *locus arbitri* is located within Japan (art. 3(1) JAA).[49] However, it is uncertain if they do apply in other situations, such as when the parties specify in the arbitration agreement a location abroad as the *locus arbitri* (art. 28(1) JAA) or when they choose Japanese law as the governing law of the arbitration agreement regardless of where the *locus arbitri* is or might be located. Some commentators have argued that the special provisions nonetheless apply in these situations as public policy or overriding mandatory rules of the forum.[50]

Formalities

Article 7(2) ML 1985 was adopted as articles 13(2), (3) and (5) JAA. Before the JAA was enacted in 2003, the Japanese courts seem to have

---

[47] Supplementary Provisions Article 3(1):
>   For the time being until otherwise enacted, any arbitration agreements [...] concluded between consumers [...] and businesses [...] subsequent to the enforcement of this Law, the subject of which constitutes civil disputes that may arise between them in the future, shall follow the provisions described in paragraphs (2) through (7).
>   (2) A Consumer may cancel a consumer arbitration agreement. Provided, this shall not apply in the event that the consumer is a claimant in arbitral proceedings based on the consumer arbitration agreement.
>   Article 4 For the time being until otherwise enacted, any arbitration agreements concluded following the enforcement of this Law, the subject of which constitutes individual labour-related disputes [...] that may arise in the future, shall be null and void.

[48] Note that the English translation, note 47, differs from the Japanese original; the provision in Japanese stipulates that these exceptions will be retained 'for the time being', without any explicit reference to future legislative amendment. For these supplementary provisions, see N. Idei, 'Shōhisha Chūsai · Rōdō Chūsai' (2015) 87-4 *Hōritsu jihō* 25 and K. Yamamoto and A. Yamada, *ADR Chūsaihō*, 2nd edn (Nipponhyōronsha, 2015) at 313–18.

[49] See Tokyo District Court Judgment 15 February 2011, 1350 Hanrei Taimuzu 189 (noting, in *obiter dicta*, that art. 4 of the Supplementary Provisions should apply only if the *locus arbitri* is located in Japan).

[50] For discussion on this point, see N. Idei et al., 'Zadankai Shin-Chūsai Hō ni tsuite UNCITRAL MODERU Hō to no no Ido wo Chūshin ni (1)' (2003) 50-10 *JCA jānaru* 18 at 23–27. See also Harata, note 4 at 609–10.

generally acknowledged the validity of arbitration agreements regardless of form.[51] The JAA, however, following the ML 1985, prescribed form requirements for arbitration agreements. Article 13(4) JAA was based on the revised draft of the ML.[52]

The provisions of article 13 JAA reveal interesting historical developments on rules of form. As discussed above,[53] Japanese case law did not insist on any formalities for choice-of-court agreements in cases involving international commerce. On the other hand, the NYC – to which Japan acceded – requires an arbitration agreement to be in writing. When the JAA was drafted, the provisions on formalities (enacted as art. 13 JAA) were modelled after the ML 1985 (which is congruent with the NYC), but broadened the scope of writing to include records in electronic and other retrievable forms (art. 13(4)), taking into consideration the then-ongoing discussion on revision of the ML.[54] By including the option for the arbitration agreement to be in the form of 'other documents', article 13(2) diverges from the stricter NYC.[55]

As to article 13(4) JAA, an issue that has arisen in the literature is whether a recorded voice should be deemed as an 'electromagnetic record', given that article 13(2) JAA provides for the 'record by words of the communicated content'.[56]

Another issue is whether an oral contract that refers to a written arbitration clause or standard-form contract including one shall be regarded as a

---

[51] See, e.g., Osaka District Court Judgment 4 April 1967, 495 *Hanrei jihō* 72.

[52] Kondo et al., note 7 at 50–51; T. Inomata, 'Chūsai Gōi no Seiritsu to Sono Hōshiki', in Kojima and Takakuwa, note 9 at 52.

As for the formalities stipulated in articles 13(2) and (3) of the JAA, see Tokyo High Court Judgment 21 December 2010, note 46 and Tokyo District Court Judgment 21 October 2005, note 44.

The Tokyo High Court in one case held that a further agreement to submit to arbitration was necessary in a case where the parties referred to a standard form contract including a clause to the effect that if a party finds it unlikely that the dispute would be settled by mediation or conciliation, the dispute is to be submitted to an arbitration in accordance with the parties' agreement. In consideration of the risk of loss of the right of access to a court, it was held that the standard form contract with the aforementioned clause was not an arbitration agreement: Tokyo High Court Judgment 10 July 2013, 1394 *Hanrei Taimuzu* 200.

[53] See note 42 and text thereto.   [54] Idei et al., note 50, K. Miki at 31.

[55] Here we can find an issue regarding the relationship between NYC and the JAA, and more specifically the interpretation of article VII (1) of the NYC. Cf. Digest, note 10 at 26 n. 96. On article VII (1) of the NYC and the issue of 'cherry-picking', see Harata, note 4 at 592–96.

[56] JAA Symposium, note 12, K. Miki and K. Yamamoto at 63. Note that the English translation of art. 13(2) JAA differs from the Japanese original text at this point.

valid arbitration agreement, as article 13(3) JAA addresses only contracts concluded in writing. In some cases, the issue can be addressed under article 13(5) JAA,[57] but otherwise there is no clear answer.[58]

Separability

Article 13(6) JAA set forth the provision regarding separability. It corresponds to the ML article 16(1) but does not limit the scope of application of this principle to the tribunal's ruling but more generally address this issue.[59]

Article 8   Arbitration Agreement and Substantive Claim before Court

Article 14 JAA stipulates the provisions which correspond by and large to article 8 ML.[60]

---

[57] Article 13(5): 'In an arbitration procedure, if a Written Allegation submitted by either party contains the contents of an Arbitration Agreement, and a Written Allegation submitted in response by the other party does not contain anything to dispute it, such Arbitration Agreement shall be deemed to be made in writing.'
　　A related issue arises in a situation where a written document containing the contents of the arbitration agreement is submitted by a party to a court and is undisputed by the other party's written pleadings. The consensus seems to be that in such a case the arbitration agreement should be considered valid, although the underlying reasoning remains a matter of debate: JAA Symposium, note 12 at 65–66.

[58] Some scholars argue that there is no provision directly dealing with such a case. JAA Symposium, note 12, K. Miki at 61–62 (arguing that during discussions at UNCITRAL, US and UK representatives supported the view that oral reference to a written clause satisfies the condition for arbitration agreement validity). Cf. UK Arbitration Act 1996, section 5(3).

[59] Kondo et al., note 7 at 52. Cases on separability include Tokyo District Court Judgment 21 October 2005, note 44; Intellectual Property High Court Judgment 28 February 2006, note 43. Cf. Supreme Court Judgment 15 July 1975, 29-6 *Minshū* 1061.

[60] For the definition of the scope of submission to arbitration, in Tokyo District Court Interlocutory Judgment 28 February 2012, *Westlaw* 2012 WLJP CA02288010, it was held that a claim for damages under article 3 of Seizōbutsu Sekinin Hō [Product Liability Law] and a claim for pre-agreed compensation are beyond the scope of the arbitration agreement, a conclusion reached primarily based on the interpretation of the agreement. See also Tokyo District Court Interlocutory Judgment 28 January 2015, 2258 *Hanrei Jihō* 100, which concerned a declaratory action on common benefit claims under the Minji Saisei Hō [Corporate Rehabilitation Law], but the court dealt with the issue not directly as a question of arbitrability, but rather as an issue of the scope of the agreement.
　　Conversely, Tokyo District Court Judgment 10 March 2011, note 44 also referred to the applicable law of the arbitration agreement in order to define the scope of submission to arbitration.

One critical difference is that Japanese courts cannot 'refer the parties to arbitration' (art. 8(1) ML, see also article II(3) of NYC); their only option is to dismiss the action.[61]

Article 9   Arbitration Agreement and Interim Measures by Court

Article 15 JAA is the equivalent to article 9 ML.[62] I discuss this in greater detail in Part. IV-A below.

Part III   Composition of Arbitral Tribunal (Articles 10 to 15)

General Observation

The provisions of the JAA regarding the composition of arbitral tribunals are almost completely consistent with the corresponding provisions of the ML, but with an additional provision on multiparty arbitration (art. 16(3) JAA).

As for the scope of mandatory disclosure, article 18(3) and (4) JAA cover 'all facts likely to give rise to doubts as to his/her impartiality

For the effect of an arbitration agreement on a third party, see Supreme Court Judgment 4 September 1997, note 46; Tokyo District Court Judgment 27 October 2008, *Westlaw* 2004 WLJP CA1027005 (concerning the representative of the defendant company); Tokyo District Court Judgment 26 March 2008, 216 *Kaijihō Kenkyū* 61 (arbitration clause printed in a bill of lading); and Tokyo District Court Judgment 17 October 2014, 1413 *Hanrei Taimuzu* 271 (on the relationship between an arbitration agreement and a tort claim by a Singaporean subsidiary company and a contract claim by the parent Singaporean company against the Japanese counterparty).

Cf. cases involving mediation agreements: Tokyo High Court Judgment 22 June 2011, 2116 *Hanrei jihō* 64 (declining to dismiss the court action based on the mediation agreement when the claim was filed in court without any attempt at mediation). See also Tokyo District Court Judgment 26 January 2004, 1157 *Hanrei Taimuzu* 267 (rejecting in *obiter* the validity of an agreement that does not deem any arbitral award to be final). For this case, see also Kensetsu Gyō Hō (Law No. 100 of 1949), art. 25(2); Kondo et al., note 7 at 50 (on art. 13(3) JAA).

[61]   I. Iwasaki and A. Takakuwa, 'Gaikoku Chūsai Handan no Shōnin oyobi Shikkō ni kansuru Jōyaku, Dai-2-jō', in Kojima and Takakuwa, note 15 at 370; M. Dōgauchi, 'Chūsai Gōi to Soshō Keizoku to no Kankei', in Kojima and Takakuwa, note 9 at 86; Kondo et al., note 7 at 55.

[62]   In Tokyo District Court Judgment 28 August 2007, note 44, the court considered the issue of a Japanese court's competence to rule on a claim for provisional remedies in a contract of sale where the arbitration agreement stipulated the *locus arbitri* to be in South Korea.

For a case decided pre-enactment of the JAA, see Tokyo District Court Judgment 19 July 1954, 5-7 *Kaminshū* 1110.

or independence'. This appears to be broader in scope than article 12(1) ML.

Article 10   Number of Arbitrators

The default number of arbitrators is three (art. 16(2) JAA).[63] Article 16 JAA implements article 10 ML, plus an additional provision regarding multiparty arbitration (art. 16(3)).[64] Nevertheless, there is a lack of clarity in both the way and the criteria by which the court appoints arbitrators in multiparty arbitration.[65] In any event, there is no definitive guidance on what would be considered 'multiparty arbitration'.[66]

Article 11   Appointment of Arbitrators

The provisions of article 17 JAA correspond to article 11 ML. However, there is no provision similar to article 11(1) ML regarding the nationality of arbitrator(s) in the JAA, even though article 17(6)(iii) JAA requires the court to take an arbitrator's nationality into consideration.[67] There

---

[63] Under the old arbitration statute, the default rule was that each of the two parties was allowed to appoint one arbitrator each: art. 788 Old Arbitration Statute. As for the appointment of arbitrators in the so-called umpire-style arbitral tribunal, see JAA Symposium, note 12 at 142–44.

[64] Article 16(3): 'If there are three or more parties, and an agreement set forth in paragraph (1) has not been reached, the number of arbitrators shall be provided by the court, upon the petition of a party.' See also art. 17(4) JAA.

[65] JAA Symposium, note 12 at 144. There is also a problem regarding the court's discretion for replacing the arbitrator who is appointed by the court.

[66] As for academic discussion, see JAA Symposium, note 12 at 145–46. There is not any provision on the similar multiparty situation referred to in the Digest, note 10 at 49–50, nos. 44–47.

[67] See Tokyo District Court Judgment 9 February 2005, 1927 *Hanrei jihō* 75, a case concerning the appointment of one of the two arbitrators in an arbitration between a Japanese shipping line and an Indian company. Although the parties agreed only on the place of arbitration (Tokyo) and not the arbitration institution, the court referred to the list of arbitrators prepared by Japan Shipping Exchange, Inc., which is the only Japanese institution of arbitration for maritime disputes and which listed only Japanese arbitrators. Despite its own insistence that the nationality of arbitrators was a necessary consideration, the court appointed a Japanese national as the other arbitrator in addition to the previously appointed Japanese arbitrator.

The issue of arbitrator nationality is also connected to the prohibition on the provision of legal services by non-attorneys: Bengoshi Hō [Attorney Act] (Law No. 205 of 10 June 1949), art. 72.

is no provision similar to article 17(4) JAA (governing multi-party arbitration) in the ML.[68]

Article 17(5) JAA only permits a party to file a petition for the appointment of an arbitrator; there is no option to 'request the court' 'to take the necessary measure' in general (art. 11(4) ML). Another difference is article 17(2) JAA, which adopts the expression 'upon the petition of said other party'; this is slightly different from article 11 ML.

In contrast with the discussions that took place under the former arbitration law, there seems to be a common understanding, in line with the ML, that post-enactment of the JAA only natural persons – not legal persons – can be appointed as arbitrators.[69]

Article 12   Grounds for Challenge

Article 18 JAA corresponds by and large to article 12 ML. Article 18(1) JAA provides for the following two grounds of challenge: '(i) the arbitrator fails to satisfy the requirements provided by the agreement of the parties' and '(ii) there are reasonable grounds to doubt the impartiality or independence of the arbitrator'. Article 18(1)(ii) JAA's 'reasonable grounds' might be different from the ML's 'justifiable doubts' (art. 12(2) ML).[70]

As for disclosure, the scope of 'all facts likely to give rise to doubts' stipulated in article 18(3) and (4) JAA[71] is broader than the grounds for

---

[68] See also, in this connection, art. 16(3) JAA (the court may decide the number of arbitrators in a multi-party arbitration where the parties fail to reach agreement).

[69] JAA Symposium, note 12 at 149. Kojima and Inomata, note 44 at 172–73. Cf. Digest, note 10 at 59, no. 5.

[70] On the *ex ante* waiver of the right to challenge an arbitrator, see JAA Symposium, note 12, M. Kondo at 166 (rejecting the possibility in view of art. 19(1) JAA). The parties' agreement to refer the challenge to a third person is asserted to be valid, while such an agreement shall not extinguish the right to bring a challenge in court. JAA Symposium, note 12 at 159.

[71] Article 18(3):

> A person who has been requested to assume the post of an arbitrator and intends to accept the negotiation shall disclose to the person that made said request all facts that would likely to give rise to doubts as to his/her impartiality or independence.
>
>   (4) During the course of the arbitration procedure, an arbitrator shall, without delay, disclose to the parties all the facts that would likely to give rise to doubts as to his/her impartiality or independence (excluding those which have already been disclosed) (emphasis added).

challenge in the ML.[72] Failure of the arbitrator to disclose any fact of this nature constitutes grounds for challenge,[73] but the scope and content of such a disclosure obligation is rather unclear.[74] Despite the discrepancies between the wording in the JAA and in the ML, commentators have argued that there is no substantial difference between the two instruments on this point, on the basis that article 12(1) ML was substantially adopted as article 18(3) and (4) JAA.[75] It is also unclear whether a breach of this obligation can be a ground for the arbitral award to be set aside (art. 44(1)(vi) JAA).[76]

Article 13   Challenge Procedure

Article 19 JAA corresponds materially to article 13 ML. However, article 19(2) and (3) JAA does not contain a condition equivalent to article 13(2) ML's 'unless the challenged arbitrator withdraws from his office or the other party agrees to the challenge'. The second paragraph of article 19(4) JAA is also worded differently from article 13(3) ML. Article 19(3) JAA includes the additional phrase 'whichever comes later', which offers greater clarity than article 13 ML. It is also important to note that article 8 JAA makes it possible for the court to intervene even before the *locus arbitri* is determined.[77] As a practical problem, it is often difficult to pinpoint the date on which a party 'became aware of the existence of' (art. 19(3)) 'reasonable grounds to suspect the impartiality or independence of the arbitrator' (art. 18(1)(ii)) in situations where different circumstances cumulatively amount to 'reasonable ground'.[78]

---

[72] JAA Symposium, note 12, K. Miki at 164. For art. 18(1)(ii) (3) and (4), see Osaka District Court Judgment 17 March 2015, 2270 *Hanrei jihō* 74.

[73] JAA Symposium, note 12 at 162–64. For opposing views on the effect of an agreement waiving the obligation to disclose, cf. JAA Symposium, note 12, K. Miki at 164 (arguing that the provision of the JAA is a default rule) with JAA Symposium, note 12) N. Idei at 166.

[74] JAA Symposium, note 12 at 161–63 and Idei et al., note 50, Idei at 34; see Supreme Court Decision 12 December 2017, 71-10 Minshū 2106.

[75] JAA Symposium, note 12 at 163.

[76] JAA Symposium, note 12 at 167; O. Mori, 'Chūsai-nin no Kihi, Kainin-tō', in Kojima and Takakuwa, note 9 at 112–13 (construing it as a ground for setting aside [Art. 44(1) (vi) JAA]).

[77] Cf. Digest, note 10 at 68, no. 3.   [78] Mori, note 76 at 115.

Article 14   Failure or Impossibility to Act

Articles 20 and 21(2) JAA correspond to article 14 ML. Although the corresponding provisions of the JAA are by and large consistent with article 14 ML, they differ in terms of composition and structure. The JAA provisions corresponding to article 14(1) ML are enacted as article 21(1) and article 22 JAA. Article 21 JAA corresponds to article 14(2) ML, but article 21(2) JAA is phrased slightly differently from article 14(2) ML. Whereas article 21(2) JAA prohibits the court from presuming the existence of any ground for challenge or termination where the arbitrator resigns or is dismissed by agreement of the parties, in this same situation article 14(2) ML states that it shall not be implied that there is 'acceptance of the validity of any ground' for challenge or termination by the arbitrator or the parties.[79] The significance of this difference, if any, is at present unknown.

Article 20 JAA, which sets out the grounds for dismissal of an arbitrator upon petition by a party, corresponds to article 14(1) sentence 2 ML which provides that the court may, upon the request of a party, decide 'on the termination of the mandate'. However, this provision of the JAA omits the specific reference to the situation in which 'a controversy remains' (art. 14(1) ML).

Where the arbitrator is dismissed by the arbitration institution, there is debate on whether such a situation should be deemed a case in which parties agree on the termination.[80]

Article 21(1)(ii) JAA contemplates the resignation of arbitrators. In this context, article 14(1) ML might seem restrictive and especially so when compared with the phrasing of 'withdrawal' in article 15 ML. In Japan, some argue that the arbitrator's freedom of resignation was acknowledged in the discussion at UNCITRAL[81] but others assert that any unilateral withdrawal of the arbitrator without any reasonable justification cannot be recognized.[82] Again, because of article 8 JAA,

---

[79] Article 21(2): 'It shall not be presumed that the grounds set forth in the items of Article 18, paragraph (1) or the items of the preceding Article are found in the relevant arbitrator from the mere fact that the arbitrator resigned or was dismissed by the agreement of the parties during the course of the challenge procedure provided for in Article 19, paragraphs (1) to (4), or the procedure for dismissal under the provision of the preceding Article' (emphasis added).

[80] JAA Symposium, note 12 at 168, 170–71.

[81] JAA Symposium, note 12, M. Kondo at 176.

[82] JAA Symposium, note 12, T. Kojima at 175. Contra Kondo et al., note 7 at 90.

it is possible for the court to intervene before the *locus arbitri* is even determined.[83]

Article 15   Appointment of Substitute Arbitrator

The words 'unless otherwise agreed by the parties' were added to article 22 JAA to clarify the corresponding provision, article 15 ML. There is also a possibility of court intervention prior to the determination of *locus arbitri*.[84]

Part IV   Jurisdiction of Arbitral Tribunal (Article 16)

Article 16 ML was adopted in article 23(1)–(4) as well as article 13(6) JAA, with some modification. Despite the ML's distinction between 'jurisdiction' and 'the scope of its authority', article 23 JAA refers simply to 'jurisdiction'.

Despite what the ML's *travaux préparatoires* suggest,[85] article 23 JAA – which corresponds to article 16 ML – is generally understood as providing that the court examines the question of jurisdiction only at the request of a party (art. 23(5) JAA).[86] However, the text of article 23(1) JAA itself does not seem to exclude the possibility that the tribunal may render a decision on its own jurisdiction on its own initiative (*proprio motu*).

It is generally accepted that a party's failure to raise a jurisdictional objection in a timely manner prevents that same party from raising the point again in the context of setting aside, or resisting recognition or enforcement of the arbitral award,[87] although the general view is that the court may examine whether there were 'justifiable grounds for a delay in making an allegation'.

Article 23(4) JAA identifies the different ways the tribunal may render a decision on jurisdiction: a preliminary decision that it has jurisdiction; an award that rules that it has jurisdiction as well as also

---

[83] Cf. Digest, note 10 at 71, no. 4 and 73, no. 2.

[84] Cf. Digest, note 10 at 71, no. 4 and 73, no. 2.   [85] Digest, note 10 at 78, no. 10.

[86] Kondo et al., note 7 at 99–100; T. Kojima, 'Chūsai-tei no Tokubetsu no Kengen', in Kojima and Takakuwa, note 9 at 139; T. Kojima and H. Shimizu, 'Chūsai-tei no Tokubetsu no Kengen', in Kojima and Takakuwa, note 9 at 141, 145 (acknowledging the tribunal's power to decide, on its own motion, whether it has jurisdiction).

[87] Kondo et al., note 7 at 101–02; Kojima and Shimizu, note 86 at 142. Cf. Digest, note 10 at 78, no. 13.

deciding substantial issues; or a decision ruling that it does not have jurisdiction.[88]

It is debated as to whether a party may file an action in court seeking a declaration of validity of the arbitration agreement on which the tribunal's jurisdiction is to be based.[89]

Article 23(5) JAA only allows judicial review of a decision in which the tribunal has affirmed its own jurisdiction, as is the case under article 16 ML. The JAA does not provide for the review of negative jurisdictional decisions by tribunals, and scholars generally reject the possibility of this kind of review.[90]

While the tribunal's decision on its own jurisdiction is said to have no binding effect on a court,[91] it is broadly acknowledged that the reverse is not necessarily true, as court decisions on arbitral tribunal jurisdiction do influence parties and arbitral tribunals as a matter of fact – notwithstanding that as a matter of strict law court decisions on tribunal jurisdiction do not bind future tribunals.[92] Some scholars go on to argue that parties can waive, *ex ante*, their right to request the court to examine and rule on the tribunal's jurisdiction.[93]

Part IV-A   Interim Measures and Preliminary Orders
(Articles 17 to 17J)

*Sub-Part I   Measures and Orders by the Tribunal
(Articles 17 to 17G)*

Article 24 JAA has explicitly acknowledged that the tribunal has power to grant interim measures for the protection of the parties. There is,

---

[88] Article 23(4):

> An arbitral tribunal shall, when the allegation set forth in paragraph (2) has been made lawfully, rule on the allegation by the decision or arbitral award specified in the following items for each category of ruling set forth in those items:
>
> (i) when ruling that the arbitral tribunal has jurisdiction: by an independent decision made before an arbitral award or by an arbitral award; and
>
> (ii) when ruling that the arbitral tribunal does not have jurisdiction: by a decision to terminate the arbitration procedure.

[89] See note 31; JAA Symposium, note 12 at 193–97; Kojima and Shimizu, note 86 at 148–49.
[90] Kondo et al., note 7 at 103–04; Kojima and Shimizu, note 86 at 144–45.
[91] Kojima and Shimizu, note 86 at 141; M. Tanabe, 'Chūsai-tei no Kengen', in Kojima and Takakuwa, note 9 at 156.
[92] Kondo et al., note 7 at 104–05; JAA Symposium, note 12 at 188–93; Kojima and Shimizu, note 86 at 146–47.
[93] JAA Symposium, note 12, N. Idei at 198; Tanabe, note 91 at 156–57 (acknowledging the validity of the agreement to confirm the tribunal's decision on competence as final and binding the court).

however, debate over the interpretation of the words 'the party' against
whom an order to provide security may be made pursuant to article 24(2)
JAA (cf. art. 17E ML).[94]

Sub-Part II   Recognition and Enforcement of Interim Measures (Articles 17H and 17I)

In this regard, there have been no subsequent legislative developments in
Japan after the ML was revised in 2006. An interim measure by an
arbitral tribunal is regarded as incapable of recognition and enforcement
by a court.[95] Tribunal decisions on provisional measures are not considered arbitral awards (cf. article 2 JAA). Therefore, to facilitate court
recognition and enforcement, separate, specific legislation is necessary.
The absence of such a provision in the JAA is attributable to the fact that
the Japanese legislator had, at the time of drafting, decided to wait for the
outcome of the ML reform project.[96]

Sub-Part III   Court-Ordered Interim Measures (Article 17J)

Parties are not disabled by virtue of an arbitration agreement from
seeking court-ordered interim measures before or during the arbitration
(art. 15 JAA). There is some debate on the relationship between court-
and tribunal-ordered interim measures, and especially on whether it is
possible for the parties to exclude recourse to judicial interim measures
by agreement.[97]

Part V   Conduct of Arbitral Proceedings (Articles 18 to 27)

General Observation

The JAA provisions governing arbitral proceedings are by and large
similar to the ML provisions. Article 27 JAA governs waiver. The
principle of party autonomy over arbitration procedure stipulated in

---

[94] Kojima and Shimizu, note 86 at 155–56.
[95] Kojima and Shimizu, note 86 at 153 and H. Takada, 'Chūsai Handan no Shikkō', in
Kojima and Takakuwa, note 9 at 275; Kobayashi and Murakami, note 17 at 216.
[96] Kondo et al., note 7 at 113–14; Kojima and Inomata, note 44 at 266; N. Idei et al.,
'Zadankai Shin-Chūsai Hō ni tsuite UNCITRAL MODERU Hō to no Ido wo Chūshin ni
(2)' (2003) 50-11 JCA jānaru 2, Miki at 3.
[97] H. Toyoda, 'Chūsai Gōi no Kōryoku', in Kojima and Takakuwa, note 9 at 81–82.

article 19 ML is adopted in the JAA. However, as we see below, the JAA takes a different position from the ML when it comes to the relationship between party autonomy and the mandatory rules of *lex loci arbitri.*

While the Digest places emphasis on the importance of party autonomy to international commercial arbitration,[98] the JAA extends the application of the ML-inspired provisions beyond international commercial disputes; generally, arbitrations of civil disputes are covered by the JAA, which did not adopt the concept of internationality. In light of this, it is doubtful whether or to what extent aspects particular to international commercial arbitration were taken into account during the drafting of the JAA.

Instead, the divergence of article 25 JAA from article 18 ML might reflect paternalistic concerns, from the perspective of Japanese domestic law as the *lex loci arbitri*, about the abuse of rights by parties. Other mandatory rules of the *lex loci arbitri* are imposed by articles 45(2) and 35 JAA.

Article 18   Equal Treatment of Parties

Article 25 JAA is the equivalent to article 18 ML. Article 25(1) seems to cover only 'arbitration procedure', which appears to be narrower than article 27 JAA (which governs waiver of the right to object). However, article 25(1) is understood to cover arbitral proceedings in a broader sense.[99]

The term 'a full opportunity' used in the English translation of article 25(2) JAA is an inaccurate translation of 'sufficient opportunity'[100] in original Japanese provision. In similar vein, the English version's 'presenting his/her case' is not a literal translation of the original Japanese text, which is better translated as 'explaining about the case'.[101] Neither usage is identical to the provisions of the ML. Some scholars speculate that as the ML's terminology could mislead parties into misinterpreting the ML provision to mean that they may change or add to their pleadings

---

[98] Digest, note 10 at 100.
[99] Kondo et al., note 7 at 118; Y. Sato, 'Shinri ni okeru Gensoku', in Kojima and Takakuwa, note 9 at 161.
[100] 'Jūbun na kikai'.   [101] 'Ji'an ni tsuite setsumei suru'.

with impunity, the JAA adopted different terminology to avoid that possibility.[102]

There is also debate on whether article 25 JAA requires formal or substantial 'equality', and if the latter what the arbitral tribunal is expected to do to place the parties on an equal footing.[103]

Article 19   Determination of Rules of Procedure

Article 19 ML was by and large adopted as article 26 JAA. However, whereas the Digest places emphasis on the 'special importance' of party autonomy in international commercial arbitration,[104] the JAA adopted the principle of party autonomy but excised the connection to its underlying basis in internationality.

Article 26(1) JAA refers to Japan's mandatory rules using the term 'provisions concerning public order'.[105] This is potentially misleading as that terminology evokes the concept of public policy or *ordre public* as it is conventionally understood in private international law. By contrast, article 26(2) JAA, which expressly refers to all 'provisions of this Act', is clearer.

As the exception to the overall dominant influence of the English language version of the ML on the JAA, it is generally agreed that article 26(3) JAA followed the French version of the ML 1985 in listing three factors instead of the four in the English version;[106] however, the significance of this difference is unclear.[107]

---

[102] Kondo et al., note 7 at 118 ('This provision does not entitle a party to supplement its claim and evidence without any restriction'); Sato, note 99 at 161.

[103] JAA Symposium, note 12 at 207. Cf. Y. Taniguchi, 'Chūsai Tetsuduki ni okeru Tetsuduki Kihonken', in K. Matsuura and Y. Aoyama (eds.), *Gendai Chūsaihō No Ronten* (Yūhikaku, 1998) at 244 (arguing [before the JAA's enactment] that art. 18 ML requires the tribunal not only to provide parties with sufficient opportunity to state and prove their case, but also to provide the parties the information necessary for them to conduct their case accordingly). Cf. Digest, note 10 at 97–99, nos. 5 to 9. On the tribunal's *ex officio* examination of evidence, see also art. 32(4) and (5) JAA. For the tribunal's duty to provide their opinion on the legal position, see JAA Symposium, note 12 at 207ff.; Taniguchi in Matsuura and Aoyama, *ibid.* at 244.

[104] Digest, note 10 at 100, no. 2.   [105] 'Hōritsu no ōyake no chitsujo'.

[106] M. Kondō et al., *Chūsai Hō Konmentāru* (Shōjihōmu, 2003) [original Japanese version of Kondo et al., note 7] at 127.

[107] Cf. Kondō et al., *ibid.* (citing both the English and French versions of the ML but quoting only from the English version) with Kondo et al., note 7 at 122 (using the terminology 'Materiality and Weight of Evidence').

Article 20   Place of Arbitration

Article 28 JAA adopted article 20 ML. However, it is also critical to recall that the ML's overarching concern was always with international commercial arbitration. By contrast, the JAA does not embody a similar specific concern, and the JAA defines its scope of application only by *locus arbitri* without regard to the international character or lack thereof of the dispute. Through this dematerialized and virtual concept of *locus arbitri*, coupled with the effect of article 8 JAA in some situations where the *locus arbitri* is likely to be in Japan, the JAA ensures that the mandatory rules in the statute will be applicable.

There remains, however, the possibility that parties might attempt to avoid the application of mandatory rules of the JAA through their own choice of the *locus arbitri*. There is no consensus on whether the arbitrator's consent is necessary for the *ex post* change of *locus arbitri* by way of parties' agreement.[108]

Article 21   Commencement of Arbitral Proceedings

Article 29 JAA corresponds to article 21 ML, albeit with slight modifications and an additional provision.[109] Article 29(1) JAA limits its own scope of application to the 'particular civil dispute'. Article 29(1) JAA also provides that the arbitral proceedings commence on the day a party gives notice to the other that arbitration procedure will be applied to the dispute, instead of the day the request by a party for the matter to be referred to arbitration is received by the counterparty as per the ML

---

[108] Y. Aoyama, 'Chūsaichi no Igi to Kōka', in Matsuura and Aoyama, note 103 at 267 (arguing that the arbitrator's consent is necessary). Contra JAA Symposium, note 12) K. Miki at 226. There is also the view that art. 28 covers only cases to which the JAA applies: Takakuwa, note 9 at 14. If so, it is necessary to define the scope of the JAA's application in a way other than using that concept of *locus arbitri* as captured in art. 28. Cf. Digest, note 10 at 102, no. 1.

[109] Article 29(1):

> Unless otherwise agreed by the parties, an arbitration procedure in respect of a particular civil dispute will commence on the date on which one party notifies the other party that the arbitration procedure shall be applied to such civil dispute (emphasis added).
>
> (2) A request in an arbitration procedure shall have the effect of interruption of prescription; provided, however, that this shall not apply to cases where the arbitration procedure has terminated other than by an arbitral award (emphasis added).

(art. 21 ML). The ML has no equivalent to article 29(2) JAA, which provides for the interruption of prescription.[110]

Article 22   Language

The provisions of article 22 ML were substantially adopted as article 30 JAA, with article 30(4) being a Japanese addition.[111]

Article 23   Statements of Claim and Defence

Article 31(1)–(4) JAA adopted article 23 ML, albeit with the contents arranged in a different order. There is no provision on set-off in the JAA.[112]

Article 24   Hearings and Written Proceedings

Article 32 JAA corresponds to article 24 ML. Article 32(1) and (2) JAA adopted article 24(1) ML, whereas Article 32(3) JAA corresponds to article 24(2) ML. Instead of 'sufficient advance notice' (art. 24(2) ML),

---

[110] Prescription is the civilian equivalent to limitation periods in common law. But note that there remains the issue of the scope of application of the provision, as the choice of law issue on limitation needs to be addressed first of all.

[111] The leading case on language is Yokohama District Court Judgment 25 August 1999, 1053 *Hanrei Taimuzu* 266; (2002) XXVII *Yearbook of Commercial Arbitration* 515. On the issue that no translation of the notice was served before the hearing, the court ruled that, in contrast to a case involving the recognition of a foreign judgment, the absence of a translation of the notice does not infringe art. V(1)(b) NYC if the parties had agreed on the individual rules of arbitration procedure (or the applicable procedural law), and especially the applicable language. However, the parties in this case did not agree upon a language to be used in an arbitration procedure. The court nonetheless found that the parties had agreed to an arbitration in which only Chinese was to be used, despite having taken into consideration the fact that the written contract, including the arbitration agreement, was concluded in both English and Chinese.

On implied agreement on language, see Kondo et al., note 7 at 160. A language choice advantageous only to one party might give rise to a problem if one subscribes to a 'substantive' version of the 'equality' principle in art. 25 JAA.

[112] T. Tsutsumi, 'Sōsai no Kōben, Hantai Seikyū', in Kojima and Takakuwa, note 9 at 187–90.

the JAA uses the term 'sufficient period of time prior to the date of the oral hearing'.[113]

Article 32(4) JAA refers to 'a written allegation, documentary evidence or any other records' instead of 'all statements, documents or other information' (art. 24(3) ML). Oral statements are not included in the former category.[114] Conversely, article 32(5) JAA broadly covers 'report of the expert witness' or other evidentiary document which is considered to include 'statements, documents or other information' (cf. 'evidentiary document' in article 24(3) ML), in so far as such information would serve as the basis for the arbitral award or other decision by the arbitral tribunal. The concept of 'serv[ing] as the basis for the Arbitral Award or other decision by the Arbitral Tribunal' (art. 35(5) JAA) is said to be identical in meaning to 'on which the arbitral tribunal may rely in making its decision' (art. 24(3) ML).[115] Irrelevant information such as administrative communication is considered to fall outside the scope of article 24(3) ML.[116]

Article 32(4) and (5) JAA requires any 'party to take measures to enable the other party to know the content' of the evidence and documents it has submitted, instead of requiring that the information be 'communicated to the other party' (art. 24(3) ML). In comparison with article 24(3) ML, which only states that the documents 'shall be communicated', article 32(4) and (5) JAA make it clear that the party who submits something has the duty to 'communicate' the submitted information to the other party.

Article 25   Default of a Party

Article 33 JAA corresponds to article 25 ML. Article 33(1) and (3) JAA uses the phrasing 'justifiable grounds' instead of 'showing sufficient cause' (art. 25 ML). However, the concept of justifiable grounds is ill-defined.[117] Seemingly different from 'sufficient cause' (art. 25 ML covering all (a), (b) and (c)), the JAA's 'justifiable reason' only applies to paragraphs (1) and (3) of article 33 JAA. An issue therefore arises as to

---

[113] For the situation where testimony is already present before the tribunal, see JAA Symposium, note 12, K. Miki at 259 (arguing that the requirement imposed by the provision be waived provided no party objects and the waiver does not cause injustice).
[114] Kondo et al., note 7 at 172.   [115] JAA Symposium, note 12, M. Kondo at 263.
[116] JAA Symposium, note 12 at 263. Cf. Kondo et al., note 7 at 172.
[117] JAA Symposium, note 12 at 265–66.

the relationship between article 25(b) and the concept of 'sufficient cause' in the ML.[118]

In contrast with article 25 ML, which uses 'statement of claim', article 33(1) JAA refers to article 31(1) JAA, a broader provision that covers 'the object of a petition, the facts supporting his/her petition and points of the dispute'.[119] Article 33(3) JAA is similar to article 25(c) ML in that the tribunal may proceed to render an award based on the available evidence without the need for the party present to make a request.[120]

There is no equivalent to article 25(c) ML, which grants the tribunal power to 'continue the proceedings', in the JAA.

Article 26   Expert Appointed by Arbitral Tribunal

The provisions corresponding to article 26 ML are found in article 34 JAA. The scope of article 34(1) JAA is defined using the term 'necessary matters', which is different from article 26(1) ML, which uses the term 'specific issues'.

Article 34(4)(ii) JAA provides that [the parties may] 'have a person who has expert knowledge and whom the party has appointed to make statements on the matters pertaining to said expert testimony'. This provision might not be completely consistent with article 26(2) ML. This is because the JAA provision seems to be broader, covering 'statements on the matters pertaining to said expert testimony' without limiting its scope of application to only 'testify[ing] on the points at issue' addressed by the court-appointed expert. One possible strict interpretation of the word 'testify' in the ML could limit the 'present[ing] expert witness' only to the issue of ascertaining whether the expert report should be accepted or refused. Conversely, it is more difficult to interpret the corresponding JAA provision in a similar way.

---

[118] JAA Symposium, note 12 at 266.

[119] The effect of termination of the arbitration proceeding is debated. One view is that no arbitration may be commenced, and no lawsuit may be filed in court on the same dispute. However, the rationale of this view, whether based on the arbitration agreement or on estoppel, remains unclear: JAA Symposium, note 12 at 264–65. Cf. art. 40(2)(i) JAA.

[120] Contra art. 244 Code of Civil Procedure.

Article 27   Court Assistance in Taking Evidence

Article 35 JAA, which is the equivalent to article 27 ML, contains several provisions not found in the ML; these additional provisions govern judicial assistance in the taking of evidence.[121] On the other hand, there is no provision in the JAA providing for the similar treatment of foreign-seated arbitrations.[122] This has caused some commentators in Japan to take the view that the court may not provide assistance in the taking of evidence for foreign-seated arbitrations.[123]

There is no provision in either the JAA or the ML contemplating the tribunal's *ex officio* examination of evidence.[124] Consequently, some Japanese observers take the view, following the ML, that the tribunal may not examine evidence *ex officio*.[125]

---

[121] Article 35(3):

> Notwithstanding the provisions of Article 5, paragraph (1), the case based on the request set forth in paragraph (1) shall be subject to the exclusive jurisdiction of the following courts:
>
> (i) the courts set forth in Article 5, paragraph (1), item (ii);
>
> (ii) the district court which has jurisdiction over the domicile or residence of the person to be examined or the person who holds the document, or the location of the subject-matter of the observation;
>
> (iii) the district court which has jurisdiction over the general venue of the claimant or respondent (limited to cases where there is no such court that corresponds to the courts set forth in the preceding two items).
>
> (4) An immediate appeal may be filed against the decision on the request set forth in paragraph (1).
>
> (5) Where the court implements the examination of evidence upon the request under paragraph (1), an arbitrator may inspect the document, verify the subject-matter of the observation, or may ask the witness or expert witness (meaning the expert witness provided for in Article 213 of the Code of Civil Procedure) questions by obtaining the permission of the presiding judge.
>
> (6) The court clerk shall prepare a record on the examination of evidence to be implemented by the court upon the request under paragraph (1).

[122] The JAA is silent on some issues; cf. Digest, note 10 at 118–19, nos. 2 and 3. On the issue of inter-state mutual legal assistance in a case where some support by a foreign court is considered to be necessary, see H. Kobayashi, 'Shōko no Shūshū to Shōko Shirabe', in Kojima and Takakuwa, note 9 at 200–01.

[123] Idei et al., note 96 at 6. For judicial support for written communications, see note 23 and text thereto.

[124] Contra Japan's former arbitration law: art. 794(1) Old Arbitration Statute.

[125] A. Takakuwa, *Kokusai Shōji Chūsai Hō no Kenkyū* (Shinzansha, 2000) at 356; Kobayashi, note 122 at 200.

Part VI   Making of Award and Termination of Proceedings
(Articles 28 to 33)

General Observation

The JAA diverges from the ML on choice of law rules governing the substantive issues in the dispute, although the practical significance of these differences remains unclear. Also, the JAA includes a provision on electing a presiding arbitrator (art. 37(1)), and the JAA does not contain any time limitation on the *ex officio* correction of the award by the tribunal (art. 41).

Article 28   Rules Applicable to Substance of Dispute

The provisions concerning choice of law are contained in article 36 JAA.[126] Although article 36 JAA refers not to 'rules of law' as article 28 ML does, but rather simply to 'law', some scholars argue that 'law' also includes any provisions and standards other than laws of a specific country.[127] However, it is not entirely clear how choice of law problems are dealt with in arbitration practice in Japan; at present there is no case law addressing this point in court proceedings to set aside, recognize or enforce arbitral awards.[128]

Article 36(2) JAA is different from article 28(2) ML. The former provides that the law of the state with 'the closest relationship to the

---

[126] Article 36(1):

> The law which the Arbitral Tribunal should comply with in making an Arbitral Award shall be as provided by the agreement of the parties. In this case, if laws and regulations of a given State have been designated, such designation shall be deemed as designating the laws and regulations of the State which shall be directly applied to the case and not the laws and regulations of the State providing the application of conflicting domestic and foreign laws and regulations, unless a contrary intention has been clearly indicated (emphasis added).
>
> (2) If an agreement set forth in the preceding paragraph has not been reached, the arbitral tribunal shall apply the laws and regulations of a State which has the closest relationship to the civil dispute that has been referred to the arbitration procedure and which should be directly applied to the case (emphasis added).

The choice of law rules laid down by JAA are different from the general rules of Japanese private international law. The JAA recognizes party autonomy not only for arbitrations on disputes arising from contract, but also for tort and property as well.

[127] Kondo et al., note 7 at 195. Idei et al., note 96, T. Nakamura at 7–8.

[128] Nonetheless, it is at least clear that the fact that the arbitral tribunal made findings of fact and rulings of law that are different from what the court would have done is not always regarded as a basis on which to set aside the award: Osaka District Court Judgment 17 March 2015, note 72. Cf. Tokyo District Court Judgment 26 January 2004, 1847 *Hanrei Jihō* 123 (a case decided under the former arbitration law).

civil dispute that has been referred to the arbitration procedure' shall be directly applied, as opposed to 'the law determined by the conflict of laws rules which [the tribunal] considers applicable' (art. 28(2) ML). A rationale offered for this difference is that 'the rule in Paragraph (2) of the present Article was more coherent in line with actual operation in practice and the fact that directly deciding the law to be applied on the basis of connection with the dispute further contributes to predictability by the parties and ensuring legal stability'.[129] However, even with the very abstract test of 'closest relationship' imposed on arbitrators, the arbitrator's discretion remains extensive. Simultaneously, even if it were technically possible for a party to raise an objection to the arbitrator's choice of applicable law, it would still be more difficult to do so given the abstract nature of the test applied.[130]

Article 36(3) JAA does not refer to *amiable compositeur* (art. 28(3) ML). Although the English translation of that provision uses the phrase 'the arbitral tribunal shall decide *ex aequo et bono*', the original Japanese provision, when literally translated, stipulates that the arbitral tribunal is deemed to decide (or to have decided) *ex aequo et bono*. This means that even in the case where the tribunal makes an award based on the application of a certain law instead of *ex aequo et bono*, any claim that the tribunal did not decide in that manner is excluded as a ground for setting aside the arbitral award.[131] This provision applies only if 'a clearly indicated request has been made by both of the parties'. It is argued that it should not apply in a case where institutional arbitration rules referred to by the parties stipulate the arbitration *ex aequo et bono*, but where the parties did not explicitly opt for this kind of arbitration.[132]

Article 36(4) JAA concerns not only 'the usage of the trade applicable to the transaction' (art. 28(4) ML) but more broadly 'the usages applicable to the relevant civil dispute.' And the same provision omitted the

[129] Kondo et al., note 7 at 196–97. See also T. Ikeda, 'Chūsai Handan', in Kojima and Takakuwa, note 9 at 207, where reference was made to similar provisions in the German and Korean arbitration statutes.
[130] It is still unclear whether the tribunal's error in choice of law could be grounds for setting aside and/or non-recognition of the award as there is yet to be a case on this point in Japan. See M. Kondo et al., note 7 at 195 (arguing that the tribunal's application of a law different from that agreed by parties should be sufficient grounds to set aside the award in view of art. 44(1)(vi)) and Ikeda, note 129 at 211 (arguing that an award rendered *ex aequo et bono*, in spite of the parties' agreement on choice of applicable law, may not be set aside or refused recognition and enforcement).
[131] Kondo et al., note 7 at 197; Ikeda, note 129 at 208.
[132] N. Idei et al., note 96, K. Miki at 8.

phrase 'in all cases' of article 28(4) ML. With this omission, it is made clear that contractual provisions or usages are not always superior to other sources. The position of contractual provisions and usages stipulated in article 36(4) shall be taken into consideration not only with a decision *ex aequo et bono*, but more generally with all other applicable legal sources.[133]

Article 29   Decision-Making by Panel of Arbitrators

The provisions corresponding to the article 29 ML are stipulated in article 37 JAA. The JAA adopted the majority principle as default rule like the ML. Additionally to the ML, article 37(1) JAA stipulates the mutual-election rule for the appointment of a presiding arbitrator.[134]

As for 'procedural matters' (or 'questions of procedure' [ML]), the JAA, like the ML, provides the presiding arbitrator with the power to decide. But the provision of article 37(3) JAA is slightly different from article 29 ML, as the former refers to 'all the other arbitrators', not to 'all members of the arbitral tribunal'. For interpretative issues on the provision, some scholars argue that an assessment on evidences shall not be deemed as 'procedural matters'.[135] There is a view that the arbitral tribunal, in the absence of parties' agreement, can decide on what is deemed to be 'procedural matters'.[136]

Article 37(4) JAA stipulates that a parties' agreement overrides the rules set forth as default rule in article 37(1)–(3). There is a possible difference in that the article 29 ML might lead to the conclusion that a parties' agreement cannot prohibit the presiding arbitrator backed with authorization of all members of the tribunal from deciding on questions of procedure.[137] The JAA explicitly gives priority to parties' agreement.

---

[133] Cf. Kondo et al., note 7 at 197–98; Ikeda, note 129 at 210.

[134] For a comparative overview on methods of appointing presiding arbitrators, see JAA Symposium, note 12 at 295.

[135] JAA Symposium, note 12, K. Miki at 301; Kojima and Inomata, note 44 at 407; Kondo et al., note 7 at 201. For the interim measure in this regard, JAA Symposium, note 12, K. Miki at 302.

[136] Kojima and Inomata, note 44 at 407.

[137] JAA Symposium, note 12, K. Yamamoto at 301. For the relation between art. 37(3) and (4) JAA, JAA Symposium, note 12 at 300–01.

Article 30   Settlement

Article 38 JAA, corresponding to article 30 ML, contains the provisions governing settlement.[138] Article 30(1) para.1 ML was adopted as article 40(2)(iii) JAA.

The phrasing of article 38(1) JAA ('the arbitral tribunal may make a decision based on the agreed matters in the settlement') is slightly different from article 30(1) ML. A decision of the tribunal so rendered has the same effect as an arbitral award (art. 38(2) JAA).

As for the substantive terms of the settlement, some scholars argue that the tribunal has the competence to review them for consistency with public order.[139] There is also the view that the tribunal must refuse to lend its imprimatur to a settlement if its terms differ from the tribunal's findings,[140] whereas others argue that it would be unreasonable for the tribunal to refuse making a decision on terms as agreed to by the parties.[141] In any event, it can be difficult to confirm whether the parties' agreement, whether to settle or to apply to the tribunal for a decision on agreed terms, is truly based on mutual consent.[142]

In the case of settlement, it is possible for arbitral proceedings to be terminated either by way of a decision amounting to an award (art. 38

---

[138] Article 38(4):

> In cases where the consent of both parties has been obtained, an arbitral tribunal or one or more arbitrators who have been appointed by the parties may attempt to arrange a settlement for the civil dispute which has been referred to an arbitral procedure (emphasis added).
>
> (5) The consent under the preceding paragraph or the revocation thereof shall be made in writing, unless otherwise agreed by the parties (emphasis added).

Cf. Digest, note 10 at 124, no. 1.

[139] JAA Symposium, note 12, N. Idei at 304. But, if so, it is unclear whether the tribunal shall and can refuse an award based on that settlement.

[140] T. Kojima, 'Wakai Chūsai Handan (Wakai ni motoduku Chūsai Handan)', in Kojima and Takakuwa, note 9 at 221.

[141] JAA Symposium, note 12, M. Kondo at 304.

[142] Kojima, note 140 at 222 and Y. Taniguchi, 'Chūsai Handan no Torikeshi', in Kojima and Takakuwa, note 9 at 246.

Live issues concerning how objections against the terms of settlement remain. The setting aside of the tribunal's decision based on parties' settlement is considered to be possible where the settlement agreement is defective, although it is unclear precisely which statutory ground for the setting aside of an award – art. 44(1)(iv), (vi) and/or (viii) JAA – is satisfied in such a case. Cf. JAA Symposium, note 12, K. Yamamoto and K. Miki at 315 with Ikeda, note 129 at 216. Cf. Digest, note 10 at 124, nos. 5 and 6.

JAA), or other means.[143] Remarkably, article 38(4) and (5) JAA stipulate that the tribunal may attempt to arrange a settlement;[144] this is in addition to (and thus different from) the ML. This is a default rule and is conditional upon the parties' agreement in writing.[145] Due to this condition, opposition by any one party is sufficient to bar the tribunal from attempting to facilitate settlement.[146]

How the tribunal should treat information acquired through an attempt to facilitate settlement is much debated in Japan due to the popularity of this practice not only with tribunals but also with the courts. However, there is no JAA provision on this point.[147]

Article 31   Form and Contents of Award

Provisions of article 31 ML were by and large adopted as article 39 JAA.[148] Article 39 JAA, following article 31 ML, requires the award to be in writing. Whether an award can be made solely in an electronic form or other retrievable record (i.e., without a formal paper document) is a matter of controversy amongst commentators;[149] in any event, awards in electronic form raise a number of as yet unresolved issues of a technical nature.[150]

Article 39(3) JAA, which corresponds to article 31 ML, requires that the award must include the date on which it is rendered. However, the

---

[143] For termination by withdrawal of claim, see art. 40(2)(i) of the JAA; for other cases, see art. 40(2)(iv) of the JAA.

[144] See Kondo et al., note 7 at 205 (explaining the spirit of the provision).

[145] The form requirement of writing here is not consistent with the prevailing practice in Japan. It is important to note that the arbitration rules prescribed by some arbitral institutions in Japan do not require similar formalities: JAA Symposium, note 12 at 310–11.

[146] JAA Symposium, note 12, N. Idei at 309.

[147] Cf. UNCITRAL Model Law on International Commercial Conciliation, art. 10. This point also has relation with the provision of art. 32(4) JAA (corresponding to the ML art. 24(3)). For the difference between Japan and other countries on the position of arbitrator in comparison with mediator, JAA Symposium, note 12, Y. Taniguchi at 312.

[148] A case pre-dating enactment of the JAA is Kobe District Court Judgment 16 November 1990, 756 *Hanrei Taimuzu* 258.

[149] For those opposed, see JAA Symposium, note 12, K. Yamamoto at 316; Kojima and Inomata, note 44 at 410. On the other hand, giving notice of the award by sending 'a copy' in electronic form is accepted by some scholars: JAA Symposium, note 12, K. Yamamoto at 317.

[150] Such issues include those of signature; enforceable title of obligation (shikkō-ryoku no aru saiken meigi) of the electronic arbitral award; and the conditions under which an arbitration, in which an electronic arbitral award is rendered, may be terminated: JAA Symposium, note 12, K. Miki at 317.

significance and legal effect of the date is quite unclear,[151] as is the purpose of article 39(4).[152] It should also be noted that the term 'copy' does not have the same meaning in article 31(4) ML 1985 and article 39(5) JAA.[153]

As the default rule that applies unless the parties agree otherwise, article 39(2) JAA requires that reasons must be given for an arbitral award.[154] Some claim that the failure to state reasons is deemed to be a ground for setting aside the award.[155] There is also the view that no dissenting opinion shall be included in an award.[156]

Article 32   Termination of Proceedings

The corresponding provisions are contained in article 40 JAA. Article 40(1) JAA refers to 'an arbitral award', and not to 'the final award' as in article 32 ML, although there is no definition of 'arbitral award' in the JAA.[157]

In Japan, an arbitral tribunal often makes the decision to dismiss a claim; this dismissal is deemed to be a decision to terminate of arbitral proceedings, instead of an arbitral award.[158]

Article 40(2)(iii) JAA is on settlement agreements (see above on article 30 ML). The part of article 32(3) referring to article 34(4) in the ML cannot find any corresponding provision in the JAA, because the JAA does not recognize the suspension of the setting aside proceedings.[159]

---

[151] Kondo et al., note 7 at 209; Kojima and Inomata, note 44 at 417; JAA Symposium, note 12 at 322–33.

[152] JAA Symposium, note 12 at 323.

[153] 'Copy' under the ML can include the 'original', but not under the JAA: JAA Symposium, note 12 at 325. Cf. Kojima and Inomata, note 44 at 419.

[154] For the former arbitration law (art. 801(1)(v)), see Supreme Court Judgment 27 October 1928, 7 *Minshū* 848.

[155] Kojima and Inomata, note 44 at 417; JAA Symposium, note 12 at 318–21.

[156] T. Ikeda, 'Chūsai Handan no Seiritsu', in Kojima and Takakuwa, note 9 at 220. Cf. Digest, note 10 at 126, no. 1.

[157] Kondo et al., note 7 at 218–19. A decision by the arbitral tribunal to terminate proceedings is not deemed to be an 'arbitral award' that can be set aside by the court (art. 44 JAA).

[158] Kondo et al., note 7 at 217; JAA Symposium, note 12 at 333; T. Inomata, in Kojima and Takakuwa, note 9 at 227.

[159] For the discussions in Japan on 'legitimate interest' of art. 40(2) JAA (but lacking sufficient reference to debates on the ML), see Kondo et al., note 7 at 215–16; Kojima and Inomata, note 44 at 465; JAA Symposium, note 12 at 328–29.

Article 33   Correction and Interpretation of Award;
Additional Award

The provisions of article 33 ML were adopted in articles 41 to 43 JAA with several differences. But the interpretative difficulty has been pointed out regarding the distinction between interpretation and correction/additional award.[160] Besides, the distinction between correction and substantive modification of award is not always easy to clarify.[161]

As for the *ex officio* correction of award by authority, there is no limitation of period different from article 33(2) ML (for the correction requested by a party, cf. article 41(2) and (4) JAA). It is explained as more rational than the ML.[162]

The part of the provision of article 33 ML regarding the interpretation of award was adopted in article 42 JAA. The *ex ante* agreement of this kind incorporated in an arbitration agreement (or clause) is deemed to be valid.[163]

There are several issues discussed by Japanese scholars which both the JAA and the ML have not directly dealt with. As for issues of how to deal with the case in which some ground for termination of arbitration proceedings occurs after the commencement of proceedings but before the composition of the arbitration tribunal, see Kondo et al., note 7 at 214; Inomata, note 158 at 231; Kojima and Inomata, note 44 at 463; JAA Symposium, note 12 at 327.

As to situations where termination is not due to a decision to terminate, e.g., the death of the sole arbitrator directly appointed by parties, see JAA Symposium, note 12 at 327–28; Kojima and Inomata, note 44 at 463.

As for the effect of termination decision, especially the effect regarding the prescription (limitation), see JAA Symposium, note 12 at 329; Kojima and Inomata, note 44 at 470. For the effect of limiting any further claim on the same matter, see JAA Symposium, note 12 at 329 and 333; Kojima and Inomata, note 44 at 467.

And for the way of objecting against the tribunal's decision on termination of proceedings, see Kondo et al., note 7 at 218–19; Inomata, note 158 at 234.

[160] JAA Symposium, note 12 at 333–35; Kojima and Inomata, note 44 at 442 n. 257.
[161] As for the conditions on substantial modification, different from simple 'correction', of arbitral award, see Kojima and Inomata, note 44 at 441–42 (arguing to acknowledge the modification before the moment when the arbitral award begins to have effect [Art. 39(5) JAA], unless parties otherwise agree).
[162] JAA Symposium, note 12 at 337; Kojima and Inomata, note 44 at 440. There are issues on the validity of *ex ante* waiver of the right of application for correction and on the validity of such an agreement as not to do so. For the latter, Kojima and Inomata, note 44 at 440; Kondo et al., note 7 at 223 (arguing such an agreement is invalid).
[163] Kondo et al., note 7 at 226. JAA Symposium, note 12 at 336. Remarkably, there is a criticism on the rationality of the condition of agreement. But in Japan there is no trace of research with scrutiny on the abusive practice of application for interpretation after the ML 1985.

As for the additional award, article 43(2) JAA stipulates the provision for the arbitral tribunal to make a decision 'on the request,' not only a decision of additional award but also a decision on whether the request is justified or not (cf. article 33(3) ML).[164]

Part VII Recourse against Award (Article 34)

As for setting aside of the arbitral award, the JAA set forth the provisions regarding the arbitration with the *locus arbitri* determined within the country (cf. articles 1 and 3 JAA). Although these provisions of the JAA are by and large similar to those of the ML, there are several differences regarding the procedure and the grounds of setting aside.[165]

The Setting Aside Procedure

The discretionary nature of the court's power to set aside the arbitral award is stipulated in article 45(6) JAA. If a ground for setting aside is technically made out but is otherwise minor and irrelevant, the court may be able to dismiss the application to set aside.[166]

The word 'only' of article 34(1) ML was deleted in article 44 JAA. Notwithstanding this difference, it is generally accepted that the setting aside procedure stipulated in the JAA is the sole recourse to a court against an award,[167] even though this point is not explicitly provided for in the JAA.

As to the procedure of the setting aside of an award, the JAA followed the former arbitration statute in adopting a non-contentious litigation procedure.[168]

---

[164] There is discussion on the case in which a party applies for the additional decision, but he/she has already waived the right of application (or agreed with his/her counterparty on it). Kojima and Inomata, note 44 at 444; Inomata, note 158 at 239. Compare with Kondo et al., note 7 at 229. Cf. Kondō et al., note 106 at 237 (referring not only to the decision of the parties but also to that of the ex-arbitrator).

[165] Article 44(1):
> If any of the following grounds exist, the parties may make an application with the court to set aside the arbitral award:
> (vi) the composition of the arbitral tribunal or the arbitration procedure is in violation of Japanese laws and regulations (if the parties have reached an agreement on the matters concerning the provisions unrelated to public order in such laws and regulations, such agreement) (emphasis added).

[166] Osaka District Court Judgment 17 March 2015, note 72.

[167] Kondo et al., note 7 at 238.   [168] Kondo et al., note 7 at 239; see also note 35.

Departing from the ML, according to article 44(2) JAA, an application for setting aside an arbitral award is not permitted 'after an enforcement decision under article 46 has become final and conclusive'.

Article 34(4) ML was not adopted in the JAA.[169]

On the other hand, article 44(2), (3)–(5) and (8) JAA are additional provisions not found in the ML; they govern discretionary transfer of the matter to another court and immediate appeal (*sokuji kōkoku*) against a first instance court's decision on a setting aside application.[170]

Grounds for Setting Aside of Arbitral Award

One difference on the grounds for setting aside regards the concept of 'proper notice' of article 34(2)(a)(ii) ML. Differently from that provision, article 44(1)(iii) JAA stipulates the necessary verification based on the Japanese domestic law as *lex loci arbitri*.[171]

As for setting aside an arbitral award with *locus arbitri* in Japan, article 44(1)(ii) JAA requires the application of Japanese laws as for the verification of validity of the arbitration agreement, failing the parties' choice of applicable law (cf. the ML 34(2)(a)(i)).

Article 44(1)(viii) JAA refers not to 'the award' (art. 34(2)(b)(ii) ML) but to 'the content of the arbitral award'. However, this provision is generally understood to cover not only the substance of content of the award in the strict sense but also the due process issues.[172]

---

[169] As to the reason, see the explanation in Kondo et al., note 7 at 247.

[170] On the relationship between setting aside and refusal of recognition or enforcement, see Taniguchi, note 142 at 244.

     There is no case law in Japan on whether it is possible to waive *ex ante* the right to apply to set aside on a specific ground or for parties to make an agreement on such terms, or whether parties may voluntarily expand the range of grounds for setting aside. On the last issue, see Taniguchi, note 142 at 246–47.

     Another live issue is the nature of the relationship between parties after the award is set aside: e.g., whether the arbitration agreement continues to have effect, and whether arbitration proceedings continue to exist. See Taniguchi, note 142 at 253–54.

     The setting aside of an award is deemed to be a discretionary decision by the court, due to the use of the term 'may' in art. 44(6) JAA: Kondo et al., note 7 at 241; Taniguchi, *ibid.* at 251.

[171] Article 44(1)(iii):

         the petitioner did not receive <u>the notice required under Japanese laws and regulations</u> (if the parties have reached an agreement on the matters concerning <u>the provisions unrelated to public order</u> in such laws and regulations, said agreement) in the procedure of appointing arbitrators or in the arbitration procedure (emphasis added).

[172] Kondo et al., note 7 at 245. The court reviewed arbitral proceedings for consistency with public policy in Osaka District Court Judgment 17 March 2015, note 72.

Part VIII Recognition and Enforcement of Awards
(Articles 35 and 36)

General Observation

The provisions corresponding to articles 35 and 36 ML were stipulated in articles 45 and 46 JAA.[173]

Very remarkably, some provisions of the JAA are not congruent with those of the ML nor of the NYC which Japan has ratified. These discrepancies may give rise to issues on the complicated relations between the JAA, the ML and NYC.[174]

Although the grounds for refusing the recognition and enforcement of an award are not exactly the same in the JAA and the ML (and NYC), Japanese scholars have not recognized the differences between them. Rather, they regard the JAA as substantially coinciding with the provisions of the ML (and therefore those of NYC) in terms of the conditions for recognition and enforcement.[175] Such an assessment, if justified, can lead us to assert that NYC has been merged into the JAA as domestic implementation.[176] In fact, some scholars argue that the JAA represents a *de facto* withdrawal of the reciprocity reservation made pursuant to article I(3) NYC because the JAA

Article 44(1)(iv) JAA was the subject of Tokyo District Court Decision 28 July 2009, 1304 *Hanrei Taimuzu* 292. The court interpreted the provision as permitting the setting aside of an arbitral award in a case where the proceedings involve an infringement of a party's procedural rights that is so serious that the party is deemed not to have been provided with the opportunity to mount a defence. Examples include the inability of the party to participate in the proceedings, and where the arbitral award was made based on materials unknown to a party. The court further held that the fact that a party had not considered the disputed issue to be relevant and crucial to the outcome of the award does not satisfy the condition for setting aside the award.

In Tokyo District Court Decision 13 June 2011, 2128 *Hanrei Jihō* 58, the court held that it was contrary to public order for the tribunal to have considered an issue to be undisputed when in fact the parties did dispute it, and when the issue was relevant to the award.

The time limit applicable to proceedings to set aside awards was also addressed in the two decisions discussed in this footnote.

[173] For the binding effect of an arbitral award as similar to *res judicata* (cf. art. 45(1) JAA), see Tokyo District Court Judgment 26 January 2004, note 60. For violation of public policy as a ground for refusal of recognition or enforcement, see Harata, note 4 at 608–10.

[174] See Harata, note 4 at 587–89.

[175] Kondo et al., note 7 at 252–53; S. Nakano, 'International Commercial Arbitration under the New Arbitration Law of Japan' (2004) 47 *Japanese Annual of International Law* 96 at 114; Kojima and Inomata, note 44 at 540, 651, 652. See also A. Takakuwa, 'Chūsai Handan no Shōnin oyobi Shikkō Kettei', in Kojima and Takakuwa, note 9 at 261.

[176] There does not seem to be any clear international standard for realizing the implementation of the New York Convention. See Report on the Survey Relating to the Legislative Implementation of the Convention on the Recognition and Enforcement of Foreign Arbitral Awards 1958, New York, A/CN.9/656.

applies the same rules to the recognition of all arbitral awards, regardless of the country where an arbitral award is made.[177]

Article 35   Recognition and Enforcement

The corresponding provisions to article 35 ML were stipulated in articles 45(1), and 46(1) and (2) JAA.

Article 45(1) JAA stipulates that the arbitral award can have the same effect as 'a final and binding judgment'. The documents requested in article 46(2) JAA for applying for the execution of an award are different from article 35(2) ML (and the ML 1985) and also from the NYC which Japan has ratified.[178]

A more remarkable divergence is found at article 45(2) JAA which seems definitively to deny the recognition (art. 45(1) JAA) by stating that such recognition '**shall** not apply', whereas the 36 ML states such recognition '**may** be refused'.[179] Yet article 46(8) JAA seems to recognize the discretion with the phrasing of '**may** dismiss'.[180] Article 45(2) might be contrary to the provisions of the ML and NYC.[181]

Article 36   Grounds for Refusing Recognition or Enforcement

The grounds for refusing recognition and/or enforcement of an arbitral award are stipulated in article 45(2) JAA, corresponding by and large to article 36 ML, with the following differences. Therefore, the enactment of the JAA,

---

[177] S. Nakano, note 175 at 114.

[178] Article 46(2):

> In filing the petition set forth in the preceding paragraph, the party shall submit a copy of the written arbitral award, a document proving that the contents of said copy are the same as those of the written arbitral award, and a Japanese translation of the written arbitral award (excluding those prepared in Japanese) (emphasis added).

[179] Article 45(2):

> The provision of the preceding paragraph shall not apply if any of the following grounds exist (for the grounds set forth in items (i) through (vii), limited to the case where any of the parties has proved the existence of said grounds) [...] (emphasis added).

[180] Article 46(8):

> If the petition set forth in paragraph (1) has been filed, the court may dismiss said petition without prejudice only when it finds that any of the grounds set forth in the items of paragraph (2) of the preceding Article exist (for the grounds set forth in items (i) through (vii) of said paragraph, limited to the case where the respondent has proved the existence of such grounds) (emphasis added).

[181] For more detailed analysis, see Harata, note 4 at 606.

allegedly modelled in principle after the ML 1985, gave rise to a problem regarding the relationship not only with the ML but also with NYC.

Difference between Article 36(1)(a)(v) ML (= Article V(1)(e) of NYC) and Article 45(2) and (vii) JAA (Regarding the Jurisdiction of Setting Aside Arbitral Awards)

The setting aside 'by a court of the country in which, <u>or</u> under the law of which, that award was made' of an arbitral awar<u>d</u> is one of the grounds on which recognition of an arbitral award may be refused: article 36(1)(a)(v) ML (= article V(1)(e) of NYC). On the other hand, article 45(2)(vii) JAA provides, as one of the grounds for refusal, where

> according to the laws and regulations of the country to which the place of arbitration belongs (<u>if the laws and regulations applied to the arbitration procedure are laws and regulations of a country other than the country to which the place of arbitration belongs, said other country</u>) the Arbitral Award is not final and binding, or the Arbitral Award has been set aside or its effect has been <u>suspended by a judicial body of that country</u>. (emphasis added)

Although the ML (and NYC) provision is not without its difficulties, the choice offered by the ML (and the NYC) has been completely excised in the JAA.[182]

Difference between Article 36(1)(a)(iv) ML (= Article V(1)(d) of NYC) and Article 45(2)(vi) JAA (Regarding One of the Dilemmas between Party Autonomy and the *Lex Loci Arbitri*)

Article 36(1)(a)(iv) ML (= article V(1)(d) of NYC) gives priority to party autonomy over the *lex loci arbitri*, as the phrasing shows: 'was not in accordance with the agreement of the parties, or, failing such agreement, was not in accordance with the law of the country where the arbitration took place'. Conversely, article 45(2)(vi) JAA always gives priority to the *lex loci arbitri*, even where the parties have agreed on the composition of an arbitral tribunal or the arbitral proceedings.[183]

---

[182] Kondo et al., note 7 at 266.
[183] Article 45(2) (vi):
> the composition of the arbitral tribunal or the arbitration procedure is in violation of <u>the laws and regulations of the country to which the place of arbitration belongs (if the parties have reached an agreement on the matters concerning the provisions unrelated to public order in such laws and regulations, such agreement)</u> (emphasis added).

Therefore, according to the JAA, the mandatory rules of the *lex loci arbitri* are considered to be always applicable; this provision differs not only from the NYC (art. V(1)(d)) but also from the ML (art. 36(1)(iv)).

It is not possible to delve into the JAA's drafting process in detail here, but it is possible to make comparative observations of the relevant provisions in the JAA and the ML, while bearing in mind the drafting process of the ML 1985. When the ML 1985 was drafted, a ground for setting aside similar to article V(1)(d) NYC was considered inappropriate because it would recognize the priority of party autonomy. Subsequently, contravention of mandatory rules of the *lex loci arbitri* – regardless of parties' agreement – came to be discussed as a possible ground for setting aside an arbitral award.[184] On the other hand, when it comes to recognition and enforcement, the division between domestic and foreign arbitral awards was originally maintained, and it was argued that mandatory rules of the *lex loci arbitri* were imposed only in the case of domestic arbitral awards as one of the conditions for recognition, and in the same way it was a ground for setting aside arbitral awards. Ultimately, rules that are the same as those of NYC were accepted as grounds for refusing recognition and enforcement, regardless of whether the arbitration was domestic or foreign (art. 36 ML). On the other hand, as for setting aside, the drafted provision regarding the application of mandatory rules of *locus arbitri* was maintained (art. 34(2)(a)(iv) ML).

Article 44(1) JAA, modelled after the ML 1985, contains the provisions for setting aside arbitral awards where the *locus arbitri* is in Japan, including article 44(1)(vi), which corresponds to article 34(2)(a)(iv) ML. However, for recognition and enforcement, the JAA (art. 45(2)(vi)) did not adopt the provision of the ML 1985 (art. 36(1)(a)(iv)) originating from the NYC; the enacted rule is the same as that for setting aside (article 44(1)(vi) JAA).[185]

---

[184] See H. M. Holtzmann and J. E. Neuhaus, *A Guide to the UNCITRAL Model Law on International Commercial Arbitration* (Kluwer, 1989) at 916–17.

[185] In Japan, the coincidence of the grounds for refusal of recognition, setting aside, and also nullity of an arbitral award does not seem to have been put into doubt, although some potential conflicts among these different contexts have been discussed. See Taniguchi, note 142 at 243–45 (but see also at 247–48); Kondo et al., note 7 at 239–40.

Difference between Article 36(a)(ii) ML (= Article V(1)(b) of NYC) and Article 45(2)(iii) JAA (Regarding the Law Applicable for Notice)

A similar causal background can also explain the difference between article 36(a)(ii) ML (= article V(1)(b) of NYC) and article 45(2)(iii) JAA.[186] The former does not explicitly refer to a choice of law issue on 'proper notice', but the latter has a provision according to which the mandatory rules of the *locus arbitri* should apply.

This provision of the JAA coincides again not with the corresponding provision of the ML (art. 36(1)(ii)) nor that of NYC but with article 44(1)(iii) JAA, which regards the conditions for setting aside arbitral awards by courts of Japan as the *locus arbitri*.

Eventually, the ML treated arbitral awards in a general manner without making any distinction between domestic and foreign arbitration in terms of their recognition and enforcement. However, it maintains the rule of the *lex loci arbitri* in the case of setting aside an arbitral award of a domestically seated arbitration. On the contrary, the JAA imposes the mandatory rule of the *lex loci arbitri* not only for setting aside but also for recognition and enforcement, regardless of whether the arbitration is domestic or foreign.[187]

Discretion regarding the Recognition and Enforcement of Arbitral Awards

The JAA sets forth several grounds for refusing to recognize or enforce an award (art. 45(2) JAA). The same article states that if there are any grounds for refusal, article 45(1), which permits recognition and enforcement, 'shall not be applied'. It seems to preclude any discretion by the

---

[186] Article 45(2)(iii):
> the party did not receive the notice required under the laws and regulations of the country to which the place of arbitration belongs (if the parties have reached an agreement on the matters concerning the provisions unrelated to public order in such laws and regulations, such agreement) in the procedure of appointing arbitrators or in the arbitration procedure (emphasis added).

[187] Note that the English translation of art. 44(2)(iii) and (vi), and art. 45(2)(iii) and (vi) JAA has used the term 'public order'. See also arts. 26(1) and 27 JAA using the same term 'public order'.

The original Japanese provision with the term 'ōyake no chitsujo' [= public order] would more broadly cover all mandatory rules of the indicated legal order rather than in the sense of public policy generally used in private international law and also in art. 45(1)(ix) JAA: Kojima and Inomata, note 44 at 508–09, 543. See also art. 19 ML.

court. To the contrary, article 46(8) JAA, which concerns the enforcement decision, stipulates that 'the court may dismiss' an application for
enforcement. This provision is generally understood to provide a court
with the discretion to make an enforcement decision even in a case in
which some ground for refusal of enforcement is verified.[188]

This apparent incoherence between these two provisions may give rise
to a serious interpretative problem. In addition, if article 36 ML
(and article V NYC) provide for a court's discretion, the provision of
article 45(2) JAA can be considered to be different from the rule of both
the ML and NYC.

With these differences considered, there is a problem of whether we can
still regard the JAA, allegedly adopting the ML 1985, as the domestic
implementation of NYC. If they were considered as respectively separated
and individual sets of provisions for recognizing and enforcing an arbitral
award it would be necessary to address the problems regarding the alternative relationship between them, as is the case with bilateral treaties.[189]

Another difference is that article 45(2)(ix) ML refers not to 'the award'
but to 'the content of the arbitral award', which 'would be contrary to the
public policy or good morals of Japan'. However, this provision is
generally construed as covering also the public policy on due process.[190]

Conclusions

Adopting Model Law as Domestic Law: What Does 'Adoption' Really Mean?

The case of Japan demonstrates powerfully three problems that arise
from the process of adopting model law as domestic law. First, although
the JAA was primarily modelled after the ML 1985, the two differ in
several critical aspects. For this reason, the Japanese 'adoption' of the ML
should be regarded as only partial, a conclusion that casts doubt on
whether it is meaningful for Japan (and UNCITRAL) to claim that Japan
has 'adopted' the ML. This should also alert us to the possibility, or,
indeed, likelihood, that other jurisdictions have been similarly and mis-
leadingly classified as having 'adopted' the ML.

---

[188] Kondo et al., note 7 at 267, and see also at 241.
[189] Harata, note 4 at 588–89. For the complicated relationship between the NYC and
bilateral treaties, see *ibid.* at 592–96.
[190] See note 172 and text thereto. See also Osaka District Court Decision 25 March 2011,
2122 *Hanrei jihō* 106.

Second, Japan is also a powerful illustration of a perennial, general problem: something is inevitably lost in the process of transforming a 'model' law into domestic law. This is particularly acute in countries such as Japan, where the official language (or even worse, languages) of law is different from that used for the model law. The necessary step of 'translating' the model law into the implementing jurisdiction's language creates distortions and discrepancies that further challenge the notion of 'adoption of a model law' – an idea which has, in any event, thus far eluded clear definition.

The final problem concerns foreign observers who are familiar with neither the legal language nor the legal system of the jurisdiction under study. For such observers, the further, artificial step of translating the text of the domestic law from the jurisdiction's legal language into the observer's language or a legal *lingua franca* (in Japan's case, from Japanese to English) is necessary. This translation is all too often a trap for the unwary and the unconscientious. Japan is an example par excellence: the English translation of the JAA provided by the Japanese government is, in substantial respects, not completely congruent with the text of the original statute in Japanese. An innocent translator's error it is not: English wording similar to that in the English version of the ML was not carelessly, but rather intentionally, used in the translation. Whatever the motives might have been, this double translation – from English (and French) into Japanese and back into English – all but ensures that differences in nuance between a model law and the domestic law purportedly 'adopting' the model is lost in translation.

Parochialism in Internationalist Clothing

At first glance, the JAA would seem to have adopted some of the principal ideas incorporated in the ML that are regarded as essential to international commercial arbitration. That is, however, where the similarity ends. First, the JAA abandoned the concept of 'internationality', extending the scope of application of such principles to civil disputes with neither an international nor a commercial dimension.[191] Second, several features of the JAA that depart from the ML suggest that the JAA leans not in favour of respect of party autonomy – a principle that is regarded as holding special importance for international commercial

---

[191] Digest, note 10 at 64, no. 3.

arbitration – but rather the strict application of mandatory rules of Japanese domestic law.[192] Illustratively, the JAA demands, in some cases, that the JAA itself must be applied as the *lex loci arbitri* regardless of the dispute's internationality or lack thereof. Finally, parts of the JAA reveal a lack of consideration for important considerations in international commercial arbitration. For instance, the JAA has no equivalent to article 11(1) ML concerning the nationality of arbitrators.[193] Another example is the fact that the principle of interpretation based on an international perspective (expressed in article 2A(1) ML) is neither adopted in the text of the JAA itself at the time of the statute's enactment, nor even mentioned thereafter either in Japanese case law or academia.

The Model Law Approach to International Harmonization: Seemingly Simple, Apparently Attractive, but Fatally Flawed

As the Digest itself makes clear, the ML is not completely consistent with the NYC,[194] a fact that complicates the trilateral relationship between the NYC, the ML and the JAA. The NYC, as an international treaty, is as an instrument first and foremost characterized by its binding effect. Conversely, the ML is, as its name suggests, a model: it necessarily leaves room for nation-states and sub-national jurisdictions to adopt it as domestic law, initially as a basis for legislative enactment and as a source for subsequent development through case law. The ML is generally considered to be a more feasible measure for improvement and progress towards international harmonization or convergence in this area of law.

However, the ML's purported strength – its optional nature – is also the source of serious issues. For instance, article 7 ML 1985, which governed form requirements in arbitration agreements, was almost entirely consistent with the NYC. However, the corresponding provision in the JAA was drafted not based on article 7 ML 1985 but rather on the new draft of the ML (which subsequently became ML 2006), which is substantially different from the NYC. The process by which the JAA became law has thus created a divergence between the ratified treaty and the domestic law based on the model law.

Last but not least, once any substantive rule has been created, included in a treaty and implemented in domestic law, it is hardly easy for a

---

[192] Digest, note 10 at 13.
[193] On how Japanese courts address the appointment of arbitrators, see note 69.
[194] Digest, note 10 at 173, no. 1.

jurisdiction's domestic legislation to keep pace with subsequent amendments to that provision made not by treaty but by model law.[195] It is far from certain – at least in Japan's case – whether the ML 2006 should be adopted, and, if so, whether this should be by legislative amendment of the statute that originally adopted the model law or simply by case law. In reality, as between Japan, which has adopted an arbitration statute based on the ML 1985, and other jurisdictions that have adopted the ML 2006, a difference has already arisen on the level of the model adopted – and this is even before taking into consideration the myriad differences on the level of individual national enactments. In addition, as we have seen in the issue of form requirements for arbitration agreements, Japan faces a difficult choice: should the ML 1985, which incorporates substantially and directly the NYC (a treaty ratified by Japan), be maintained as the model going forward? Or should Japan follow future revisions of the ML and proceed to adopt, as domestic law, rules inconsistent with those of the NYC? If Japan should opt for the latter, the relationship between the NYC as domestically implemented and domestic law that is different from the NYC will become a live issue.[196]

It is certainly the case that the model law approach is more flexible, and supposedly more feasible, than a multilateral treaty in today's international context. Nevertheless, as the conflict between the JAA and the ML 1985, the ML 2006, and the NYC powerfully shows, mixing treaty and model law is a sure recipe for complications in any domestic legal system.

---

[195] As further instance, UNCITRAL Recommendation Regarding the Interpretation of Article II, Paragraph 2, and Article VII, Paragraph 1, of the New York Convention, Document N 25/ 276, A/61/17 (SUPP).

[196] This point is connected to the interpretation of art. VII (1) NYC. However, this rule is nothing more than a judgment call, made from the NYC's own perspective, on its relationship with other systems. When it comes to states that have ratified the NYC – which necessarily includes art. VII (1) – but have also enacted laws on arbitration that differ from the NYC, the question of the relationship between the NYC as domestic law and their own respective domestic arbitration laws is yet to be adequately addressed.

Republic of Korea

Model Law in Asia: The Case for Korea

HI-TAEK SHIN

Introduction

Korea legislated its first arbitration law, the Arbitration Act, in 1966[1] as a stand-alone statute governing both domestic and international arbitrations. While the first arbitration law was influenced by the arbitration provisions of the German Code of Civil Procedure, unlike Germany, the Korean legislature opted to enact the arbitration law as an independent statute, separate from the Civil Procedure Act governing judicial proceedings conducted by the national court system.[2] This first legislation comprised only eighteen articles. As the number of arbitration cases have increased in Korea with the growth of the Korean economy since the 1970s, the need to modernize the arbitration law better to meet the demands of the domestic and international business community and to be consistent with international standards and practice was keenly felt in the Korean legal community. After the adoption of the UNCITRAL Model Law on International Commercial Arbitration 1985,[3] Korea started to look into the

Hi-Taek Shin retired as a professor at Seoul National University (SNU) School of Law in August 2017. The author thanks the EW Barker Centre for Law & Business at the Faculty of Law of the National University of Singapore for financing his participation in the conference entitled, 'The UNCITRAL Model Law on International Commercial Arbitration in Asia', which led to this book. The author also thanks Jinho Suh for his invaluable assistance in research and preparation of this chapter.

[1] Arbitration Act (Jung Jae Beop), Law No. 1767, effective as of 16 March 1966.

[2] For a detailed account of the historical background of the enactment of the first arbitration law, see Byeong-Hoi Yang (ed.), *Ju Seok Jung Jae Beop* [Commentaries on the Arbitration Act] (KCAB/Korean Association of Arbitration Studies, 2005), p. xii; according to this commentary, the first arbitration law of Korea was modelled after the arbitration provisions found in the tenth book of the German Code of Civil Procedure.

[3] UNCITRAL Model Law on International Commercial Arbitration 1985, UN General Assembly Resolution 40/72 (11 December 1985) ('ML 1985').

desirability of adopting ML 1985 to replace or supplement the existing arbitration law of 1966. In December 1998, a committee was established within the Ministry of Justice (MOJ) to draft an amendment to the arbitration act. Based upon the work of this committee, the National Assembly approved a sweeping amendment to the arbitration act which incorporated ML 1985 to a very substantial degree.[4] In making this amendment in 1999, the Korean legislature stated that the purpose of this amendment was to promote international commercial arbitration by adopting international standards for arbitration, minimizing court interference in arbitration and facilitating enforcement of arbitral awards. Minor amendments were subsequently made in 2001, 2002 and 2013.

After the adoption of the UNCITRAL Model Law on International Commercial Arbitration 2006,[5] scholars and practitioners have advocated further amendment of the arbitration law to reflect the new features adopted in ML, in particular, provisions relating to interim measures. A special task force was organized by the MOJ in 2014. This task force has recommended that the amendments embrace the new provisions relating to interim measures in ML as well as the developments of arbitration law and practice in major jurisdictions since 1999. In 2015, based upon the recommendation of the task force, the MOJ submitted a bill for the amendment of the arbitration law to the National Assembly, which approved the bill in May 2016. The amendment went into effect on 30 November 2016.[6]

KAA has embraced the principle as well as the text of the ML to a very substantial degree. KAA is currently composed of fifty articles. Of the forty-six articles of the ML (including those relating to interim measures and preliminary orders from Article 17A to 17J), KAA has adopted the texts of sixteen articles verbatim[7] and twenty-seven articles,

---

[4] Arbitration Act, Law No. 6083, effective as of 31 December 1999. For a detailed explanation of the efforts leading to the 1999 amendment of the Korean Arbitration Act, see Bae, Kim & Lee, *Arbitration Law of Korea: Practice and Procedure* (JurisNet, 2012), 14–17. The adoption of ML 1985 by Germany greatly facilitated the discussion in Korea in favour of the adoption of ML 1985 in the Korean arbitration law.

[5] UNCITRAL Model Law on International Commercial Arbitration 2006, UN General Assembly Resolution 61/33 (4 December 2006) ('ML').

[6] Arbitration Act, Law No. 14176, effective as of 30 November 2016. The Arbitration Act, as amended, will be referred to as KAA, while the amendment made in 2016 will be referred to as 2016 amendment.

[7] KAA is in the Korean language. In this chapter, the expression that KAA has adopted an ML article verbatim is used to mean that KAA has adopted the Korean translation of an ML article verbatim. There are two publicly available English translations of the KAA: the

with some modifications. Some of these twenty-seven articles have been broken down into paragraphs or regrouped without altering the meaning, whereas others have been modified or partially adopted to reflect that KAA governs both domestic and international arbitration and to remain consistent with the Korean legal and judicial system which is based upon a civil law system. Only three ML articles – 17B, 17C and 17J have not been adopted at all. In addition to forty-three ML articles KAA has embraced in full or in part, KAA has added five articles to reflect the particulars of Korean law-making practice and to provide a legal basis of the Korean Commercial Arbitration Board (KCAB), which is the only officially recognized arbitration institution in Korea. The order and the title of KAA articles closely follow those of the ML. The article numbering up to article 33 of KAA corresponds to the ML article plus one – the Korean legislature added article 1 of KAA to state the purpose of the legislation as a general practice of Korean law-making. For instance, ML article 12 (Grounds for challenge) has been adopted as KAA article 13 (Grounds for challenge of arbitrators), and ML article 33 (Correction and interpretation of award; additional award) has been adopted as KAA article 34 (Correction and interpretation of award and additional award). The titles of twenty-nine articles of KAA are exactly the same as the corresponding articles of the ML, and the titles of thirteen articles are very similar to the corresponding ML articles.

first is the version on the website of the National Law Information Center. This website has an English translation of the most current Arbitration Act that was put into effect on 30 November 2016 (www.law.go.kr/eng/engLsSc.do?menuId=1&query=Arbitration+Act&x=0&y=0#liBgcolor2). This translation is the product of the Korea Legislation Research Institute. The same English translation is also available at the website of the Korea Legislation Research Institute (http://elaw.klri.re.kr/kor_service/lawView.do?hseq=38889&lang=ENG). The second translation is the version available on the website of the Korean Commercial Arbitration Board. As of 5 November 2017, this website has the English translation of the Arbitration Act prior to the 2016 amendment (www.kcab.or.kr/servlet/kcab_kor/medshar ebrd/1020?sb_clsf=1&sNum=3&dNum=0&mi_code=medsharebrd). There are some minor discrepancies between these two versions, mostly regarding the selection of particular English terms for Korean words. The English translation used in this chapter is based on the version posted by the Korean Commercial Arbitration Board with a few modifications by the author where necessary to reflect the fact that the Korean version of the KAA originates from the English version of the UNCITRAL Model laws. The English translation of the 2016 amendment used in this chapter is the author's own.

In 1973, Korea ratified the Convention on the Recognition and Enforcement of Foreign Arbitral Awards of 1958.[8] KAA makes an explicit reference to NYC in article 39 (Foreign arbitral awards).

Part I   General Provisions of the Model Law (Articles 1 to 6)

In line with the general practice of the Korean National Assembly of stating the purpose of the legislation in the very first article of the statute it enacts, KAA article 1 provides the legislative purpose of KAA. It states that '[t]he purpose of this Act is to ensure the proper, impartial and prompt settlement of disputes in private laws by arbitration.' This first article clearly declares that KAA is, in principle, a pro-arbitration legislation. In addition, it signals two important features of KAA which deviate from ML: first, KAA delimits the use of arbitration to 'disputes in private laws' and, second, it governs both domestic and international arbitration. These two key deviations will be discussed later in detail when we address relevant articles.

Article 1   Scope of Application

ML article 1 has been partially adopted by KAA as article 2 (Scope of application) with the same title. KAA deviates from ML in that it applies to both domestic and international arbitration.[9] As KAA does not limit its application to international commercial arbitration, it does not need to include any definition of what is 'commercial' nor distinguish between international and domestic arbitration. As a result, ML article 1(3) and article 1(4) dealing with the definition of 'international' have not been adopted by KAA. However, ML article 1(2) and article 1(5) have been adopted as KAA article 2(1) and article 2(2) respectively.

---

[8] Convention on the Recognition and Enforcement of Foreign Arbitral Awards, New York, 10 June 1958, in force 7 June 1959, 330 UNTS 4739 ('NYC'). In acceding NYC as the 43rd contracting state with effect from 9 May 1973, Korea has made reciprocity and commercial reservations.

[9] The Korean legislature decided also to apply KAA to domestic arbitration because a single arbitration statute would create less confusion for the parties and the arbitrators. See Yong-Deug Ha, 'Jung Jae Beop Ui Gae Jeong Gyeong Gwa Mit Ju Yo Nae Yong' [Revision Process of the Arbitration Act and its Main Contents] (2000) 295 *Jung Jae* 8; Moon-Chul Chang, *Hyeon Dae Jung Jae Beop Ui I Hae* [Understanding Contemporary Laws on Arbitration] (2000), 19.

KAA article 2(1) has adopted the territorial principle as embodied in ML article 1(2). However, it deviates from ML in the treatment of articles carved out as exceptions to the territorial principles. Specifically, KAA article 9 (Arbitration agreement and substantive claim before court) and article 10 (Arbitration agreement and interim measures by court), which correspond to ML articles 8 and 9, shall apply when the place of arbitration has not yet been determined as well as when the place of arbitration is not in Korea. Unlike ML, no provisions relating to the interim measures adopted in the 2016 amendment to KAA have been carved out as exceptions to the territorial principles.

Article 2   Definitions and Rules of Interpretation

While ML article 2 provides the definitions of three terms (arbitration, arbitral tribunal and court) and three rules of interpretation, KAA article 3 (Definitions) provides the definitions for a different set of three terms (arbitration, arbitration agreement and arbitral tribunal) and has not adopted any rules of interpretation.

While the focus of the definition of 'arbitration' under ML article 2(a) is to cover both institutional and ad hoc arbitrations, KAA article 3(a) attempts to provide a more generic definition of arbitration by defining 'arbitration' to mean 'a procedure to settle disputes involving property rights and disputes not involving property rights, but where parties are entitled to conclude a settlement on the issue in dispute, not by the judgment of a court, but by the decision of an arbitrator, as agreed by the parties.' Two points need to be mentioned in this connection. First, as arbitration is defined as a procedure to settle disputes, as agreed by the parties, it is interpreted to include both institutional and ad hoc arbitrations as provided for in ML. Secondly, the definition touches upon the issue of arbitrability by limiting the arbitration to the disputes involving property rights and disputes not involving property rights, but where the parties are entitled to conclude a settlement on the issue in dispute. Prior to the 2016 amendment, the same article of KAA defines arbitration to mean 'a procedure to settle disputes in private laws', repeating the text of KAA article 1. The new definition in the 2016 amendment, which follows the approach taken by article 1030(1) of the German Code of Civil Procedure,[10] has been adopted to clarify that disputes not involving

---

[10] Code of Civil Procedure as promulgated on 5 December 2005, last amended by Article 1 of the Act dated 10 October 2013 (Federal Law Gazette, p. 3786); translation available at

property rights, but where the parties are entitled to conclude a settlement on the issues in disputes, could be resolved by arbitration. In light of this new definition, read together with the purpose provision in KAA article 1, it is generally interpreted in Korea that disputes pertaining to criminal, constitutional or administrative law matters are not arbitrable. While questions remain concerning the arbitrability of disputes arising under civil or commercial laws with important public interest objectives, such as competition laws, bankruptcy laws and environmental laws, the private law consequences of these laws should be arbitrable in Korea as long as public policy is not otherwise violated. Korean courts tend to interpret arbitrability rather broadly to include torts claims and private law consequences of intellectual property disputes.

The definition of an 'arbitration tribunal' in KAA is the same as that of the ML. KAA does not define the word 'court' as it is self-evident under Korean law.

KAA defines an 'arbitration agreement' to mean an 'agreement between the parties to settle, by arbitration, all or some disputes which have already occurred or might occur in the future with regard to defined legal relationships, whether contractual or not.' It is in essence the same as the first sentence of the ML article 7(1). However, the Korean legislature felt that it is logical to locate the definition of 'arbitration agreement' in article 3 where other terms are defined.

KAA has not adopted rules of interpretation as embodied in ML article 2, paragraphs (d), (e) and (f). However, the interpretation should be the same under KAA as suggested by ML.

Article 3   Receipt of Written Communications

ML article 3 gives equal effect to personal delivery and delivery at a place of business, habitual residence or mailing address. KAA article 4 (Receipt of written communications) deviates from this rule by stipulating that (i) unless the parties agree otherwise, any written communication should be delivered to the addressee personally (article 4(1)), and (ii) delivery at residence, the place of business or mailing address is allowed only when personal delivery is not possible (article 4(2)). The other elements in ML article 3 have been adopted by KAA.

Bundesministerium der Justiz und für Verbraucherschutz website, https://www.gesetze-im-internet.de/englisch_zpo/englisch_zpo.html.

Article 4   Waiver of Right to Object and Article 5 Extent
of Court Intervention

The text of ML article 4 (Waiver of right to object) and article 5 (Extent of court intervention) have been adopted by KAA verbatim as article 5 and article 6 respectively.

Article 6   Court or other Authority for Certain Functions
of Arbitration Assistance and Supervision

ML article 6 (Court or other authority for certain functions of arbitration assistance and supervision) has been adopted as KAA article 7 (Competent court) which specifies the competent court having jurisdiction over the various issues in accordance with the Korean judicial system. It is noteworthy that this article provides that the competent court is a district court or its branch which is a first instance court level. Thus, all of the matters listed in KAA article 7, including the recognition or enforcement of an arbitral award, are subject to a three-level review by the district court, high court and finally Supreme Court unless an appeal is prohibited by the explicit provisions of KAA. KAA article 7 omits a reference to 'other authority'.

Specifically, the competent court for the following matters is the district court (or its branch) designated by an arbitration agreement or, failing such designation, the district court (or its branch) of the place of arbitration or, if the place of arbitration has not yet been determined, the district court (or its branch) of the respondent's residence or place of business or, if none of those can be found, his place of abode or, if it cannot be found, his last-known residence or place of business (article 7(1)): (a) appointment of an arbitrator and designation of an arbitration institution under article 12(3) and (4); (b) decision on the request for challenging an arbitrator under article 14(3); (c) decision on the request for terminating the mandate of an arbitrator under article 15(2); (d) decision on the jurisdiction of the arbitral tribunal under article 17(6); (d-2) decision on the application for recognition or enforcement of interim measures, and ruling of provision of security under article 18-7; or (e) decision on the request for challenging an expert under article 27(3).

The competent court for the taking of evidence under article 28 is the district court (or its branch) of a place where it is performed (article 7(2)). With respect to (a) deposit of the original arbitral award under article 32(4) or (b) application for setting aside an award to court under article 36(1), the competent court is the district court (or its branch) of the place of arbitration (article 7(3)). Finally, the competent court for an application for the recognition or enforcement of an arbitral award under articles 37 to 39 is (a) the district court (or its branch) designated by an arbitration agreement, (2) the district court (or its branch) of the place of arbitration, (c) the district court (or its branch) of the place where a respondent's property is located or (d) the district court (or its branch) of the respondent's residence or place of business or, if none of those can be found, his place of abode or, if it cannot be found, his last-known residence or place of business (article 7(4)).

Part II   Arbitration Agreement (Articles 7 to 9)

Article 7   Definition and Form of Arbitration Agreement

Prior to the 2016 amendment, KAA in its article 8 essentially adopted all elements of article 7 of ML 1985 regarding definition and form of arbitration agreement in different articles by breaking down the elements in several paragraphs. The 2016 amendment virtually adopted all essential elements of the Option I of ML article 7 in article 8 (Form of arbitration agreement) of KAA. The text of KAA article 8 (Form of arbitration agreement), as amended, reads as follows:

(1) An arbitration agreement may be in the form of a separate agreement or in the form of an arbitration clause in a contract.
(2) An arbitration agreement shall be in writing.
(3) An agreement shall be deemed to be an arbitration agreement in writing:
   (a) If its content is recorded in any form, whether or not the arbitration agreement or contract has been concluded orally, by conduct, or by other means;
   (b) If it is contained in an exchange of electronic communication such as telegrams, telexes, facsimiles, electronic emails, or other means of telecommunication; however, if the contents of the arbitration agreement cannot be ascertained, it would not be deemed as such;
   (c) If it is contained in an exchange of statements of claims or defence in which the existence of an agreement is alleged by one party and not denied by the other.

> (4) The reference in a contract to a document containing an arbitration
> clause constitutes an arbitration agreement, provided that the refer-
> ence is such as to make that clause part of the contract.

Specifically, KAA separated article 7(1) of ML Option I into two parts: as
explained earlier, the definition of arbitration agreement has been
relocated to article 3 together with definitions of 'arbitration' and 'arbitral
tribunal', while the second sentence addressing the form of arbitration
agreement has been retained verbatim as paragraph (1) of article 8. Article
7(2) of ML Option I has been adopted verbatim in KAA article 8(2). ML
Option I article 7(3) to 7(6) are all reflected in KAA article 8(3) and (4).

Korean courts have tended to interpret the ambit of arbitration agreements broadly. There are a number of Supreme Court decisions interpreting the scope and validity of arbitration agreement under KAA
article 8.

In a decision rendered in 2005, the Supreme Court held that 'an
arbitration agreement shall apply not only to the disputes arising from
the agreement in which an arbitration clause is included but also to
disputes which are directly related to, or closely relevant to the consum-
mation, performance and effectiveness of, such agreement.'[11] In another
decision, the Supreme Court held that:

> if there is an agreement between the parties to submit to arbitration future
> disputes arising from a defined legal relationship between them, unless
> there is a special circumstance evidencing that the parties have limited the
> scope of disputes to a certain dispute, it is reasonable to interpret such
> agreement to arbitration to cover all future disputes between them arising
> from such defined legal relationship.[12]

Therefore, if parties intend to limit the category of disputes they intend to
refer to arbitration, such intention must be clearly expressed.

In a case which involved a challenge to an award of an arbitration
conducted under the KCAB rules on various grounds, including that a
claim for tort damages in respect of an explosion caused by latent defects
in certain transferred assets was outside the scope of the arbitration
agreement in the relevant business transfer agreement, the Supreme
Court held that:

---

[11] Supreme Court, 2004 Da 67264. Unless otherwise stated, the English translation of the
court decisions are the author's.
[12] Supreme Court, 2010 Da 76573.

Article 14 (arbitration clause) of the Business Transfer Agreement (Exhibit A2) provides that 'a legal dispute over the terms of the Agreement that cannot be resolved between the parties' may be subject to arbitration. Here, a dispute over the terms of the Agreement should be deemed to refer to not only a dispute over the interpretation of the terms and conditions of the Agreement, but also a dispute that is directly or closely related to the establishment of the terms and conditions of the Agreement, performance of the Agreement and existence/non-existence of validity of the Agreement. As in this case at hand, in case where a latent defect in the Transferred Assets has caused damage, the liability for defects to be borne by the Transferor against the Transferee is imperfect performance liability in nature and is directly related to the performance of the terms of the Agreement. Thus, based on the same fact situation, in cases where performance liability and tort liability are concurrent, a dispute over the existence/non-existence of the tort liability is a dispute closely related to the performance of the terms of the Agreement, and thus it is reasonable to find that the dispute should be deemed to be included in the category of disputes that may be subject to arbitration as prescribed in the arbitration clause in Paragraph A above.[13]

The Digest suggests that the constituent elements of an arbitration agreement are listed exhaustively in article 7(1) of the ML, and that other issues need not be addressed in order to validate the arbitration agreement.[14] In a decision rendered in 2007, the Supreme Court expressed the same position in the following terms:

For purposes of the Korean Arbitration Act, an arbitration agreement is an agreement between the parties to resolve, by arbitration, all or a part of disputes which have already arisen or which may arise in the future in respect of a defined legal relationship, whether contractual or not. Accordingly, as long as there has been a clear declaration of intent to resolve future disputes by arbitration, an arbitration agreement will be found to satisfy the requirements of validity even if it does not specify any particular arbitral institution, governing law or place of arbitration.[15]

On the other hand, the Supreme Court has repeatedly held that so-called 'split' dispute resolution clauses that offer a choice between litigation and arbitration are unenforceable as an arbitration agreement, and that split clauses offering a choice between mediation and arbitration are unenforceable as an arbitration agreement where the decision of the mediator

---

[13] Supreme Court, 91 Da 14146, 91 Da 17153.
[14] UNCITRAL, 2012 Digest of Case Law on the Model Law on International Commercial Arbitration, 28 (para. 10).
[15] Supreme Court, 2005 Da 74344; same holding by Supreme Court, 2005 Da 76573.

may be appealed to a court for adjudication on the merits. An otherwise unenforceable split clause will, however, become enforceable if one party initiates arbitration proceedings and the other party participates in those proceedings without challenging the arbitrator's jurisdiction, or otherwise alleging the non-existence of a valid arbitration agreement, by no later than the submission of its first statement of defence on the merits of the dispute in accordance with KAA article 17(2).[16]

Article 8   Arbitration Agreement and Substantive Claim before Court

ML article 8 (Arbitration agreement and substantive claim before court) has been adopted in substance as KAA article 9 (Arbitration agreement and substantive claim before court), with one modification to reflect the Korean judicial system. While ML article 8 prescribes that the court, in principle, refer the parties to arbitration when an action is brought before the court in a matter which is the subject of a valid arbitration agreement, KAA article 9(1) requires the court to dismiss an action. Korean courts have consistently dismissed action before the court when a valid arbitration agreement is found.

Article 9   Arbitration Agreement and Interim Measures by Court

This article of the ML has been adopted verbatim as KAA article 10 (Arbitration agreement and interim measures by court).

Part III   Composition of Arbitral Tribunal (Articles 10 to 15)

Article 10   Number of Arbitrators

ML article 10 has been adopted verbatim as KAA article 11 (Number of arbitrators).

Article 11   Appointment of Arbitrators

ML article 11 has been adopted as KAA article 12 (Appointment of arbitrators), but with the following modifications:

---

[16] Supreme Court, 2004 Da 42166.

(1) While ML provides for a thirty-day limit to appoint an arbitrator in an arbitration with three arbitrators, it does not impose the same thirty-day limit in an arbitration with a sole arbitrator. In contrast, KAA applies the thirty-day limit to an arbitration with a sole arbitrator as well (article 12(3)(a)).

(2) While ML provides for the court or other authority specified in article 6 as an appointing authority, KAA provides that the competent court as designated in article 7 of KAA or the arbitration institution designated by the competent court is the appointing authority under article 12. Prior to the 2016 amendment, the appointing authority under article 12 was limited to the competent court. The 2016 amendment allows the competent court to designate an arbitration institution for the appointment of an arbitrator to facilitate the process of a qualified arbitrator as an arbitration institution is better positioned to identify an arbitrator suitable for the nature of the dispute in question (article 12(4)).

(3) KAA article 12(5) retains the first sentence of ML article 11(5) (i.e., no appeal to the decision), but omits the second sentence (i.e., due regard to qualification agreed upon by the parties and independence and impartiality of an arbitrator). However, even without an explicit provision, it is expected that the court will take this into consideration in making an appointment.

There are two notable Supreme Court decisions interpreting KAA article 12. In a decision rendered in 2009, the Supreme Court held that 'when the court receives an application for appointment of an arbitrator, the court is obligated to appoint an arbitrator if it finds that the particular dispute is covered by an arbitration agreement', and it may not dismiss such application 'on the basis of its finding that the underlying claims of the claimant do not exist after its own review of the merits of the dispute'.[17] It could be inferred from this holding that Korean courts would reject the application for an appointment of an arbitrator if the court finds that there is no valid arbitration agreement or the dispute in question falls outside the scope of disputes covered by the arbitration agreement.

With respect to the 'no appeal' clause in KAA article 12 (corresponding to the first sentence of ML article 11(5)), the Supreme Court held that 'the decision which shall be subject to no appeal is limited to the decision of the court to appoint an arbitrator. It does not include a decision of

---

[17] Supreme Court, 2009 Ma 1395.

the court dismissing the application for appointment of an arbitrator.'[18]
Such narrow interpretation is supported by the Digest, which refers to
several cases which stood for the proposition that the rule of no appeal
applies where the grounds of appeal directly relate to one of the appointment procedures set out in paragraphs (3) and (4) as opposed to matters
that are peripheral to these procedures.[19]

Article 12   Grounds for Challenge

ML article 12 has been adopted as KAA article 13 (Grounds for challenge) with technical modification of wording which does not alter the
meaning. Specifically, KAA article 13(1) combines two sentences of ML
article 12(1) into a single sentence. KAA article 13(2) is a Korean
translation verbatim of ML article 12(2). In line with the cases referred
in the Digest,[20] the Supreme Court has also recognized KAA article 13(1),
which obligates arbitrators to disclose circumstances giving rise to justifiable doubts concerning their independence and impartiality as a 'mandatory' provision. The Supreme Court held that KAA article 13(1)
relating to the disclosure obligation shall not be treated as a provision
which could be deemed waived for the purpose of the application of
article 5 (Waiver of right to object) but shall be deemed as mandatory
provisions which cannot be waived.[21]

Neither ML nor KAA sets forth the relevant standard or test to assess
an arbitrator's independence or impartiality. A decision of the Supreme
Court rendered in 2004[22] is illustrative of the standard that the Korean
court applies in determining the independence and impartiality of an
arbitrator. The factual background of this case is as follows. In this first
arbitration case, the parties involved were the Korean Government and a
private construction company. The legal counsel to the construction
company ('counsel A') was appointed as legal counsel of another construction company in an unrelated arbitration case against the Korean
Government ('the second arbitration case'). After the first arbitration
case had commenced, the arbitrator on the first case was appointed as
joint legal counsel to the second arbitration case with counsel A and they
appeared together at the hearing for the second arbitration case as joint

---

[18] Supreme Court, 2007 Gue 154.
[19] UNCITRAL, 2012 Digest of Case Law, note 14 at 63 (para. 28).
[20] UNCITRAL, 2012 Digest of Case Law, note 14 at 65 (para. 5).
[21] Supreme Court, 2004 Da 47901.   [22] Supreme Court, 2003 Da 21995.

counsel. Both disputes dealt with similar legal issues and the Korean Government sought to set aside the award in the first arbitration case on the grounds that the arbitrator was not impartial. The court agreed with the Korean Government and held that an arbitrator should refrain from contacting the parties or their agents outside the arbitral proceedings. In case a practising attorney is appointed as an arbitrator, although he or she may still practise as a lawyer notwithstanding the arbitrator appointment, in principle, he or she should not accept cases from the parties or their agents as counsel regardless of whether the case is related to the arbitration or not. The court further held that if the arbitrator accepted a case from a party as counsel and the case involved the same or similar legal or factual issues with the arbitration case in which he acted as an arbitrator, 'it would provide material grounds for removing the arbitrator from the arbitral proceeding as it would give rise to suspicion as to the arbitrator's impartiality and independence' and that 'it would also provide grounds for setting aside the award if the arbitrator had not been removed'.

Article 13   Challenge Procedure

ML article 13 has been adopted as KAA article 14 (Challenge procedure), with the following minor modifications:

(1) While ML article 13(2) provides for 'fifteen days after becoming aware of the constitution of the arbitral tribunal', KAA article 14(2) provides for 'fifteen days after the constitution of the arbitral tribunal'. Thus, KAA takes a rather rigid approach as compared to ML in terms of the time limit for the challenge.
(2) While ML article 13(2) refers to 'a written statement of the reasons for the challenge', KAA article 14(2) uses 'written application for the challenge'. However, this change would not alter any meaning as the application for the challenge would include a statement of the reasons for the challenge in any event.
(3) While ML article 13(3) provides for 'the court' or 'other authority' to decide on the challenge, KAA article 14(3) allows only the competent court to decide on the challenge.

Article 14   Failure or Impossibility to Act

ML article 14 has been adopted in substance as KAA article 15. The title of this article is further elaborated in KAA as 'Termination of mandate of arbitrator due to his failure or impossibility to act'.

Specifically, ML article 14(1) has been broken down into three separate paragraphs as article 15(1), 15(2) and 15(3), but with one modification: consistent with articles 11 and 13, it deletes reference to 'other authority'. ML article 14(2) has not been adopted by KAA as this clause was not viewed as necessary to be included in the arbitration law.

Article 15   Appointment of Substitute Arbitrator

ML article 15 has been adopted as KAA article 16 (Appointment of substitute arbitrator) in a simplified wording without specifying the reasons for such termination. It provides that 'when the mandate of an arbitrator terminates, a substitute arbitrator is appointed.'

Part IV   Jurisdiction of Arbitral Tribunal (Article 16)

Article 16   Competence of Arbitral Tribunal to Rule on its Jurisdiction

ML article 16 has been adopted by KAA as article 17 (Ruling of arbitral tribunal on its jurisdiction), with some modification. Paragraph (1) has been retained though in simplified wording. Paragraph (2) has been broken down into three separate paragraphs (2), (3) and (4) without altering the meaning. Paragraph (3) has also been broken down into four separate paragraphs (5), (6), (7) and (8).

The 2016 amendment is noteworthy in two aspects:

(1) ML article 16(3) permits the objecting party to appeal a tribunal's positive jurisdictional finding to the competent court but is silent on the question of recourse against a tribunal's negative jurisdictional finding. The 2016 amendment explicitly allows a party to appeal a tribunal's ruling that it does not have jurisdiction as well (article 17(6)).

(2) A new paragraph was added as article 17(9) addressing the consequences of the court's positive ruling on the jurisdictional issue. This paragraph provides that '[i]f the court rules [...] that the arbitral tribunal has jurisdiction, the arbitral tribunal must continue the proceedings. If an arbitrator cannot or does not wish to continue the proceedings, the mandate of the arbitrator is terminated and a substitute arbitrator shall be appointed under article 16.'

The Supreme Court held that as the jurisdiction of the arbitral tribunal directly relates to the issue of the existence or validity of the arbitration agreement, the challenge of the jurisdiction of the tribunal should include a challenge as to the existence or validity of the arbitration agreement.[23]

Under KAA, before the 2016 amendment, Korean courts did not allow recourse against a negative jurisdictional finding by an arbitral tribunal. In a case rendered in 2004, the Supreme Court upheld a lower court's rejection of an action seeking to set aside an arbitral award in which the arbitral tribunal had refused to accept a request for arbitration on the ground that it did not have jurisdiction to hear the case.[24] However, the explicit provision allowing an appeal to the negative jurisdictional decision will require the court to reverse its position in the future.

Part IV-A   Interim Measures and Preliminary Orders (Articles 17 to 17J)

Sub-Part I   Measures and Orders by the Tribunal (Articles 17 to 17G)

Prior to the 2016 amendment, KAA article 18 (Interim measures) adopted article 17 of ML 1985 in substance, with a few modifications that do not alter the meaning. As stated earlier, the core elements of the 2016 amendment to KAA is the adoption of the provisions relating to interim measures of ML to a very substantial degree. KAA created a new Chapter III-2 with the title of 'Interim Measures' under which ML articles 17A–17I have been adopted, with some deviations to be discussed below, as KAA article 18, article 18-2 to article 18-8. While the 2016 amendment to KAA accepted ML provisions relating to interim measures, it did not accept the provisions relating to a 'preliminary order' which is foreign to the Korean judicial system.

Article 17   Power of Arbitral Tribunal to Order Interim Measures

ML article 17 has been adopted as KAA article 18 with slight wording changes which do not alter the meaning. Specifically, KAA article 18(1) states that '[u]nless otherwise agreed by the parties, the arbitral tribunal may, at the request of a party, decide on such interim measure of protection as the arbitral tribunal may consider necessary.' KAA article 18(2) adopted ML article 17(2) verbatim after deleting the phrase 'whether in the form of an award or in another form'. Prior to the

---

[23] Supreme Court, 2005 Da 12452.   [24] Supreme Court, 2003 Da 70249, 70256.

2016 amendment, KAA article 18 specified that the interim measures be in the form of an order. The deletion of this limitation in the 2016 amendment will grant the arbitral tribunal discretion to grant an interim measure in the form of an award or an order.

Article 17A Conditions for Granting Interim Measures KAA adopted this ML article verbatim as article 18-2 (Conditions for granting interim measures).

Article 17B Applications for Preliminary Orders and Conditions for Granting Preliminary Orders and Article 17C Specific Regime for Preliminary Orders As explained earlier, KAA has not adopted these two articles relating to preliminary orders.

Article 17D Modification, Suspension, Termination This article has been adopted as KAA article 18-3, with the following two modifications: (1) reference to the preliminary orders was deleted; and (2) KAA added a requirement that '[t]he arbitral tribunal shall question the parties prior to modification, suspension, or termination of an interim measure.'

Article 17E Provision of Security ML article 17E(1) has been adopted verbatim as KAA article 18-4 (Provision of security). ML article 17E(2) dealing with preliminary orders has not been adopted.

Article 17F Disclosure ML article 17F(1) has been adopted verbatim as KAA article 18-5 (Disclosure). ML article 17F(2) dealing with preliminary orders has not been adopted.

Article 17G Costs and Damages This article has been adopted verbatim as KAA article 18-6 (Costs and damages), except for the reference to a preliminary order.

Sub-Part II   Recognition and Enforcement of Interim Measures
(Articles 17H and 17I)

Article 17H Recognition and Enforcement ML article 17H has been adopted as KAA article 18-7 (Recognition and enforcement of interim measures) with two important deviations:

(1) KAA article 18-7(1) which adopted ML article 17H(1) did not adopt the phrase 'irrespective of the country in which it was issued, subject to the provisions of article 17I'. As a result, only an interim measure issued by an arbitral tribunal which is governed by KAA could be recognized and enforced pursuant to KAA article 18-7(1).

(2) KAA added a new paragraph (4) to further define the rules governing the recognition and enforcement of interim measures as follows: 'The provisions of Civil Execution Act regarding preservative measures shall apply *mutatis mutandis* to the enforcement of interim measures.'

Article 17I   Grounds for Refusing Recognition or Enforcement
While ML article 17I has been adopted as KAA article 18-8 (Grounds for refusing recognition or enforcement), some modifications were made to this article to further clarify the grounds for refusing recognition or enforcement. Specifically, while embracing ML article 17I(1), KAA article 18-8(1) added the following two grounds for refusing recognition or enforcement: (i) the party against whom the interim measure was invoked has not received proper notification regarding the appointment of arbitrators or rules of arbitration procedure, or was unable to present his case for reasons other than the above; and (ii) the interim measure deals with a dispute falling outside or beyond the scope of an arbitration agreement, provided that, if the interim measure deals with matters within the scope of an arbitration agreement which can be separated from those outside of an arbitration agreement, only that part of the interim measure which deals with matters not covered by an arbitration agreement may be refused.

ML article 17I(2) has been broken down as KAA article 18-8(2) and 18-8(3), without altering the meaning.

Sub-Part III   Court-Ordered Interim Measures (Article 17J)

Article 17J   Court-Ordered Interim Measures   This article has not been adopted by KAA. However, Korean courts have power to order interim measures under the Code of Civil Procedure and article 10 of KAA.

Part V   Conduct of Arbitral Proceedings (Articles 18 to 27)

Article 18   Equal Treatment of Parties

This article has been adopted verbatim as KAA article 19 (Equal treatment of parties).

Article 19   Determination of Rules of Procedure

This article has been adopted verbatim as KAA article 20 (Rules of procedure).

Article 20   Place of Arbitration

The text of this article has been adopted verbatim as KAA article 21 (Place of arbitration), while ML article 20(1) has been broken down into two separate paragraphs in KAA.

Article 21   Commencement of Arbitral Proceedings

The text of ML article 21 has been adopted verbatim by KAA as article 22(1). KAA added a new paragraph (2) as follows: 'In the request referred to in paragraph (1), the parties, the subject-matter of the dispute and contents of the arbitration agreement shall be contained.'

Article 22   Language

This article has been adopted by KAA as article 23 (Language), with two important modifications: first, KAA deleted the words 'or languages'. However, this deletion is more of linguistic adjustment to the Korean language which does not clearly distinguish between the singular and plural form of nouns. Thus, parties will be able to agree to the use of more than one language. Second, KAA added a new sentence to the effect that, in the absence of the determination by the arbitral tribunal on the language, the Korean language shall be used. Therefore, in the unlikely event that the tribunal fails to agree on the language, Korean will be the language of the arbitration proceeding under KAA.

Article 23   Statements of Claim and Defence

This article has been adopted by KAA as article 24 (Statement of claim and defence), with two insignificant omissions:

(1) Paragraph 1, which closely follows ML article 23(1), omitted a reference to 'the points at issue'. However, this omission would not alter the overall meaning of ML article 23(1).

(2) Paragraph 1 omitted the phrase in ML article 23(1) 'unless the parties have otherwise agreed as to the required elements of such statements'.

Article 24   Hearings and Written Proceedings

The text of this article has been adopted virtually verbatim as KAA article 25 (Hearings), while ML article 24(3) has been broken down into two separate paragraphs as KAA article 25(3) and article 25(4). The 2016 amendment to KAA added the words 'without delay' to article 25(3).

Article 25   Default of a Party

The text of this article has been adopted as KAA article 26 (Default of a party). KAA restructured it into four separate paragraphs without altering the meaning.

Article 26   Expert Appointed by Arbitral Tribunal

This article has been adopted by KAA as article 27 (Expert) with some significant modification as follows:

(1) ML article 26(1) has been adopted verbatim as KAA article 27(1).
(2) ML article 26(2) has been adopted with modification as KAA article 27(2). ML article 26(2) states that '[u]nless otherwise agreed by the parties, if a party so requests or if the arbitral tribunal considers it necessary, the expert shall, after delivery of his written or oral report, participate in a hearing where the parties have the opportunity to put questions to him and to present expert witnesses in order to testify on the points at issue.' However, KAA article 27(2) omitted the words 'after delivery of his written or oral report' and rephrased the entire sentence to state that an expert witness could be called to participate in the hearing for the parties to put questions to him.
(3) KAA added a new paragraph (3) to the effect that '[t]he provisions of articles 13 and 14 shall apply *mutatis mutandis* to an expert appointed by the arbitral tribunal.' This is to ensure impartiality of experts. As a result, under KAA, an expert could be challenged on the same ground and the same manner as in the case of an arbitrator. This addition, modelled after the provision in the German Code of

Civil Procedure,[25] apparently intends to ensure the independence
and impartiality of the expert appointed by the tribunal.

Article 27   Court Assistance in Taking Evidence

ML article 27 has been adopted in substance by KAA as article 28 (Court
assistance in taking evidence) with a number of modifications as follows:

(1) KAA makes it clear that the arbitral tribunal may either entrust the
court to take evidence on its behalf or seek the court's assistance in
taking evidence. KAA article 28(1) provides that '[t]he arbitral tribunal may, either on its own initiative or upon the request of a party,
entrust to, or request assistance from, a competent court, in taking
evidence.

(2) Under KAA, only the arbitral tribunal may entrust to, or request
assistance from, a competent court either on its own initiative or
upon the request of a party. A party is not allowed to make such
request directly to a competent court.

(3) In lieu of the second sentence in ML article 27, KAA added five
additional paragraphs to elaborate further details. The text is provided below:

  (a) KAA article 28(2): When entrusting the court for taking evidence, the arbitral tribunal may, in writing, specify the matters to
  be recorded in the protocol of the court and other particulars
  necessary for investigation.

  (b) KAA article 28(3): With the approval of the presiding judge, the
  arbitrator(s) and the party(ies) may participate in the process of
  the taking evidence by the court in accordance with paragraph
  (2) above.

  (c) KAA article 28(4): The court referred to in paragraph (2) shall,
  without delay after taking evidence, send the records on taking
  evidence such as a certified copy of protocol for examination of
  witness or inspection of property to the arbitral tribunal.

  (d) KAA article 28(5): When the arbitral tribunal requests assistance
  of the court in taking evidence, the court may order a witness to
  appear before the arbitral tribunal or order a person who pos-
  sesses a document to submit the document to the arbitral
  tribunal.

---

[25] German Code of Civil Procedure, art. 1049.

(e) KAA article 28(6): The arbitral tribunal shall pay necessary expenses for taking evidence to the court referred to in paragraph (1).

Part VI Making of Award and Termination of Proceedings (Articles 28 to 33)

Article 28 Rules Applicable to Substance of Dispute

This article has been adopted as KAA article 29 (Law applicable to substance of dispute) with the following two significant modifications:

(1) In paragraph 1, it replaced the words 'such rules of law' with 'such law'. Commentators differ as to the significance of this change of words. Some scholars are of the opinion that the use of the word 'law' rather than 'rules of law' in KAA was to avoid complications that could arise from potential application of multiple rules of law.[26] Other scholars opine that the concept of law in this paragraph should be interpreted to include 'rules of law' as provided for in the ML article 28(1) as there is no rational reason to restrict the parties' ability to choose rules of law.[27]

(2) While ML article 28(2) provides that '[f]ailing any designation by the parties, the arbitral tribunal shall apply the law determined by the conflict of laws rules which it considers applicable', KAA article 29(2) provides that in such a case the arbitral tribunal shall apply 'the law of the State with which the subject-matter of the dispute is most closely connected'.

Therefore, where the seat of arbitration is in Korea and the parties have not chosen the applicable substantive law, KAA article 29(2) requires arbitrators to 'apply the law of the state which has the closest connection to the subject-matter of the dispute' rather than 'the law determined by the conflict of laws rules which the tribunal considers applicable' as provided for in ML.

While there are not many reported cases on point, Korean courts seem to distinguish between the law governing the main contract and the law governing the arbitration agreement contained therein.

---

[26] Moon-Chul Chang, note 9 at 53–54.
[27] See Young Joon Mok, *Sang Sa Jung Jae Beop* [Commercial Arbitration Law] (2011), 117.

This position is reflected in a 1990 decision of the Supreme Court where the plaintiff sought enforcement of an English award in Korea.[28] The substantive law applicable to the arbitration agreement became an issue when the defendant resisted enforcement of the award on the ground that the arbitration agreement was allegedly invalid, having been previously revoked by the defendant. The Supreme Court held that:

> Whether or not an arbitration agreement may be revoked is ultimately a matter of the effect of the said agreement. As to the foregoing, Article V(1)(a) of the New York Convention provides that such an issue shall be primarily determined 'under the law to which the parties have subjected it or, failing any indication thereon, under the law of the country where the award was made'. In the event that a sales agreement contains a provision stating that 'all disputes arising out of or in connection with this contract shall be determined by arbitration pursuant to the rules of the London Court of Arbitration [sic] in effect as of the date of this contract', it can be concluded that the parties have designated English law as a law governing their arbitration agreement and, according to English law, a written arbitration agreement as above may not be revoked arbitrarily by one of the parties thereto.

In deciding that the applicable substantive law was English law, the Supreme Court relied on the reference in the arbitration agreement to the rules of the London Court of Arbitration [sic], concluding that such reference reflected an agreement not only to designate the arbitral institution and applicable procedural rules as stated, but also to situate the place of arbitration in London. Finding that the parties had implicitly agreed to situate the place of arbitration in London, the Court held that this amounted to an agreement that English law was to be the substantive law applicable to the arbitration agreement.

Although the main contract contained a governing law clause stating that '[t]he validity, interpretation and performance of this contract shall be governed by the English law' the Court did not rely on that provision but on the reference in the arbitration clause to 'the rules of the London Court of Arbitration [sic]', from which the court inferred an agreement to designate English law as the 'law governing their arbitration agreement'.

On this basis and a few other judgments, commentators have concluded that the Supreme Court recognizes a distinction between the substantive law applicable to the arbitration agreement and the governing law applicable to the contract as a whole and that the court's

---

[28] Supreme Court, 89 Da 20252.

preferred choice of law method for determining the substantive law applicable to the arbitration agreement is to apply the law of the place of arbitration in priority to the governing law of the main contract.

In a decision rendered in 2001, the Seoul High Court indicated its recognition of a possible distinction amongst arbitral procedural law, the substantive law governing the arbitration agreement and the law applicable to the substance of the dispute. The court held that:

> [i]n general, governing laws related to arbitration are classified into (1) law governing the arbitral procedure, (2) substantive law applicable to the arbitration agreement, and (3) law applicable to determine the substance of the dispute [...] With regard to the procedural law applied to the arbitral award of this case, in general, an arbitral procedural law may be determined upon agreement between the parties. In case there is no such agreement, one opinion is that the law of the place of the arbitration shall be applied and another is that the arbitrator determines which arbitral procedural law is applicable.[29]

In practice, however, the author is not aware of any case in which Korean courts have considered the foreign arbitral procedural law chosen by the parties to apply in their arbitration.

Article 29 Decision-Making by Panel of Arbitrators

This article has been adopted verbatim as KAA article 30 (Decision-making by arbitral tribunal).

Article 30 Settlement

This article has been adopted verbatim as KAA article 31 (Settlement).

Article 31 Form and Contents of Award

This article has been adopted by KAA as article 32, with the following modifications:

(1) In the second sentence of paragraph 3, the words 'on that date' were added in addition to 'at that place'.
(2) Paragraph 4 introduced an option of the parties to make a request to the arbitral tribunal that the original award be sent to and deposited

---

[29] Seoul High Court, 2000 Na 36448.

with the competent court. The text reads as follows: 'The duly authenticated award made and signed in accordance with paragraphs (1)
through (3) of this Article shall be delivered to each party in accordance with paragraphs (1) through (3) of Article 4, and, upon the
request by a party, the original award shall be sent to and deposited
with the competent court, accompanied by a document verifying such
delivery.' This is a novel feature in KAA whose purpose is to enable the
parties to be able to verify the award against the original copy deposited
with the competent court should a dispute arise over the contents of
the award in the future. In particular, it will be useful in ad hoc
arbitrations in which arbitral institutions have not been engaged.

With respect to the requirement of the award to state the reasons upon
which it is based in the context of setting aside claims based upon failure
to state reasons, Korean courts have required a high threshold standard.
In a decision rendered in 2010, the Supreme Court held that:

> [t]he arbitral tribunal's failure to state the reasons upon which it is based
> refers to the cases (i) where there is a total absence of the reasons upon
> which the award is based, (ii) even if the reasons stated are so unclear that
> it is impossible to understand the legal or factual basis of the tribunal's
> determinations, or (iii) where there is contradiction. As far as the reasons
> are stated, the reasons could be based upon equitable principles as well as
> law. The reasons need not be clear and detailed on the underlying rights
> and obligations. It is sufficient as long as it is possible to follow how the
> arbitrators reached their decision. Unless such reasoning is manifestly
> against common sense or contradictory, inadequate or incomplete
> reasons do not constitute a failure to state reasons.[30]

Article 32   Termination of Proceedings

This article has been adopted verbatim as KAA article 33 (Termination
of proceedings) except that it omitted reference to ML article 34(4). KAA
article 33 corresponding to ML article 34 did not adopt ML article 34(4).

Article 33   Correction and Interpretation of Award; Additional Award

The text of this article has been adopted in substance as KAA article 34
(Correction and interpretation of award, and additional award). KAA
rephrased and restructured the text of this article without altering the
meaning.

---

[30] Supreme Court, 2007 Da 73918.

Part VII   Recourse against Award (Article 34)

KAA added an article as article 35 which declares that an arbitral award has the same effect on the parties as 'the final and conclusive judgment of the court, unless the recognition or enforcement is refused in accordance with article 38'. KAA article 38 provides for grounds for refusal of recognition or enforcement of domestic arbitral awards which are subject to KAA. While ML is silent on this point, this article confirms the principle that recourse against an arbitral award to the courts is not allowed apart from recourse on the procedural grounds such as those listed in KAA article 36 (corresponding to ML article 34).

Article 34   Application for Setting Aside as Exclusive Recourse against Arbitral Award

ML article 34(1) prescribing that recourse to a court against an arbitral award may be made only by an application for setting aside in accordance with paragraphs (2) and (3) of the same article has been adopted in substance as KAA article 36(1).

ML article 34(2) providing for a list of grounds for setting aside has been adopted by KAA as article 36(2) with one modification regarding the public policy provision. While ML article 34(2)(b)(ii) provides that 'the award is in conflict with the public policy of this State', KAA article 36(2)(b)(ii) stipulates that 'the recognition and enforcement of the award is in conflict with the good morals or other public policy of the Republic of Korea'. KAA also makes it explicit that the court may find the article 36(2)(b) grounds 'on its own initiative'.

KAA has not adopted ML article 34(4) of ML, which allows the court to suspend temporarily its setting aside proceedings to give the arbitral tribunal an opportunity to resume the arbitral proceedings or to take such other action as in the arbitral tribunal's opinion will eliminate the grounds for setting aside. Some commentators explained that the reason for not adopting ML article 34(4) was because the concept of suspension of court proceedings was rather uncommon under the Korean judicial system and practice. Other explanations included that it is not always realistic to expect that the original arbitral tribunal take corrective measures to eliminate grounds of setting aside and it might be a simple solution for the court to set aside the decision to leave the matter to the parties and the tribunal to address the matter in consideration of the court's decision. However, some commentators are of the view that the Korean court would not be prohibited from taking such action on its own initiative or where so requested by a party.[31]

Instead, KAA adds a new provision as article 36(4) to the effect that after a final and conclusive decision for recognition or enforcement of the relevant award by a court of the Republic of Korea is rendered, no action for setting aside the award may be brought.

The Supreme Court clearly held that Korean courts can only set aside arbitral awards where the arbitral tribunals were seated in Korea. In a decision rendered in 2003, the Supreme Court upheld the lower court's decision which dismissed an application for setting aside an ICC award where the place of arbitration was Hong Kong and the governing law was Korean law.[32] In its reasoning, the Supreme Court first referred to the New York Convention under which an arbitration award may not be enforced or recognized if the award was set aside by a competent authority of the 'country where the award was made' or the 'country under the law of which that award was made'. Then the Supreme Court held that 'the law of which that award was made' referred to *lex arbitri* rather than the governing law of the dispute. Therefore, the Korean court lacked jurisdiction to set aside the award for which Hong Kong was the place of arbitration.

In applying KAA article 36(4), the Seoul High Court held that although the arbitral award lacks the requisite specificity for execution, a legitimate interest exists to bring a legal action for an enforcement judgment of the arbitral award that cannot be executed. The plaintiff has a legitimate interest to bring a legal action for the enforcement judgment because the setting aside action would be barred by the enforcement judgment pursuant to KAA article 36(4).[33]

Part VIII   Recognition and Enforcement of Awards
(Articles 35 and 36)

Article 35   Recognition and Enforcement

While KAA embraces the principle embodied in this article, it deals with the recognition and enforcement in its own logic and manner in article 35 (Effect of Arbitral Awards), article 37 (Recognition and enforcement

---

[31] Bae, Kim & Lee, note 4 at 24.   [32] Supreme Court, 2001 Da 77840.
[33] Seoul High Court, 2013 Na 13506.

of an arbitral award), article 38 (Domestic Arbitral Awards) and article 39 (Foreign Arbitral Awards).

Notable deviations from ML include: (i) the different treatment of domestic arbitral awards (article 38) and foreign arbitral awards (article 39) and (ii) KAA's attempt to distinguish the concept of 'recognition' and that of 'enforcement'.

As explained earlier, KAA article 35 (Effect of Arbitral Awards) provides that '[a]rbitral awards shall have the same effect on the parties as the final and conclusive judgment of the court, unless the recognition or enforcement is refused in accordance with article 38.' This article applies to the arbitral awards rendered in Korea as the carved-out exception to the territorial principle in KAA article 2(1) does not include article 35. However, article 37 is carved out as an exception to the territorial principle in KAA article 2(1), and thus applicable to foreign arbitral awards.

The substance of ML article 35(1) has been adopted by KAA in articles 37(1) and 37(2). With respect to recognition, KAA article 37(1) reads that '[a]n arbitral award shall be recognized, unless there is a ground to refuse recognition in accordance with article 38 or article 39, provided that the court may make a ruling recognizing an arbitral award upon application by a party.' KAA article 38 relates to domestic arbitral awards, while article 39 relates to foreign arbitral awards. With respect to enforcement, KAA article 37(2) provides that '[e]nforcement based upon an arbitral award shall be granted by a ruling of a court upon application by a party.'

ML article 35(2) has been accepted verbatim as KAA article 37(3) which specifies Korean as the language of the state.

KAA article 37 has five additional paragraphs which address the procedural details of the recognition or enforcement proceedings, as follows: (i) Upon application by a party for recognition or enforcement, the court shall set a hearing date in which both parties may participate, and notify the parties of that date (article 37(4)); (ii) The ruling of the court shall state reasons, provided, however, that if there was no hearing, a summary of reasons should suffice (article 37(5)); (iii) The ruling of the court shall be subject to an immediate appeal (article 37(6)); (iv) The immediate appeal under article 37(6) shall not have the effect of suspending the execution of the ruling, provided, however, that the appellate court (if the case docket remains in the court of the first instance, then that court) may, with or without ordering a party to provide security, suspend the execution of the original ruling or suspend all or part of the execution process until there is a decision on the immediate appeal. An appellate court may also order a party to provide a security as a condition of continuing the execution (article 37(7)); and (v) The decision in accordance with the proviso of article 37(7) above shall not be subject to an appeal (article 37(8)). These additional paragraphs have been added by the 2016 amendment to give exceptional treatment to the court 'ruling' to be rendered in connection with the recognition or enforcement of arbitral awards as compared to general characteristics of court 'rulings' in other matters.

Article 36   Grounds for Refusing Recognition or Enforcement

The principle embedded in ML article 36(1) has been adopted by KAA in a different formulation. As explained earlier, KAA governs both domestic and international arbitration. KAA addresses recognition and enforcement of awards in two separate articles.

First, KAA article 38 (Domestic arbitral awards) provides that:

> Arbitral awards made in the territory of the Republic of Korea shall be recognized or enforced, unless it falls under any of the following:
>
> (a) a party to an arbitral award proves any one of the following facts:
>   (i) any of the circumstances referred to in article 36(2)(a); or
>   (ii) any one of the following: the arbitral award has not yet become binding on the parties; or the arbitral award has been set aside by the court
> (b) any of the circumstances referred to in article 36(2)(b) exist.

Second, for foreign awards which were rendered outside the territory of Korea, KAA article 39 (Foreign arbitral awards) provides as follows:

> (1) Recognition or enforcement of a foreign award which is subject to the Convention on the Recognition and Enforcement of Foreign Arbitral Awards shall be governed by that Convention.
> (2) Article 217 of the Civil Procedure Act and articles 26(1) and 27 of the Civil Execution Act shall apply *mutatis mutandis* to the recognition or execution of a foreign arbitral award which is not subject to the Convention on the Recognition and Enforcement of Foreign Arbitral Awards.

In essence, with respect to international arbitral awards rendered outside of Korea, but within the territories of the signatory state of the NYC, the NYC will directly apply by operation of KAA article 39(1). In these instances, grounds for refusing recognition or enforcement are exactly the same as those enumerated in Article V of the NYC. On the other hand, KAA subjects a foreign arbitral award which was not rendered in a member state to the NYC to a procedure under article 217 of the Civil Procedure Act and articles 26(1) and 27 of the Civil Execution Act, which are the procedures applicable to the recognition and enforcement of a foreign court judgment.[34] The rationale behind this different treatment is due to the reciprocity reservation Korea has made at the time it accepted the NYC.

ML article 36(2) has not been adopted by KAA. However, the Korean court where recognition or enforcement of a foreign arbitral award (to which NYC is applicable) is sought will apply NYC Article VI, which is in substance identical to ML article 36(2).

---

[34] Civil Procedure Act Article 217(1) provides as follows:

> A final and conclusive judgment by a foreign court shall be acknowledged to be valid, only upon the entire fulfilment of the following requirements:

> 1. That an international jurisdiction of such foreign court is recognized in the principles of an international jurisdiction pursuant to the Acts and subordinate statutes of the Republic of Korea, or to the treaties;
> 2. That a defeated defendant received, pursuant to a lawful method, a service of a summons or a document equivalent thereto, and a notice of date or an order, with a time leeway sufficient to defend (excluding the case pursuant to a service by public notice or similar service), or that he responded to the lawsuit even without being served;
> 3. That such judgment does not violate good morals and other social order of the Republic of Korea; and
> 4. That there exists a mutual guarantee.

Article 26(1) and Article 27 of Civil Execution Act provide as follows:

> Article 26 (Compulsory Execution by Foreign Judgment) (1) A compulsory execution based upon the judgment of a foreign court may be conducted only if a court of the Republic of Korea has made a declaration of its legality by means of a judgment of execution.

> Article 27 (Judgment of Execution) (1) A judgment of execution shall be made without making any examination as to whether the judgment is right or wrong.

> (2) A lawsuit seeking a judgment of execution shall be dismissed if it falls under any of the following subparagraphs:

> 1. When it has not been proved that the judgment of a foreign court has become final and conclusive;
> 2. When the foreign judgment fails to fulfil the conditions under Article 217 of the Civil Procedure Act.

The notion of 'public policy' as stated in NYC is generally interpreted narrowly by Korean courts and challenges to arbitration awards on grounds of violation of public policy are mostly unsuccessful. Commentators are generally in agreement that Korean courts maintain a pro-enforcement attitude to both domestic and foreign awards, strictly applying the NYC.[35]

The Supreme Court held that 'when determining whether the public policy has been violated, the public policy ground must be interpreted restrictively, taking into account the international aspect of the business in question as well as Korean laws and policy.'[36] In another case, the Supreme Court stated that:

> Article 36(2)(b)(ii) of KAA which provides that 'the recognition and enforcement of the award is in conflict with the good morals or other forms of social order of the Republic of Korea' refers to a situation where the execution and enforcement of the award results in conflict with the good morals or other forms of social order of the Republic of Korea. It does not include all situations where there are errors in the factual determination of the arbitrators or the legal determination of the arbitrators is in conflict with laws and regulations. The fact that the arbitral award is based upon interpretation of laws or contracts different from the decisions of the Supreme Court does not itself fall under article 36(2)(b)(ii).[37]

In a case rendered in 1995 where the governing law of the arbitration was the law of the Netherlands, and the tribunal rendered an award in accordance with Dutch law's extinctive prescription period of thirty years which was longer than that of the Korean law, the Supreme Court held that the award cannot be denied recognition merely because the applied foreign law is directly in violation with the Korean mandatory laws. The court further held that it must be additionally shown that as the result of recognition there may be actual violation of Korea's moral standards and public policy.[38] In a more recent case, rendered in 2010, the Supreme Court held that an award that is not consistent with previous Supreme Court precedents in similar cases is not a violation of public policy unless the result of the award is clearly in violation of the moral standards and other social order of Korea.[39] This position of the Korean courts is in line with the case law in the Digest which states the mere fact that the arbitral award violated certain laws or regulations

[35] Bae, Kim & Lee, note 4 at 27.   [36] Supreme Court, 2001 Da 20134.
[37] Supreme Court, 2007 Da 73918.   [38] Supreme Court, 93 Da 53054.
[39] Supreme Court, 2007 Da 73918.

of the enforcing state is not sufficient to constitute a violation of public policy.[40]

The Digest introduces a decision in Thailand where the court refused to enforce an award based on a contract obtained by bribery.[41] The Korean Supreme Court has shown a careful approach regarding the award allegedly obtained by the fraudulent acts of the party. The Supreme Court held that 'the award cannot be denied recognition on grounds of public policy unless (i) such fraud has been clearly proved; (ii) the other party was unaware of the fraud and could not defend himself from such fraud during the arbitral proceedings; and (iii) such fraud was closely related to the issues of the arbitration case.'[42] The rationale for this ruling is that the enforcement court is not permitted substantively to review the arbitral tribunal's findings and judgment to assess whether fraud has been committed.

Additional Articles in KAA

KAA Article 34-2 (Apportionment of the Cost of the Arbitration) The 2016 amendment to KAA introduced a new article on apportionment of arbitration costs. The article reads as follows:

> Unless otherwise agreed by the parties, the arbitral tribunal may, taking into consideration all circumstances of the case, determine the apportionment of the costs incurred in connection with the arbitration procedure.

KAA Article 34-3 (Default Interest) The 2016 amendment to KAA also introduced a new article on the default interest as follows:

> Unless otherwise agreed by the parties, the arbitral tribunal may, taking into consideration all circumstances of the case, order a payment of an appropriate default interest when making an award.

KAA Article 40 (Assistance to Commercial Arbitration Institution) KAA article 40 provides that for the purpose of promoting the impartial and prompt settlement of commercial disputes through arbitration, governmental financial support may be given to an arbitral institution when incorporated as a non-profit association as designated by the Minister of Commerce, Industry and Energy (MOCIE). Currently, the Korean Commercial Arbitration Board (KCAB) is the only institution designated by the MOCIE.

---

[40] UNCITRAL, 2012 Digest of Case Law, note 14 at 184 (para. 59).
[41] UNCITRAL, 2012 Digest of Case Law, note 14 at 185 (para. 62).
[42] Supreme Court, 2006 Da 20290.

KAA Article 41   (Establishment and Approval of Arbitration Rules)
This article provides that the arbitration rules of the arbitral institution
designated by the MOCIE in accordance with article 40 of KAA are
subject to the approval of the Chief Justice of the Korean Supreme Court.
It serves as legal basis for the Supreme Court to review and supervise the
arbitral rules of the KCAB.

Conclusion

A detailed comparison of ML and KAA as set forth above reveals that the
overall structure, the sequence of articles and the core principles of ML
have been very closely adopted by KAA through its amendments in 1999
and 2016.

In particular, effective as of 30 November 2016, KAA has been
amended to incorporate the 2006 amendment to the ML and also to
reflect recent developments in the field of arbitration law in major
jurisdictions which have transpired since the 1999 amendment. The
National Assembly approved the amendment in about a year after
the MOJ submitted the amendment bill. This reflects the urgency felt
by the Korean legal and business community on the need to modernize
KAA in order to facilitate arbitration as an efficient and cost-effective
alternative means of dispute resolution. It is evident that the
2016 amendment to KAA is in the direction of further harmonizing
the Korean arbitration law regime with international standards and
practice so that impartial, efficient and prompt resolution of disputes
through arbitration based upon the principle of party autonomy might
be promoted. It is generally viewed that KAA contains 'no provisions
that are unduly restrictive of party autonomy, that undermine the
enforceability of arbitral awards, or that conflict with prevailing international best practices'.[43]

As illustrated by Korean court decisions reviewed earlier in this
chapter, Korean courts have recognized the international origin of the
articles adopted from ML. They have made conscious efforts faithfully
to interpret and apply the core elements of ML as well as its object and
purpose, as incorporated in KAA. It is generally viewed that Korean
courts have consistently shown pro-enforcement attitudes to both

---

[43] Bae, Kim & Lee, note 4 at 23.

domestic and foreign arbitral awards. Only a very small number of reported court decisions have set aside an arbitral award. Korean courts have also strictly applied the NYC with no foreign award having been refused recognition and enforcement in Korea by the Korean Supreme Court on any of the substantive grounds provided in Article V of the NYC.[44]

---

[44] Bae, Kim & Lee, note 4 at 27.

Malaysia

The Arbitration Regime in Malaysia: A De Jure Model Law Jurisdiction?

SUNDRA RAJOO AND CHOONG YEOW CHOY

Introduction

A brief history of the arbitration regime in Malaysia can be elucidated by dividing the timeline into three distinct periods. The first is pre-2005. The Arbitration Ordinance XIII of 1809 was the first statutory law on arbitration in pre-independence Malaya.[1] That ordinance governed arbitration law and practice for nearly 150 years before it was replaced by the Arbitration Act 1952.[2] This piece of legislation was based almost word for word on the United Kingdom's Arbitration Act 1950. This Act was in force until it was repealed by the Arbitration Act 2005 ('2005 Act').[3] This period of just over half a century was dictated by the jurisprudence whereby the courts were given wide discretionary powers to intervene in and govern the arbitral process.[4]

The year 2005 marks an important year as it heralded the espousal of a new arbitration landscape for Malaysia.[5] In the Explanatory Statement,

Datuk Professor Sundra Rajoo is the Director of the Asian International Arbitration Centre (formerly known as the Kuala Lumpur Regional Centre for Arbitration) and visiting professor at the Faculty of Built Environment, University of Technology Malaysia. Choong Yeow Choy is a professor and former dean at the Faculty of Law, University of Malaya, Malaysia. The authors thank the EW Barker Centre for Law & Business at the Faculty of Law of the National University of Singapore for financing their participation in the conference entitled, 'The UNCITRAL Model Law on International Commercial Arbitration in Asia', which led to this book. This chapter was up to date on 28 May 2015.

[1] Prior to independence, Malaysia was known as Malaya.   [2] Act 93.   [3] Act 646.

[4] For a discussion of the application of the Arbitration Act 1952, see W. S. W. Davidson and Sundra Rajoo, 'The New Malaysian Arbitration Regime 2005', http://sundrarajoo .com/portfolio-posts/the-new-malaysian-arbitration-act-2005-by-w-s-w-davidson-and-sundra-rajoo-sweet-maxwell-reprinted-from-2006-72-arbitration-257-264/.

[5] Although the 2005 Act was enacted on 30 December 2005, it only came into force on 15 March 2006.

it is stated that the Arbitration Bill 2005[6] seeks to, *inter alia*, 'promote international consistency of arbitral regimes based on the model law adopted by the United Nations Commission on International Trade Law on 21 June 1985'. The 2005 Act is said to have brought about 'much needed change clamoured for by the business and arbitral communities in Malaysia'.[7]

The extent to which Malaysia as a jurisdiction has adopted the texts and/or principles of the UNCITRAL Model Law on International Commercial Arbitration 1985, UN General Assembly Resolution 40/72 (11 December 1985) ('ML 1985') and achieved the aim of promoting 'international consistency of arbitral regimes' will be discussed in the text that follows. Suffice it to say at this juncture that while the business and arbitral communities had welcomed the 2005 Act there was a realization that there was an urgent need for further tweaking to add certainty and consistency to the application and implementation of the 2005 Act. This led to the introduction of the Arbitration (Amendment) Act 2011,[8] marking the beginning of the third significant period in the area concerning the law and practice of arbitration in Malaysia. The Arbitration (Amendment) Act 2011 amended nine of the main provisions in the 2005 Act. The Explanatory Statement in the Bill that introduced the Arbitration (Amendment) Act 2011 alluded to the ML 1985 in two specific instances.[9] The ensuing sections in this chapter will no doubt deliberate on the successes or otherwise of the objectives sought by Parliament.

Malaysia has declared to the UNCITRAL that it has adopted the ML 1985.[10] It has adopted the original and English version of the ML 1985. More than 90 per cent of the provisions of the ML 1985 have been adopted in full without any amendment and these are reflected in the current statutory law on arbitration in Malaysia, namely the 2005 Act as amended in 2011. While these have made Malaysia, to all intents and

[6] D.R. 30/2005.   [7] See note 4.   [8] Act A1395.
[9] The first is with regards to the amendment to section 8 of the 2005 Act. The amendment was 'to adopt, with modification, the language used' in ML 1985 art. 5. The Explanatory Statement went on to state that: 'This provision is to limit court intervention to situations specifically covered by Act 646 and to discourage the use of inherent powers.' The second concerns the amendment to section 39 of the 2005 Act. One of the two purposes of the amendment to section 39 was to provide for severability provision to be consistent with ML 1985 art. 36.
[10] See www.uncitral.org/uncitral/en/uncitral_texts/arbitration/1985Model_arbitration_status .html.

purposes, a Model Law jurisdiction, there are aspects where the legislator has deemed necessary a departure or modification. Likewise, the approach and interpretations adopted by the courts in Malaysia when dealing with issues relating to arbitral proceedings and the arbitration legislation have a profound impact on the adoption and implementation of the text and principles of the ML 1985. A discourse on all these matters will be undertaken in the succeeding sections of this chapter.

Part I   General Provisions of the Model Law (Articles 1 to 6)

Articles 1–6 of the ML 1985 are listed under the heading of general provisions. The 2005 Act has adopted the 1985 original version of article 1 concerning the scope of application of the ML 1985, with some modifications. There are two notable features in the 2005 Act that illustrate the departure from the provision in article 1.

First, the 2005 Act specifically states that it shall apply to both domestic and international arbitration. The reasoning and decision to have both domestic and international arbitration governed by a single statute would be similar to those made in other jurisdictions. Be that as it may, a number of additional provisions are provided in Part III of the 2005 Act and these provisions apply to domestic arbitration and not international arbitration unless the parties agree otherwise in writing.[11]

Second, while the term 'commercial' is used in ML 1985 article 1 and the footnote states that the term is to be given a wide definition, the 2005 Act has omitted the term 'commercial'.

ML 1985 article 2 (Definitions and rules of interpretation) has been adopted with some necessary modifications. It is, however, noteworthy that the 2005 Act does not provide a definition of arbitration. In addition, article 2A (International origin and general principles) has not been adopted in any form. The adoption of article 2A would go a long way in underscoring the need for the courts in Malaysia always to have regard to the international origin of arbitration law and practice, the need to promote uniformity in its application and the need to conform to the general principles of arbitration law and practice.

The provision concerning the receipt of written communications has been adopted with slight modification in the 2005 Act. Unlike ML

---

[11] See section 3(2)(b) and 3(3)(b) of the 2005 Act.

1985 article 3, section 6(2) of the 2005 Act includes electronic communication.[12]

While ML 1985 article 4 (Waiver of right to object) has been adopted verbatim without amendments into section 7 of the 2005 Act, there is no specific provision in the form of ML 1985 article 6 in the 2005 Act. Be that as it may, the principle behind article 4 has been adopted in the 2005 Act.

A matter of vast significance relates to the extent of court intervention in matters governed by arbitration law and in arbitral proceedings. This aspect is expressed in ML 1985 article 5.

The provision in the Malaysian arbitration statute regulating the extent of court intervention is section 8. Prior to 2011, the relevant section read:

> 'Unless otherwise provided, no court shall intervene in any of the matters governed by this Act.'
> This was substituted with:
> 'No court shall intervene in matters governed by this Act, except where so provided in this Act.'[13]

Two comments are germane at this juncture. First, it would appear that the amendment merely rephrases the sentence without changing the substance. To a lay person, there is no difference between the pre-2011 and post-2011 versions.

Perhaps, there is a subtle distinction between the wordings of the provisions in the pre-2011 and post-2011 versions. The pre-2011 version may be interpreted to mean that a court may intervene if it can find some provisions, whether in the 2005 Act itself or outside the 2005 Act, justifying intervention. The post-2011 version makes it clear that intervention can only be made if and only if there are specific provisions in the Act permitting intervention.

Indeed, the 2005 Act makes specific provisions allowing court intervention. This is evident from sections 10 (stay of proceedings), 11 (interim measures), 37 (setting aside), 39 (grounds for refusing recognition or enforcement) and 42 (reference on questions of law). However, it should also be noted that the High Court in Malaysia in *Sunway*

---

[12] Section 6(2) of the 2005 Act reads as follows: 'Unless otherwise agreed by the parties, a written communication sent electronically is deemed to have been received if it is sent to the electronic mailing address of the addressee.'

[13] Section 8 was wholly substituted by the Arbitration (Amendment) Act 2011 (Act A1395) s. 3 with effect from 1 July 2011 vide PU(B) 342/2011.

Damansara Sdn Bhd v. Malaysia National Insurance Bhd[14] had in 2008 interpreted section 8 as only permitting the court to intervene if it is so expressly permitted in the 2005 Act. Thus, this begs the question of the necessity to amend section 8 in 2011.

Perhaps the amendment was necessary. Besides providing certainty, one could see the motive of the amendment by making reference to the Explanatory Statement to the Arbitration (Amendment) Bill 2010. This is the second aspect pertaining to section 8. The Explanatory Statement states that the amendment to section 8 seeks to adopt, with modification, the language used in the ML 1985. More importantly, it further explained that the purpose of this provision is 'to limit court intervention to situations specifically covered by the Arbitration Act and to discourage the use of inherent powers by the court'.

The catalyst for the recasting of the wordings may have been prompted by a number of decisions that failed to give due credence to two of the underlying principles of arbitration law, that is, the principle of party autonomy and certainty as to the extent of judicial intervention. In *Taman Bandar Baru Masai Sdn Bhd v. Dindings Corporations Sdn Bhd*,[15] the High Court went on to say that it may interfere if a matter involves 'patent injustice'. In *Albilt Resources Sdn Bhd v. Casaria Construction Sdn Bhd*,[16] one of the judges delivering the judgment of the Court of Appeal held that curial intervention may be permitted in the exercise by the court of its 'inherent jurisdiction'.

With the adoption of ML 1985 article 5 into section 8 of the 2005 Act via the 2011 amendment, it should now be clear to the courts in Malaysia that they are 'discouraged' from invoking their inherent powers, and any form of intervention is only to the extent as allowed in the 2005 Act. Indeed, it is heartening to note that the High Court in *Twin Advance (M) Sdn Bhd v. Polar Electro Europe BV*[17] clearly understood the underlying rationale behind section 8 and gave effect to this section in that case. The High Court emphasized the principle behind ML 1985 article 5 in the following terms:

> [39] The ensuing question is whether this court can invoke its inherent jurisdiction to permit the plaintiff's application under s. 37 of the AA 2005 to be pursued vide this OS. In the cited case of *Mitsui Engineering & Shipbuilding Co. Ltd v. Easton Graham Rush & another* [2004] 2 SLR 14, Justice Woo Bik Lik has referred to article 5 of the Model Law and amplifies that the effect of it is to 'exclude any general or residual powers' given to the court of

---

[14] [2008] 3 MLJ 872.   [15] [2010] 5 CLJ 83 at 98.   [16] [2010] 7 CLJ 785 at 799–804.
[17] [2013] 7 MLJ 811.

the enacting state by statutes other than the ML 1985. I am of the view that our s. 8 of the AA 2005 which is akin to article 5 of the Model Law as adopted by the AA 2005 should similarly be interpreted in line with the Model Law that the court should exclude its general or residual powers or its inherent jurisdiction to indirectly vary the substantive provisions of AA 2005 which does not categorically provide or intend so.

Part II   Arbitration Agreement (Articles 7 to 9)

The articles in the ML 1985 governing the arbitration agreement, namely articles 7–9, take the form and shape of sections 9–11 of the 2005 Act. These three articles/sections refer to three distinct but related matters, namely (i) definition of arbitration agreement, (ii) enforcement of arbitration agreement and (iii) interim measures. These will now be discussed separately.

Definition of Arbitration Agreement

The 2005 Act adopts the 1985 original version of article 7. The Malaysian courts have consistently adopted the liberal approach when interpreting this provision. In *Bauer (M) Sdn Bhd* v. *Daewoo Corp*,[18] Gopal Sri Ram JCA opined that the word 'written agreement' in the definition of 'arbitration agreement' does not demand of a formal agreement executed by the parties to the dispute. His Lordship said that the agreement to which the definition refers 'may be gathered from either a single document or series of documents, or in some cases, a party may be estopped from asserting that there is an agreement'. This was followed by *Usahasama SPNB-LTAT Sdn Bhd* v. *Borneo Synergy (M) Sdn Bhd*.[19] However, the Court of Appeal has also demanded that the existence of an arbitration agreement must be clearly established.[20] In *Sebor (Sarawak) Marketing & Services Sdn Bhd* v. *SA Shee (Sarawak) Sdn Bhd*,[21] the High Court accepted the minutes recording an oral agreement to arbitrate as a valid written arbitration agreement. In interpreting the term 'written agreement', the courts in Malaysia have referred to decisions from other jurisdictions. These include judgments from Hong Kong, India and the United Kingdom.[22]

---

[18] [1999] 4 MLJ 545 at 565. This case was decided under the former Arbitration Act 1952.
[19] [2009] 2 MLJ 308.
[20] *Duta Wajar Sdn Bhd* v. *Pasukhas Construction Sdn Bhd* [2012] MLJU 355.
[21] [2006] 6 MLJ 1.
[22] For a list of the cases, see Sundra Rajoo, *The Malaysian Arbitration Act 2005 (Amended 2011): An Annotation* (LexisNexis 2013) at 41–48.

Enforcement of Arbitration Agreements

The importance of the need to enforce agreements to arbitrate cannot be overstated. The ML 1985 makes provision for this in the form of article 8 and the 2005 Act makes similar provision, albeit not in verbatim, but in the form of section 10. This section was also amended in 2011.

The courts in Malaysia have made it abundantly clear that agreements to arbitrate will be consistently enforced. This position has been reiterated on a number of occasions by the superior courts. For example, the Supreme Court in *Seloga Jaya Sdn Bhd* v. *Pembangunan Keng Ting (Sabah) Sdn Bhd*,[23] emphasized that 'those who make a contract to arbitrate their disputes should be held to their bargain.'[24] Likewise, in *Accounting Publication Sdn Bhd* v. *Ho Soo Furniture Sdn Bhd*,[25] the Court of Appeal held in no uncertain terms that 'it is settled law that, given a dispute, a court must compel the parties to adhere to the terms of the arbitration agreement entered into by them even though it may appear from the evidence presented upon the application for a stay that the defendant is unlikely to succeed before the arbitrator.'[26] More recently, the Court of Appeal in *Albilt Resources Sdn Bhd* v. *Casaria Construction Sdn Bhd*[27] reiterated the point that parties who contract to arbitrate their disputes should be held to their bargain and noted that 'it is the prima facie duty of the court to act upon such an arbitration agreement.'[28]

The Arbitration (Amendment) Act 2011 amended section 10 of the 2005 Act in three respects. First, one of the grounds to stay arbitration proceedings, namely, 'that there is in fact no dispute between the parties with regard to the matters to be referred', was deemed as unnecessary and thus removed.[29] The Arbitration (Amendment) Act 2011 also introduced special provisions which empower the court to order the retention of the property or provision of security pending the determination of the arbitration proceedings related to admiralty disputes and to provide for the definition of 'admiralty proceeding'.[30] The third aspect concerns the introduction of a new subsection (3) which clarifies that this section shall also apply in respect of an international arbitration even though the seat of arbitration is not in Malaysia.

---

[23] [1994] 2 CLJ 716.   [24] *Ibid.* at 728.   [25] [1999] 1 CLJ 765.   [26] *Ibid.* at 772.
[27] [2010] 3 MLJ 656.   [28] *Ibid.* at 667.
[29] This was the ground in section 10(1)(b) of the 2005 Act.
[30] This was done by the insertion of the new subsections (2A) (2B) and (2C) in section 10 of the 2005 Act. See the Explanatory Statement attached to the Arbitration (Amendment) Bill.

The language of section 10 of the 2005 Act has led some commentators to interpret section 10 as making it mandatory for a court to stay proceedings when it can be shown that an arbitration agreement exists between the parties. Indeed, it is clear that section 10 uses the term 'shall' as opposed to the term 'may' as used in the erstwhile Arbitration Act 1952. Further, the Court of Appeal in *Albilt Resources Sdn Bhd* v. *Casaria Construction Sdn Bhd*[31] has also acknowledged that the term 'shall' that appears in section 10 must necessarily mean 'directory' or 'mandatory'.

However, notwithstanding the above, to understand the legal position under section 10 in the correct perspective, it is important to consider the decisions in three cases, namely, *Standard Chartered Bank Malaysia Bhd* v. *City Properties Sdn Bhd*,[32] *Innotec Asia Pacific Sdn Bhd* v. *Innotec GMBH*[33] and *Ace Synergy Insurance Bhd* v. *Teng Yed Lan*.[34]

In dealing with section 10 of the 2005 Act, the High Court in *Standard Chartered Bank Malaysia Bhd* v. *City Properties Sdn Bhd* regarded stay of proceedings as mandatory and described the court's discretion as 'encumbered'. On the other hand, the High Court in *Innotec Asia Pacific Sdn Bhd* v. *Innotec GMBH* read the effect of the provision as not excluding the general jurisdiction to grant stay on justifiable grounds, but as qualifying it by making the requirement to stay 'generally mandatory'. In *Ace Synergy Insurance Bhd* v. *Teng Yed Lan*, the High Court preferred the interpretation adopted in *Standard Chartered Bank Malaysia Bhd* v. *City Properties Sdn Bhd*, due to the imperative wording of the provision and the use of the word 'shall' instead of the word 'may'.

Furthermore, while comparing section 6 of the erstwhile Arbitration Act 1952 with section 10 of the 2005 Act, the High Court in *FSBM Holdings* v. *Technitium Sdn Bhd*[35] relied on the opinion of one of the authors of this Report, which stated that:

> The main difference between section 6 of the 1952 Act and section 10 of the Act is that the general discretion vested in the court under section 6 no longer applies and the substantial case law which defined the judicial approach to the general discretion is no longer applicable. Instead the requirement to stay is mandatory unless the court finds either that:

---

[31] See note 27.
[32] *Standard Chartered Bank Malaysia Bhd* v. *City Properties Sdn Bhd* [2008] 1 CLJ 496.
[33] *Innotec Asia Pacific Sdn Bhd* v. *Innotec GMBH* [2007] 8 CLJ 304.
[34] *Ace Synergy Insurance Bhd* v. *Teng Yed Lan* [2009] MLJU 1719.
[35] *FSBM Holdings* v. *Technitium Sdn Bhd* [2010] MLJU 1103.

(a) the Arbitration Agreement is null and void, inoperative or incapable of being performed; or

(b) that there is in fact no dispute between the parties with regard to the matters to be referred.[36]

Ultimately, it is submitted that to interpret section 10 of the 2005 Act as a mandatory provision without any qualification whatsoever is incorrect. It is further submitted that a Malaysian court retains certain discretion when called upon to stay a proceeding by a party invoking an arbitration agreement. While the scope of the discretion does not extend beyond the circumstances prescribed in the 2005 Act, the qualifications provided in the relevant provision leave the courts with much room to exercise their discretion based on the factual matrix of each case.

The arbitration agreement being 'null and void, inoperative or incapable of being performed' is merely one of the grounds that a party seeking to challenge an arbitration agreement can rely upon. It is possible to plead other grounds, such as: (i) that the other party has taken 'any other steps in the proceedings'; or (ii) that there is in fact no dispute between the parties with regard to the matters to be referred; or (iii) that the matter is not arbitrable; or (iv) that the arbitration agreement is contrary to Malaysian public policy.[37]

In relation to the first of the above grounds, the Federal Court, in *Sanwell Corp v. Trans Resources Corp Sdn Bhd*,[38] held that, in an application under section 6 of the erstwhile Arbitration Act 1952 (now replaced by section 10 of the 2005 Act), if the applicant has taken any other action in the proceedings other than entering appearance, then the court would have to consider whether such action amounted to a 'step in the proceedings' and whether such action indicated an unequivocal intention on the part of the applicant to proceed with the suit and to abandon its right to have the dispute disposed of by arbitration. If the applicant had served any pleadings, then it had clearly taken a step in the proceedings within the meaning of section 6 of the erstwhile Arbitration Act 1952. In such a case, the applicant had elected to proceed with the proceedings in the High Court and it would be barred from applying for a stay of proceedings to refer the dispute to arbitration.

---

[36] *Ibid.* at 1104–05.   [37] See sections 4 and 10 of the 2005 Act.   [38] [2002] 2 MLJ 625.

Interim Measures

ML 1985 article 9 provides that 'It is not incompatible with an arbitration agreement for a party to request, before or during arbitral proceedings, from a court an interim measure of protection and for a court to grant such measure.' The 2005 Act has heeded the suggestion made in the ML 1985 and now vests the courts with the powers through section 11 of the 2005 Act to make a variety of interim measures. The orders listed in section 11(1) are for: (a) security for costs; (b) discovery of documents and interrogatories; (c) giving of evidence by affidavit; (d) appointment of a receiver; (e) securing the amount in dispute, whether by way of arrest of property or bail or other security pursuant to the admiralty jurisdiction of the High Court; (f) the preservation, interim custody or sale of any property which is the subject matter of the dispute; (g) ensuring that any award which may be made in the arbitral proceedings is not rendered ineffectual by the dissipation of assets by a party; and (h) an interim injunction or any other interim measure. Section 11(2) further provides that 'Where a party applies to the High Court for any interim measure and an arbitral tribunal has already ruled on any matter which is relevant to the application, the High Court shall treat any findings of fact made in the course of such ruling by the arbitral tribunal as conclusive for the purposes of the application'.

Section 11 was amended in 2011. A new subsection (3) was inserted to extend the powers of the court to grant the interim measures listed in this section to an international arbitration where the seat of arbitration is not in Malaysia. The addition of this new subsection is not without any significance. Prior to the introduction of section 11(3), the High Court in *Aras Jalinan Sdn Bhd* v. *Tipco Asphalt Public Company Ltd*[39] was confronted with the issue of whether it had the jurisdiction to grant injunctive relief in respect of matters where the seat of arbitration was outside Malaysia. The High Court ruled that since it had not been conferred with such jurisdiction by the 2005 Act (prior to the 2011 amendment) or any federal law, it did not have the jurisdiction to grant injunctive relief in respect of matters where the seat of arbitration was outside Malaysia. With the introduction of the new subsection (3), the position is now clear.

The phrase 'whether by way of arrest of property or bail or other security pursuant to the admiralty jurisdiction of the High Court' was

---

[39] [2008] 5 CLJ 654.

inserted after the word 'dispute' in paragraph (1)(e) so as to 'clarify' the power of the court in making an interim order to 'secure the amount in dispute'.[40]

Although the 2005 Act has not adopted article 17J of the Model Law as amended in 2006 'to put it beyond any doubt that the existence of an arbitration agreement does not infringe on the powers of the competent court to issue interim measures',[41] it can safely be surmised from the reported decisions that the courts in Malaysia will interpret section 11 as not barring a party from requesting from a court any interim protection despite the existence of an arbitration agreement. In *Intramas Technology Sdn Bhd* v. *AmBank (M) Bhd*,[42] Mary Lim JC expressed the view that the court has jurisdiction and full discretion to decide on the applications made pursuant to section 11 and that the law with regard to granting interim relief would apply. Parties to an arbitration agreement have successfully invoked section 11 and granted an interim injunction and a Mareva injunction in *Plaza Rakyat Sdn Bhd* v. *Datuk Bandar Kuala Lumpur*[43] and *Jasa Keramat Sdn Bhd* v. *Monatech (M) Sdn Bhd*.[44] In the former, Mah JC explained that the purpose of section 11 is to preserve the subject matter which has been referred to arbitration.

In *Ikatan Inovasi Sdn Bhd* v. *KACC Construction Sdn Bhd*,[45] the High Court examined the orders listed in paragraph (f) concerning the preservation, interim custody or sale of any property which is the subject matter of the dispute, and paragraph (g) on ensuring that any award which may be made in the arbitral proceedings is not rendered ineffectual by the dissipation of assets by a party, and opined that paragraph (g) has a wider application than paragraph (f). The learned judge suggested that the court may make orders it thinks just and appropriate to ensure an award that may be obtained in arbitration

---

[40] This phrase was inserted by the Arbitration (Amendment) Act 2011 s. 5(a) with effect from 1 July 2011 vide PU(B) 342/2011. See also the Explanatory Statement attached to the Arbitration (Amendment) Bill 2010.

[41] See paragraph 30 of the Explanatory Note as provided by the UNCITRAL secretariat on the ML 1985 on International Commercial Arbitration as amended in 2006.

[42] [2009] MLJU 855.

[43] [2012] 7 MLJ 36. In this case, the High Court was of the view that justice lay in maintaining the status quo pending arbitration.

[44] [1999] 4 MLJ 217. In this case, the High Court was satisfied that the plaintiff had a good arguable case and there was a risk that the defendant could have dealt with its assets within the jurisdiction as to render them unavailable or untraceable to satisfy any award that the plaintiff may obtain against the defendant.

[45] [2008] 3 CLJ 48.

would be valuable and this gives the courts the power to restrain both movable and immovable assets.

Finally, the phrase 'before or during arbitral proceedings' was considered in *I-Expo Sdn Bhd* v. *TNB Engineering Corporation Sdn Bhd*.[46] In this case, the defendant had raised the argument that the words 'before or during arbitral proceedings' means that any application for interim injunction is to be made when parties are contemplating commencing arbitral proceedings and commencing an action in court. The High Court rejected such a narrow reading of the provision and held that the power to grant an interim injunction for the purpose of preserving the status quo of a dispute applies in all instances, whether before or during arbitral proceedings.

Part III   Composition of Arbitral Tribunal (Articles 10 to 15)

The provisions of the ML 1985 relating to the composition of arbitral tribunal (articles 10–15) have been adopted as sections 12–17 in the 2005 Act, with some modifications.

The principles that parties are free to agree on the number of arbitrators has been codified in the 2005 Act.[47] In the event that the parties fail to determine the number of arbitrators, section 12 of the 2005 Act follows article 10 in providing that the number of arbitrators shall be three. However, the 2005 Act also makes provision for domestic arbitration, which shall consist of a single arbitrator.[48]

The principle of non-discrimination of arbitrators based on nationality has been adopted by the 2005 Act. However, the parties are at liberty to appoint or exclude the nationals of certain states as arbitrators.[49] The principle that parties are free to agree on the procedure for appointing arbitrators is also preserved in the 2005 Act. In addition, the 2005 Act also espouses the principle that court(s) or other authorities shall be called upon to appoint the arbitrator(s) in the event of a defect in the appointment procedure and such a decision is final. The 'other authorities' is specifically identified as the Director of the Asian International Arbitration Centre.[50]

As for the grounds for challenging the appointment of an arbitrator and the procedure for mounting such a challenge, the 2005 Act has

---

[46] [2007] 3 MLJ 53.   [47] See section 12(1) of the 2005 Act.
[48] See section 12(2)(b) of the 2005 Act.   [49] See section 13(1) of the 2005 Act.
[50] See section 13(4)–(9) of the 2005 Act (as amended by the Arbitration (Amendment) Act 2018).

adopted ML 1985 articles 12 and 13 without any noteworthy modification.[51] The gist as contained in ML 1985 article 14 (failure or impossibility to act) has also been codified in the 2005 Act.[52] If a need arises for the appointment of a substitute arbitrator, section 17 of the 2005 Act sets out the procedure for the appointment of the substitute arbitrator in detail. The consequences of the new appointment are also explained. Like ML 1985 article 15, section 17 of the 2005 Act preserves the rights of the parties to freely agree to terminate an arbitrator's mandate. It also adheres to the principle that arbitrators are free to resign for any reason.

Part IV   Jurisdiction of Arbitral Tribunal (Article 16)

Section 18 of the 2005 Act provides powers to an arbitral tribunal to decide on its own jurisdiction or the validity of an arbitration agreement. In this respect, ML 1985 article 16 has been adopted in its entirety and the principle of *kompetenz-kompetenz/compétence-compétence* and the principle of separability or severability are espoused in the 2005 Act. In *Chut Nyak Isham bin Nyak Arif* v. *Malaysian Technology Corp Sdn Bhd*,[53] the Malaysian High Court acknowledged the competency of the arbitral tribunal to decide on its own jurisdiction without interference.

The aspect relating the power of an arbitral tribunal to decide on the validity of an arbitration agreement must be read and reconciled with section 10 of the 2005 Act, that is, ML 1985 article 8. The High Court in *Chut Nyak Isham bin Nyak Arif* alluded to these two provisions and concluded that arbitration proceedings take precedence over court proceedings. In *Standard Chartered Bank Malaysia Bhd* v. *City Properties Sdn Bhd*,[54] the learned judge said:

> The only conclusion I can draw from the import of this entirely new provision in s. 10 when read with s. 18 of the 2005 Act, is that with this new Act, Parliament has clearly given the arbitral tribunal much wider jurisdiction and powers. And, such powers would extend to cases even when its own jurisdiction or competence or scope of its authority, or the existence or validity of the arbitration agreement is challenged.[55]

However, the court in *Total Safe Sdn Bhd* v. *Tenaga Nasional Berhad*[56] ruled that since section 18 provides that 'the arbitral tribunal *may* rule on

---

[51] See sections 14 and 15 of the 2005 Act.   [52] See section 16 of the 2005 Act.
[53] [2009] 6 MLJ 729.   [54] [2008] 1 MLJ 233.   [55] *Ibid.* at 244.
[56] [2010] MLJU 1247.

its own jurisdiction [...] with respect to the existence or validity of the arbitration agreement', this does not oust the jurisdictions of the courts in ruling on the existence or validity of the arbitration agreement. It should also be noted that the court in *Cyber Business Solutions Sdn Bhd v. Elsaga Datama SPA*[57] has held that the power conferred on arbitral tribunals are only to decide on its own jurisdiction and not the jurisdiction of others. Thus, if there are jurisdictional issues in competing forums, the courts are seised with jurisdiction to determine the forum with the authority to hear the dispute.

Part IV-A   Interim Measures and Preliminary Orders (Articles 17 to 17J)

Sub-Part I   Measures and Orders by the Tribunal (Articles 17 to 17G)

Sub-Part II   Recognition and Enforcement of Interim Measures (Articles 17H and 17I)

Sub-Part III   Court-Ordered Interim Measures (Article 17J)

The 2005 Act in Malaysia has not adopted ML 1985 article 17 and nor articles 17 to 17J of the UNCITRAL Model Law on International Commercial Arbitration 2006, UN General Assembly Resolution 61/33 (4 December 2006) ('ML').

The powers of an arbitral tribunal to order interim measures are set out in section 19 of the 2005 Act. A parallel can be drawn with section 11 of the same Act which sets out the orders that may be made by the court. The list of orders under section 19 is not as extensive as that conferred on the court under section 11. The orders listed in section 19(1) are for (a) security for costs; (b) discovery of documents and interrogatories; (c) giving of evidence by affidavit; and (d) the preservation, interim custody or sale of any property which is the subject matter of the dispute. The powers under the foregoing paragraphs may be further reinforced with the arbitral tribunal requiring any party to provide appropriate security in connection with such measures as ordered in section 19(1).[58] Section 19(3) goes on to provide that unless otherwise agreed by the parties, the provisions on 'recognition and enforcement of awards' and the 'grounds for refusing recognition or enforcement' under sections 38 and 39 respectively shall apply to the orders made by an

---

[57] [2012] 1 CLJ 115.   [58] Section 19(2) of the 2005 Act.

arbitral tribunal under section 19 as if a reference to sections 38 and 39 to an award were a reference to such an order.

Part V   Conduct of Arbitral Proceedings (Articles 18 to 27)

The conduct of arbitral proceedings (articles 18–27) are governed by sections 20 to 29 of the 2005 Act.

The principle of equality as laid down in ML 1985 article 18 has been adopted into section 20 of the 2005 Act. Interestingly, the principle that parties must be given a 'full' opportunity of presenting their case is replaced with the assurance of a 'fair and reasonable' opportunity of presenting their case.[59]

The principles that parties are free to agree on the arbitral procedure and in the absence of parties' agreement, the arbitral tribunal may consider the arbitration in such manner as it considers appropriate, have been adopted in the 2005 Act.[60] The 2005 Act lists the powers of the arbitral tribunal when it conducts such proceedings and these include the power to (a) determine the admissibility, relevance, materiality and weight of any evidence; (b) draw on its own knowledge and expertise; (c) order the provision of further particulars in a statement of claim or statement of defence; (d) order the giving of security for costs; (e) fix and amend time limits within which various steps in the arbitral proceedings must be completed; (f) order the discovery and production of documents or materials within the possession or power of a party; (g) order the interrogatories to be answered; (h) order that any evidence be given on oath or affirmation; and (i) make such other orders as the arbitral tribunal considers appropriate.[61]

The courts in Malaysia have reaffirmed the point that the Evidence Act 1950 does not apply to arbitration. The court in *Jeuro Development Sdn Bhd* v. *Teo Teck Huat (M) Sdn Bhd*[62] held that there can be no valid objection to the conduct of arbitral proceedings that the arbitral tribunal has departed from a technical rule of the Evidence Act 1950 unless the rule of evidence violated is one which is based on natural justice and an infringement of it is, therefore, repugnant to a sense of justice and

---

[59] For a discussion of the application of this section, see Rajoo, *Malaysian Arbitration Act 2005* at 88.
[60] See section 21(1) and (2) of the 2005 Act.   [61] See section 21(3) of the 2005 Act.
[62] [1998] 6 MLJ 545 at 552.

fairness. This was approved by the Court of Appeal in *Hartela Contractors Ltd* v. *Hartecon JV Sdn Bhd.*[63]

Both these cases were decided under the now repealed Arbitration Act 1952 but there is no reason to suggest that the above pronouncements will not be applied with equal force under the 2005 Act.

ML 1985 article 20 concerning the place of arbitration has been adopted in the 2005 Act but the term 'place' is substituted with the term 'seat'.[64]

Likewise, ML 1985 article 21 has also been adopted, with minor modifications. Section 23 of the 2005 Act provides that: 'Unless otherwise agreed by the parties, the arbitral proceedings in respect of a particular dispute *shall* commence on the date on which a request *in writing* for that dispute to be referred to arbitration is received by the respondent.' The words 'shall' and 'in writing' are not found in ML 1985 article 21.

On the other hand, the provisions of the ML 1985 on language (art. 22) and the statements of claim and defence (art. 23) have been adopted without modification by the 2005 Act.[65]

The 2005 Act also contains provisions governing the hearing and written proceedings.[66] The principles such as the freedom of the parties to agree on oral hearings or written proceedings and that in the absence of parties' agreement the decision on the mode shall then be made by the tribunal have been maintained.[67] Likewise, the principle that parties have a fundamental right to oral hearings which cannot be excluded by the arbitral tribunal unless the parties have agreed that there would be no oral hearings has also been incorporated into the 2005 Act.[68]

Be that as it may, some wordings used in section 26 of the 2005 Act differ from those in ML 1985 article 24. In the context of the giving of notice, the 2005 Act chose the phrase 'reasonable prior notice' over the phrase 'sufficient advance notice' as recommended in ML 1985 article 24(2).

The principles concerning the consequences of a party in failing to communicate his statement of claim, statement of defence or appearing at a hearing or to produce documentary evidence have been maintained in the 2005 Act.[69] However, the 2005 Act provides for an additional default not found in ML 1985 article 25, that is, when a claimant fails to proceed with the claim. In such a case, section 27(d) gives the power

---

[63] [1999] 2 MLJ 481 at 490.   [64] See section 22 of the 2005 Act.
[65] See sections 24 and 25 of the 2005 Act.   [66] See section 26 of the 2005 Act.
[67] See section 26(1) of the 2005 Act.   [68] See section 26(2) of the 2005 Act.
[69] See section 27 of the 2005 Act.

to the arbitral tribunal to make an award dismissing the claim or give directions, with or without conditions, for the speedy determination of the claim.

On the issue of the appointment of expert(s), the principles as contained in ML 1985 article 26 have found their way into section 28 of the 2005 Act.

While the principle concerning an application to the court for assistance in taking evidence (article 27) has been adopted into section 29 of the 2005 Act, there is a slight departure in the way in which the provision is phrased. Section 29 has two subsections and they read as follows:

(1) Any party may with the approval of the arbitral tribunal, apply to the High Court for assistance in taking evidence.

(2) The High Court may order the attendance of a witness to give evidence or, where applicable, produce documents on oath or affirmation before an officer of the High Court or any other person, including the arbitral tribunal.

It is unfortunate that, to date, there have not arisen other opportunities for the courts in Malaysia to interpret the provisions of the 2005 Act relating to the provisions governing the conduct of arbitral proceedings. Based on the courts' interpretation of the provisions in the other chapters of the 2005 Act, there is nothing to suggest that the courts in Malaysia will not consider other decisions or doctrinal writings from outside the jurisdiction in order to give regard to the international origin of the articles and the need to promote uniformity in their application.

Part VI   Making of Award and Termination of Proceedings (Articles 28 to 33)

The rules governing the making of awards and the termination of proceedings have been primarily adopted by the 2005 Act. However, ML 1985 article 28 has been adopted, with some modifications.

First, section 30 the 2005 Act uses the term 'law' instead of 'rules' in the heading (article 28). Second, domestic and international arbitrations are treated differently. In the case of 'domestic arbitration where the seat of arbitration is Malaysia', the parties are allowed to determine the substantive law to be applicable. However, in the absence of such determination by the parties, 'the arbitral tribunal shall decide the dispute in accordance with the substantive law of Malaysia'.[70] Prior to 2011, all domestic arbitrations where the seat of arbitration was in Malaysia were to be determined in accordance with the substantive law of Malaysia.[71] Third, in the case of international arbitration, the principles enunciated in ML 1985 article 28 have been fully adopted by the 2005 Act. The only notable point is that ML 1985 article 28(3) has been omitted (*ex aequo et bono* or *amiable compositeur*).

The law concerning the decision-making process (article 29) is provided for in section 31 of the 2005 Act. It contains the gist of the principles as encapsulated in ML 1985 article 29. The principles as proposed in ML 1985 article 30 relating to the settlement of disputes have also been wholly adopted in the 2005 Act.[72]

The provisions governing the form and contents of an award (article 31) can be traced to section 33 of the 2005 Act. The principles that (i) the arbitral award shall be made in writing and signed by the arbitrator(s) for the sake of certainty; (ii) the signatures of a majority of the arbitral tribunal will suffice; (iii) the arbitral tribunal shall state the reasons upon which the award is based; (iv) the parties are free to agree that no reasons are to be given; (v) dissenting opinions are neither required nor prohibited in the award; (vi) the arbitral award is deemed to be made at the place of arbitration; and (vii) a copy of the award which has been signed by the arbitrator(s) shall be delivered to each party have all been adopted by the 2005 Act. There is no reason to suspect that the courts in Malaysia will not respect these principles.

This section departs from ML 1985 article 31 in one important respect. An additional provision is inserted in section 33 of the 2005 Act. Section 33(6) of the 2005 Act, which is not found in article 31, provides as follows:

> Unless otherwise provided in the arbitration agreement, the tribunal may –
>
> (a) award interest on any sum of money ordered to be paid by the award from the date the award to the date of realization; and
> (b) determine the rate of interest.

---

[70] See section 30(1) of the 2005 Act and the Explanatory Statement to the Arbitration Bill 2005 (D.R.42/2010).
[71] See the Arbitration (Amendment) Act 2011 (Act A1395) s. 6 with effect from I July 2011 vide PU(B) 342/2011.
[72] See section 32 of the 2005 Act.

The circumstances leading to the termination of the arbitral proceedings as outlined in ML 1985 article 32 have all been incorporated by the 2005 Act.[73] One noteworthy difference is the additional provision in the form of section 34(4) of the 2005 Act. The Malaysian Parliament deemed that it was necessary to add that:

> Unless otherwise provided by any written law, the death of a party does not terminate –
>
> (a) the arbitral proceedings; or
> (b) the authority of the arbitral tribunal.

The principles in ML 1985 article 33 conferring the mandate on the arbitral tribunal to make corrections and interpret awards have been implemented in the 2005 Act.[74]

Part VII   Recourse against Award (Article 34)

The principles governing applications to set aside an arbitral award is of paramount importance in the law and practice of arbitration. In this respect, the 2005 Act adheres to the underlying principles as enunciated in ML 1985 article 34. A reading of section 37 of the 2005 Act will show that in Malaysia an application to set aside an arbitral award can only be made to the High Court and such an application must be based on one of the grounds as provided therein. The grounds in section 37(1)(a) and (b) of the 2005 Act are analogous to those in ML 1985 article 34(2)(a) and (b). The courts in Malaysia have given effect to this principle.[75]

While the principle that an application for setting aside an arbitral award may only be made to a court in the place of arbitration can be inferred from section 37, it may be argued that there is nothing in that section or in the 2005 Act to suggest that the courts in Malaysia are prohibited from exercising jurisdiction over an application to set aside an award made elsewhere. However, the High Court in *Twin Advance (M) Sdn Bhd* v. *Polar Electro Europe BV*[76] made it clear that a party will not be allowed to invoke section 37 of the 2005 Act to set aside an award made

---

[73] See section 34 of the 2005 Act.   [74] See section 35 of the 2005 Act.

[75] See cases such as *Government of Lao Democratic People's Republic* v. *Thai-Lao Lignite Co. Ltd* [2013] 3 MLJ 409 and *The Government of India* v. *Cairn Energy India Pty Ltd* [2014] 9 MLJ 149, HC (setting aside of the second award); [2012] 3 CLJ 423, FC (setting aside of the first award) and *Perwira Bintang Holdings Sdn Bhd* v. *Kerajaan Malaysia* [2014] 11 MJ 561.

[76] [2013] 7 MLJ 811.

outside Malaysia. The learned judge made the following observations at paragraphs 37 and 38 in his judgment:

[37] From the Model Law perspective and the other jurisdictions which adopt the Model Law on international commercial arbitration, one clear principle which I term it as the 'entrenched principle' that the arbitration laws have accepted and adhered to is that the right to challenge the arbitral award, as distinct from the recognition of arbitration agreement and recognition and enforcement of arbitral award, ought to be in the courts of the place or seat of arbitration.

[38] Will our AA 2005 depart from that entrenched principle accepted internationally? The answer is obviously in the negative. The rationale of our AA 2005 is to achieve consistency between the international and our domestic arbitral regimes. It will be inconsistent with such intent and purpose if the AA 2005 were to depart from that internationally entrenched principle. Our AA 2005 was indeed enacted to be consonant with the Model Law. There must therefore be harmonisation between our AA 2005 and the Model Law. It is unconceivable for the AA 2005 which bears resemblance to the Model Law to have enacted provisions inconsistent and/or contrary to the Model Law and/or the international arbitral regimes in commercial arbitration. For that reason, I do not agree with the plaintiff's contention that s. 37 of the AA 2005 can be interpreted to be applicable to set aside an arbitral award which was made at a seat outside Malaysia. Section 37 itself does not provide so. To attempt to extend the scope of s. 37 as the plaintiff has contended would not only usurp the express consensus of the parties to the joint venture contract but must be seen as a violation of the AA 2005 where it does not provide specifically in s. 37 with clear expression that a foreign or international arbitral award where the seat is outside Malaysia may be set aside by our High Court as well as by reference to the Model Law and the law of other jurisdictions as narrated above. Consequently, I hold that s. 37 of the AA 2005 is not applicable to the arbitral award in the instant case where the seat of arbitration is in Singapore. I find that this court has no jurisdiction to entertain such an application to set aside an award where the seat of arbitration is in a foreign country. In the instant case, the Singapore High Court is the proper jurisdiction for the plaintiff to challenge the said award. The contracting parties have agreed to such process of arbitration and it must be adhered to as they have covenanted to the exclusion of any intervention by this court.

The High Court in this case also made reference to section 8 of the 2005 Act, which is *in pari materia* with ML 1985 article 5, and rightly refused to exercise its inherent jurisdiction to allow the plaintiff to invoke section 37.

On the ground of public policy,[77] the 2005 Act provides further clarification as to what may constitute a 'conflict with the public policy of Malaysia'. Section 37(2) expressly states that:

> Without limiting the generality of subparagraph (i)(b)(ii), an award is in conflict with the public policy of Malaysia where –
>
> (a) the making of the award was induced or affected by fraud or corruption; or
> (b) a breach of the rules of natural justice occurred –
>   (i) during the arbitral proceedings; or
>   (ii) in connection with the making of the award.

The question of what amounts to public policy, or in this instance the public policy of Malaysia, is a difficult one. By and large, the courts in Malaysia have taken a conservative approach when determining whether an award is in conflict with the public policy of Malaysia. In the context of section 37, the case of *The Government of India* v. *Cairn Energy India Pty Ltd & Ors*[78] noted as follows:

> [122] Within sub-paras 37 (1)(a)(iv) and (v) is also this clear restriction, and that is the discretion ought to be exercised only if it is proved to the court the matters complained of. First of all, the phrase 'only if' is indicative of the intention of Parliament that the courts be conferred a limited discretion. By limited, it is to say that the discretion is subject to the provision of proof of any or all the matters complained of in (a)(i) to (vi) and/or (b)(ii).

In that case the court went on to say that while the ML 1985 recognizes that each state has its own concept of what is required of public policy it is nonetheless subject to overlying conditions. The requirement of law provides that while making an allegation of conflict one also has to prove the basis of the allegation, how it is conflicted or breached and how the said breach has prejudiced the rights of the Plaintiff.

The minimum interventionist approach of the courts was also demonstrated in the case of *Government of the Lao People's Democratic Republic* v. *Thai-Lao Lignite Co. Ltd*[79] where a breach of the principles of natural justice was alleged. The High Court noted that since the term 'public policy' was not defined in the 2005 Act nor in the ML 1985 the term should only encompass a narrow scope.

---

[77] Article 34(1)(b)(ii) of the ML 1985 art. 34(1)(b)(ii) and section 37(1)(b)(ii) of the 2005 Act.
[78] [2014] 9 MLJ 149.   [79] [2013] MLJU 165.

In the case of *Perwira Bintang Holdings Sdn Bhd* v. *Kerajaan Malaysia*,[80] the High Court of Malaysia held that this minimum intervention must not be construed as an abdication of the basic and fundamental role of the courts in matters of justice.[81]

On the limitation issue that an application for setting aside cannot be made after the expiry of ninety days,[82] the 2005 Act differs from the ML 1985 in one important respect. Section 37(5) of the 2005 Act provides that the limitation period does not apply where an application for setting aside is based on the ground that the award was induced or affected by fraud or corruption. It is also noteworthy that in the context of such a time frame, the Malaysian court in *Dato Dr Muhammad Ridzuan bin Mohd Salleh* v. *Syarikat Air Terengganu Sdn Bhd*[83] held that the court has a discretion to extend the time period. In that case, Lee Swee Seng JC noted as follows:

> [16] It was submitted by the plaintiffs that this court has the discretion to extend time for the application to set aside an award beyond the 90 days period as the word used is 'may' and not 'shall'. I agree that there is a discernible difference between a peremptory 'shall' and a permissive 'may'. The former is mandatory whereas the latter is not. The former takes away any discretion for extension of time, for instance, whereas the latter leaves some room for the exercise of discretion to extend time in the context of a time frame to do a particular act. Parliament could have used the word 'shall' if they had wanted to as 'shall' is used in the context of a time frame to make an application in s. 42(2) of the Act as follows:
>
> A reference shall be filed within forty-two days of the publication and receipt of the award, and shall identify the question of law to be determined and state the grounds on which the reference is sought. (emphasis added)

In interpreting section 37 of the 2005 Act, the courts in Malaysia have been very liberal in referring to decisions from other jurisdictions so as to have regard to the international origin of ML 1985 article 34 and thus have promoted uniformity in its application.

Part VIII   Recognition and Enforcement of Awards
(Articles 35 and 36)

Section 38(1) of the 2005 Act expressly states that all awards made in respect of an arbitration where the seat of arbitration is in Malaysia or all

---

[80] [2014] 11 MLJ 561.   [81] See also Rajoo, *Malaysian Arbitration Act 2005* at 110–11.
[82] ML 1985 art. 34(3) provides for 'three months' whilst section 37(4) of the 2005 Act provides for 'ninety days'.
[83] [2012] 3 MLJ 737.

awards from a foreign State shall be recognized as binding and shall be enforced by the High Court.[84] The phrase 'an arbitration where the seat of arbitration is in Malaysia' was inserted to replace the words 'a domestic arbitration' in 2011.[85] The Explanatory Statement to the Arbitration Bill 2005 states that the purpose of this amendment is to 'provide for the enforcement of any awards made in Malaysia be it in respect of domestic or international arbitration'. Previously, an international arbitration held in Malaysia could be interpreted as one which does not fall within the meaning of a domestic arbitration and thus could not be enforced by entry as a judgment. Such confusion is no longer present after the 2011 amendment. The present position is that all international arbitral awards, irrespective of their place of origin, are treated uniformly on recognition and enforcement under the 2005 Act and this is in line with the principle as envisaged in article 35 of the ML 1985.

It is also clear that under the 2005 Act, all awards in international commercial arbitration are recognized as binding between the parties and will be enforced when an application is made to the High Court if no grounds to refuse enforcement exist. However, it is incumbent on the party making the application to produce a duly authenticated original award or a duly certified copy of the award *and* the original arbitration agreement or a duly certified copy of the agreement.[86] The 2005 Act also clarifies that where the award or arbitration agreement is in a language other than the national language or the English language the application shall supply a duly certified translation of the award or agreement in the English language.

Section 38 was invoked and considered by the High Court in *Bauer (M) Sdn Bhd* v. *Embassy Court Sdn Bhd*.[87] The High Court explained the ambit and application of section 38 in the following terms.

> [17] It is pertinent at this point to examine section 38 of the 2005 Act which empowers the Court to grant an application to enter a judgment in

---

[84] Section 38(4) defines 'foreign State' as 'a state which is a party to the Convention on the Recognition and Enforcement of Foreign Arbitral Awards adopted by the United Nations Conference on International Commercial Arbitration in 1958'. *Lombard Commodities Ltd* v. *Alami Vegetable Oil Products Sdn Bhd* [2010] 2 MLJ 23 in authority for the proposition that while a Gazette notification declaring a particular state a contracting state to the New York Convention is conclusive evidence, the lack of such a Gazette notification does not render an award unenforceable.

[85] See the Arbitration (Amendment) Act 2011 (Act A1395) s. 7 with effect from 1 July 2011 vide PU(B) 342/2011.

[86] See section 38(2) of the 2005 Act.   [87] [2010] MLJU 1323.

the terms of an award, including an interim award. Section 38 has to be considered together with Section 39 which restricts the specific grounds only upon which recognition (to register as judgment) or enforcement of an Award can be refused by the Courts.

[...]

[19] This was a marked departure from the regime that existed under the erstwhile Arbitration Act 1952, for the recognition and enforcement of arbitral awards. There was no restrictive provision there similar to the current Section 39 which goes to specify grounds or circumstances, under which only recognition or judgment could be refused. It was clearly therefore the intention of the legislature when the 2005 Act was brought into force to accord to arbitral awards a status and recognition that could only be defeated or challenged on those specific grounds or circumstances now entrenched as law. In other words, it should be as a matter of course that arbitral awards be recognised, and judgments entered by the courts on those awards for purposes of enforcement, unless the court is satisfied that its discretion to do so is restricted by Section 39.

[20] After noting that Section 39 corresponds with article 36 of the Model Law and does closely follow similar grounds for setting aside of awards found in section 37 of our 2005 Act, the learned authors, Sundra Rajoo and W. S. W. Davidson of the seminal book titled *The Arbitration Act 2005; UNCITRAL Model Law as Applied in Malaysia*, has this comment on the effect of Section 39 of the 2005 Act, at page 185 of that commentary:

> The grounds for refusal of recognition are exhaustive and if none of these grounds are present the award must be recognized: *Rossel NV v. Oriental Commercial & Shipping Co (UK)* [1991] 2 Lloyd's Rep 625. However, once one of the grounds is established, the court is still left with a discretion whether or not to enforce. In some cases, there is little latitude for discretion, e.g. where there is a lack of capacity, but in other cases, e.g. where there is a minor departure from the agreed procedure, the court may exercise its discretion to allow enforcement. See on this subject *Russell on Arbitration* (1997), p. 404.

[21] A Court called upon to recognize and register an Award of an arbitral tribunal under the 2005 Act, is therefore not in my view required to enter into a minute examination or analysis of the Award save where there is sufficient 'proof placed before the Court, to satisfy any of the grounds enumerated in that sub-subsection (i.e. section 39(1) (a)) or on the grounds of subsection (b) of that section.'

As noted in the above case, the recognition and enforcement of arbitral awards under section 38 is of course subject to section 39. Section 39 of the 2005 Act provides several grounds for the refusal of recognition or enforcement of a foreign arbitral award and these grounds are similar to those provided in ML article 36 and analogous to article V of the Convention on the Recognition and Enforcement of Foreign Arbitral

Awards, New York, 10 June 1958, in force 7 June 1959, 330 UNTS 4739 ('NYC'). The ambit of section 39 of the 2005 Act was examined and explained by the High Court in *Bauer (M) Sdn Bhd* v. *Embassy Court Sdn Bhd.*[88]

A number of observations are germane at this juncture.

First, to date, there have been no reported cases where the courts in Malaysia have recognized or enforced a foreign arbitral award even though a ground has been established that would permit them to deny recognition or enforcement of the award.

Second, the question of whether the existence of a ground to deny recognition or enforcement of a foreign arbitral award may be waived by the parties has not been directly addressed by the courts in Malaysia.

Third, it can be concluded that the Malaysian courts apply a minimalist approach to judicial intervention, tending to avoid interfering with arbitral awards or decisions made by foreign courts. This applies both to issues of substance raised in relation to a final award as well as procedural decisions on issues such as jurisdiction. This is evident from cases such as, for example, *Open Type Joint Stock Co. Efirnoye ('EFKO')* v. *Alfa Trading Ltd.*[89] In this case, the plaintiff made an application pursuant to section 38 of the 2005 Act for the recognition and enforcement of an award issued by the International Commercial Arbitration Court in Russia. The defendant sought to resist enforcement pursuant to section 39(1)(a) of the 2005 Act on the grounds that: (i) the arbitral procedure was not in accordance with the agreement of the parties; and (ii) the award was in conflict with the public policy of Malaysia. The High Court declined to consider an issue sought to be raised before it by the defendant as that issue had already been considered and decided by two arbitral tribunals. It noted that the issue in question, namely, that once a party had initiated arbitral proceedings in the forum of its choice under the arbitration clause then the other party was bound to submit to that jurisdiction, had already been considered by two arbitral tribunals in great detail. Both arbitral tribunals had disagreed with the interpretation put forward by the defendant and there was an express finding by one arbitral tribunal that the defendant had submitted to its jurisdiction after its initial objections. The High Court decided that since the defendant had submitted to the jurisdiction of the arbitral tribunal the defendant

---

[88] *Ibid.* See also the recent decision of the High Court in *CTI Group Inc* v. *International Bulk Carriers SPA* [2014] 11 MLJ 205.
[89] [2012] 1 MLJ 685.

should not be allowed to renege from that position by raising the jurisdiction issue again.

Some of the grounds in section 39 of the 2005 Act that have been invoked and considered by the courts in Malaysia will be briefly highlighted.

Invalidity of the Arbitration Agreement

This ground was examined and discussed at length by the High Court in *Food Ingredients LCC* v. *Pacific Inter-Link Sdn Bhd.*[90] Based on the facts in the case, the High Court arrived at the conclusion that there was no valid arbitration agreement from which the tribunal could validly render an award. This case demonstrates that in appropriate cases the courts in Malaysia will not adopt a hands-off approach when a challenge against the recognition and enforcement of an arbitral award is made by a party.

When this decision went on appeal before the Court of Appeal in *Agrovenus LPP* v. *Pacific Inter-Link Sdn Bhd and another appeal,*[91] the decision of the High Court was reversed. The Court of Appeal concluded that the arbitral tribunal had jurisdiction over the dispute as the subsequent oral agreement must be read together with an earlier sale contract. The Court of Appeal agreed with the observation by the High Court that the burden of proving any of the grounds in section 39(1)(a)(i)–(vii) of the 2005 Act rests with the party resisting recognition or enforcement. However, the Court of Appeal refused to entertain the objection in question as to the jurisdiction of the arbitral tribunal. The Court of Appeal was influenced by two considerations. The first was the fact that the respondent only raised the objection concerning the jurisdiction of the arbitral tribunal for the first time before the High Court when the appellant sought recognition or enforcement of the arbitral award and not when the matter was still before the arbitral tribunal. Having fully participated in the arbitration, the Court of Appeal was of the view that the respondent was thus estopped from raising an objection at the stage when the appellant sought recognition and enforcement of the award. More importantly, the Court of Appeal referred to the position under English law, in particular, to sections 31 and 73 of the English Arbitration Act 1996.

---

[90] [2012] 8 MLJ 585.   [91] [2014] 3 MLJ 648.

These provisions provide that the right to object on grounds of jurisdiction may be lost if such objection is not taken up before the arbitral
tribunal within the time frames allowed. Although the Court of Appeal
noted that these provisions had not been imported by section 39(1)(a)
(ii) of the 2005 Act, the parties had agreed that English law shall apply
in relation to the arbitration agreement.[92] It appears that both the High
Court and the Court of Appeal came to the conclusion that the arbitration agreement was indeed invalid and thus attracted the application of
such a ground to challenge the enforcement of the award. However, the
Court of Appeal was influenced by the fact that English law only
permits a 'one-shot remedy' when a party seeks to object on the
grounds of jurisdiction. This is to be contrasted with the concept of
active and passive remedies as explained by the Singapore Court of
Appeal in its recent judgment in *PT First Media TBK (formerly known
as PT Broadband Multimedia TBK) v. Astro Nusantara International
BV and others and another appeal.*[93]

Inadequate Notice or Opportunity to Present One's Case

This ground was raised in *Infineon Technologies (M) Sdn Bhd v. Orisoft
Technology Sdn Bhd.*[94] In considering the ground of failure to give proper
notice or inability to present one's case, the High Court said that the
provision that provides for this ground must be read in connection with
another provision which relates to the final award being in conflict
'with the public policy of Malaysia'. The ground of public policy is
discussed below.

Disputes Outside the Terms of Submission

This ground was discussed in *Taman Bandar Baru Masai Sdn Bhd
v. Dindings Corporations Sdn Bhd.*[95] In this case, the High Court held
that it must be proved that an arbitrator acted outside his jurisdiction in
order for a challenge pursuant to section 39 of the 2005 Act to succeed.
Of relevance is the pronouncement by the High Court that parties to

---

[92] On the question of when an issue relating to excess of jurisdiction can or ought to be
raised and what form it should take, see also the recent decision of the Court of Appeal in
Thai-Lao Lignite Co. Ltd v. Government of the Lao People's Democratic Republic [2014] 1
LNS 525.
[93] [2013] SGCA 57.   [94] [2011] 7 MLJ 539.   [95] [2010] 5 CLJ 83.

arbitration cannot complain that the arbitrator has exceeded his jurisdiction by simply relying on pre-2005 Act cases. The High Court referred to section 9 of the 2005 Act[96] and held that this provision shows that 'Parliament has in its wisdom given wider powers to the arbitrator to bring to an end all issues whether pleaded or not as long as it is relevant and arises in consequence of the arbitration agreement to reach its finality.' On the basis of section 9 of the 2005 Act, the High Court concluded that 'the court's jurisdiction to intervene is almost prohibited'. The High Court also made the following remarks:

> The AA 2005 must be seen to be a new chapter to the law, practice, and intervention of court etc in arbitration proceedings. The jurisdiction to ensure that courts do not intervene and meddle with arbitration proceedings is clearly set out in various provisions of the Act. Pre-2005 cases which provide room for interference with arbitrator's decision must now be treated as otiose, as AA 2005 has been shrewdly worded to ensure that courts ordinarily do not interfere with arbitration awards.[97]

Improper Composition of Arbitral Tribunal or Non-Compliance of Arbitral Procedure

This ground was considered by the High Court in *Open Type Joint Stock Company Efirnoye ('EFKO')* v. *Alfa Trading Ltd.*[98] In that case, the arbitration agreement provided for a Ukrainian arbitral tribunal in case the defendant filed a claim and also provided for a Russian arbitral tribunal in case the plaintiff filed a claim. The defendant's contention in essence was that since it had filed the Ukrainian claim which invoked the jurisdiction of Ukrainian laws and procedure, any further claim relating to the contract should have been brought or maintained before the Ukrainian arbitral tribunal. The plaintiff, by later initiating arbitral proceedings before the Russian tribunal, had failed to adhere to the procedure stipulated in the contract and this failure was sufficient reason to refuse to recognize or enforce the arbitral award under section 39(1)(a)(vi) of the 2005 Act. The defendant further submitted that the defendant's claim before the Ukrainian arbitral tribunal and the plaintiff's claim before the Russian tribunal concerned the same issues, albeit from opposing perspectives.

---

[96] This provision stipulates the definition and form of an arbitration agreement.
[97] See note 96 at 98.   [98] See note 89.

The High Court rejected these arguments and reasoned in the following terms:

> Although it concerned me initially that matters arising out of the same contract were being determined by different tribunals, once I had read the awards it became clear that the arbitrators had addressed their minds to this issue, as had the parties who effectively agreed that the subject matter in terms of adjudication was different. Therefore, this is another reason for concluding that there was no failure to comply with arbitral procedure. This is not a case where two tribunals dealt with the same subject matter and arrived at two differing decisions;
>
> (c) another relevant fact is the finding of the Russian tribunal that the defendant here effectively submitted to the jurisdiction of the Russian arbitral tribunal after the initial objections taken to jurisdiction when it filed a counterclaim in the Russian proceedings. There is an express finding of the Russian arbitral tribunal that the defendant submitted to its jurisdiction. This was upheld by the arbitration court when the defendant sought to have the award cancelled. Having so submitted to the jurisdiction of the Russian tribunal it ill behoves the defendant to now seek to renege from that position by alleging in this, the enforcement jurisdiction once again, that arbitral procedure was not adhered to;
>
> (d) having perused the arbitration cl 6 as amended and having considered the entirety of the awards in Ukraine and Russia as well as the conduct of parties therein and taking note of the findings of these respective tribunals it appears to this court that arbitral procedure was adhered to. The parties exercised their rights as set out expressly in cl 6 to have their respective but different issues under the contract determined by the respective arbitral tribunals. This was in accordance with the consensus of the parties. The alternative construction put forward by the defendant with regards to cl 6 is not tenable as it effectively allows whichever party that first initiates the arbitral process to impose upon the other party both its choice of jurisdiction as well as choice of law. This would be contrary to the express intention of cl 6 as objectively assessed. In these circumstances I conclude that the parties complied with cl 6 without detriment or deprivation of any parties' rights.[99]

Based on the above findings, the High Court was of the view that the defendant had failed to show that there was a failure to adhere to arbitral procedure as envisaged in section 39(1)(a)(vi) of the 2005 Act.

---

[99] See note 89 at 700–01.

Non-Arbitrability of the Dispute

Arbitrability as a ground to challenge the recognition and enforcement of an arbitral award is recognized in section 39(b)(i) of the 2005 Act. This provision must be read together with section 4 of the 2005 Act, which provides that:

(1) Any dispute which the parties have agreed to submit to arbitration under an arbitration agreement may be determined by arbitration unless the arbitration agreement is contrary to public policy.

(2) The fact that any written law confers jurisdiction in respect of any matter on any court of law but does not refer to the determination of that matter by arbitration shall not, by itself, indicate that a dispute about that matter is not capable of determination by arbitration.

The meaning or ambit of arbitrability has not been directly dealt with by the courts in Malaysia. Be that as it may, a decision that discussed this point in an indirect way and warrants close scrutiny is *Shaharuddin bin Ali* v. *Superintendent of Lands and Surveys Kuching Division.*[100] This was a case that involved native customary rights. The plaintiffs had submitted their claims for compensation to the defendant following an action by the defendant to extinguish rights over certain parcels of land. The plaintiffs' contention was that they had native customary rights over those parcels of land. The claims by the plaintiffs were rejected by the defendant. Dissatisfied, the plaintiff commenced an action in the High Court and sought a number of declarations. Of interest to us is the fact that the defendant had applied for an order to stay the proceedings on the ground that the matter should be referred to arbitration. The defendant relied on an arbitration provision in the Sarawak Land Code. Therefore, unlike a typical commercial contract where the parties to the contract elect to insert an arbitration clause or enter into an agreement to refer any dispute to arbitration, there was no such 'contract' between the plaintiffs and the defendant in this case. However, arbitration was imposed by statute. One of the issues before the court was whether the plaintiff could be compelled to refer their dissatisfaction with the decision of the defendant to arbitration pursuant to the Sarawak Land Code and thus an order for stay should be granted to the defendant. The High Court held that since the operative word of the provision in the Sarawak Land Code uses the word 'may', the plaintiffs could not be compelled to refer

---

[100] [2005] 2 MLJ 555.

the matter to arbitration.[101] If the provision in the Sarawak Land Code had used the word 'shall' or 'must' instead of 'may', would the High Court have arrived at the same conclusion? The question is: should a dispute or claim based on native customary rights be regarded or not as arbitrable? This issue was not directly addressed by the High Court, but it was nevertheless answered.[102] In applying the public law–private law dichotomy to the factual matrix of the case, Skinner J explained as follows:

> 26 So although the plaintiffs say that the native customary rights which they claim to have acquired (through persons who had created those rights before 1958) are proprietary in nature, the fact remains that the rights which they claim are rights created or recognised by statute, or put in another way, they are rights protected by public law. The plaintiffs' alleged native customary rights do not arise out of any private contract or arrangement between the plaintiffs and the Government (the defendants here), or put in another way, there is no infringement of a right of the plaintiffs arising under private law.[103]

Based on the above reasoning, it is submitted that even if the Sarawak Land Code had used the word 'shall', the subject matter in this case was not arbitrable. As his Lordship rightly conceded in this case, the plaintiffs' remedy to enforce or protect rights created or acquired or recognized in accordance with the provisions of the Land Code 'must be sought under public law and not private law'.[104]

Violation of Public Policy

Public policy is the most frequently invoked ground. The courts in Malaysia have shown their commitment to upholding foreign arbitral awards and have interpreted the public policy exception narrowly.

---

[101] The Deputy Registrar had earlier rejected the application by the defendant for an order for a stay on the ground that the relevant section in the erstwhile Arbitration Act 1952 can only be invoked by 'a party to an arbitration agreement'. Since there was no arbitration agreement in this case, the defendant could not be said to be a party to an arbitration agreement.

[102] Ironically, the defendant had argued in this case that the matter fell within the realm of public law and not private law. The defendant had raised the technical argument or objection that the plaintiffs should have commenced proceedings under Order 53 of the Rules of the High Court 1980, namely sought judicial review of the decisions of the defendant in ordering the reversion of the parcels of land in question to the government and in rejecting the claims by the plaintiffs.

[103] See note 100 at 566.   [104] Ibid.

The most recent decisions support the above contention. These decisions are *Open Type Joint Stock Company Efirnoye ('EFKO')* v. *Alfa Trading Ltd*,[105] *Infineon Technologies (M) Sdn Bhd* v. *Orisoft Technology Sdn Bhd*[106] and *Colliers International Property Consultants (USA) and Anor* v. *Colliers Jordan Lee and Jaafar (Malaysia)*.[107]

In *EFKO*, the party challenging the enforcement of an arbitral award argued that an identical dispute had been decided by two tribunals resulting in two different decisions and to allow the enforcement of one of the awards would be contrary to the public policy of Malaysia. The High Court rejected the above argument based on the factual matrix in the case. The more vital point in this case concerns the public policy argument.

The High Court made reference to decisions from common law countries such as New Zealand, Australia and Hong Kong to underscore its conclusion that a higher threshold is required to invoke this public policy exception. It explained that the fact that a case would have been decided differently under the law of the country where an award is sought to be recognized and enforced is not sufficient to invoke the public policy exception. The High Court further clarified that in the instant case there had not been a lack of fairness of procedure or breach of natural justice or illegality of a fundamental nature. Thus, *res judicata* did not apply and there was no question of moral and ethical policy that arose on the facts of this case. The High Court also made the following point concerning the public policy exception to the enforcement of arbitral awards:

> The enforcing court should guard against attempts made to go behind the award or to argue or reargue matters which have been comprehensively dealt with in the course of the arbitration. The provisions of s. 39, particularly the contravention of public policy argument ought not to be utilised as a guise to re-open settled matters in the arbitration. This the court ought to vigilantly guard against.[108]

In *Infineon Technologies*, the High Court referred to the leading cases on this issue from Hong Kong, Singapore, New Zealand and the USA and concluded that the correct approach is not to refuse to register a foreign arbitral award on the ground of conflict of public policy unless the most basic notions of morality would be offended. It is understandable that the

---

[105] See note 89.   [106] [2011] 7 MLJ 539.   [107] [2010] MLJU 650.
[108] See note 89 at 705.

High Court did not venture to explain the term 'basic notions of morality and justice'. This term strongly resists easy definition and it is best that an attempt is not made to define it. However, the High Court did say that in examining whether the basic notions of morality and justice would be offended the approach ought to be very restrictive, 'being grounded in the upholding of international comity'.

Colliers International Property Consultants concerned a dispute relating to the ownership of the 'Colliers' trade name and mark. Two arbitral awards were handed down by a foreign arbitral tribunal in favour of the plaintiff. The seat of arbitration was in the United Kingdom. The enforcement of the awards was challenged in Malaysia on the ground that the awards were in conflict with the public policy of Malaysia, and therefore, pursuant to section 39 of the 2005 Act, they should not be registered and enforced in Malaysia. The Court of Appeal was not persuaded by the defendant's argument that the relevant agreement, and consequent thereon the awards, violated the provisions of the Valuers, Appraisers and Estate Agents Act 1981. The learned judge noted that 'even if they did, which I disagreed, there was nothing that conflicted with fundamental principle of justice or morality or otherwise offensive to the public policy of Malaysia'. This decision should be contrasted with the decision in *Sami Mousawi v. Kerajaan Negeri Sarawak*[109] (discussed below), where breaches of local laws were upheld as offending the public policy of Malaysia.

However, notwithstanding the above, when the occasion calls for intervention, the courts in Malaysia have acted to prevent a foreign arbitral award from being enforced. This can be seen in cases such as *Sami Mousawi*[110] and *Equitas Ltd v. Allianz General Insurance Co. (Malaysia) Bhd.*[111]

In *Sami Mousawi v. Kerajaan Negeri Sarawak*, a British architectural firm called Sami Mousawi International (SMI), with Sami Mousawi as its principal, entered into a consultancy services agreement with Amanah Kebajikan Mesjid Negeri Sarawak, whereby SMI had to provide comprehensive consultancy services for the design and supervision of a proposed new state mosque in the state of Sarawak. As a result of a dispute over the non-payment of fees, domestic arbitration proceedings were instituted pursuant to an arbitration clause in the consultancy services agreement. A preliminary issue was raised as to whether the

---

[109] [2004] 2 MLJ 414.   [110] *Ibid.*   [111] [2009] MLJU 1334.

appellant was entitled to claim professional fees. This issue was raised because the appellant was found to have breached the Architects Act 1967, the Registration of Engineers Act 1967 and the Quantity Surveyors Act 1967. The arbitral tribunal ruled in favour of the appellant and eventually made an award in favour of the appellant. However, the respondent was successful in its application before the High Court to have the award set aside. When the matter came before the Court of Appeal, the appellate court explained that those laws were enacted to regulate the professions involved and to protect the public from unqualified and unregistered architects, engineers and quantity surveyors. Thus, any award made in contravention of any written law would be contrary to the public policy of Malaysia and should accordingly be set aside or refused recognition.

Admittedly, the decision in *Sami Mousawi* did not involve the enforcement of a foreign arbitral award. Further, it is undeniable that the ambit of a national public policy cannot be equated with that of an international public policy. Thus, in principle, a more rigid approach towards public policy should apply where the award is a foreign arbitral award. However, notwithstanding this tentative conclusion, as rightly cautioned by the High Court in *Infineon Technologies*, 'the comparative jurisprudence on this matter cannot as yet be said as approximating a uniform approach'. Since the issue of whether a breach of Malaysian domestic laws will render a foreign arbitral award unenforceable on the ground of public policy was not dealt with by the Court of Appeal, it cannot be ruled out that the appellate or apex court in Malaysia may adopt the same approach even when dealing with a foreign arbitral award.

In *Equitas Ltd* v. *Allianz General Insurance Co. (Malaysia) Bhd*, a number of arbitral awards were awarded in the United Kingdom against Malaysian British Assurance Berhad (MBAB). MBAB later became known as Allianz General Insurance Malaysia Berhad, the defendant in this case. One of the arguments raised by the defendant was that an award can only be registered against the party against whom the award was obtained. This technical argument was upheld by the High Court. More importantly, the High Court correlated a breach of natural justice with the concept of public policy. The relevant part of the judgment reads as follows:

> In the instant case there is clear evidence to show that the defendant was not given an opportunity to participate in the U.K. arbitral proceedings. *And the conduct of the plaintiff is a blatant abuse of rules of natural justice and the court can, in the exercise of its inherent jurisdiction and/or public*

policy reason, refuse to register an award taking into consideration the particular circumstance of the facts of the case, notwithstanding there is no application by the defendants to set aside the arbitral award [see *Ngo Chew Hong Oils & Fats (M) Sdn Bhd* v. *Karya Rumpun Sdn Bhd*, High Court (Kuala Lumpur) Suit No: R3-24-45-3009]. In this case the defendants could not have made an application to set aside the award as the award was not against them. It will not be correct exercise of discretion to grant the order when principles of justice, equity and good conscience have been compromised by the conduct of the plaintiff by failing to give proper opportunity to the defendants to arbitrate the matter in U.K.[112]

Another case worthy of mention is *Harris Adacom Corporation* v. *Perkom Sdn Bhd*.[113] In this case, the defendant had sought to challenge the enforcement of an award on the ground that the plaintiff was an Israeli company and to allow the award to be enforced would be contrary to public policy. The High Court made a finding of fact that the plaintiff was a US corporation and as such the award could be enforced in Malaysia. However, the High Court said that if indeed it had been proven that the plaintiff was an Israeli company, it would be against public policy to enforce the award. This is because trade with Israel is prohibited. The defendant had produced in the High Court a declaration from the foreign office indicating that trade with Israel is prohibited. However, based on the facts of the case, the High Court found that the Malaysian Government's stand vis-à-vis the state of Israel was not applicable and had no relevance in this case and did not support the defendant's argument that the award should not be recognized and enforced on the ground of public policy. The High Court noted that the plaintiff 'like any other company has a 68% stake in a subsidiary company engaged in development and manufacturing operations in Israel'. However, notwithstanding the above, it relied on the fact that 'the products covered by the distribution agreement have been and would have continued to be developed, manufactured and supported from the plaintiff's United States operation', and this fact had an important bearing on the outcome of the case.[114]

---

[112] Emphasis supplied. On the nexus between a breach of the rule of natural justice and public policy, see the decision of the Supreme Court of Victoria in *IMC Mining Inc* v. *Altain Khuder LLC* (2011) 282 ALR 717.

[113] [1994] 3 MLJ 504.   [114] *Ibid.* at 508.

Conclusion

From the foregoing, it can be concluded that Malaysia has not just adopted the text but the principles of the Model Law.

The enactment of the 2005 Act followed by the amendments made in 2011 to the 2005 Act are a manifestation of the seriousness on the part of the government of Malaysia to adhere to the principles enshrined in the Model Law. The 2011 amendment to adopt, with modification, the language used in ML 1985 article 5 will no doubt limit the courts' intervention to situations specifically covered by the 2005 Act and to discourage the use of the courts' inherent powers. Be that as it may, the courts' power cannot be totally curtailed as the occasions for the courts to intervene under the 2005 Act are still copious and when any of these provisions are invoked the courts are at liberty to exercise their jurisdiction and discretion. However, Malaysian courts have demonstrated their disposition in observing the principles of the Model Law. The courts have consistently referred to decisions from other jurisdictions when interpreting the provisions of the 2005 Act and this will help achieve the aim of promoting international consistency of arbitral regimes.

It has been noted that the 2011 amendment has clarified and severely limited the occasions for intervention by the courts to only the circumstances provided in the 2005 Act. Be that as it may, the 2005 Act contains a provision not found in the Model Law. Section 42 of the 2005 Act provides that any party may refer to the High Court any question of law arising out of an award. The 2011 amendment inserted a new subsection (1A) to provide that:

> The High Court shall dismiss a reference made under subsection (1) unless the question of law substantially affects the rights of one or more of the parties.[115]

This additional occasion for intervention may not further the objective of the Model Law in limiting judicial intervention in arbitral proceedings. While it is true that section 42 is in Part III of the 2005 Act and this provision shall not apply to international arbitration unless the parties agree otherwise in writing, the reverse position is adopted in cases of domestic arbitration.[116] As one commentator rightly noted, the expression 'substantially affects the rights of one or more of the parties' is

---

[115] Subsection (1A) was inserted by the Arbitration (Amendment) Act 2011 (Act A1395) s. 9 with effect from 1 July 2011 vide PU(B) 342/2011.

[116] See section 3(3)(b) and (2)(b) of the 2005 Act respectively.

unclear and 'may be fertile ground for litigation until such time that the Malaysian courts make an authoritative ruling as to the circumstances that fall within the ambit of that expression'.[117]

It would be helpful if Malaysia were to adopt ML article 2A. The adoption of such a provision would serve as a reminder to the courts when they are called upon to interpret or apply the provisions of the domestic arbitration laws. Nevertheless, it is submitted that since the courts in Malaysia have dependably considered decisions or doctrinal writing from other jurisdictions and alluded to the fact that there is a need to promote uniformity in the application of the laws of arbitration, the omission to incorporate ML article 2A into the 2005 Act will not have any adverse effect on the implementation of the principles of the Model Law.

---

[117] See Ashok Kumar, The Arbitration (Amendment) Act 2011, www.skrine.com/the-arbi tration-amendment-act-2011 (accessed 23 April 2015). For a discussion of the other subsections of section 42 of the Arbitration Act 2005, see Rajoo, *Malaysian Arbitration Act 2005* at 123–25.

6

Myanmar

The Model Law: A New Model for a New Era in Myanmar from the 1944 Arbitration Act to the 2016 Arbitration Law

MINN NAING OO

Introduction

Since 2011, Myanmar has seen a renewed effort at reforming its political, social and economic landscape. Apart from sweeping changes to the political and rights regime, efforts have been made to open up the economy, encourage foreign investment, relax import restrictions and export taxes, reform the anti-corruption regime and unify the currency exchange systems.

In this background, Myanmar also recognizes the crucial importance in providing a strong and certain dispute resolution framework to foreign investors in the country.

Important measures have been adopted by Myanmar to reform the law in this respect. This chapter provides a summary of the key developments in Myanmar arbitration law.

Past

Arbitration in Myanmar was governed until recently by the Arbitration Act of 1944 (the '1944 Act').[1] The 1944 Act was not based on the

Minn Naing Oo is Managing Director, Allen & Gledhill (Myanmar) Co. Ltd and Partner, Allen & Gledhill Singapore LLP. Email: minn.naingoo@allenandgledhill.com. The author thanks the EW Barker Centre for Law & Business at the Faculty of Law of the National University of Singapore for financing his participation in the conference entitled, 'The UNCITRAL Model Law on International Commercial Arbitration in Asia', which led to this book. The author would also like to thank Mr Vivekananda N for his invaluable assistance in writing this chapter.
[1] The 1944 Act can be found at http://www.burmalibrary.org/docs15/1944-Arbitration_Act-en.pdf.

UNCITRAL Model Law on international commercial arbitration. The 1944 Act primarily applied to domestic arbitrations, i.e., arbitrations conducted in Myanmar.

The 1944 Act provided for a large degree of deference to court involvement in the commencement, conduct and post-award stages of an arbitration. Courts had wide powers to appoint arbitrators or umpires;[2] set aside appointments of arbitrators;[3] remove arbitrators for misconduct;[4] terminate the effectiveness of the arbitration agreement;[5] provide its opinion on any point or issue submitted to it by an arbitrator;[6] direct an award to be filed in court;[7] modify or correct an award;[8] remit an award to the arbitrator for reconsideration;[9] extend the time for submission of an award;[10] pronounce judgment according to an award and pass a decree;[11] pass interim orders;[12] summon parties and witnesses;[13] and punish parties and witnesses for failing to give evidence.[14]

Awards could be set aside on broad grounds including on the basis of an arbitrator's misconduct, or that the arbitration had been superseded by an order of court, or that the award was improperly procured or was otherwise invalid.[15]

An award could be remitted by the court to the arbitrator(s) if it did not determine all matters referred to arbitration; it determined a matter not referred to arbitration; it was so indefinite as to be incapable of execution; or an objection to its legality was apparent on the face of it.[16]

An award could be modified or corrected by the court if it appeared that a part of the award was upon matters not referred to arbitration and such part could be separated from the other part and did not affect the decision on the matter referred to court; the award was imperfect in form or contained any obvious error which could be amended without affecting the decision; or the award contained a clerical mistake or an error arising from an accidental slip or omission.[17]

The 1944 Act was not clear as to whether parties could select a governing law of their choice including a foreign law to govern the

[2] Section 8, Arbitration Act 1944.   [3] Section 9, Arbitration Act 1944.
[4] Section 11, Arbitration Act 1944.   [5] Section 12(2), Arbitration Act 1944.
[6] Section 13(b), Arbitration Act 1944.   [7] Section 14, Arbitration Act 1944.
[8] Section 15, Arbitration Act 1944.   [9] Section 16, Arbitration Act 1944.
[10] Section 28, Arbitration Act 1944.   [11] Section 17, Arbitration Act 1944.
[12] Section 18, Arbitration Act 1944.   [13] Section 43(1), Arbitration Act 1944.
[14] Section 43(2), Arbitration Act 1944.   [15] Section 30, Arbitration Act 1944.
[16] Section 16, Arbitration Act 1944.   [17] Section 15, Arbitration Act 1944.

substantive contract between the parties. The 1944 Act also did not clearly delineate arbitrable disputes. However, some matters were understood to fall within the exclusive jurisdiction of the courts such as adjudication under the Insolvency Act or the winding up of a company.

As to the enforcement of awards, the 1944 Act provided for the enforcement of domestic awards. However, Myanmar is also party to the Geneva Convention on the Execution of Foreign Arbitral Awards 1927 and the Geneva Protocol on Arbitration Clauses 1923, which are codified in the Arbitration (Protocol and Conventions) Act 1939. Myanmar therefore provided for the enforcement of foreign arbitral awards from Geneva Convention countries, which had reciprocal arrangements for such enforcement. This was a limited regime since the number of signatories to the Geneva Convention is small. As such, there are no reported instances of enforcement of foreign arbitral awards in Myanmar under the Arbitration (Protocol and Conventions) Act 1939.

The 1944 Act and the regime for enforcement of awards in Myanmar therefore required updating for them to be brought in line with international jurisprudence and practice.

Present

As part of the wide reforms instituted by the government from 2011, on 15 July 2013, Myanmar formally acceded to the New York Convention on the Recognition and Enforcement of Foreign Arbitral Awards 1958 ('NYC' or 'New York Convention'). The New York Convention obliges Myanmar courts to give effect to contractual provisions that provide for disputes to be resolved by arbitration and to enforce foreign arbitral awards. Myanmar's accession represents a significant step by the government in creating a certain legal framework for the enforcement of foreign arbitral awards, and consequently for foreign investment in the country.

It has formed the foundation of the success of international arbitration as a dispute resolution mechanism for cross-border disputes. The ability to enforce arbitration agreements and arbitral awards across signatory jurisdictions is an important reason why arbitration is chosen in cross-border contracts. It gives parties confidence that their agreements and awards will be recognized and enforced by national courts in each of those jurisdictions irrespective of where the seat of arbitration is located.

The main object of this chapter is the comparison of the new arbitration law of Myanmar with the UNCITRAL Model Law on International Commercial Arbitration 1985 with amendments as adopted in 2006 ('ML').[18]

On 5 January 2016, the Union Parliament of Myanmar adopted the Arbitration Law (Union Law No. 5/2016) (the 'Arbitration Law').[19] Unlike some major arbitration forums such as England, France, Switzerland, Sweden and the USA that have largely developed their legislations on arbitration on their own, much of Myanmar's Arbitration Law is based on the ML.

Myanmar joins several other Asian jurisdictions in doing so, including notably Singapore and India (from which Myanmar has traditionally borrowed elements of its law).

Part I   General Provisions of the Model Law (Articles 1 to 6)

The foremost feature of the Arbitration Law is its effort to provide for the paramount place to the 'seat of the arbitration'.

Section 2(a) of the Arbitration Law incorporates article 1(2) ML to clarify that the law will apply where the place of arbitration is Myanmar. This is also apparent from section 2(b) which provides that certain provisions relating to grant of interim measures of protection, court assistance in securing evidence in support of arbitration and for enforcement of a tribunal's 'orders and directive' continue to apply even where the place of arbitration is not in Myanmar. This provision mirrors article 1(2) ML and the ML 1985.

The term 'award' is defined as a decision of the arbitral tribunal and includes any interim award.[20]

Section 3(i) of the Arbitration Law defines 'international arbitration' in language similar to article 1(3) of the ML.

---

[18] UNCITRAL Model Law on International Commercial Arbitration 1985, UN General Assembly Resolution 40/72 (11 December 1985) ('ML 1985'); UNCITRAL Model Law on International Commercial Arbitration 2006, UN General Assembly Resolution 61/33 (4 December 2006).

[19] The summary presented in this chapter of the Arbitration Law is based on an unofficial English translation of the Arbitration Law (from the Myanmar original) available on file with the author.

[20] Section 3(e).

However, the Arbitration Law does not adopt article 2A of the ML (International origin and general principles), as the Arbitration Law covers both domestic and international arbitrations.

The Arbitration Law adopts the provisions of the ML in relation to the receipt of written communications (article 3 ML).[21] It further seeks to improve upon article 4 of the ML by setting out the specific instances where a party must state its objection without undue delay, failing which it will be deemed to have waived such an objection. These include pleas that the arbitral tribunal has no jurisdiction; the arbitral proceedings were not conducted properly; any provision of the arbitration agreement or the arbitration law was not complied with; and that the arbitral tribunal or the arbitral proceedings were affected in some manner leading to the proceedings not being conducted properly.[22] If a party proceeds with the arbitration without stating any such objections, he shall be deemed to have waived his right to object.[23]

Section 7 of the Arbitration Law codifies the important principle contained in article 5 of the ML that a court shall not intervene in any matters governed by the Arbitration Law except as provided therein.

Section 8 of the Arbitration Law entitled 'Administrative Support' incorporates article 6 of the ML.

Part II   Arbitration Agreement (Articles 7 to 9)

In defining an arbitration agreement, the Arbitration Law substantially adopts Option 1 of article 7 suggested in the ML but not the text itself. The first sentence of article 7(1) as well as article 7(2) (Option 1) of the ML defining the arbitration agreement is adopted in substance at section 3 of the Arbitration Law. The rest of article 7 ML is substantially adopted in section 9 of the Arbitration Law. The Arbitration Law mandates that the arbitration agreement be in writing,[24] but also enumerates the situations where the arbitration agreement may be deemed to be in writing.

An agreement signed by the parties is deemed to be an agreement in writing.[25] An arbitration agreement made by electronic communication is in writing if the information contained in the electronic communication is accessible so as to be usable for subsequent reference.[26]

An arbitration agreement is in writing if it is contained in an exchange of statements of claim and defence in which the existence of an

---

[21] Section 5.   [22] Section 6(a)(1) to (4).   [23] Section 6(b).   [24] Section 3(b).
[25] Section 9(a).   [26] Section 9(b).

agreement is alleged by one party and not denied by the other.[27] Lastly, the Arbitration Law acknowledges that an arbitration agreement may be in the form of an arbitration clause in a contract or in the form of a separate agreement.[28]

The Arbitration Law also substantially adopts, and adds details to, article 8 of the ML and article II of the New York Convention in respect of the enforcement of arbitration agreements. Accordingly, section 10 of the Arbitration Law requires a court in Myanmar before which an action is brought that is otherwise the subject matter of an arbitration agreement to refer such parties to arbitration, on application by a party no later than when submitting the first statement on the substance of the dispute. The only exception to the rule is where the court finds that the agreement is null and void, inoperative or incapable of being performed.[29] A decision of the court to refer parties to arbitration is not appealable while a decision refusing to refer parties to arbitration may be appealed against.[30]

Importantly, the provision applies irrespective of whether the seat selected by the parties in such an arbitration agreement is in Myanmar or not.[31] This provides the necessary recognition for arbitration agreements involving Myanmar parties where the seat of the arbitration may be offshore.

In addition, where such an action is brought before a court, arbitral proceedings may nevertheless be commenced or continued, and an award may be made while the issue is pending before the court.[32] If the court refers the parties to arbitration, it is required to suspend (or stay) the court action.[33]

The Arbitration Law does not adopt the text of article 9 of the ML, but section 11 of the Arbitration Law makes clear the power of the court to grant interim measures.

Part III   Composition of Arbitral Tribunal (Articles 10 to 15)

Article 10   Number of Arbitrators and Article 11 Appointment of Arbitrators

Like in the ML, under the Arbitration Law, parties are free to determine the number of arbitrators; however, if there is more than one arbitrator,

---

[27] Section 9(c).   [28] Section 9(2).   [29] Section 10.
[30] Section 10(e) and (f) read with Sections 43(c)(1) and 47(a)(1).   [31] Section 2(b).
[32] Section 10(b).   [33] Section 10(d).

the Arbitration Law provides that the number of arbitrators shall not be an even number.[34] Contrary to the ML,[35] the default position, if the parties have not agreed on a number of arbitrators in the arbitration agreement, is that a sole arbitrator is to be appointed.[36]

Parties are free to agree on a procedure to appoint the arbitral tribunal (article 11(2) of the ML),[37] and are also free to appoint a person of any nationality as an arbitrator (article 11(1) of the ML).[38] This will provide further encouragement to parties to select an institutional set of arbitral rules to arbitrations seated in Myanmar, and for procedures prescribed in such institutional rules to apply to the appointment of an arbitral tribunal.

The default appointment power is vested in the Chief Justices of the regional/state High Court having jurisdiction (in respect of domestic arbitrations) and the Chief Justice of the Union (in respect of international arbitrations).

The Arbitration Law substantially adopts article 11(3) and (4) of the ML. Therefore, in an arbitration with three arbitrators, each party is required to appoint one arbitrator. The two arbitrators so appointed must appoint the third arbitrator, who shall act as the presiding arbitrator. If a party fails to appoint an arbitrator within thirty days of receipt of a request to do so from the other party, or if the two appointed arbitrators fail to appoint a third arbitrator within thirty days of their appointment, a party may request the appropriate Chief Justice to make the appointment.[39]

Similarly, in an arbitration with a sole arbitrator, if the parties fail to jointly appoint a sole arbitrator within thirty days of receipt of a request to do so from either party, a party may request the appropriate Chief Justice to make the appointment.[40]

In the discharge of the function to appoint arbitrators, the Chief Justice and his delegates are required to take into account the criteria and qualifications of the arbitrators, agreed to by the parties, and also endeavour to secure the appointment of an independent and impartial arbitrator.[41]

Importantly, the Arbitration Law provides that the Chief Justice may appoint an arbitrator of a neutral nationality to those of the parties to the arbitration in the case of the appointment of a sole arbitrator or the presiding arbitrator in an international arbitration where parties are

---

[34] Section 12(a).   [35] Article 10 ML.   [36] Section 12(b).   [37] Section 13(b).
[38] Section 13(a).   [39] Section 13(d)(1).   [40] Section 13(d)(2).   [41] Section 13(e).

citizens of different countries.[42] This is an important provision that is likely to lend greater confidence to foreign parties if they should find themselves in an arbitration seated in Myanmar.

Also, the Arbitration Law provides that the powers of appointment of the Chief Justice may be exercised by 'any person or organization determined by the Chief Justice'.[43]

Article 12   Grounds for Challenge and Article 13 Challenge Procedure

The grounds and procedure for challenging arbitrators as well as grounds to terminate the mandate of an arbitrator mirror articles 12 and 13 of the ML.[44]

Broadly, an arbitrator may be challenged on the basis that there are circumstances that give rise to justifiable doubts as to his impartiality or independence,[45] or that he does not possess qualifications agreed to by the parties.[46]

Parties are free to agree on a procedure for challenging an arbitrator including selecting an institutional set of arbitration rules which contain such a procedure.[47] Failing such an agreement among the parties, a party who intends to challenge an arbitrator must do so within fifteen days of becoming aware of the constitution of the tribunal or the circumstances giving rise to the challenge.[48] The party must make the challenge in writing with reasons and provide the written statement of challenge to the arbitral tribunal. The tribunal shall decide the challenge unless the arbitrator whose appointment is challenged steps down voluntarily, or the other party agrees to the challenge.[49]

If the challenge is not successful, a party may apply to the court to rule on the challenge within thirty days of the rejection of the challenge.[50] However, the arbitral tribunal is entitled to continue with its proceedings and make an award even when such an application is pending before the court.[51]

---

[42] Section 13(g).   [43] Section 13(c), (d), (e), (f), (g) and (h).   [44] Sections 14 to 16.
[45] Section 14(c)(1).   [46] Section 14(c)(2).   [47] Section 15(a).   [48] Section 15(b).
[49] Section 15(c).   [50] Section 15(d).   [51] Section 15(e).

Article 14   Failure or Impossibility to Act and Article 15
Appointment of Substitute Arbitrator

The Arbitration Law also contains detailed provisions on the termination of the mandate of an arbitrator and for replacement of an arbitrator. These provisions incorporate articles 14 and 15 of the ML. In effect, they provide that the mandate of an arbitrator shall terminate if he becomes *de jure* or *de facto* unable to perform his functions or fails to act without undue delay for other reasons.[52] Alternatively, the mandate of an arbitrator shall terminate if he withdraws from his office or the parties agree on the termination of his mandate.[53]

The Arbitration Law adds to the ML by stating that in the event of any dispute concerning whether any of the grounds for the termination of the mandate of the arbitrator is triggered, a party may request the court to decide the issue.[54] However, no appeal lies from a decision of the court on the issue.

In the event that an arbitrator is removed as a result of a challenge to his appointment or due to the termination of his mandate or due to a voluntary withdrawal, a replacement arbitrator must be appointed in accordance with the procedure agreed by the parties for the appointment of the arbitrator who is sought to be replaced.[55] In the event of the appointment of a replacement arbitrator, the arbitral tribunal may repeat any hearings conducted previously unless the parties agree otherwise.[56] Similarly, unless agreed otherwise by the parties, any orders or awards made by the arbitral tribunal prior to replacement of the arbitrator are not invalidated merely because the composition of the arbitral tribunal is subsequently altered.[57]

Part IV   Jurisdiction of Arbitral Tribunal (Article 16)

The Arbitration Law recognizes and codifies the principle of separability, i.e., the arbitration agreement is a distinct agreement from the substantive contract it forms a part of. The principle of separability is embedded in article 16 of the ML.

The Arbitration Law also recognizes and codifies the principle of *kompetenz-kompetenz/compétence-compétence*, i.e., the arbitral tribunal shall have the power to rule on its own jurisdiction.[58] Like the ML,

---

[52] Section 16(a)(1).   [53] Section 16(a)(2).   [54] Section 16(b).   [55] Section 17(a).
[56] Section 17(b).   [57] Section 17(c).   [58] Section 18.

the Arbitration Law requires that a plea by a party that the arbitral tribunal does not have jurisdiction be raised no later than the submission of the statement of defence.[59]

A plea that the arbitral tribunal is exceeding the scope of its authority is to be raised as soon as the matter alleged to be beyond the scope of its authority arises during the arbitral proceedings.[60] It is, however, open to the arbitral tribunal to admit a later plea in either situation above if it considers the delay to be justified.[61]

The Arbitration Law, going beyond the ML, appears to have adopted the position under the Singapore International Arbitration Act[62] (the 'Singapore IAA') in granting a right of appeal against both positive and negative determinations of jurisdiction by an arbitral tribunal. Therefore, the Arbitration Law provides that a party may appeal against a jurisdictional decision of the arbitral tribunal within thirty days of such decision.[63]

Part IV-A   Interim Measures and Preliminary Orders (Articles 17 to 17J)

Sub-Part I   Measures and Orders by the Tribunal (Articles 17 to 17G)

The Arbitration Law also confers specific powers on an arbitral tribunal to grant interim measures of protection and orders although the formulation of the powers of the tribunal does not follow the text of the ML, but is modelled closely on Section 12 of the Singapore IAA.[64] Therefore, Myanmar did not adopt the 2006 version of the ML on measures and orders by the tribunal but rather that addition to the ML 1985 which Singapore has adopted.

Sub-Part II   Recognition and Enforcement of Interim Measures (Articles 17H and 17I)

Importantly, the Arbitration Law specifically provides that orders, decisions and directions issued by an arbitral tribunal may be enforced with the permission of the court as if they were court orders.[65] This is an important adoption of the principle of article 17H of the ML but not its

---

[59] Section 18(b).   [60] Section 18(c).   [61] Section 18(d).
[62] International Arbitration Act, Statutes of Singapore, Cap. 143A.
[63] Sections 43(d)(1), 43(d)(2) and 47(b)(1).   [64] Section 19(a).
[65] Section 19(e) read with Section 31.

text – in fact the text adopted is similar to section 12(6) of the Singapore IAA which provides for the enforceability of interim orders rendered by arbitral tribunals in Singapore-seated arbitrations.

The Arbitration Law also provides for the enforceability of orders and directions rendered by an arbitral tribunal in an arbitration seated outside Myanmar.[66]

Sub-Part III   Court-Ordered Interim Measures (Article 17J)

Under the Arbitration Law, a court can order interim measures of protection in aid of arbitration.

The Arbitration Law expands on articles 9 and 17J of the ML and sets out in some detail the nature of interim measures of protection that may be ordered by a court in aid of arbitration. Further, an order made by the court granting any such interim measures of protection will cease to have effect if the arbitral tribunal makes an order on the same issues.[67]

Importantly, such interim measures of protection are normally only to be granted after due notice is provided to the other party and the arbitral tribunal, and if permission is provided by the tribunal or the other party in writing. This requirement applies only where the interim measure requested is not urgent in nature.[68] On the other hand, where the interim measure requested by a party is urgent in nature, the court may issue any order it deems necessary particularly for the preservation of evidence or property.[69] Further, the court may normally only exercise its jurisdiction to grant interim measures of protection where an institution or arbitral tribunal does not have the power in that respect.[70] An appeal lies against any decision of the court granting interim measures of protection.[71]

Importantly, the power of courts in Myanmar to grant interim measures of protection applies equally to aid an arbitration that is seated outside Myanmar.[72]

Part V   Conduct of Arbitral Proceedings (Articles 18 to 27)

Section 21 of the Arbitration Law adopts article 18 of the ML (Equal treatment of the parties) verbatim.[73]

---

[66] Section 31(a).   [67] Section 11(f).   [68] Section 11(c).   [69] Section 11(b).
[70] Section 11(d).   [71] Section 11(e).   [72] Section 2(b).
[73] The English translation of the Arbitration Law is identical to the ML.

Section 22 of the Arbitration Law adopts article 19 of the ML almost verbatim. It provides for the freedom of parties to agree on the procedure to be followed by the arbitral tribunal in conducting the proceedings (article 19(1) of the ML) so long as such procedure is not contrary to the provisions of the Arbitration Law. The provision further confers complete discretion on the tribunal to conduct the arbitration in such manner as it considers appropriate. This includes, for instance, the power of the tribunal to determine the admissibility, relevance, materiality and weight of any evidence (article 19(2) of the ML).[74]

The Arbitration Law adopts almost verbatim article 20 ML. The Arbitration Law also recognizes the freedom of parties to select a place of their choice (article 20(1) of the ML).[75] If the parties fail to agree on a seat of arbitration, the arbitral tribunal has the power to determine the place with regard to the circumstances of the case and the convenience of the parties.[76] Importantly, the Arbitration Law recognizes the distinction between place and venue of arbitration and specifically provides that the arbitral tribunal may, unless otherwise agreed by the parties, meet at any appropriate place for consultation among its members, for hearing witnesses, experts or the parties, or for inspection of goods, other property or documents (article 20(2) of the ML).[77]

Article 21 of the ML on the commencement of arbitration is adopted verbatim.

The parties also have the freedom to select the language or languages to be used in the proceedings (article 21 of the ML).[78] If the parties fail to agree on the language, the arbitral tribunal has the power to determine the most appropriate language or languages to be used.[79]

The Arbitration Law adopts article 23 of the ML (Statements of claim and defence) almost verbatim.[80]

The Arbitration Law adopts article 24 of the ML (Hearings and written proceedings) verbatim. The arbitral tribunal is free to decide if oral hearings must be held for the presentation of evidence or oral arguments. Alternatively, the tribunal may decide to conduct the proceedings on the basis of documents and other materials alone. This is of course subject to the agreement of the parties and unless parties have agreed that no hearings are to be held the arbitral tribunal shall hold such hearings at an appropriate stage of the proceedings.[81]

---

[74] Section 22(c).   [75] Section 23(a).   [76] Section 23(b).   [77] Section 23(c).
[78] Section 25(a).   [79] Section 25(b).   [80] Section 26.   [81] Section 27(a).

The Arbitration Law adopts article 25 of the ML (Default of a party) verbatim. Where a claimant fails to communicate its statement of claim, the arbitral tribunal is permitted to terminate the proceedings. Where a respondent fails to communicate its statement of defence, the arbitral tribunal may continue the proceedings, without treating such failure in itself as an admission of the claimant's claims and allegations.[82] Where any party fails to appear at an oral hearing or to produce documentary evidence, the arbitral tribunal may continue the proceedings and make the award on the evidence before it.[83] These provisions are in line with the ML and international practice.

The Arbitration Law adopts article 26 of the ML (Expert appointed by arbitral tribunal) almost verbatim. The Arbitration Law provides that the tribunal may, unless otherwise agreed by the parties, appoint one or more experts to report on specific issues.[84] The tribunal may also require a party to give the expert relevant information or to produce or provide access to relevant documents, goods or other property for the expert's inspection.[85] Subject to the agreement of the parties, the expert must participate in the hearing if requested by the parties or if the tribunal considers it necessary.[86] Further, any expert report or evidentiary document on which the tribunal may rely in making its decision shall be communicated to the parties.[87]

The tribunal or a party with the approval of the arbitral tribunal may request assistance from a court in taking evidence (article 27 of the ML).[88] However, the Arbitration Law goes further than article 27 of the ML in prescribing the powers of the courts in this respect. The Arbitration Law specifically confers powers upon the courts to obtain testimony, issue subpoenas for examination of witnesses and production of documents and to send any such evidence gathered to the arbitral tribunal directly.[89]

The power of the courts to assist in taking such evidence may also be utilized where the seat of the arbitration is outside Myanmar.[90]

Part VI   Making of Award and Termination of Proceedings
(Articles 28 to 33)

The Arbitration Law also recognizes that in an 'international arbitration', i.e., where a foreign element is involved, parties are free to choose a

---

[82] Section 28(b).   [83] Section 28(c).   [84] Section 29(a).   [85] Section 29(b).
[86] Section 29(c).   [87] Section 27(c).   [88] Section 30(a).   [89] Section 30(c) and (d).
[90] Section 2(b).

substantive law of the contract of their choice.[91] However, when the parties fail to make a choice of law, the Arbitration Law does not adopt the indirect approach of article 28(2) of the ML which requires reference to rules of conflicts of law ('the arbitral tribunal shall apply the law determined by the conflict of laws rules which it considers applicable') but rather the direct approach which does not require reference to any rules of conflicts of law ('the arbitral tribunal shall apply the rules of law which it considers applicable').[92] It should also be noted that whereas the ML allows the parties to choose 'rules of law', the Arbitration Law only allows the tribunal to choose 'the law', thus limiting the tribunal to a choice of a national law rather than some other rules such as the UNIDROIT Principles of International Commercial Contracts.

However, when both parties are from Myanmar (i.e., in a domestic arbitration), the tribunal shall decide the dispute in accordance with the prevailing substantive law of Myanmar. There is no equivalent provision in the ML.

The Arbitration Law adopts article 29 of the ML (Decision-making by panel of arbitrators) and article 30 of the ML (Settlement) verbatim.[93]

Article 31   Form and Contents of Award

Article 31 of the ML (Form and contents of award) is largely imported into the Arbitration Law particularly as to the requirements of the form and content of an award. Broadly, the award must be in writing and signed by the arbitrators.[94] Where there is more than one arbitrator, the signatures of the majority of the members of the tribunal are sufficient as long as the reason for any omitted signature is stated.[95]

The award must state the reasons upon which it is based unless the parties have agreed that no reasons are to be given or the award is an award on agreed terms.[96] The award must also state the date and the seat of arbitration. The award is deemed to have been made at that place.[97]

However, in the section on 'Form and contents of award', the Arbitration Law additionally confers on the arbitral tribunal the power to determine, in the award, the costs of arbitration and its apportionment among the parties.[98] The term 'costs' includes the fees and expenses for arbitrators and witnesses; solicitor fees and expenses; administrative fees

---

[91] Section 32(2)(aa) and (bb).   [92] Section 32(2)(cc).
[93] Sections 33 and 34 respectively.   [94] Section 35(a).   [95] Section 35(b).
[96] Section 35(c).   [97] Section 35(d).   [98] Section 35(f).

for the organization (or institution) handling the arbitration; and other costs in connection with arbitral proceedings and award.[99]

The Arbitration Law also adopts Article 32 of the ML (Termination of proceedings) almost verbatim. It provides that the arbitral proceedings are terminated by the final award or by an order of the arbitral tribunal. An arbitral tribunal may order the termination of the proceedings if the claimant withdraws his claim (unless the respondent objects thereto and the arbitral tribunal recognizes a legitimate interest on the respondent's part in obtaining a final settlement of the dispute). Alternatively, the tribunal may also order a termination of proceedings if the parties agree on the termination or the tribunal finds that the continuation of the proceedings has become unnecessary or impossible for any reason.[100]

The Arbitration Law substantially adopts article 33 of the ML, which provides for parties to apply to the tribunal for the correction of computational, clerical or typographical errors,[101] or for the interpretation of a specific point or part of the award,[102] within thirty days of the receipt of the award.

In addition, a party may also request the tribunal to make an additional award as to claims presented in the arbitral proceedings but omitted from the award, within thirty days of the receipt of the award.[103]

Part VII   Recourse against Award (Article 34)

Recourse Even before a Domestic Award is Issued

Unlike the ML, under the Arbitration Law, any party may, unless agreed otherwise by the parties and with notice to the arbitral tribunal and other parties, apply to the court for a ruling on an issue of law arising from the arbitral proceedings even before the award is issued. The court may rule on such an issue of law if it is convinced that the rights of parties are materially prejudiced.[104] This recourse is only available to domestic arbitrations and not international arbitrations.

The court will, however, not consider such an application if it is convinced that such an application was not made in accordance with the agreement of the parties, or was made without notice to the arbitral

---

[99] Explanation to Section 35(f).   [100] Section 36(b).   [101] Section 37(a) and (b).
[102] Section 37(c) and (d).   [103] Section 37(e) and (f).   [104] Section 39(a).

tribunal, or that the consideration of such an application will increase costs or delay the proceedings.[105]

An arbitral tribunal may continue with the arbitral proceedings notwithstanding that such an application is pending before the court.

Setting Aside of Awards

With respect to domestic awards, the Arbitration Law adopts article 34 of the ML (Setting aside) in entirety in setting out the grounds for setting aside an award, by a court, arising from an arbitration seated in Myanmar.[106]

An application to set aside an award cannot be made after three months have elapsed from the receipt of the award by the party making the challenge.[107] The decision of a court to set aside or reject an application to set aside an award is appealable.[108]

In respect of an international or foreign award, an application to set aside the award would have to be made to the competent authority of the country in which, or under the law of which, that award was made. The Arbitration Law does not empower the Myanmar Courts to set aside a foreign award under any circumstances.

Unlike the ML, a party may also appeal on an issue of law arising from a domestic award.[109] However, parties may agree to exclude such a right.[110]

The court shall allow the appeal if it is convinced that its ruling upon the issue materially prejudices the rights of a party or the award of the arbitral tribunal in respect of the dispute submitted for its decision is completely wrong.[111] Consequently, the court may confirm the award, vary the award, return the award to the arbitral tribunal for reconsideration of the whole or any part of the award, or set aside the whole or part of the award.[112]

If the court makes an order to remand the matter to the tribunal for its fresh consideration, the tribunal is required to review the award to make a new award in respect of such matters.[113] The court may also stipulate an appropriate time period for the arbitral tribunal to do so.[114]

---

[105] Section 39(b).   [106] Section 41(a)(1) to (7).   [107] Section 41(b).
[108] Section 43(c)(4).   [109] Section 42(a).   [110] Section 42(b).   [111] Section 43(a).
[112] Section 43(b).   [113] Section 44(b).   [114] Section 44(c).

Part VIII   Recognition and Enforcement of Awards
(Articles 35 and 36)

Execution of Domestic Award

The Arbitration Law also provides that the execution of a domestic award shall be carried out according to the procedure employed for enforcement of a decree under the Code of Civil Procedure.[115] The only defence to such an execution is that the arbitral tribunal had no mandate to make the award.[116]

Enforcement of Foreign Awards

The Arbitration Law codifies Myanmar's international law obligations under the New York Convention to recognize and enforce international arbitration agreements and awards.

In doing so, the Arbitration Law incorporates article IV of the New York Convention on the procedural requirements for enforcement of a foreign arbitral award.[117] Further, the Arbitration Law mirrors article V of the New York Convention and article 36 of the ML in setting out the grounds upon which a court may refuse to enforce a foreign award.[118]

The codification of the New York Convention in the Arbitration Law brings in line Myanmar's position with other prominent New York Convention jurisdictions and ensures that foreign awards from 155 other jurisdictions are readily enforceable in Myanmar.

The Arbitration Law also repeals the Arbitration (Protocol and Convention) Act of 1937, which hitherto applied for the enforcement of foreign arbitral awards from Geneva Convention countries.[119]

Conclusion

Myanmar is at the cusp of history today. A new government is in place and foreign investment in the country is growing. A modern and up-to-date arbitration legislation based on international practice will go a long way in securing investor confidence. However, much will depend on its implementation in practice, its adoption by parties and its apposite interpretation by the courts.

---

[115] Section 40(a).   [116] Section 40(b).   [117] Section 45.
[118] Section 46(b)(1) to (6) and 46(c)(1) to (2).   [119] Section 49.

7

Philippines

The Application of the UNCITRAL Model Law on International Commercial Arbitration in The Philippines

RENA M. RICO-PAMFILO

Introduction

Alternative dispute resolution in the Philippines is governed by a distinct set of laws, foremost of which is the Republic Act No. 9285, also known as the Alternative Dispute Resolution Act of 2004 ('ADR Act'), promulgated on 2 April 2004. The ADR Act covers arbitration, mediation and other forms of alternative dispute resolution [ADR] such as third-party evaluation, mini-trial and mediation-arbitration. However, many provisions of the ADR Act are devoted to arbitration, specifically international commercial arbitration. The ADR Act adopts the 1985 version of the UNCITRAL Model Law on International Commercial Arbitration 1985, UN General Assembly Resolution 40/72 (11 December 1985) ('ML 1985'), which is annexed to the ADR Act. The relevant provision of the ADR Act states:

> SECTION 19. Adoption of the Model Law on International Commercial Arbitration. – International commercial arbitration shall be governed by the Model Law on International Commercial Arbitration (the 'Model Law') adopted by the United Nations Commission on International Trade Law on 21 June 1985 (United Nations Document A/40/17) and recommended for enactment by the General Assembly in Resolution No. 40/72 approved on 11 December 1985, copy of which is hereto attached as Appendix 'A'.

Rena M. Rico-Pamfilo is Professor of International Commercial Arbitration at the Ateneo de Manila University Law School. The author thanks the EW Barker Centre for Law & Business at the Faculty of Law of the National University of Singapore for financing her participation in the conference entitled, 'The UNCITRAL Model Law on International Commercial Arbitration in Asia', which led to this book.

There has been no amendment to the ADR Act, including the version of the UNCITRAL Model Law adopted. The Philippines has substantially adopted the provisions of the ML 1985 with revisions meant to localize specific references in the law.

The ADR Act recognizes three distinct types of arbitration and each is governed by a specific law: (a) domestic arbitration, governed by the Republic Act No. 876[1] enacted in 1953, (b) construction arbitration governed by Executive Order No. 1008,[2] conducted under the auspices of the Construction Industry Arbitration Commission and (c) international commercial arbitration governed by the ADR Act, specifically by ML 1985. The distinction between international commercial arbitration and domestic arbitration is simple under the ADR Act. Under the ADR Act, domestic arbitration is an arbitration that is not international as defined in ML 1985 article 1(3).[3] Construction arbitration refers to the arbitration of disputes arising from, or connected with, contracts entered into by parties involved in construction in the Philippines. These disputes may involve government or private contracts.

The ADR Act limits the application of the ML 1985 to international commercial arbitration. However, the ADR Act makes certain provisions of the ML 1985 and of the chapter on international commercial arbitration applicable to domestic arbitration.[4]

In addition to legislation, the Philippine legal framework allows for the issuance of specific regulations or procedures to implement legislation or prescribe details for the execution or application of legislation. In the case of the ADR Act, the implementing rules and regulations of the law were drafted by an Oversight Committee specifically created by the ADR Act. The ADR Act also created a special agency called the Office of Alternative Dispute Resolution which is attached to the Department of Justice, to promote, develop and expand the use of alternative dispute resolution in the Philippines in both the public and private

---

[1] Republic Act No. 876 is entitled, 'An Act to Authorize the Making of Arbitration and Submission Agreements, to Provide for the Appointment of Arbitrators and the Procedure for Arbitration in Civil Controversies, and for Other Purposes', 19 June 1953.

[2] Executive Order No. 1008 is entitled, 'Creating an Arbitration Machinery in the Construction Industry of the Philippines', 4 February 1985.

[3] ADR Act, section 32.

[4] Section 33 of the ADR Act enumerates the provisions of ML 1985 that apply to domestic arbitration which include provisions on mandatory referral to arbitration, constitution and appointment of the tribunal, equal treatment of parties and termination of proceedings.

sectors, to study and evaluate the use of ADR and lobby for needful changes in the law or in relevant regulations to strengthen and improve ADR.[5]

With respect to the implementation by the courts of the ADR Act, the Philippine Supreme Court has the power to adopt specific rules of procedure in relation to legislation that requires the intervention or participation by the court. In September 2009, the Philippine Supreme Court issued the Special Rules of Court on Alternative Dispute Resolution [Special ADR Rules] which are procedural rules for actions or remedies in court that are available to parties in relation to alternative dispute resolution processes, specifically arbitration and mediation.[6] The Special ADR Rules is noteworthy in that it contains specific policy provisions, which are meant to guide the courts when making decisions primarily with respect to international arbitration matters.[7]

When discussing the decisions of Philippine courts in relation to international arbitration, this chapter shall be limited to promulgated decisions of the Philippine Supreme Court. Only decisions of the Philippine Supreme Court are published and have the effect of *stare decisis* or are considered as binding precedents. While the ADR Act has been in effect for more than ten years, there are only a few decisions of the Supreme Court on international commercial arbitration. This may be partly due to the few international arbitration cases seated in the Philippines or involving Philippine parties or involving parties with assets in the Philippines. There is no centralized database or registry of arbitration cases involving a Philippine party or seated in the Philippines. However, the Philippine Dispute Resolution Center (PDRC), an organization which administers arbitration in the Philippines, regularly compiles statistics with respect to arbitration matters referred to it. These statistics give a helpful indication of the level of activity in the Philippines. Table 7.1 shows the number of domestic and international arbitration cases administered by the PDRC or that have made use of its facilities.

Since the enactment of the ADR Act, there are still very few international arbitration cases filed with or referred to the PDRC either as administered arbitration cases or for use of facilities only (in case of ad hoc arbitration). Based on the statistics provided by the PDRC, for the

---

[5] ADR Act, section 49.   [6] A.M. No. 07-11-08-SC (1 September 2009).
[7] Special ADR Rules, r. 2.

Table 7.1 *Domestic and international arbitration cases administered by the Philippine Dispute Resolution Center, 2004–2015*

	2004	2005	2006	2007	2008	2009	2010	2011	2012	2013	2014	2015
Domestic	2	4	3	2	2	5	3	9	5	7	4	4
International	0	0	1	1	0	4	1	3	0	2	4	2
Totals	2	4	4	3	2	9	4	12	5	9	8	6

past five years, on average, 70 per cent of the cases each year are administered under the Arbitration Rules of the PDRC and the majority of the cases filed would have a Philippine party.

In the few decisions of the Supreme Court on international arbitration, the Supreme Court does not generally refer to specific provisions of the ML 1985 as the basis for its decisions. Reference is usually made to previous decisions of the Supreme Court upholding certain principles of arbitration that are also reflected in ML 1985. Specific reference to legislation will be to provisions of the ADR Act rather than to ML 1985 even if more specific and direct support of the ruling can be found in ML 1985. There is very little reference or citation to international decisions or publications in the rulings of the Court. In general, reference or citation to foreign sources by the Philippine Supreme Court is rare and is usually resorted to in cases where there is no applicable Philippine jurisprudence on the matter.

In any event, the few cases promulgated by the Supreme Court on international arbitration, specifically on the implementation of provisions or key principles of the ML 1985, are generally encouraging and point to an interpretation of the ML 1985 that is consistent with the internationally accepted principles of international arbitration.

Part I   General Provisions of the Model Law (Articles 1 to 6)

The Philippine legislature did not make any material or substantive changes to ML 1985 and in fact it is posited that additions or revisions of the ADR Act on ML 1985 give further clarity or detail to the provisions of the ML 1985. Other changes involve 'localizing' the provisions to ML 1985 as they specifically apply in the Philippine setting. There is no significant modification to ML 1985 and any changes or additions made under the ADR Act do not modify but only supplement certain

provisions in ML 1985. Key provisions of the ML 1985 are not changed –
for example, the definition of international commercial arbitration, Article 5 on the limited role of the courts, the definition of an arbitration
agreement, mandatory referral to arbitration and grounds to set aside an
arbitral award.

Concrete examples of the direction of the law to give further clarity or
detail to ML 1985 can be found in the first few provisions of the ADR Act.
While ML 1985 defines 'arbitration' as 'any arbitration whether or not
administered by a permanent arbitral institution',[8] the ADR Act defines
'arbitration' as 'a voluntary dispute resolution process in which one or
more arbitrators, appointed in accordance with the agreement of the
parties, or rules promulgated pursuant to this Act, resolve a dispute by
rendering an award'.[9] The ADR Act does not define an 'arbitral tribunal'
but defines an 'arbitrator' as a 'person appointed to render an award, alone
or with others, in a dispute that is the subject of an arbitration agreement.'[10] Reference to a 'court' under ML 1985 is a reference to the Regional
Trial Court or a court of general jurisdiction in the Philippines that is
designated in every judicial region in the country.[11] All the other provisions of article 2 of the ML 1985 on definitions and rules of interpretation
are adopted verbatim under the ADR Act.

The concept of 'commercial' arbitration is not given much importance
in ML 1985 and the definition of the term 'commercial' is relegated to a
footnote to article 1 of the ML 1985. The ADR Act gives some significance to the definition of a 'commercial arbitration' by expressly
adopting a definition in section 3(g) of the ADR Act, i.e., '[a]n arbitration
is "commercial" if it covers matter arising from all relationships of a
commercial nature, whether contractual or not' and defining the term
'commercial' again in section 21 of the ADR Act. The definition of the
term 'commercial' in section 21 reproduces almost verbatim the footnote
to article 1 of the ML 1985.[12]

The rules of interpretation in ML 1985 echo the principle of party
autonomy which is expressly declared in the ADR Act as the principle
which governs the enactment and implementation of the law. Section 2
of the ADR Act provides:

---

[8] ML 1985 art. 2(a).   [9] ADR Act, section 3(d).   [10] ADR Act, section 3(e).
[11] ADR Act, section 3(k).
[12] There is a slight modification in that the phrase 'exploitation agreement or concession'
contained in the footnote to Article 1 of ML 1985 is omitted from section 21 of the ADR Act.

Section 2. *Declaration of Policy*. – it is hereby declared the policy of the State to actively promote party autonomy in the resolution of disputes or the freedom of the party to make their own arrangements to resolve their disputes. Towards this end, the State shall encourage and actively promote the use of Alternative Dispute Resolution (ADR) as an important means to achieve speedy and impartial justice and declog court dockets. As such, the State shall provide means for the use of ADR as an efficient tool and an alternative procedure for the resolution of appropriate cases. Likewise, the State shall enlist active private sector participation in the settlement of disputes through ADR. This Act shall be without prejudice to the adoption by the Supreme Court of any ADR system, such as mediation, conciliation, arbitration, or any combination thereof as a means of achieving speedy and efficient means of resolving cases pending before all courts in the Philippines which shall be governed by such rules as the Supreme Court may approve from time to time.

It is therefore a declared policy of the law to uphold party autonomy in dispute resolution. The law takes a further step by declaring the active promotion of the use of alternative dispute resolution as a viable, credible and efficient alternative to court litigation.

A distinct feature of the ADR Act is that the law expressly states that in interpreting the provisions of the ML 1985, 'regard shall be had to its international origin and to the need for uniformity in its interpretation and resort may be made to the *travaux preparatories* [*sic*] and the report of the Secretary General of the United Nations Commission on International Trade Law dated 25 March 1985 entitled, "International Commercial Arbitration: Analytical Commentary on Draft Text identified by reference number a/CN. 9/264".'[13] There is a new provision in the UNCITRAL Model Law on International Commercial Arbitration 2006, UN General Assembly Resolution 61/33 (4 December 2006) ('ML') to this effect. However, in the Philippines, this provision is express in the law and was effective even prior to the issuance of the ML 1985. However, as will be shown later in this chapter, while the law already prescribes the manner by which ML 1985 shall be interpreted, Philippine courts have not specifically invoked or applied this provision and instead would cite previously decided cases of the Supreme Court or general principles of international arbitration.

---

[13] ADR Act, section 20.

Section 25 of the ADR Act contains a specific provision on interpretation of the law:

> SEC. 25. *Interpretation of the Act.* – In interpreting the Act, the court shall have due regard to the policy of the law in favor of arbitration. Where action is commenced by or against multiple parties, one or more of whom are parties who are bound by the arbitration agreement although the civil action may continue as to those who are not bound by such arbitration agreement.

The last sentence of section 25 is an interesting one and possibly a reaction to a series of cases decided by the Philippine Supreme Court on the effect of a pending arbitration proceeding on a similar court action where not all of the parties to the court action are parties to the arbitration agreement.[14] In those cases, the Supreme Court gave due course to and decided on the petitions despite being aware that an arbitration proceeding involving similar facts and causes of action had commenced, on the basis that not all of the parties before the court action are parties to the arbitration agreement from which the arbitration proceeding arises. Section 25 now expressly allows a situation for both the civil action and arbitration proceeding to continue and be resolved, hence a possibility of conflicting results or that the decision in one will influence the other, where not all of the parties in the civil action are parties to the arbitration agreement.

Articles 3 and 4 of the ML 1985 are adopted verbatim by the ADR Act. Article 3 on communications between parties are standard and accepted procedures in the Philippines and excludes communications in relation to court proceedings. The Philippine Rules of Court governing procedures before the courts have specific rules on filing and service of pleadings, judgments and other papers.[15] The Special ADR Rules also contain specific provisions of the filing and service of pleadings and other court documents for summary and non-summary proceedings covered by the Special ADR Rules.[16] The rule on waivers in article 4 is also not controversial and clearly places the onus on the parties to the arbitration to be vigilant in the enforcement of their rights.

---

[14] *Agan, et al.* v. *PIATCO, et al.*, G.R. Nos. 155001, 155547 and 155661, 5 May 2003; *Del Monte Corporation-USA* v. *Court of Appeals*, G.R. No. 136154, 7 February 2001; *Salas, Jr.* v. *Laperal Realty Corporation*, G.R. No. 135362, 13 December 1999.
[15] Rules of Court of the Philippines, r. 13.   [16] Special ADR Rules, rr. 1.3 and 1.8.

One key provision of the ML 1985 is article 5, which expressly limits the intervention of the courts only in instances provided by ML 1985. This is not changed by the ADR Act. In addition, the Special ADR Rules provide for general policies which reinforce this provision:

> Rule 2.1. *General policies.* – It is the policy of the State to actively promote the use of various modes of ADR and to respect party autonomy or the freedom of the parties to make their own arrangements in the resolution of disputes with the greatest cooperation of and the least intervention from the courts. To this end, the objectives of the Special ADR Rules are to encourage and promote the use of ADR, particularly arbitration and mediation, as an important means to achieve speedy and efficient resolution of disputes, impartial justice, curb a litigious culture and to de-clog court dockets.
>
> The court shall exercise the power of judicial review as provided by these Special ADR Rules. Courts shall intervene only in the cases allowed by law or these Special ADR Rules. (emphasis added)

The above policy in the Special ADR Rules is complemented by the following direction to the court:

> Rule 2.2. *Policy on arbitration.*
> [. . .]
> (B) Where court intervention is allowed under ADR Laws or the Special ADR Rules, courts shall not refuse to grant relief, as provided herein, for any of the following reasons:
>
> a. Prior to the constitution of the arbitral tribunal, the court finds that the principal action is the subject of an arbitration agreement; or
> b. The principal action is already pending before an arbitral tribunal.

The above provision clarifies that notwithstanding the existence of a valid arbitration agreement or a pending arbitration proceeding the court is still authorized to act as prescribed by the Special ADR Rules. This highlights that the role of the court, as embodied in the Special ADR Rules, is to support and give effect to the arbitral process and naturally contemplates the existence of an arbitration agreement between the parties or the pendency of arbitral proceedings.

The designation of the default appointing authority under ML 1985 is localized and is prescribed by the ADR Act to refer to the National President of the Integrated Bar of the Philippines. Hence, for ad hoc arbitration seated in the Philippines, in the absence of any specific agreement of the parties, the appointing authority is the National President of the Integrated Bar of the Philippines. The Integrated Bar of the Philippines is a national organization comprising the entire membership of the Philippine Bar. It was formally established in 1973 as a body corporate possessing corporate legal power and capacity under Presidential Decree No. 181.[17] Section 27 of the ADR Act provides that in the event that the National President of the Integrated Bar of the Philippines fails or refuses to act within thirty days from receipt of a request, the party may apply before the Regional Trial Court.

Part II   Arbitration Agreement (Articles 7 to 9)

The ADR Act does not modify article 7 of the ML 1985 on the definition and form of the arbitration agreement. Article 7 is undoubtedly one of the most important provisions of the ML 1985 as the determination of the existence of an arbitration agreement, specifically an international arbitration agreement, has specific consequences.

One important decision of the Supreme Court in international arbitration, particularly on the validity of an international commercial arbitration agreement, is the case of *Korea Technologies Co., Ltd* v. *Lerma and Pacific General Steel Manufacturing Corporation*[18] [*Korea Tech*]. However, *Korea Tech* is a double-edged sword. While there are key rulings in the case which affirm ML 1985 and the application of international arbitration in the Philippines, there are certain statements by the Supreme Court in *Korea Tech* (as will be seen later in this chapter) which contradict ML 1985. With respect to the arbitration agreement, *Korea Tech* is the first clear case where the Supreme Court expressly and clearly upheld the validity of an international arbitration agreement, i.e., an arbitration agreement involving at least one party residing outside of the Philippines, providing for a foreign seat of arbitration and governed by foreign arbitral rules of procedure. *Korea Tech* involves a contract between a Korean supplier, Korea Technologies Co., Ltd ('KOGIES') and a Philippine manufacturer, Pacific General Steel Manufacturing Corp. ('PGSMC') for the supply and installation of the machinery and facilities necessary for manufacturing of liquefied petroleum gas cylinders. The contract provided for arbitration of disputes in Seoul, Korea under the rules of the Korean Commercial Arbitration Board (KCAB). Disputes arose between the parties resulting in the unilateral termination by

---

[17] Entitled, 'Constituting the Integrated Bar of the Philippines into a Body Corporation and Providing Government Assistance Thereto for the Accomplishment of its Purposes', 4 May 1953.
[18] G.R. No. 143581, 7 January 2008; 542 SCRA 1.

PGSMC of the contract. KOGIES initiated arbitration proceedings in KCAB. Subsequently, KOGIES also instituted an action before the Philippine courts for specific performance against PGSMC and requested the court to issue a restraining order to prevent PGSMC from dismantling the machinery and equipment installed by KOGIES. KOGIES also argued that the termination/rescission by PGSMC of the contract was premature in view of the arbitration agreement, i.e., that the parties needed to resort to arbitration prior to any party having the right to terminate the agreement. PGSMC argued that the arbitration agreement is null and void as it ousted Philippine courts of jurisdiction.

The Supreme Court upheld the validity of the arbitration agreement and expressly stated that an arbitration clause providing for arbitration of disputes in Korea under the rules of the KCAB and stating that the resulting arbitral award shall be final and binding is valid and not contrary to public policy. While previous cases of the Supreme Court have upheld the validity of an arbitration agreement, this is the first clear case where an international arbitration agreement is clearly upheld and found valid. The Court expressly referred to the ADR Act and its adoption of the ML 1985 to govern international commercial arbitration.[19] While the Supreme Court in this case did not expressly cite any specific provision of the ML 1985 to support its ruling on the validity of an international arbitration agreement, the principle behind the ruling on the affirmation of the arbitration agreement is consistent with ML 1985. The Court, in view of the arbitration agreement, ultimately directed the parties to resolve their dispute through arbitration.

Note also that in *Korea Tech*, the Supreme Court ruled that the ADR Act, being a procedural law, had retroactive effect and applied to cases that were filed prior to the effectivity of the ADR Act. The Court cited the rule that 'the retroactive application of procedural laws does not violate any personal rights because no vested right has yet attached nor arisen from them.'[20]

---

[19] Note that the Supreme Court in *Korea Tech* referred to the ADR Act as having incorporated ML 1985 to which the Philippines is a 'signatory'. This is obviously an incorrect statement as ML 1985 is not an instrument to which countries 'sign' or ratify or accede to.

[20] Citing *In the Matter to Declare in Contempt of Court Hon. Simeon A. Datumanong, Secretary of DPWH*, G.R. No. 150274, 4 August 2006; citing *Calacala* v. *Republic*, G.R. No. 154415, 28 July 2005.

Article 8 of the ML 1985, which mandates a court to refer the parties to arbitration with respect to a dispute within the scope of a valid arbitration agreement, is slightly modified by the ADR Act. Section 24 of the ADR Act localizes the procedure for a party to request referral by requiring that this be done no later than the pre-trial conference. The pre-trial conference is a distinct stage in the litigation process and occurs after the initial pleadings are filed, signalling the joinder of issues. Once the issues are joined, the plaintiff or the court sets the case for pre-trial where the parties may enter into a stipulation of facts, manifest availment of discovery proceedings, declare witnesses, the substance of their testimony and other related incidents. Pre-trial is also the stage where the possibility of amicable settlement is explored between the parties.

The decisions of the Philippine Supreme Court that are relevant to article 8 of the ML 1985 do not refer to or cite article 8 but the basis or *ratio* of the decisions are on principles that are consistent with article 8.[21] In *Fiesta World Mall Corp* v. *Linberg Philippines*,[22] the Supreme Court directed the suspension of court proceedings commenced by Linberg and directed the parties to submit their dispute to arbitration in accordance with the arbitration clause in the contract. The Supreme Court held that the arbitration agreement is 'the law between the parties', and since the arbitration agreement is binding, 'the parties are expected to abide by it in good faith.'[23] The Court found that the dispute between the parties is one that is covered by the scope of the arbitration agreement, hence upheld the right of Fiesta World to demand recourse to arbitration. The Court rejected the argument of Linberg that a separate clause of the contract referring to disputes arising from the agreement to be resolved by court action applied. The Court effectively ruled that the applicable provision is the arbitration clause which provided for reference to arbitration for a specific type of dispute, i.e., payment disputes, and since the dispute fell within the scope of the arbitration clause, the arbitration clause should prevail.

In another and more recent case of *Gilat Satellite Networks Ltd* v. *United Coconut Planters Bank General Insurance Co. Inc.* [*Gilat*],[24] the Supreme Court refused the request for referral to arbitration on the

---

[21] In *Korea Tech*, section 24 of the ADR Act is mentioned by way of *obiter* as one of the 'pertinent features of the (ADR Act) applying and incorporating the (ML 1985)'.

[22] G.R. No. 152471, 18 August 2006.

[23] See art. 1159 of the Civil Code of the Philippines, Republic Act No. 386, 18 June 1949.

[24] G.R. No. 189563, 7 April 2014.

basis that the party requesting the referral is not a party to the arbitration agreement. The Supreme Court expressly referred to section 24 of the ADR Act and held that the 'party' being referred to in section 24 of the ADR Act (and effectively article 8 of the ML 1985) is the party to the arbitration agreement. A non-party to an arbitration agreement is not entitled to the remedy of seeking prior recourse to arbitration. In *Gilat*, a company called One Virtual placed an order with Gilat Satellite Networks Ltd for the purchase of various telecommunications equipment and accessories. To secure the payment by One Virtual, respondent United Coconut Planters Bank (UCPB) issued a surety bond in favour of Gilat. One Virtual failed to pay certain instalment payments prompting Gilat to sue UCPB as surety. UCPB argued that the dispute must be referred to arbitration on the basis of the arbitration clause in the purchase agreement between Gilat and One Virtual. There is no arbitration clause in the contract of suretyship between Gilat and UCPB. The Supreme Court rejected UCPB's argument and went into an analysis of the liability of a surety vis-à-vis the principal obligor and the ancillary contract of suretyship. In reference to UCPB's ability to demand referral to arbitration, the Court recognized that UCPB was not a party to the arbitration agreement, and neither Gilat nor One Virtual demanded any referral to arbitration, hence UCPB is not entitled to demand referral of the dispute to arbitration.

The clearest expression of curial support in favour of mandatory referral of matters to arbitration is r. 2.2(A) of the Special ADR Rules:

> Rule 2.2. *Policy on arbitration.* – (A) Where the parties have agreed to submit their dispute to arbitration, courts shall refer the parties to arbitration pursuant to Republic Act No. 9285 bearing in mind that such arbitration agreement is the law between the parties and that they are expected to abide by it in good faith. Further, the courts shall not refuse to refer parties to arbitration for reasons including, but not limited to, the following:
>
> a. The referral tends to oust a court of its jurisdiction;
> b. The court is in a better position to resolve the dispute subject of arbitration;
> c. The referral would result in multiplicity of suits;
> d. The arbitration proceeding has not commenced;
> e. The place of arbitration is in a foreign country;
> f. One or more of the issues are legal and one or more of the arbitrators are not lawyers;
> g. One or more of the arbitrators are not Philippine nationals; or
> h. One or more of the arbitrators are alleged not to possess the required qualification under the arbitration agreement or law.

The above policy is a definitive rejection of previous rulings of the Supreme Court on arbitration (almost all of which were issued prior to the entry into force of the ADR Act) declaring an arbitration agreement invalid on one or more of the reasons enumerated above. This provision and the decisions of the Supreme Court after the passage of the ADR Act are a clear signal to the Philippine courts of a shift in treatment and outlook on arbitration agreements and arbitral processes.

Article 9 of the ML 1985 refers to the power of the court to issue interim measures of protection despite the existence of an arbitration agreement. This is not modified by the ADR Act. The power of the court to grant interim measures of protection in support of arbitration is given further detail and colour in section 28 of the ADR Act:

> Section 28. *Grant of Interim Measure of Protection.* –
>
> (a) It is not incompatible with an arbitration agreement for a party to request, before constitution of the tribunal, from a Court an interim measure of protection and for the Court to grant such measure. After constitution of the arbitral tribunal and during arbitral proceedings, a request for an interim measure of protection, or modification thereof, may be made with the arbitral tribunal or to the extent that the arbitral tribunal has no power to act or is unable to act effectively, the request may be made with the Court. The arbitral tribunal is deemed constituted when the sole arbitrator or the third arbitrator, who has been nominated, has accepted the nomination and written communication of said nomination and acceptance has been received by the party making the request.
>
> (b) The following rules on interim or provisional relief shall be observed:
>
> (1) Any party may request that provisional relief be granted against the adverse party.
> (2) Such relief may be granted:
>   (i)   to prevent irreparable loss or injury;
>   (ii) to provide security for the performance of any obligation;
>   (iii) to produce or preserve any evidence; or
>   (iv) to compel any other appropriate act or omission.
> (3) The order granting provisional relief may be conditioned upon the provision of security or any act or omission specified in the order.
> (4) Interim or provisional relief is requested by written application transmitted by reasonable means to the Court or arbitral tribunal as the case may be and the party against whom the relief is sought, describing in appropriate detail the precise relief, the party against whom the relief is requested, the grounds for the relief, and the evidence supporting the request.
> (5) The order shall be binding upon the parties.

(6) Either party may apply with the Court for assistance in implementing or enforcing an interim measure ordered by an arbitral tribunal.

(7) A party who does not comply with the order shall be liable for all damages resulting from noncompliance, including all expenses, and reasonable attorney's fees, paid in obtaining the order's judicial enforcement.

Section 28 of the ADR Act states when interim relief may be requested before the court or the arbitral tribunal, the grounds by which interim relief may be issued by the court, the procedure for filing the application in court or the arbitral tribunal (as the case may be) and the consequences of non-compliance with an order granting interim protection. Section 28 expressly states that an interim measure of protection issued by the arbitral tribunal may be enforced by the court. Section 28 also states that an interim measure of protection issued by the court before the constitution of the arbitral tribunal may be modified by the arbitral tribunal upon its constitution.[25] It is also clear in section 28 that despite the constitution of the arbitral tribunal, a party may request the court for interim relief 'to the extent that the arbitral tribunal has no power to act or is unable to act effectively'.

Section 28 of the ADR Act is an important provision of the law and displays a clear pro-arbitration policy. A party is given a broad range of remedies for the application of interim relief and the court is given express powers to support the arbitral process. In addition, the law gives muscle to the enforcement of interim measures in support of arbitration as mandatory penalties for non-compliance are expressly provided by law.

The decisions of the Supreme Court on this topic do not discuss any direct interpretation or application of section 28 of the ADR Act or article 9 of the ML 1985 but simply affirm that these remedies are available and recognized. In *Korea Tech*, the petitioner KOGIES also filed with the court an application for the issuance of a restraining order to prevent PGSMC from dismantling and transferring the equipment and accessories supplied and installed by KOGIES in the manufacturing plant of PGSMC. While the trial court denied the restraining order, which denial was upheld by the Supreme Court, the Supreme Court affirmed the power of the trial court to hear and determine applications

---

[25] Section 28 provides in part: 'After constitution of the arbitral tribunal and during arbitral proceedings, a request for an interim measure of protection, or modification thereof, may be made with the arbitral tribunal . . .' (emphasis added).

218 RENA M. RICO-PAMFILO

for interim relief in support of arbitration, citing section 28 of the ADR
Act. While the restraining order applied for by KOGIES before the trial
court was technically not an interim measure of protection in support of
an arbitration proceeding as KOGIES had also initiated an action before
the court for specific performance against PGSMC, the Supreme Court
noted the trial court's jurisdiction to hear the petition for a restraining
order on the basis of section 28 of the ADR Act.[26]

In the case of *Transfield Philippines, Inc.* v. *Luzon Hydro Corporation, et al.*[27] one of the issues addressed by the Supreme Court was
whether petitioner Transfield was guilty of forum shopping for filing
various cases in the Philippine courts in relation to a pending arbitration seated in Australia. One of the cases filed was a petition for the
issuance of an injunction preventing certain banks from releasing
monies or proceeds held as security in favour of Luzon Hydro. The
Supreme Court held that there was no forum shopping with respect to
the petition for injunction as there was no identity of parties (Transfield
having also impleaded the banks which granted security in favour of
Luzon Hydro) and that, in any event, section 28 of the ADR Act
expressly recognizes the ability of a party to seek relief from the courts
in relation to an arbitration proceeding during the pendency of such
arbitral proceeding.

With respect to the issuance of interim relief prior to the constitution of the arbitral tribunal, in *Department of Foreign Affairs and
Bangko Sentral ng Pilipinas* v. *Falcon and BCA International Corporation,*[28] the Supreme Court affirmed the power of the trial court to
issue a writ of injunction, in support of arbitration proceedings
filed by BCA against the Department of Foreign Affairs with the
Philippine Dispute Resolution Center, Inc. prior to the constitution
of the tribunal, citing section 28 of the ADR Act. The Supreme Court
held, however, that section 28 of the ADR Act should give way to
special laws such as Republic Act No. 8975,[29] which prohibits the

---

[26] Note that *Korea Tech* also cited Articles 17 and 17J of the 2006 version of ML 1985 as the basis to affirm the trial court's jurisdiction to hear the interim relief application which were not adopted in the Philippines.

[27] G.R. No. 146717, 19 May 2006.   [28] G.R. No. 176657, 1 September 2010.

[29] Republic Act No. 8975 is entitled, 'An Act to Ensure the Expeditious Implementation and Completion of Government Infrastructure Projects by Prohibiting Lower Courts from Issuing Temporary Restraining Orders, Preliminary Injunctions or Preliminary Mandatory Injunctions, Providing Penalties for Violations Thereof, and for Other Purposes', 7 November 2000.

courts, except the Supreme Court, from issuing injunctions in cases involving national government projects. This notwithstanding, the Supreme Court held that in this case the trial court had jurisdiction to issue interim relief and found that Republic Act No. 8975 is inoperative as petitioners failed to prove that the e-Passport Project is a national government project as defined therein. The Supreme Court ultimately denied the application for injunction for lack of factual basis.

Part III   Composition of Arbitral Tribunal (Articles 10 to 15)

Articles 10 to 15 of the ML 1985 on the arbitral tribunal are generally procedural in nature. These provisions are adopted and not modified by the ADR Act. The default number of arbitrators for an ad hoc arbitration seated in the Philippines is three. The PDRC amended its arbitration rules and with respect to the appointment of arbitrators the rules appear to follow the model/structure of the International Chamber of Commerce International Court of Arbitration or the Singapore International Arbitration Centre requiring confirmation of the appointment of arbitrators and providing for the appointment of arbitrators in a multi-party arbitration. With respect to the number of arbitrators, where there is no agreement between the parties, the Arbitration Rules of the PDRC (PDRC Rules) provide that the PDRC will determine the number of arbitrators to be appointed, taking into account the circumstances of the case.[30]

The procedure for the appointment of a sole arbitrator or a three-member tribunal is provided in article 11 of the ML 1985 and reflects general practice. As stated above, in ad hoc arbitration, the default appointing authority under the ADR Act is the National President of the Integrated Bar of the Philippines. In the event that the National President of the Integrated Bar of the Philippines is required to act, a party must submit a written request. In the event that the National President of the Integrated Bar of the Philippines fails or refuses to act within thirty days from receipt of the request, a party may request the Regional Trial Court to make the appointment.

Rule 6 of the Special ADR Rules governs the appointment by the court of an arbitrator under the specific circumstances allowed by the ADR Act. The Special ADR Rules further provide that appointment of

---

[30] PDRC Rules, art. 11.

arbitrators by the court shall be a summary proceeding where the court is directed to set the hearing on the petition no later than five days from the lapse of the period for filing a comment to the petition.[31] The hearing shall be one day only and for the purpose of clarifying facts. The petition shall be decided within thirty days from the day of hearing. While the Special ADR Rules provide a summary procedure, it may take more than one month for an appointment of an arbitrator to take place and allows the opposing party to comment on the application. In the event that the court grants the petition and appoints an arbitrator, such decision is immediately executory and will not be subject of any motion for reconsideration, appeal or certiorari.[32] If the court denies the petition to appoint, a motion for reconsideration, appeal or certiorari may be filed.

The PDRC Rules provide that for multi-party arbitration, where there are multiple parties as claimants or respondents, the multiple claimants or the multiple respondents shall jointly appoint the arbitrator.[33] Article 11 of the ML 1985 also provides that an appointment made by the default appointing authority stated in the law is final and is not subject to appeal. A party that objects to the appointment of an arbitrator by the appointing authority will have the remedy of challenge under articles 12 and 13 of the ML 1985.

The duty of the arbitrator to disclose any fact or information that would give rise to justifiable doubts as to his impartiality or independence is stated in article 12 of the ML 1985. Article 12 also clarifies that such duty exists at the time the arbitrator is approached for a possible appointment and throughout the arbitral proceedings. The grounds to challenge an arbitrator are also expressly provided. Where a challenge is brought against an arbitrator, the tribunal shall decide on the challenge. If the challenge is unsuccessful, under the ADR Act, the party may request the National President of the Integrated Bar of the Philippines to decide on the challenge, which decision shall not be subject to appeal.[34] While such challenge is pending, the arbitral tribunal may continue the arbitration proceedings and render an award. Section 27 of the ADR Act provides that in the event that the National President of the Integrated Bar of the Philippines fails or refuses to act on the challenge within thirty days, the party may renew its challenge before the Regional Trial Court.

---

[31] Special ADR Rules, r. 1.3.   [32] Special ADR Rules, r. 6.9.   [33] PDRC Rules, art. 14.
[34] ADR Act, sections 26 and 27.

Rule 7 of the Special ADR Rules states the process for the filing of a petition to challenge the appointment of an arbitrator before the court, the contents of the petition, the grounds upon which the challenge is based and the bases for court action. Rule 7.9 expressly allows the court to grant the arbitrator reasonable compensation and reimbursement of reasonable expenses incurred prior to the grant of the challenge, where there is no bad faith on the part of the arbitrator, which amount shall be paid by the party challenging the appointment. This is a unique provision and deviates from general practice, whether in ad hoc or institutional arbitration, where the fees of the arbitrator are generally split between the parties, subject to the award on costs at the end of the proceedings.

Article 14 of the ML 1985 sets out the instances when the mandate of the arbitrator is considered terminated. Any issue with respect to the termination of the mandate of the arbitrator shall, for ad hoc arbitration under the ADR Act, be decided by the National President of the Integrated Bar of the Philippines or in the event of his failure or refusal to act within thirty days, by the court. Rule 8 of the Special ADR Rules governs the process for a petition for the termination of the mandate of an arbitrator before the court. The Special ADR Rules consider such a petition to be summary in nature, hence the shortened period for a response, hearing and resolution apply.[35] Any order of the court on the petition, whether granting or denying the petition, is immediately executory and shall not be subject to reconsideration, appeal or certiorari.[36]

Where the appointment of a substitute arbitrator is required, due to resignation, withdrawal, successful challenge or termination of mandate, article 15 of the ML 1985 provides that the appointment of the replacement arbitrator shall be in accordance with the rules or procedures applicable to the appointment of the arbitrator being replaced. This is also not changed in the ADR Act.

Part IV   Jurisdiction of Arbitral Tribunal (Article 16)

Article 16 is an important provision of the ML 1985 and can be said to be the 'heart' of international arbitration. This is not modified by the ADR Act. The ability of the arbitral tribunal to rule on its own jurisdiction despite any allegation that the contract containing the arbitration agreement is null and void *ab initio* and the corollary principle of separability

---

[35] Special ADR Rules, r. 1.3.   [36] Special ADR Rules, r. 8.7.

of the arbitration clause from the contract which it forms part are the primary pillars in the international arbitral process. This provision is not changed in the ADR Act. The case of *Jorge Gonzales and Panel of Arbitrators* v. *Climax Mining Ltd, et al.* [*Gonzales*][37] involves a domestic arbitration proceeding. However, the Supreme Court cited Article 16(1) of the ML 1985 to affirm the applicability of the principle of separability and the power of the tribunal to determine the issue of whether the contract containing the arbitration agreement is null and void. The case involves a contract between Filipino parties containing an arbitration clause. Petitioner Jorge Gonzales filed an action before the trial court alleging that the contract is null and void. Climax, on the other hand, petitioned the court to direct the parties to arbitration pursuant to the arbitration clause in the contract. Petitioner argued that since the contract is null and void the arbitration clause is necessarily void and the court has no basis to refer the parties to arbitration. The Supreme Court upheld the referral of the parties to arbitration. While this involves a purely domestic arbitration, hence ML 1985 should not apply, the Supreme Court cited article 16(1) of the ML 1985 to affirm the applicability of the doctrine of separability in Philippine law. Under Republic Act No. 876, which was in effect even prior to the ADR Act, for domestic arbitration proceedings, the rule is that a court is mandated to direct the parties to arbitration where it finds that an arbitration agreement exists between the parties.[38] The Supreme Court held that any allegation on the validity of the agreement is for the arbitral tribunal to determine. The Court also cited the US case of *Prima Paint Corp.* v. *Flood & Conklin Manufacturing Co.* [*Prima Paint*].[39] *Prima Paint* involved an allegation of fraudulent inducement in the execution of a consulting contract containing an arbitration clause. The US court directed the parties to arbitration despite the allegation of fraud in the contract by Prima Paint on the basis that Prima Paint's allegations of fraud are not directed to the arbitration agreement itself but on the consulting agreement which contains the arbitration clause. The citation of *Prima Paint* appears odd as the factual circumstances are not directly on point in the issue before the Supreme Court in *Gonzales*. Nevertheless, the principle in *Prima Paint* which upholds the validity of the arbitration agreement and directs parties to comply with such agreement despite an allegation of invalidity or fraud in the commercial contract containing such clause applies.

---

[37] G.R. Nos. 161957 and 167994, 22 January 2007.   [38] Republic Act No. 876, section 6.
[39] 388 US 395, 87 S. Ct. 1801, 18 L. Ed. 2d 1270 (1967).

The ruling of the Supreme Court in *Gonzales* regarding the separability of the arbitration agreement was cited and affirmed in the later case of *Cargill Philippines, Inc.* v. *San Fernando Regala Trading, Inc.*[40] In this case, San Fernando Regala Trading, Inc. [Regala] filed a complaint before the Regional Trial Court for rescission of contract with damages alleging that Cargill Philippines, Inc. [CPI] failed to deliver molasses as agreed. CPI filed a Motion to Dismiss/Suspend Proceedings on the basis of an arbitration clause contained in a contract between the parties referring disputes to arbitration in New York under the arbitration rules of the American Arbitration Association. CPI also alleged that there was no binding agreement for CPI to supply molasses because Regala did not sign the contract nor did Regala open a letter of credit. The Regional Trial Court denied the Motion to Dismiss/Suspend Proceedings stating that the arbitration clause in question had no basis under Republic Act No. 876 or the law governing domestic arbitrations. CPI filed a petition for certiorari before the Court of Appeals. The Court of Appeals rejected the ruling of the Regional Trial Court that the arbitration clause referring the dispute to arbitration in New York under the arbitration rules of the American Arbitration Association is not supported by law. Nevertheless, it affirmed the ruling of the lower court denying the Motion to Dismiss/ Suspend Proceedings. The Court of Appeals held that since CPI alleged as one of its grounds in its Motion to Dismiss/Suspend Proceedings that the contract on which the complaint was based did not exist, it was proper that such issue be resolved by the trial court, being an issue of fact. The Court of Appeals held that arbitration is not proper when one of the parties repudiated the existence or validity of the contract. The Supreme Court rightfully reversed the rulings of the Regional Trial Court and the Court of Appeals. The Supreme Court affirmed that an arbitration clause referring parties to a foreign seat and adopting arbitration rules of a foreign arbitration institution is valid, binding and recognized in the Philippines. The Supreme Court then examined the case of *Jorge Gonzales and Panel of Arbitrators* v. *Climax Mining Ltd, Climax-Arimco Mining Corp., and Australasian Philippines Mining Inc.*[41] cited by the Court of Appeals to support its ruling. The Supreme Court noted that this ruling was modified by the Supreme Court in *Gonzales* on Motion for Reconsideration. The Supreme Court affirmed its ruling in *Gonzales* that 'the validity of the contract containing the arbitration agreement

---

[40] G.R. No. 175404, 31 January 2011.   [41] G.R. No. 161957, 28 February 2005.

does not affect the applicability of the arbitration clause itself and applied the doctrine of separability. The Supreme Court also ruled that even the party who has repudiated the main contract is not prevented from enforcing the arbitration clause.

The principle of *kompetenz-kompetenz/compétence-compétence* and separability are also expressly adopted and explained in the Special ADR Rules using language directly borrowed from article 16(1) of the ML 1985:

> Rule 2.2. *Policy on arbitration.* –
> [. . .]
> The Special ADR Rules recognize the principle of competence-competence, which means that the arbitral tribunal may initially rule on its own jurisdiction, including any objections with respect to the existence or validity of the arbitration agreement or any condition precedent to the filing of a request for arbitration.
> The Special ADR Rules recognize the principle of separability of the arbitration clause, which means that said clause shall be treated as an agreement independent of the other terms of the contract of which it forms part. A decision that the contract is null and void shall not entail ipso jure the invalidity of the arbitration clause.
> Rule 2.4. *Policy implementing competence-competence principle.* – The arbitral tribunal shall be accorded the first opportunity or competence to rule on the issue of whether or not it has the competence or jurisdiction to decide a dispute submitted to it for decision, including any objection with respect to the existence or validity of the arbitration agreement. When a court is asked to rule upon issue/s affecting the competence or jurisdiction of an arbitral tribunal in a dispute brought before it, either before or after the arbitral tribunal is constituted, the court must exercise judicial restraint and defer to the competence or jurisdiction of the arbitral tribunal by allowing the arbitral tribunal the first opportunity to rule upon such issues.
> Where the court is asked to make a determination of whether the arbitration agreement is null and void, inoperative or incapable of being performed, under this policy of judicial restraint, the court must make no more than a prima facie determination of that issue.
> Unless the court, pursuant to such prima facie determination, concludes that the arbitration agreement is null and void, inoperative or incapable of being performed, the court must suspend the action before it and refer the parties to arbitration pursuant to the arbitration agreement.

The statement of policy in the Special ADR Rules is fairly detailed and is meant to guide and educate the judge in making his or her rulings with respect to applications for referral to arbitration or petitions relating to the validity or invalidity of an arbitration agreement.

It is worthwhile to note that Rule 2.4 requires the court to make no more than a prima facie determination of whether the arbitration agreement is null and void, inoperative or incapable of being performed. The court is not required to undertake an in-depth inquiry on the existence or validity of the arbitration agreement, consistent with the principle of *kompetenz-kompetenz/compétence-compétence*. Thus, if on its face, the court is able to determine that an arbitration agreement exists and is valid, the court is required to refer the parties to arbitration. This approach is intended to encourage the courts to take a liberal interpretation of the arbitration agreement. It is only when it is plain on its face that an arbitration agreement does not exist or is invalid or unenforceable will the courts refuse a referral to arbitration.

Rules 3.12 to 3.22 govern the procedure for an application to the court to decide a jurisdictional question where the arbitral tribunal decides this as a preliminary matter, prior to an award on the merits. It is interesting that article 16 of the ML 1985 provides a remedy of recourse to the courts only if the tribunal upholds its jurisdiction.[42] This necessarily implies that if the tribunal rules as a preliminary matter that it has no jurisdiction, there is no recourse to the courts and that is the end of the proceedings. *Expressio unius est exclusio alterius*.[43] However, r. 3.12 of the Special ADR Rules appears to allow recourse to the court even where the tribunal declines jurisdiction:

> Rule 3.12. *Who may file petition*. – Any party to arbitration may petition the appropriate court for judicial relief from the ruling of the arbitral tribunal on a preliminary question <u>upholding or declining its jurisdiction.</u> <u>Should the ruling of the arbitral tribunal declining its jurisdiction be</u> <u>reversed by the court, the parties shall be free to replace the arbitrators</u> <u>or any one of them in accordance with the rules that were applicable for</u> <u>the appointment of arbitrator sought to be replaced.</u> (emphasis added)

The Special ADR Rules go beyond the ability of the court to review a decision of the tribunal declining jurisdiction and provide consequences in the event that the court reverses the decision of the tribunal. The framers of the Special ADR Rules realized that an awkward situation will arise where the arbitrator or tribunal who has declined jurisdiction will be ordered by the court to proceed with the arbitration. The Special ADR Rules therefore allow the parties to replace all or some of the arbitrators in the event that the court orders the arbitration to proceed. This gives

---

[42] ML 1985 art. 16(3).   [43] The expression of one thing is the exclusion of the other.

rise to some uncertainty in the arbitral process as the parties will need to agree on whether all or some of the arbitrators need to be replaced and if not all of the arbitrators will be replaced, who among the arbitrators will be replaced. A party that does not wish to proceed with the arbitration can easily delay the proceedings.

Rule 3.18(B) of the Special ADR Rules clearly provide that the court shall have no power to enjoin the arbitral process while a petition questioning the decision of the tribunal upholding its jurisdiction is pending before the court. In the event that the tribunal renders its award on the merits prior to any decision of the court on the jurisdiction issue, Rule 3.21 of the Special ADR Rules provides that the petition shall become ipso facto moot and academic and shall be dismissed by the court. The dismissal, however, shall be without prejudice to the right of the aggrieved party to raise the same issue in a timely petition to set aside the award. The Special ADR Rules appear to provide a practical solution to the possible conflicting decisions. Given the heavy court dockets that most courts possess, it is not unlikely that a decision by the tribunal on the merits will be issued ahead of a court decision.

Part IV-A   Interim Measures and Preliminary Orders
(Articles 17 to 17J)

Sub-Part I   Measures and Orders by the Tribunal (Articles 17 to 17G)

Sub-Part II   Recognition and Enforcement of Interim Measures (Articles 17H and 17I)

Sub-Part III   Court-Ordered Interim Measures (Article 17J)

It should be restated here that the Philippines did not adopt the extensive provisions of the 2006 version of the ML on interim measures and preliminary orders. Therefore, only article 17 of the ML 1985 was adopted.

Article 17 of the ML 1985 is not significantly changed in the ADR Act. Section 29 of the ADR Act states that the grounds for the grant of an application for interim relief before the court similarly apply to applications for interim relief before the tribunal, effectively specifying by law the grounds upon which an application for interim relief before the tribunal may be granted. Section 29 also provides the specific types of relief that may be granted by the tribunal and that a party may apply to the court for the enforcement of interim relief issued by the tribunal. Such interim measures include, but are not limited to, preliminary injunction directed against a party, appointment of receivers or detention, preservation, inspection of property that is the subject of the dispute in arbitration. Section 29 also expressly states that a party may apply to the court for the enforcement of an interim measure of protection issued by the arbitral tribunal.

Part V Conduct of Arbitral Proceedings (Articles 18 to 27)

The provisions on the conduct of the arbitral process under ML 1985 generally remain unmodified under the ADR Act. The modifications are only meant to localize the application of certain provisions in the Philippines.

Article 18 of the ML 1985 prescribing the equal treatment of parties and the principle of due process is another important provision of the ML 1985 and is not modified under the ADR Act. The power of the parties to determine the rules of procedure, failing which the tribunal may prescribe the rules of procedure, is also not modified under the ADR Act and is reiterated in the Special ADR Rules.[44] With respect to the place of arbitration, the ADR Act provides that in the absence of agreement, the place of arbitration shall be Metro Manila.[45] With respect to the language of the arbitration, the ADR Act provides that in the absence of agreement, the English language shall be used for international arbitration and English or Filipino for domestic arbitration, unless otherwise determined by the arbitral tribunal.[46]

The provisions on the commencement of arbitration, submission of pleadings by the parties, conduct of hearings and reception of evidence are adopted and not modified by the ADR Act. The consequences of failure by a party to submit its statement of claim or statement of defence, as the case may be, or to appear during a hearing without sufficient cause are provided in article 25 of the ML 1985. It is clear under article 25 that failure by the respondent to submit its statement of defence shall not be deemed an admission of the claim. This means that the tribunal is required to apply its independent mind on the facts and evidence before it. A respondent that does not participate in the arbitration proceedings without justification, despite due notice, takes the risk that the arguments and evidence before the tribunal, while not considered admitted, will stand uncontroverted.

---

[44] Special ADR Rules, r. 2.3.   [45] ADR Act, section 30.   [46] ADR Act, section 31.

The process for the appointment of expert witnesses and reception of expert testimony are also adopted and not changed in the ADR Act. With respect to the power of the court to assist in the taking of evidence in relation to an arbitration proceeding, there are specific provisions in the Special ADR Rules. The court can grant the following types of assistance in the taking of evidence:

a. To comply with a subpoena *ad testificandum* and/or subpoena *duces tecum*;
b. To appear as a witness before an officer for the taking of his deposition upon oral examination or by written interrogatories;
c. To allow the physical examination of the condition of persons, or the inspection of things or premises and, when appropriate, to allow the recording and/or documentation of condition of persons, things or premises (i.e., photographs, video and other means of recording/documentation);
d. To allow the examination and copying of documents; and
e. To perform any similar acts.[47]

In addition to the above types of assistance, the Special ADR Rules allow the perpetuation of testimony in accordance with the Rules of Court:

> Rule 9.10. *Perpetuation of testimony before the arbitral tribunal is constituted.* – At any time before arbitration is commenced or before the arbitral tribunal is constituted, any person who desires to perpetuate his testimony or that of another person may do so in accordance with Rule 24 of the Rules of Court.

Perpetuation of testimony is a remedy allowed under Rule 24 of the Rules of Court of the Philippines to preserve the testimony of a witness for future use on a matter that is cognizable by the court. The Special ADR Rules allows the exercise of the same remedy in relation to arbitration proceedings.

The Special ADR Rules provide that an order granting assistance in the taking of evidence shall be immediately executory and not be subject of a motion for reconsideration or appeal.[48] However, an order denying the request for assistance may be subject of a motion for reconsideration or appeal.[49]

---

[47] Special ADR Rules, r. 9.5.   [48] Special ADR Rules, r. 9.9.
[49] Special ADR Rules, r. 9.9.

The Special ADR Rules allow the court to impose 'appropriate sanctions' in the event of disobedience by any person who disobeys an order of the court to testify or perform any act required by the court.[50]

Part VI Making of Award and Termination of Proceedings (Articles 28 to 33)

The provisions of the ML 1985 on the rules governing the substance of the dispute, manner of decision-making by a panel of arbitrators, settlement, form and contents of the award, termination of proceeds and correction of the award are largely uncontroversial and are not modified by the ADR Act.

The PDRC Rules provide that where there is more than one arbitrator, an award shall be made within one year from the constitution of the tribunal and shall be made by a majority of the tribunal. If there is no majority, the award may be made by the Chairman of the tribunal alone.[51]

Part VII Recourse against Award (Article 34)

Article 34 on setting aside of arbitral awards is not changed under the ADR Act. There is no separate rule under the Special ADR Rules which governs procedures purely on setting aside of an arbitral award governed by ML 1985. The Special ADR Rules combine court procedures for setting aside an award and enforcement of an international commercial arbitration award seated in the Philippines in r. 12 of the Special ADR Rules entitled 'Recognition and Enforcement or Setting Aside of an International Commercial Arbitration Award'. A petition for recognition and enforcement of an arbitration award and a petition for setting aside are treated as two sides of the same coin in r. 12, and not as distinct remedies available under ML 1985. Rule 12.2 of the Special ADR Rules provides that a petition for recognition and enforcement of an award issued in an international arbitration proceeding governed by ML 1985 can be filed anytime from receipt of the award. However, in the event that a timely setting aside petition is filed, 'the opposing party must file therein and in

[50] Special ADR Rules, r. 9.11.   [51] PDRC Rules, art. 42(1).

opposition thereto the petition for recognition and enforcement of
the same award within the period for filing an opposition.' Rule 12.2
further provides that in the event that a petition to set aside the award
is not filed within three months from receipt of the award or from
receipt of a decision on a motion to correct or interpret an award or
issue an additional award, a petition to set aside an award shall be
barred and 'shall preclude a party from raising grounds to resist
enforcement of the award'. It is submitted that ML 1985 provides
for two distinct remedies, i.e., set aside an award within the time and
under the grounds provided and recognize and enforce an award. The
treatment of r. 12 of the ADR Rules of one remedy being a corollary
of the other is inconsistent with ML 1985. Rule 12 denies a winning
party in an arbitration proceeding, for strategic or practical reasons,
not to initiate enforcement proceedings in the Philippines and simply
oppose an application to set aside. Instead, r. 12 requires the winning
party to oppose a petition to set aside by petitioning the court to
recognize and enforce the award. Moreover, r. 12 denies the losing
party the option (possibly for strategic or practical reasons) not to
initiate any petition for setting aside an award and instead legitim-
ately oppose any application to enforce an arbitration award. Under
r. 12, if a party fails to file a petition to set aside an award within the
period prescribed, it is precluded from opposing an application to
enforce the award.

Rule 12.5 of the Special ADR Rules makes clear that setting aside
an award is the only recourse against an award issued in international
arbitration proceedings under ML 1985 and only under the grounds
specified under ML 1985. This is an important provision that prevents any other remedy from being entertained by the court. Rule
12.12 also expressly provides a presumption in favour of enforcement
of the award unless any ground to set aside or refusal to enforce is
established.

Judicial Commentary on Setting Aside of an Arbitral Award

As mentioned at the beginning of this chapter, *Korea Tech*, while
providing a definitive pronouncement of the validity and enforceability of an international arbitration agreement and express judicial
recognition to the adoption and applicability of the ML 1985 through
the ADR Act, the case also provides doubtful and disturbing

pronouncements with respect to the role of Philippine courts in the setting aside and enforcement of a foreign arbitral award. Although arguably *obiter*, the Supreme Court seems to suggest that an arbitral award rendered in an arbitration with a seat outside of the Philippines is subject to 'judicial review' by Philippine courts. The Court stated:[52]

> Sec. 42 in relation to Sec. 45 of RA 9285 designated and vested the [Regional Trial Court] with specific authority and jurisdiction to set aside, reject, or vacate a foreign arbitral award on grounds provided under Art. 34 (2) of the UNCITRAL Model Law.
>
> [...]
>
> Thus, while the RTC does not have jurisdiction over disputes governed by arbitration mutually agreed upon by the parties, still the foreign arbitral award is subject to judicial review by the RTC which can set aside, reject, or vacate it. In this sense, what this Court held in Chung Fu Industries (Phils.), Inc. relied upon by KOGIES is applicable insofar as the foreign arbitral awards, while final and binding, do not oust courts of jurisdiction since these arbitral awards are not absolute and without exceptions as they are still judicially reviewable. Chapter 7 of RA 9285 has made it clear that all arbitral awards, whether domestic or foreign, are subject to judicial review on specific grounds provided for.

Recall that in *Korea Tech* the arbitration clause provided a seat of arbitration in Korea. The above paragraph is disturbing as it declares that a foreign arbitral award is subject to 'judicial review' and may be interpreted to include the ability by a Philippine court to set aside a foreign arbitral award. This interpretation is incorrect and is not supported by the law. There is nothing in ML 1985, Chapter 7 of the ADR Act or any part of the ADR Act which suggests that a foreign arbitral award may be set aside by a Philippine Court. Rule 12.1 of the Special ADR Rules, adopted after *Korea Tech*, however, makes clear that a petition to set aside an award may be filed only by a party to an international arbitration seated in the Philippines:

> Rule 12.1. *Who may request recognition and enforcement or setting aside.* – Any party to an international commercial arbitration in the Philippines may petition the proper court to recognize and enforce or set aside an arbitral award.

[52] 542 SCRA 1, 28–29.

It may be argued that the pronouncement of the Court in *Korea Tech* regarding remedies that a party may have upon issuance of the award is *obiter* as the issue before the Court was the enforceability of the arbitration agreement and the application for interim relief by KOGIES. The arbitration proceeding in Korea was pending and was not resolved at that time and no issue with respect to the arbitral award was submitted to the Court for resolution. The author is not aware of any subsequent Supreme Court decision which affirms this pronouncement in *Korea Tech*. It is also unclear whether Rule 12.1 of the Special ADR Rules 'neutralizes' the pronouncement in *Korea Tech* and will be considered as the prevailing or correct rule. This uncertainty can hopefully be settled in a subsequent decision of the Supreme Court categorically affirming r. 12.1 of the Special ADR Rules.

Part VIII   Recognition and Enforcement of Awards
(Articles 35 and 36)

The provisions on recognition and enforcement of an award under ML 1985 are adopted and not modified under the ADR Act. The Philippines is also a signatory to the Convention on the Recognition and Enforcement of Foreign Arbitral Awards, New York, 10 June 1958, in force 7 June 1959, 330 UNTS 4739 ('NYC'). The Philippines acceded to the NYC on 6 July 1967 and it entered into force in the Philippines on 4 October 1967.[53] While the Philippines was one of the first countries in Asia to accede to the NYC, it was only in 2004 under the provisions of the ADR Act that specific legislation on the NYC was enacted. Section 42 of the ADR Act states that the NYC shall govern the recognition and enforcement of awards covered by the NYC. The procedure for enforcement of arbitral awards that are not covered by the NYC shall be governed by the rules of procedure enacted by the Supreme Court of the Philippines. The court may, on grounds of comity and reciprocity, recognize and enforce a non-NYC award as a NYC award.[54]

---

[53] The Philippines adopted reservations on applying the Convention only to awards rendered in contracting states and that the Philippines will only apply the Convention to differences arising out of legal relationships, whether contractual or not, that are considered commercial under national law.

[54] ADR Act, section 43.

Thus, while the language of articles 35 and 36 of the ML 1985 covers foreign awards and not just international arbitration awards rendered in the Philippines and considering that under section 42 of the ADR Act the NYC applies to foreign arbitral awards, it is submitted that to reconcile these laws, articles 35 and 36 would govern the recognition and enforcement of international arbitration awards seated in the Philippines. While not expressly stated, this appears to be the treatment under the Special ADR Rules, specifically under r. 12. It would be interesting to see how the Supreme Court will interpret and view the enforcement of international arbitration awards seated in the Philippines and whether the Supreme Court will adopt a pro-enforcement policy that is consistent with the NYC.

The recognition and enforcement of a foreign arbitral award is separately dealt with in the Special ADR Rules under r. 13, with the NYC as its statutory basis. Rule 13.12 repeats the provisions of the ADR Act on the enforcement of non-NYC award, and adds that in the event that the country of the seat of arbitration does not extend comity or reciprocity to awards made in the Philippines the court 'may nevertheless treat such award as a foreign judgment enforceable as such under Rule 39, Section 48, of the Rules of Court'.

With respect to the enforcement of foreign arbitral awards, one case worth mentioning is *Tuna Processing, Inc.* v. *Philippine Kingford, Inc.*[55] [*Tuna Processing*]. In that case, an arbitration award was issued in favour of petitioner Tuna Processing, Inc. (TPI) a company based in California, USA in an arbitration proceeding between Tuna Processing and Philippine Kingford, Inc., a Philippine corporation. The arbitration was seated in California, USA. TPI applied for the enforcement of the arbitral award before the Regional Trial Court of Makati City pursuant to the NYC. The trial court dismissed the petition on the basis of a provision in the Corporation Code of the Philippines which prohibits foreign corporations doing business in the Philippines without a licence from commencing any suit, action or proceeding before any Philippine court or agency. The court, having found that TPI is a foreign corporation doing business in the Philippines without the requisite licence, denied the petition for enforcement of the arbitral award. On appeal, the Supreme Court reversed the ruling of the

[55] G.R. No. 185582, 29 February 2012.

trial court and held that the specific provisions of the NYC on the enforcement of foreign arbitral awards prevail over the general provisions of the Corporation Code. The Supreme Court cited the ADR Act as having specifically 'incorporated' the NYC as the law governing the enforcement of foreign arbitral awards and held that a foreign arbitral award can be refused enforcement only on the grounds specified by the NYC. Considering that the absence of a licence to do business in the Philippines is not one of the grounds to refuse enforcement, and no other ground under the NYC has been established, the Supreme Court ruled that the award must be enforced. The Supreme Court stated:

> Indeed, it is in the best interest of justice that in the enforcement of a foreign arbitral award, we deny availment by the losing party of the rule that bars foreign corporations not licensed to do business in the Philippines from maintaining a suit in our courts. When a party enters into a contract containing a foreign arbitration clause and, as in this case, in fact submits itself to arbitration, it becomes bound by the contract, by the arbitration and by the result of arbitration, conceding thereby the capacity of the other party to enter into the contract, participate in the arbitration and cause the implementation of the result.

While the case does not directly discuss any provision of the ML 1985,[56] the ruling of the Supreme Court in *Tuna Processing* is a clear signal from the Court of its support for international arbitration. *Tuna Processing* effectively creates an exception from the express prohibition in the Corporation Code on foreign corporations doing business in the Philippines without the required licence from maintaining or intervening in any action or proceeding before any court or agency in the Philippines.

Tuna Processing is also a clear indication that the Supreme Court recognizes the ADR Act as *lex specialis* or a special law governing a specific subject matter, such that the special law shall take precedence over a general law. While *Tuna Processing* primarily dealt with the NYC, it is believed that this interpretation should extend to the ADR Act considering that the ADR Act is the comprehensive body of law on

---

[56] The case mentions Article 36 of ML 1985 and states that the grounds to refuse enforcement of an arbitral award under Article 36 are substantially the same as in Article V of the NYC. The statements of the Court on Article 36 are *obiter* as the award being enforced is a foreign arbitral award and NYC should apply.

alternative dispute resolution. It can be argued that the ADR Act, as *lex specialis*, should govern and prevail in the interpretation of international arbitration matters, in the event of any inconsistency with any other general law.

The ruling of the Supreme Court in *Tuna Processing* is a clear signal of a pro-arbitration and pro-enforcement stand of the Court. It is a good precedent that will hopefully steer the Court towards a pro-enforcement attitude even with respect to awards issued pursuant to international arbitration proceedings seated in the Philippines.

Conclusion

As seen from the above discussion, the Philippines has closely adopted the provisions of the ML 1985. The changes or modifications to ML 1985 introduced in the ADR Act are either required modifications or meant to localize certain provisions, e.g., designating an appointing authority or court required to act, place of arbitration, language, or add implementing details to the provisions of the ML 1985 to strengthen enforcement, e.g., interim measures of protection. The ADR Act provides a solid framework for the growth and development of alternative modes of dispute resolution in the Philippines, particularly international commercial arbitration.

Based on the survey of jurisprudence on the application of the ML 1985 and the Special ADR Rules, Philippine courts are generally supportive of international arbitration. There is a general expectation that Philippine courts will continue to support and look favourably towards international arbitration and other modes of dispute resolution as an effective approach to achieving speedy and impartial justice and to unclog heavily burdened court dockets. More importantly, the outlook is hopeful that Philippine courts will continue to apply and interpret the provisions of the ML 1985 and the NYC in a manner that is consistent with the international decisions and accepted principles in international arbitration.

As mentioned above, while the Philippines has not adopted the 2006 version of the ML 1985 which contains, under Article 2A, a rule of interpretation where due regard is given to the international origin of the ML 1985 and the general principles upon which it is based, the ADR Act in 2004 already provided a similar rule of interpretation. However, as can be seen from the cases discussed, despite the clear proscription of the law, the Supreme Court rarely looks to foreign cases as guides to interpretation or application of the ML 1985 or of the ADR Act. This can be explained by the historical or traditional tendency of the Supreme Court to look to local precedents as a basis for interpretation or application of the law rather than foreign precedents. Generally, it is only in the absence of local precedent, possibly due to the novelty of the issue or circumstances, that the court will be looking to foreign precedents. Given that there are only a few cases decided by the court on international arbitration, and as international arbitration gains momentum in the Philippines, it is likely that more sophisticated issues will be brought before the court which will lead the court to refer to foreign precedents or commentaries on international best practices. This situation is in fact expressly encouraged and directed by section 20 of the ADR Act.

As seen from the above discussion, there are a number of areas for improvement with respect to court interpretation and implementation of the ML 1985. The ADR Act provides a good framework from which a pro-arbitration policy can be built. The Special ADR Rules correctly echo and emphasize the important international arbitration principles that should guide the courts in the exercise of their discretion in relation to curial support for arbitration proceedings. While the Special ADR Rules and jurisprudence, as seen from the above discussion, may not be completely consistent with ML 1985 in certain areas, it is hoped that as the number of arbitration matters increase and more awareness of best practices in international arbitration is developed in the bench and bar, the court will be steered towards interpreting ML 1985 and the ADR Act in a manner that is consistent with, and reflective of, the pro-arbitration policy in the law. The development of confidence by the international community in the Philippines in dispute resolution matters, specifically in international arbitration, will depend not just on the laws and rules which the Philippines adopts, but the attitude and approach which the Philippine courts take in these matters. The challenge is not just with the courts but is also on the international arbitration practitioners to educate themselves on best practices in international arbitration and correctly advocate these principles. While the ADR Act has been in effect in the Philippines for more than ten years, because of the small number of arbitration cases, particularly in international arbitration, the development of the law on arbitration is still very much in its infancy. Nevertheless, the attitude in the Philippines towards international arbitration has been generally positive and the road ahead appears to be optimistic that the courts will continue to adopt an approach and interpretation that is consistent with ML 1985 and international best practices.

Singapore

Singapore's Implementation of the Model Law: If at First You Don't Succeed . . .

GARY F. BELL

Introduction

Singapore is a Model Law country, but in this introduction, before going into the details, it is worth mentioning that, first, the way in which the Model Law was adopted and amended in Singapore's legislation can be a bit confusing and, second, Singapore Courts in the past have radically departed from the internationally accepted interpretation of the Model Law, only to be corrected by the Legislature. Luckily, the Courts are now much better at interpreting the Model Law (though not perfect – who is?).

The Model Law as Adopted by Singapore

As I have mentioned elsewhere:[1]

> Singapore being a former British colony, it is not surprising that until 1995 its arbitration law was similar in principles to the English arbitration

Gary F. Bell is an associate professor at the National University of Singapore. I want to express my thanks to my research assistant, Mr Toh Cher Han for his invaluable help in preparing this chapter. Special thanks to the EW Barker Centre for Law & Business at the Faculty of Law of the National University of Singapore for financing my participation in the conference entitled, 'The UNCITRAL Model Law on International Commercial Arbitration in Asia', which led to this book.
[1] Gary F. Bell, 'Singapore's Arbitration Laws', in Eric E. Bergsten, *International Commercial Arbitration* (Oxford University Press, 2012–2014) ('Bell/Oxford'). Some parts of this chapter will resemble the chapter published in *International Commercial Arbitration*. This is unavoidable as I am commenting on the same provisions and the law has not changed much since that earlier publication and my views have also not changed much. I have, however, updated the law when necessary and have reorganized the presentation to follow closely the organization of the ML.

law. In the mid-nineties as England decided not to adopt the *UNCITRAL Model Arbitration Law of 1985*[2] (hereinafter 'ML') in its reform of its arbitration law,[3] Singapore decided to largely abandon the English model and adopt the ML for international arbitrations in 1994 through its *International Arbitration Act* (hereinafter 'IAA').[4] It was decided that if Singapore were to become a leading arbitration hub in Asia, it could ill-afford to resist the international uniformisation the ML offered, especially since the ML was likely to become a model in Asia. The adoption of the ML would allow Singapore to adopt international best practices which would be familiar to both civil law and common law jurisdictions in Asia and beyond.[5]

For domestic arbitrations, however, Singapore has decided to keep its old English-inspired law.[6] That law was reformed in 2002 by the adoption of the new Arbitration Act (AA).[7] The AA does not implement the ML. I will, in this chapter only consider the International Arbitration Act (IAA) implementing the ML and will not account for the domestic AA, although parties to an international arbitration could in fact opt for the latter.[8]

---

[2] UN Document A/40/17, annex 1, available at www.uncitral.org/pdf/english/texts/arbitra tion/ml-arb/06-54671_Ebook.pdf.

[3] See the English Arbitration Act 1996, 1996 c. 23.

[4] International Arbitration Act, c. 143A, rev. S. Sing. ('IAA').

[5] 'The step of incorporating the Model Law as part of Singapore law is one which takes the country further along the road toward becoming an international arbitration centre. The adoption of a regime (albeit with modifications) which has been accepted in several other jurisdictions signals a desire to belong to a community which adopts a uniform, neutral standard for the governing of international arbitrations. Foreign investors in these jurisdictions can now be advised that the international arbitration system in Singapore is patterned after the same model as their own. This familiarity, it is hoped, will create a greater willingness to have international commercial disputes conducted in Singapore.' Hsu Locknie, 'The Adoption of the UNCITRAL Model Law on International Commercial Arbitration in Singapore' [1994] *Sing. J. Legal Stud.* 387 at 391–92.

[6] See section 5(1) of the International Arbitration Act, c. 143A, rev. S. Sing.

[7] C. 10, rev. S. Sing., originally enacted in 2001 and in force in 2002.

[8] See section 15(1) IAA: 'If the parties to an arbitration agreement (whether made before or after 1st November 2001*) have expressly agreed either –

(a) that the Model Law or this Part shall not apply to the arbitration; or

(b) that the Arbitration Act (Cap. 10) or the repealed Arbitration Act (Cap. 10, 1985 Ed.) shall apply to the arbitration,

then, both the Model Law and this Part shall not apply to that arbitration but the Arbitration Act or the repealed Arbitration Act (if applicable) shall apply to that arbitration.'

Having adopted the ML in 1994 through the IAA, Singapore has obviously adopted the 1985 version of the ML, not the 2006 version. Section 3(1) IAA simply states that 'Subject to this Act, the Model Law, with the exception of Chapter VIII thereof, shall have the force of law in Singapore.'[9] The 1985 ML is therefore in force verbatim (in English) unless the IAA specifically makes an exception to it. Notwithstanding many modifications by the IAA, probably 80 per cent of the text of the articles of the ML (that is the 1985 version of the ML) are in force without modification. A notable exception is Chapter VIII of the ML which is not in force – rather, the IAA implements the New York Convention ('NYC')[10] for the enforcement of foreign award and provides separately for the enforcement of domestic awards.

Although the 2006 version of the ML ('ML 2006')[11] was never adopted verbatim, as we will see, the IAA has adopted many of its principles, and some amendments to the IAA adopted some of the text of the ML 2006.

The IAA has been amended frequently since its adoption, as recently as in 2016. On 1 June 2012, a series of important amendments to the IAA came into force.[12] These amendments adopted some of the principles found in the 2006 version of the ML and included: 'a relaxation of the writing requirement of the arbitration agreement' (effectively implementing part of option 1 of article 7 ML 2006), 'the power for Singapore Courts to review negative jurisdiction rulings and grant costs for reviews of jurisdiction rulings, an expansion of the power of the tribunal to award interest, and new provisions making awards and orders of emergency arbitrators enforceable, and making orders and directions of interim

---

[9] Section 2(1) IAA defines the ML as follows: '"Model Law" means the UNCITRAL Model Law on International Commercial Arbitration adopted by the United Nations Commission on International Trade Law on 21st June 1985, the text in English of which is set out in the First Schedule.'

[10] Convention on the Recognition and Enforcement of Foreign Arbitral Awards, New York, 10 June 1958, in force 7 June 1959, 330 UNTS 4739 ('NYC').

[11] UN Documents A/40/17, annex I and A/61/17, annex I, available at www.uncitral.org/pdf/english/texts/arbitration/ml-arb/07-86998_Ebook.pdf.

[12] See International Arbitration (Amendment) Act 2012, Act 12 of 2012. The amendments came into force on 1 June 2012, see International Arbitration (Amendment) Act (Commencement) Notification 2012, S 235/2012. However, section 12 of this Amendment Act provides that the amendments will only apply to arbitral proceedings commenced on or after that date unless the parties agree in writing that the amendments will apply to proceedings started before that date (s. 12(1)). Arbitral proceedings are taken to have commenced when the Respondent has received a request for arbitration or if the parties have agreed to another date as the commencement of the arbitration (for example, as provided by some arbitration rules), on that date (s. 12(3)).

measures made by a tribunal outside Singapore enforceable in Singapore'[13] (a principle of the ML 2006).

Although it is indeed good that Singapore has adopted the very text of the ML, the way in which the ML was amended through the IAA may sometimes lead to confusion, especially for foreign lawyers unfamiliar with Singapore law. First, it may be difficult for an outsider to understand exactly which articles of the ML are in force and which are not – the ML is reproduced in full as the 'First Schedule' to the IAA even though many of its provisions in fact do not have the force of law in Singapore. One has to be very familiar with the detailed and sometimes convoluted provisions of the IAA to know which articles of the ML apply and which do not. In that respect Hong Kong's new Arbitration Ordinance[14] is much clearer and user-friendly – it follows the order of the ML and clearly amends the provisions of the ML as it goes along when need be. In Hong Kong, one need not juggle between the ML and a domestic statute to try to figure out what articles of the ML apply, and which do not – the Hong Kong Ordinance makes that very clear and is therefore more user-friendly.

In summary, in Singapore, the presumption is that the ML applies verbatim unless amended by the IAA amendments. Therefore, Singapore truly is a ML country as the majority of its arbitration law is governed by the very text of the ML and only some provisions of the ML have been modified.

The Singapore Courts' Interpretation of the ML

Singapore never adopted article 2A(1) of the ML 2006 that states: 'In the interpretation of this Law, regard is to be had to its international origin and to the need to promote uniformity in its application and the observance of good faith', or a similar principle, and in the early days of the ML in Singapore, it showed.

As will be seen below, the Singapore Courts in the early days rendered many decisions that were at odds with the generally accepted interpretation of the ML and with very basic principles of international commercial arbitration accepted in so-called arbitration-friendly jurisdictions. The Singapore Parliament had to intervene repeatedly to correct mistaken interpretations of the ML given by the Courts, which explains

---

[13] Bell/Oxford, note 1 at 1–2.
[14] Arbitration Ordinance, Cap. 609 adopted in 2010 in force in 2011.

the few provisions of the IAA that start with the words 'for the avoidance of doubt' and then provide the correct interpretation of the ML that the Courts should have implemented. Even some relatively recent decisions of the Singapore Courts can be seen as inconsistent with generally accepted interpretations of the ML and of the principles of international commercial arbitration.

Luckily, the performance of the Courts in interpreting the ML has improved drastically lately and recent decisions of the Court of Appeal have been excellent, as well as international and forward looking in outlook.

But it is worth remembering that it was not always like this. Not that we should reminisce in order to be overly negative about Singapore's past performance at implementing the ML (especially since the present is indeed very positive), but, since many Asian jurisdictions may be struggling to implement the ML or its principles, it is worth remembering that even in Singapore, now a successful arbitration centre, not so long ago the Courts were not always adept at implementing the ML and even today, occasionally, they get it wrong (in my view). This fact should be encouraging: it takes time for the Courts, the legislature and the legal profession of any jurisdiction which is new to international arbitration to figure out what is needed to implement an arbitration regime which serves the country well, as well as can earn the trust of the international commercial arbitration community.

Part I   General Provisions of the Model Law (Articles 1 to 6)

As stated above, section 3 of the IAA states: 'subject to this Act, the Model Law, with the exception of Chapter VIII thereof, shall have the force of law in Singapore.' Again, the version of the ML adopted by Singapore is the 1985 version.[15] Article 1 of the ML states that it 'applies to international commercial arbitration' and defines what an international arbitration is at paragraphs (3) and (4).

The IAA, however, adopts its own definition of what constitutes an international arbitration. Section 5 IAA resembles article 1 ML, yet modifies it significantly if subtly (the modified text is in bold):

> (2) **Notwithstanding Article 1 (3) of the Model Law**, an arbitration is international if –

---

[15] See above.

(a) **at least one of the parties** to an arbitration agreement, at the time of the conclusion of the agreement, **has its place of business in any State other than Singapore**; or

(b) one of the following places is situated outside the State in which the parties have their places of business:

    (i) the place of arbitration if determined in, or pursuant to, the arbitration agreement;

    (ii) any place where a substantial part of the obligations of the commercial relationship is to be performed or the place with which the subject-matter of the dispute is most closely connected; or

(c) the parties have expressly agreed that the subject-matter of the arbitration agreement relates to more than one country.

(3) For the purposes of **subsection (2)** –

    (a) if a party has more than one place of business, the place of business **shall be** that which has the closest relationship to the arbitration agreement;

    (b) if a party does not have a place of business, **a** reference **to his place of business shall be construed as a reference** to his habitual residence.

As I have explained elsewhere:

> Therefore, if one of the parties has its place of business outside Singapore, the arbitration is deemed international. This is a modification of article 1(3)(a) ML which requires that the parties have their place of business in different States. If the parties have their place of business in the same State other than Singapore, the arbitration would be international under s. 5(2)(a) IAA but would not be under art 1(3)(a) ML.
>
> The wording of the next paragraph (s. 5(2)(b) IAA) is taken word for word from the ML but in the ML the paragraph is an alternative when the parties have their place of business in the same State (had they been from different States, para. (a) would have applied). In the IAA the paragraph is an alternative when no party is from a State other than Singapore - i.e. when all the parties are from Singapore. The arbitration is international if one of the following places is outside Singapore: the place of arbitration, any place where a substantial part of the obligations is to be performed, or the place to which the subject matter is most closely connected.[16]

At first the High Court in interpreting section 5(2)(b) IAA seemed to suggest that the requirement was that 'the place of substantial

---

[16] Bell/Oxford, note 1 at [15–16].

performance of the commercial obligations of the parties to the contract
was outside Singapore'.[17] In a later case, however, the High Court
rejected the use of the concept of 'the place of substantial performance'
and decided that 's. 5(2)(b)(ii) refers to "*any* place where a substantial
part of the obligations of the commercial relationship is to be performed"
[emphasis added] and not *the* place of substantial performance.'[18] One
therefore only need a substantial part of the obligations to be performed
outside Singapore for the IAA to apply even if most of the obligations are
to be performed in Singapore.

In summary, Singapore's definition of what is an 'international' arbitration is in fact broader than the definition given by the ML.

Article 2 of the ML provides definitions and rules of interpretation
which are in force in Singapore, except that the IAA provides its own
definition of an arbitral tribunal: '"arbitral tribunal" means a sole arbitrator or a panel of arbitrators or a permanent arbitral institution, and
includes an emergency arbitrator appointed pursuant to the rules of
arbitration agreed to or adopted by the parties including the rules
of arbitration of an institution or organization.'[19] The IAA also provides
its own definition of an award.[20]

As mentioned above, Singapore did not adopt article 2A of the ML
2006. However, in interpreting the ML, the IAA specifically authorizes
reference to the documents of UNCITRAL and the working group on
the ML[21] but falls short of article 2A(1) ML 2006 which would have
required that 'in the interpretation of this Law, regard is to be had to its
international origin and to the need to promote uniformity in its application and the observance of good faith', which would have encouraged

---

[17] *Vanol Far East Marketing Pte Ltd* v. *Hin Leong Trading (Pte) Ltd* [1996] SGHC 108,
[1996] 2 SLR(R) 172 at [14].

[18] *Mitsui Engineering & Shipbuilding Co. Ltd* v. *PSA Corp Ltd* [2003] 1 SLR(R) 446, [2002]
SGHC 170 at [27]. The words '[emphasis added]' are in the original judgment as well as
all emphases found in the quote above. The case also interprets section 5(3) IAA defining
the place of business and the judge appropriately referred to a case from Hong Kong and
a law review article on article 1(4) of the ML which is worded similarly.

[19] Section 2(1) of the IAA.

[20] '"Award" means a decision of the arbitral tribunal on the substance of the dispute and
includes any interim, interlocutory or partial award but excludes any orders or directions
made under section 12', section 2(1) IAA.

[21] Section 4(1) IAA: 'For the purposes of interpreting the Model Law, reference may be
made to the documents of – (a) the United Nations Commission on International Trade
Law; and (b) its working group for the preparation of the Model Law, relating to the
Model Law.' Section 4(2) reminds the Courts that section 9A of the Interpretation Act,
c. 1 rev. S. Sing. continues to apply to the interpretation of the IAA.

the Singapore Courts to consult international doctrine and precedents. International doctrine and precedents could nevertheless be considered as the Interpretation Act also allows the courts to consider other relevant documents in interpreting Acts such as the ML and the IAA.[22] Unfortunately, Singapore lawyers, and therefore Singapore Courts, have the habit of citing English cases even when interpreting the ML even though England is not a ML jurisdiction. Fortunately, in a few cases, Singapore Courts have recently started to refer to precedents from other ML jurisdictions.

Article 3 (Receipt of written communications) and article 4 (Waiver of right to object) were adopted verbatim, but there have been no Court cases on them.

Article 5 (Extent of Court intervention) has been adopted verbatim and has been interpreted correctly by the Courts: the powers of the Courts to intervene in arbitration matters are listed exhaustively in the ML and the IAA, and all other residual powers are excluded.[23]

Article 6 of the ML invites the jurisdiction to identify the Court that will have jurisdiction over arbitration matters. Section 8 IAA states that the Singapore High Court will exercise the powers listed at article 6 ML, except for the power to appoint arbitrators,[24] which section 8(2) IAA (as amended in 2016) confers to the President of the Court of Arbitration of the Singapore International Arbitration Centre (SIAC).[25]

Part II   Arbitration Agreement (Articles 7 to 9)

In 1994, Singapore adopted article 7 of the 1985 version of the ML – the arbitration agreement had to be in writing signed by the parties or found in an exchange of letters or other telecommunications or found in an exchange of statements of claims and defence in which one party alleges the existence of the agreement and the other does not deny it. The IAA also extended the definition to include 'a reference in a bill of lading to a

---

[22] Section 9A, Interpretation Act.

[23] *L W Infrastructure Pte Ltd* v. *Lim Chin San Contractors Pte Ltd* [2013] 1 SLR 125 at [36]; *NCC International AB* v. *Alliance Concrete Singapore Pte Ltd* [2008] 2 SLR(R) 565 at [22]–[23]; *Mitsui Engineering & Shipbuilding Co. Ltd* v. *Easton Graham Rush* [2004] 2 SLR(R) 14 at [23].

[24] Article 11(3) and (4) ML.

[25] In addition, section 8(3) IAA allows the Chief Justice to appoint any other person to exercise the power of President of the Court of Arbitration of the SIAC. The IAA, unlike the ML, grants immunity to the appointing authority – see section 25A IAA.

charterparty or some other document containing an arbitration agreement' and to include a reference to an arbitration agreement in an arbitral or legal proceedings which is not denied when it should have been by the other party.[26]

On 1 January 2010, an amendment to the IAA came into force which adopted paragraph 4 of option I of article 7 of the 2006 ML, almost word for word. The definition of an arbitration agreement was therefore extended to include 'an agreement made by electronic communications if the information contained therein is accessible so as to be useable for subsequent reference'.[27]

For arbitrations started on 1 June 2012 or later,[28] the IAA adopts, in part verbatim, the approach found at option I of section 7 of the ML 2006.[29] Therefore, an agreement is deemed to be in writing 'if its content is recorded in any form, whether or not the arbitration agreement or contract has been concluded orally, by conduct or by other means'.[30] Singapore, however, did not adopt option II of article 7 of the ML 2006 – a writing is still required. It has recently been held that an arbitration clause is presumed to be governed by the same law as the law governing the main contract.[31]

Article 8 of the ML, which requires a Court to refer to arbitration matters which are the subject of an arbitration agreement, has not been adopted. It is replaced by section 6 IAA, which has a similar effect but is more detailed and allows Courts to make interim and supplementary orders to preserve the rights of parties. Section 6(4) IAA also provides that 'Where no party to the proceedings has taken any further step in the proceedings for a period of not less than 2 years after an order staying the proceedings has been made, the Court may, on its own motion, make an order discontinuing the proceedings [. . .].' Section 6(5) also makes clear that all Courts in Singapore have to stay the proceedings.[32]

---

[26] Section 2(3) and (4) IAA as they stood until 2012.

[27] Section 2(1) IAA as it stood until 2012. The definitions of 'electronic communication' and of 'data message' found in option 1 of article 7 of 2006 ML were also reproduced in section 2(1) IAA as it stood until 2012.

[28] See note 12.

[29] See section 2A of the IAA as amended in 2012 which adopts for the most part the very wording of option I of section 7 of ML 2006 but keeps the additional example of a reference in a bill of lading to a charterparty or another document containing an arbitration clause and a slightly broader description of the instances where the undenied allegation of the existence of an arbitration clause in a proceeding constitutes an arbitration agreement.

[30] Section 2A(4) of the IAA as amended in 2012. [31] BCY v. BCZ [2016] SGHC 249.

[32] 6. –(1) Notwithstanding Article 8 of the Model Law, where any party to an arbitration agreement to which this Act applies institutes any proceedings in any Court

Article 9 states that 'it is not incompatible with an arbitration agreement for a party to request, before or during arbitral proceedings, from a Court an interim measure of protection and for a Court to grant such measure.' The article does not confer powers on the Courts to grant interim measures but intends to preserve the powers Courts already have to grant such measures. In 2006, the Court of Appeal in Singapore held that Singapore Courts had no power to grant interim measures, such as a Mareva injunction, in support of an arbitration not seated in Singapore.[33] Luckily the effect of the Court of Appeal's decision was reversed by legislation that came into force on 1 January 2010[34] – more on this below in the discussion of interim measures.

Part III   Composition of Arbitral Tribunal (Articles 10 to 15)

It should be noted that whenever parties choose a set of arbitration rules, these rules will usually replace articles 10 to 15 and therefore the articles are not very frequently used.

against any other party to the agreement in respect of any matter which is the subject of the agreement, any party to the agreement may, at any time after appearance and before delivering any pleading or taking any other step in the proceedings, apply to that Court to stay the proceedings so far as the proceedings relate to that matter.

(2) The Court to which an application has been made in accordance with subsection (1) shall make an order, upon such terms or conditions as it may think fit, staying the proceedings so far as the proceedings relate to the matter, unless it is satisfied that the arbitration agreement is null and void, inoperative or incapable of being performed.

(3) Where a Court makes an order under subsection (2), the Court may, for the purpose of preserving the rights of parties, make such interim or supplementary orders as it may think fit in relation to any property which is the subject of the dispute to which the order under that subsection relates.

(4) Where no party to the proceedings has taken any further step in the proceedings for a period of not less than 2 years after an order staying the proceedings has been made, the Court may, on its own motion, make an order discontinuing the proceedings without prejudice to the right of any of the parties to apply for the discontinued proceedings to be reinstated.

(5) For the purposes of this section and sections 7 and 11A –

   (a) a reference to a party shall include a reference to any person claiming through or under such party;

   (b) 'Court' means the High Court, District Court, Magistrate's Court or any other Court in which proceedings are instituted.

[33] *Swift-Fortune Ltd* v. *Magnifica Marine SA* [2006] SGCA 42 at [31]–[33].
[34] New section 12A(1)(b) IAA.

Article 10 of the ML provides that if the parties have not agreed on a number of arbitrators, the default number of arbitrators shall be three. However, section 9 IAA modifies article 10 ML: in Singapore the default is a single arbitrator.

Article 11 of the ML on the appointment of arbitrators is adopted by Singapore with one significant modification in arbitrations with three arbitrators: instead of the third arbitrator being appointed by the first two arbitrators, in Singapore, the third arbitrator must be appointed by the parties.[35]

Article 12 of the ML (Grounds for challenge) was adopted without modifications and so were article 13 ML (Challenge procedure), article 14 (Failure or impossibility to act) and article 15 (Appointment of substitute arbitrator). Except for one case directly on article 13[36] and another considering its legislative history,[37] there has been no case on these articles.

Part IV   Jurisdiction of Arbitral Tribunal (Article 16)

Singapore has adopted article 16 of the ML. Therefore, tribunals have jurisdictions to decide on their own jurisdiction (*kompetenz-kompetenz/ compétence-compétence*) (16(1) ML),[38] and Singapore law recognizes the separability of arbitration clauses (16(2) ML).

As is well known, article 16(3) of the ML only provides a recourse (in Singapore, to the High Court) against a preliminary decision by a tribunal that it has jurisdiction.[39] It does not provide a recourse if the tribunal decides as a preliminary question that it does not have jurisdiction, i.e. a negative ruling.[40] In Singapore, the standard of review under article 16(3) is a *de novo* review.[41]

---

[35] Section 9A IAA adopted in 2001.

[36] In *Mitsui Engineering & Shipbuilding Co. Ltd* v. *Easton Graham Rush* [2004] 2 SLR(R) 14 at [23]–[29], it was rightly held that the Court had no residual power to stay the arbitral proceedings while it considered a challenge to an arbitrator.

[37] *PT First Media TBK* v. *Astro Nusantara International BV* [2014] 1 SLR 372 at [127]–[128] and [130] comparing 13(3) ML to 16(3) ML on the consequence of their non-use on resisting enforcement.

[38] *Tjong Very Sumito and Others* v. *Antig Investments Pte Ltd* [2009] 4 SLR(R) 732 at [24]; *The 'Titan Unity'* [2013] SGHCR 28 at [14].

[39] Section 16(3) of the ML. Section 8(1) IAA indicates that the review is made by the High Court in Singapore.

[40] *PT Asuransi Jasa Indonesia (Persero)* v. *Dexia Bank SA* [2007] 1 SLR(R) 597 at [45] and [68].

[41] *Insigma Technology Co. Ltd* v. *Alstom Technology Ltd* [2009] 1 SLR(R) 23 at [21].

Contrary to article 16(3) of the ML, which does not provide an appeal from the Court of first instance, in Singapore, a decision of the High Court under article 16(3) is not final and, with leave of that Court, can be appealed to the highest Court, the Court of Appeal.[42] The arbitration is not suspended while the review is ongoing,[43] though in Singapore the Court at its discretion could suspend the arbitration.[44] It should be noted that courts in Singapore are very efficient and therefore no significant delays should ensue from the fact that the decision of the High Court is not final.

For arbitrations commenced after 1 June 2012, the IAA now allows for a review of negative decisions of a tribunal on jurisdiction. Section 10 IAA, as amended in 2012, is rather long,[45] but essentially allows for a

---

[42] Section 10 IAA. There is no appeal against a refusal to grant leave to appeal, section 10(2) IAA.

[43] '[W]hile such a request is pending, the tribunal may continue the arbitral proceedings and make an award.' Article 16(3) ML.

[44] See section 10(9)(*a*) IAA: 'Where an application is made pursuant to Article 16(3) of the Model Law or this section – (a) such application shall not operate as a stay of the arbitral proceedings or of execution of any award or order made in the arbitral proceedings unless the High Court orders otherwise; and (b) no intermediate act or proceeding shall be invalidated except so far as the High Court may direct' (emphasis added). See *BLY* v. *BLZ* [2017] 4 SLR 410, [2017] SGHC 59.

[45] The new s. 10 IAA states:

Appeal on Ruling of Jurisdiction

(1) This section shall have effect notwithstanding Article 16(3) of the Model Law.
(2) An arbitral tribunal may rule on a plea that it has no jurisdiction at any stage of the arbitral proceedings.
(3) If the arbitral tribunal rules –
   (a) on a plea as a preliminary question that it has jurisdiction; or
   (b) on a plea at any stage of the arbitral proceedings that it has no jurisdiction,
   any party may, within 30 days after having received notice of that ruling, apply to the High Court to decide the matter.
(4) An appeal from the decision of the High Court made under Article 16(3) of the Model Law or this section shall lie: to the Court of Appeal only with the leave of the High Court.
(5) There shall be no appeal against a refusal for grant of leave of the High Court.
(6) Where the High Court, or the Court of Appeal on appeal, decides that the arbitral tribunal has jurisdiction –
   (a) the arbitral tribunal shall continue the arbitral proceedings and make an award; and
   (b) where any arbitrator is unable or unwilling to continue the arbitral proceedings, the mandate of that arbitrator shall terminate and a substitute arbitrator shall be appointed in accordance with Article 15 of the Model Law.

review by the High Court of any preliminary decision of an arbitral tribunal on the issue of jurisdiction, whether it decides that it has or does not have jurisdiction. Such decisions can still be appealed to the Court of Appeal. In another innovation, section 10 IAA now makes clear that the Courts have the power to grant costs on such decisions of theirs. If a Court reverses the negative decision of a tribunal, that same tribunal is given the authority and power to continue to hear the case and to make an award. An arbitrator who is unable or unwilling to resume his or her duties will be replaced by a substitute arbitrator.

With this provision, Singapore can enforce the arbitration agreement the parties have agreed to, even when the tribunal mistakenly denies jurisdiction. Parties do not risk being caught in a *double-renvoi*, between a court that holds that they must go to arbitration and a tribunal that holds that they should go to court.

Part IV-A   Interim Measures and Preliminary Orders (Articles 17 to 17J)

Singapore has not adopted the text of the ML 2006, but this is not to say that it does not allow for interim measures and preliminary orders from both the tribunal and the Courts.

(7) In making a ruling or decision under this section that the arbitral tribunal has no jurisdiction, the arbitral tribunal, the High Court or the Court of Appeal (as the case may be) may make an award or order of costs of the proceedings, including the arbitral proceedings (as the case may be), against any party.

(8) Where an award of costs is made by the arbitral tribunal under subsection (7), section 21 shall apply with the necessary modifications.

(9) Where an application is made pursuant to Article 16(3) of the Model Law or this section –
   (a) such application shall not operate as a stay of the arbitral proceedings or of execution of any award or order made in the arbitral proceedings unless the High Court orders otherwise; and
   (b) no intermediate act or proceeding shall be invalidated except so far as the High Court may direct.

(10) Where there is an appeal from the decision of the High Court pursuant to subsection (4) –
   (a) such appeal shall not operate as a stay of the arbitral proceedings or of execution of any award or order made in the arbitral proceedings unless the High Court or the Court of Appeal orders otherwise; and
   (b) no intermediate act or proceeding shall be invalidated except so far as the Court of Appeal may direct.

As we know, article 17 of the 1985 version of the ML, which Singapore has adopted, is not very detailed on interim measures by the tribunal – it is a very general article that simply states that the tribunal may order interim measures of protection. The ML 1985 is also silent on interim measures by the Courts in support of arbitration except for article 9 of the ML which states that such measures by the Courts (which are not defined and presumably to be found in national law) are not incompatible with an arbitration agreement.

Singapore was not satisfied with this position of the ML 1985 and even before the 2006 version of the ML was adopted by UNCITRAL section 12 IAA provided for extensive powers for the tribunal to order interim measures, for their enforcement in Singapore (and more recently for the enforcement in Singapore of measures ordered by tribunals seated outside Singapore) and for the Courts in Singapore also to have similar powers to order interim measures for arbitrations seated in Singapore.

Sub-Part I   Measures and Orders by the Tribunal (Articles 17 to 17G)

Singapore never adopted articles 17 to 17G ML 2006, but even before the ML 2006, in a clear desire to empower the tribunal to order interim measures and make other orders and directions independently of the Courts, section 12 IAA, when amended in 2001 and subsequently, went well beyond what the ML 1985 provided.

As I have described elsewhere:[46]

> Section 12(1) (as amended in 2001) added to article 17 ML by providing a long list of powers of the tribunal, including the power to make orders for security for costs,[47] for the discovery of documents, for the taking of samples and custody of evidence, for the preservation of property, for securing the amount in dispute, even for interim injunctions and for 'any other interim measure'.[48] The tribunal has the power to administer oaths and affirmations.[49] Interestingly for a common law jurisdiction, s. 12(3) IAA empowers the tribunal to adopt the inquisitorial processes of the civil law if it thinks fit[50] (not so much an interim order – rather a power of the tribunal).
>
> All the orders or directions of the tribunal (since 2012, including orders by an emergency arbitrator), by leave of the High Court or a judge thereof, shall be enforceable in Singapore as if made by the Court.[51]

---

[46] Bell/Oxford, note 1 at [51–52].   [47] See also section 12(4) IAA.   [48] See 12(1) IAA.
[49] Section 12(2) IAA.   [50] Section 12(3) IAA.   [51] Section 12(6) IAA.

When the new version of the ML was adopted in 2006 giving lots of detailed powers to the arbitral tribunal on interim measures and preliminary orders,[52] Singapore did not feel the need to adopt these provisions of the 2006 version of the ML as it already had granted wide powers to arbitral tribunals. It seems that Singapore also decided not to allow for ex parte proceedings the way the ML 2006 does.[53]

Sub-Part II   Recognition and Enforcement of Interim Measures (Articles 17H to 17I)

Singapore has not adopted articles 17H and 17I ML 2006 on the recognition and enforcement of interim measures.

Singapore adopted and supplemented article 17 ML 1985, which gives the arbitral tribunal powers to make orders on interim measures of protection but left a lacuna in the law by being silent on the status and enforceability of such orders. Section 12(6) IAA was thus introduced to remedy this lacuna with a *sui generis* enforcement mechanism allowing such orders to be enforceable as Court orders,[54] but not as an award, thus not broadening the definition of an 'award' and therefore no Court can set aside these orders under article 34 ML.[55] The underlying policy consideration was that Courts should intervene minimally in procedural and administrative issues which fall within the province of the tribunal and which should be decided solely by the tribunal.[56] However, the Singapore approach is the exact opposite of the approach adopted by article 17I ML 2006, which in fact does allow Courts to refuse to enforce such interim measures on the very same grounds on which an award may be refused enforcement (article 36 ML).

Note also that section 12(6) IAA does not provide for the international enforcement of interim measures ordered by tribunals seated in Singapore or the enforcement in Singapore of interim measures ordered by

---

[52] See new article 17 and article 17A–17 G of the ML 2006.

[53] Article 17B and C of ML 2006.

[54] Section 12(6) IAA states: 'All orders or directions made or given by an arbitral tribunal in the course of an arbitration shall, by leave of the High Court or a Judge thereof, be enforceable in the same manner as if they were orders made by a court and, where leave is so given, judgment may be entered in terms of the order or direction.'

[55] The definition of 'award' at s. 2(1) IAA specifically excludes 'any orders or directions made under section 12', i.e., any interim measures.

[56] *PT Pukuafu Indah and Others v. Newmont Indonesia Ltd* [2012] 4 SLR 1157 at [21]–[23].

tribunals seated outside of Singapore. The adoption of article 17I ML 1985 would have allowed the latter.

However, Singapore has found a different way to enforce in Singapore interim measures ordered by tribunals seated outside of Singapore.

Singapore did not adopt articles 35 and 36 of the ML on the recognition and enforcement of award but Part III of the IAA (ss. 27–33) is devoted to the implementation of the NYC without reference to the ML. The provision for the enforcement of foreign interim measures in Singapore has been added to this Part III of the IAA on the enforcement of foreign arbitral awards.

As I wrote elsewhere:

> In 2012, the definition of 'arbitral award' for the purpose of enforcement of foreign awards found at section 27(1) IAA was modified. That section now states '"arbitral award" has the same meaning as in the convention, but also includes an order or direction made or given by an arbitral tribunal in the course of an arbitration in respect of any of the matters set out in section 12(1)(c) to (i)' i.e. Courts in Singapore can enforce interim measures ordered by a foreign-seated tribunal. This goes beyond the *NY Convention*.[57]

Can interim measures issued by a tribunal seated in Singapore be enforced in another country? It will depend on the laws of that country – the NYC is of no help to the extent that these measures are not awards under the NYC. But even the ML 2006 does not provide for the recognition and enforcement of a tribunal's interim measures outside of the jurisdiction where that tribunal is seated, unless that jurisdiction where the enforcement is sought has itself also adopted article 17I ML 2006 (which is rather rare at this point).

Sub-Part III   Court-Ordered Interim Measures (Article 17J)

Singapore did not adopt article 17J ML 2006 which states that 'A Court shall have the same power of issuing an interim measure in relation to arbitration proceedings, <u>irrespective of whether their place is in the territory of this State</u>, as it has in relation to proceedings in Courts. The Court shall exercise such power in accordance with its own

---

[57] Bell/Oxford, note 1 at [105]. For an argument that interim measures ordered by an emergency arbitrator should be similarly enforced, see Bell/Oxford, note 1 at [106]–[107].

procedures in consideration of the specific features of international arbitration' (emphasis added).

Until 1 January 2010, section 12(7) IAA granted the Singapore Courts the same powers as those provided to the tribunal to grant interim measures under the IAA. Of course, the Court could grant interim measures (such as orders freezing assets) when the tribunal was seated in Singapore, but could the Court do so when the tribunal was seated abroad?

In 2006, the High Court issued two contradicting decisions on this question. Justice Belinda Ang held that section 12(7) IAA and article 9 ML empowered the Singapore Courts to grant interim orders in support of arbitrations seated outside of Singapore,[58] whereas Justice Judith Prakash held that the High Court had no such power.[59] That latter decision was appealed to the Court of Appeal.

The Court of Appeal held that it did not have jurisdiction to grant interim measures in support of foreign seated arbitration. It had been argued that the court should take into account the fact that Singapore's reputation as an arbitration-friendly jurisdiction would be hurt if its Courts could not issue such measures in favour of foreign-seated arbitrations. The Court, however, said that this was a policy issue for Parliament and narrowly interpreted the law. It stated:

> Thus, whilst we can accept counsel's realistic assessment of how international arbitrations are conducted today, the potentially adverse consequences spelt out by counsel are par excellence policy considerations within the purview of Parliament. Secondly, it is reasonable to assume that the framers of the IAA were aware of these considerations and would have factored them into the drafting of the IAA. If they have not been taken into account in the IAA, we doubt very much that we can do so, without arrogating to ourselves the power to decide such policy issues. Thirdly, the duty of the Court is to determine what the law is, i.e., the true meaning of s 12(7), and to apply it to the facts of the case. It should not second-guess Parliament on such matters.[60]

It seems that, indeed, the law as interpreted by the Court of Appeal was bad for Singapore as Parliament intervened to correct the course and re-establish Singapore's reputation as an arbitration-friendly jurisdiction.

---

[58] *Front Carriers Ltd* v. *Atlantic & Orient Shipping Corp* [2006] SGHC 127.
[59] Except in the limited situations covered by sections 6(3) and 7(1) IAA. See *Swift-Fortune Ltd* v. *Magnifica Marine S.A.* [2006] SGHC 36, [2006] 2 SLR(R) 323.
[60] *Swift-Fortune Ltd* v. *Magnifica Marine S.A.* [2006] SGCA 42 at [16].

The Court of Appeal's decision was effectively reversed by legislation that came into force on 1 January 2010.[61]

Parliament introduced a new section 12A IAA on 'Court-ordered interim measures'. It reaffirms the earlier position to the effect that Courts may grant the same interim measures a tribunal may grant,[62] but states very clearly that a Singapore Court may order such measures 'irrespective of whether the place of arbitration is in the territory of Singapore'.[63] However, it adds that '[the High Court [...] may refuse to make an order [...] if, in the opinion of the High Court or Judge, the fact that the place of arbitration is outside Singapore or likely to be outside Singapore when it is designated or determined makes it inappropriate to make such order.'[64]

However, the Court is authorized to make such orders only if 'the arbitral tribunal [...] has no power or is unable for the time being to act effectively'.[65] Singapore therefore takes the position that the parties should seek interim measures from the tribunal rather than the Courts whenever the tribunal may do so effectively. An order of the Court will cease to have effect 'if the arbitral tribunal [...] makes an order which expressly relates to the whole or part of the order'.[66] The tribunal, not the Courts, has the final word on interim measures.

Part V   Conduct of Arbitral Proceedings (Articles 18 to 27)

Article 18 of the ML (Equal treatment of parties) has been adopted without amendment. A Court has even looked at both civil law and common law jurisdictions to determine what equality and a full opportunity of presenting one's case should mean under article 18.[67]

Rules of Procedure: Relationship between the ML and Arbitration Rules

Article 19 of the ML (Determination of rules of procedure) was adopted without modification. The article is rather simple, and its interpretation should not be difficult. It simply states 'subject to the provisions of this

---

[61] International Arbitration (Amendment) Act 2009, Statute of Singapore No. 26 of 2009, which came into force on 1 January 2010.
[62] Old section 12(7) IAA now repealed and replaced by section 12A(2) IAA.
[63] Section 12A(1)(b) IAA.   [64] Section 12A(3) IAA.   [65] Section 12A(6) IAA.
[66] Section 12A(7) IAA.
[67] *Soh Beng Tee & Co. Pte Ltd* v. *Fairmount Development Pte Ltd* [2007] 3 SLR(R) 86 at [42]–[65].

Law, the parties are free to agree on the procedure to be followed by the arbitral tribunal in conducting the proceedings' and that failing such agreement the tribunal will determine the procedure. This article is an instance of the arbitration principle of party autonomy[68] which should allow the parties to choose not only the procedure to be followed for the proceedings but also the arbitration rules that will replace the content of the arbitration law to the extent that the provisions of the law are not mandatory.

For a while, however, the Courts in Singapore did not properly understand the relationship between the arbitration rules chosen by the parties and the applicable arbitration law. Part of the early confusion stemmed from the fact that, in Singapore, the parties are free to opt out of the IAA and ML in favour of the domestic AA and Courts sometimes mistakenly interpreted the choice of a set of arbitration rules as a tacit opting out of the IAA and ML when these rules were different from the IAA and ML.

The infamous 2001 High Court case of *John Holland* clearly and surprisingly held that the adoption of the ICC Arbitration Rules was a rejection of the ML and the IAA.[69] To my knowledge, in no other ML jurisdiction were the ICC Rules ever held to be incompatible with the ML. The problem is that the Court did not look at other ML jurisdictions. The Court cited mainly cases from common law jurisdictions which are not ML jurisdictions and only cited one case from Hong Kong, a ML jurisdiction, but distinguished it. This came as a shock to the international arbitration community and the Government addressed the issue by immediately amending the IAA. Section 15 IAA was amended in the same year as *John Holland* to make clear that '[f]or the avoidance of doubt, a provision in an arbitration agreement referring to or adopting any rules of arbitration shall not of itself be sufficient to exclude the application of the Model Law or this Part to the arbitration concerned.'[70]

---

[68] Article 19 reflects the widely accepted principle of party autonomy: see *Jurong Engineering Ltd* v. *Black & Veatch Singapore Pte Ltd* [2004] 1 SLR(R) 333 at [27].

[69] *John Holland Pty Ltd* v. *Toyo Engineering Corp (Japan)* [2001] SGHC 48, [2001] 1 SLR(R) 443 (High Ct). See also the earlier case of *Coop International Pte Ltd* v. *Ebel SA* [1998] SGHC 425, [1998] 1 SLR(R) 615 (High Ct) at [146] (*obiter dictum*): 'By choosing procedures [Rules of Arbitration of the Chamber of Commerce and Industry of Geneva] which are alien and contrary to the mandatory provisions in the Model Law or Part II for arbitration in Singapore, I think parties would have successfully opted out by implication.'

[70] Section 15(2) IAA.

Unfortunately, this provision was not sufficient to put an end to the Courts' misinterpretation of the relationship between arbitration rules and arbitration law. Almost immediately after the amendment of the IAA came the 2002 High Court case of *Dermajaya*. In that case, the Court held that the UNCITRAL Rules were incompatible with the ML and the IAA and made the following astonishing statement:

> The question then is, if the Model Law applies, does this mean that the other incompatible set of rules is totally excluded or is it excluded only in so far as it is not inconsistent with the Model Law? From what I have said above, my view is that the other set of rules is completely excluded.[71]

This decision directly went against the principle of party autonomy which allows the parties to opt out of non-mandatory provisions of an arbitration law by choosing a set of arbitration rules. The Court called the differences between the arbitration law and the arbitration rules 'inconsistencies' and effectively made mandatory all the provisions of the IAA and the ML thus completely excluding the arbitration rules chosen by the parties as soon as it found the slightest 'inconsistency'. The proper interpretation would have been that a particular provision of a set of arbitration rules (and not the whole set of rules) should be rejected only if it is inconsistent with a mandatory provision of the ML or IAA. It would be quite a challenge to find in rules such as the ICC Rules or the UNCITRAL Rules any provision that is inconsistent with a mandatory rule of the ML or IAA, especially since most of the provisions of the ML and IAA are not mandatory. Unfortunately, the Court did not look at any precedent from any other ML jurisdiction.

This decision could not be allowed to stand – not respecting the choice of rules made by the parties would have killed Singapore as an arbitration centre. The Government acted very quickly and proposed amendments to the IAA that would try to restore the proper relationship between arbitration rules and arbitration law. The same year, in 2002, a new version of section 15 IAA was adopted and a new section 15A was also adopted which explains clearly the proper relationship between arbitration rules and arbitration law. The provision is in fact so clear that I use it as a pedagogical tool when I teach the relationship between rules and law to my students. Section 15A(5) states:

> A provision of rules of arbitration is not inconsistent with the Model Law or this Part [of the IAA] merely because it provides for a matter which is

---

[71] *Dermajaya Properties Sdn Bhd* v. *Premium Properties Sdn Bhd* [2002] SGHC 53, [2002] 1 SLR(R) 492 at [69] (High Ct).

covered by a provision of the Model Law or this Part which allows the parties to make their own arrangements by agreement but which applies in the absence of such agreement.

The other paragraphs of section 15A are also very detailed and explain very well the relationship between rules and law. This latest amendment seems to have worked and we have not had any new egregious case. Singapore now applies international standards and understandings to the relationship between the arbitration rules and the arbitration law.

Other Articles on the Conduct of Proceedings

Article 20 of the ML (Place of arbitration) has been adopted without modification and cases have shown that the Courts do understand the difference between the place (or seat) of the arbitration and the venue of hearings.[72]

Article 21 (commencement of arbitral proceedings) and Article 22 (language) were adopted verbatim and there has been no case on these articles in Singapore.

Article 23 (Statements of claim and defence), which was also adopted without modification, was referred to by the Court of Appeal in explaining that 'in order to determine whether an arbitral tribunal has the jurisdiction to adjudicate on and make an award in respect of a particular dispute, it is necessary to refer to the pleaded case of each party to the arbitration and the issues of law or fact that are raised in the pleadings to see whether they encompass that dispute.'[73]

Article 24 of the ML (Hearings and written proceedings) was adopted without modifications and is well understood by the Courts.[74]

Article 25 of the ML (Default of a party), Article 26 ML (Expert appointed by arbitral tribunal) and Article 27 ML (Court assistance

---

[72] *PT Garuda Indonesia v. Birgen Air* [2002] 1 SLR(R) 401 at [21]–[24] and [36].

[73] *PT Prima International Development v. Kempinski Hotels SA and other appeals* [2012] 4 SLR 98 at [34]. See also at [32]–[34] and [47].

[74] Article 24(1) does not require an oral hearing unless either the parties or the arbitral tribunal require one: *Government of the Republic of the Philippines v. Philippine International Air Terminals Co., Inc.* [2007] 1 SLR(R) 278 at [33]; a party's legitimate expectation to cross-examination under article 24(1) does not extend to cross-examination on a specific issue that had not been pleaded: *Kempinski Hotels SA v. PT Prima International Development* [2011] 4 SLR 633 at [87]–[89].

in taking evidence) have been adopted verbatim but have not been the object of any case in Singapore.

Part VI   Making of Award and Termination of Proceedings (Articles 28 to 33)

Article 28 of the ML (Rules applicable to substance of dispute), article 29 ML (Decision-making by panel of arbitrators) and article 30 ML (Settlement) were adopted verbatim and have not been commented upon by the Courts.

Article 31 of the ML (Form and contents of award) was adopted verbatim and in a case the Court commented that the level of detail to which a tribunal must give reasons is similar to the obligation of a Court to give reasons.[75]

Article 32 of the ML (Termination of proceedings) was adopted verbatim but in 2001 the Court of Appeal interpreted the meaning of 'final award' in paragraph 1 in a way that was inconsistent with international interpretations and practices. The Court of Appeal held that a partial award, because it was not a final award, could be reopened and rewritten at will by the tribunal until it had delivered its final award.[76] This was yet another instance in which Parliament had to intervene rapidly and in the same year the IAA was amended by the adoption of section 19B IAA which states that an award (including a partial award) is final when signed and delivered and that 'the arbitral tribunal shall not vary, amend, correct, review, add to or revoke the award'.[77]

Article 33 of the ML (Correction and interpretation of award; additional award) was adopted verbatim. A Court held that implicit in the requirement of giving notice to the other party of any request to have the tribunal issue an additional award was a duty for the tribunal to hear the other party before issuing such an award.[78]

---

[75] *TMM Division Maritima SA de CV* v. *Pacific Richfield Marine Pte Ltd* [2013] 4 SLR 972 at [97]–[105].

[76] *Tang Boon Jek Jeffrey* v. *Tan Poh Leng Stanley* [2001] 2 SLR(R) 273 at [33]–[38].

[77] Section 19B(2) IAA.

[78] *L W Infrastructure Pte Ltd* v. *Lim Chin San Contractors Pte Ltd* [2012] SGCA 57. Although this case was governed by the AA rather than the IAA and the ML, the Court of Appeal held that the ML should be used to interpret the AA and therefore the decision in this case could serve as a precedent on the ML.

Part VII   Recourse against Award (Article 34)

Article 34 of the ML was adopted verbatim, but in addition to the many grounds provided by article 34 for setting aside an award[79] a Court in Singapore may set aside the award if: '(a) the making of the award was induced or affected by fraud or corruption; or (b) a breach of the rules of natural justice occurred in connection with the making of the award by which the rights of any party have been prejudiced'.[80]

The Courts have understood and respected the fact that the grounds for setting aside an award are exhaustive and exclusive.[81] The Singapore Courts are not quick to set aside awards. The Court of Appeal held that 'findings of fact made in an IAA award are binding on the parties and cannot be reopened except where there is fraud, breach of natural justice or some other recognized vitiating factor.'[82] In an earlier case, that Court stated that 'errors of law or fact, *per se*, do not engage the public policy of Singapore',[83] and held that it can normally only review errors of law, not of facts, when reviewing an award on grounds of public policy.[84]

The Court of Appeal also decided to apply, when considering setting aside an award,[85] the same concept of Singapore public policy used when considering the enforcement of a foreign arbitral award.[86]

---

[79] Incapacity, invalidity of agreement, improper notice, inability to present one's case, lack or excess of jurisdiction, improper composition of tribunal or conduct of procedure, non-arbitrability or award is against public policy of the state of the seat.

[80] Section 24 IAA. For a case setting aside an award due to a breach of fundamental justice, see *JVL Agro Industries Ltd* v. *Agritrade International Pte Ltd* [2016] 4 SLR 768, [2016] SGHC 126.

[81] *ABC Co.* v. *XYZ Co. Ltd* [2003] 3 SLR(R) 546 at [3].

[82] *AJU* v. *AJT* [2011] SGCA 41, [2011] 4 SLR 739 at [65].

[83] *PT Asuransi Jasa Indonesia (Persero)* v. *Dexia Bank SA* [2006] SGCA 41, [2007] 1 SLR(R) 597 at [57] cited in *AJU* v. *AJT*, note 82 at [66].

[84] 'In our view, limiting the application of the public policy objection in Art. 34(2)(b)(ii) of the Model Law to findings of law made by an arbitral tribunal – to the exclusion of findings of fact (save for the exceptions outlined at [65]) – would be consistent with the legislative objective of the IAA that, as far as possible, the international arbitration regime should exist as an autonomous system of private dispute resolution to meet the needs of the international business community.' *AJU* v. *AJT*, note 82 at [69].

[85] Section 19B(4) of the IAA, read with article 34(2)(b)(ii) of the ML.

[86] Section 31(4)(b) of the IAA implementing article 5(2)(b) of the New York Convention. See *AJU* v. *AJT*, note 82 at [37]–[38].

In another decision, the High Court held that a tribunal's interpretation of a choice of law clause, even if it were erroneous, was not a matter that could lead to setting aside an award provided the tribunal properly considered the choice made by the parties.[87]

Regarding the time period during which one can seek to set aside an award, the Courts have held that the words 'may not be made after three months have elapsed from the date on which the party making that application had received the award' in article 34(3) ML were clearly mandatory and imposed a time bar. As the article does not provide for any extension, and as the Court derives its jurisdiction to hear the application from this article alone, the Court does not have the power to grant an extension. The proper interpretation of article 34(3) must be that a party seeking to set aside an award must, within the three-month period, file an application which states the ground or grounds he intends to rely on.[88]

Part VIII   Recognition and Enforcement of Awards
(Articles 35 and 36)

Singapore did not adopt Chapter VIII of the ML (article 35 and article 36) on the recognition and enforcement of awards.[89] These articles do not make a distinction between foreign and domestic awards – 'irrespective of the country in which [the award] was made', says article 35 ML. Singapore does make a distinction. The IAA, in its Part III entitled 'Foreign Awards', implements the NYC for the recognition and enforcement of foreign awards[90] and section 19 of the IAA provides a means for enforcing Singapore-seated awards.

Recognition and Enforcement of Singapore-Seated Awards

The awards of tribunals seated in Singapore can be enforced through section 19 IAA: 'An award on an arbitration agreement may, by leave of the High Court or a Judge thereof, be enforced in the same manner as a judgment or an order to the same effect and, where leave is so given,

---

[87] Quarella SpA v. Scelta Marble Australia Pty Ltd [2012] SGHC 166.

[88] See ABC Co. v. XYZ Co. Ltd [2003] 3 SLR(R) 546 at [9]-[10]; PT Pukuafu Indah v. Newmont Indonesia Ltd [2012] 4 SLR 1157 at [28]-[30].

[89] Section 3(1) IAA.

[90] In Singapore, as in most Commonwealth countries, treaties are not self-implementing and must be implemented by legislation. The IAA implements Singapore's obligations under the NYC.

judgment may be entered in terms of the award.' That section was copied from the English Arbitration Act.[91]

Section 19 IAA plays the role that would be played by article 35 ML (enforcement of awards) if it were in force, but it should be noted that the IAA does not have a list of grounds for refusing recognition or enforcement – there is no equivalent to article 36 of the ML in the IAA. Does this mean that the Court must enforce awards even if there is no valid arbitration agreement or even if the tribunal has exceeded its jurisdiction, for example? The answer is obvious: of course not. But how can a Court refuse enforcement when there is no authority whatsoever in the IAA to do so? Obviously, Parliament has mistakenly left a lacuna in the IAA – it seems that Parliament forgot to enact the usual grounds for refusing enforcement in section 19 IAA and left the matter at the discretion of the Courts ('<u>may</u> be enforced' says art. 19 IAA).

In the past, the Court would probably have done what Courts in Singapore have done so often before – see *John Holland*,[92] *Dermajaya*,[93] *Swift-Fortune Ltd*[94] and *Tang Boon Jek Jeffrey*,[95] for example – it would have taken an extremely narrow approach by interpreting the provisions of the law painstakingly mechanically, in complete isolation from the interpretation given to that provision of the ML or to similar provisions all around the world, thus going against the very spirit of the ML and forsaking the kind of uniform law Parliament had intended to adopt. It probably would have then stated that it is for Parliament to deal with policy issues, not the Courts. It would have added that it was simply enforcing the words of the Statutes which must be reflecting the clear intent of Parliament. Parliament would then immediately amend the law to undo what the Court had got wrong (thus proving that the Court was wrong as to the true intent of Parliament) and would re-establish the correct interpretation consistent with the ML and its spirit by adding yet one more oddly numbered section to the IAA (15A, 19A, 19B etc.) often starting with the words 'for the avoidance of doubt'.

---

[91] The chapter is only concerned with international arbitration as defined by the IAA and therefore is here concerned with the enforcement of Singapore-seated awards issued in an international arbitration. The enforcement of Singapore seated awards issued in a domestic arbitration would be governed by the AA.

[92] *John Holland Pty Ltd*, a 2001 case, note 69.

[93] *Dermajaya Properties Sdn Bhd*, a 2002 case, note 71.

[94] *Swift-Fortune Ltd v. Magnifica Marine SA*, a 2006 case, note 31 and following discussion.

[95] *Tang Boon Jek Jeffrey*, a 2001 case, note 76.

We are of course thankful that the Singapore Parliament has soldiered on all these years, rapidly undoing the mistakes of the Courts in interpreting the ML, but it could not have been good for the reputation of Singapore that Parliament constantly had to correct the Courts to reestablish its clear intent – i.e., that the ML should be interpreted as a uniform law consistent with its general principles and its generally accepted interpretation worldwide.

Over the past decade, however, the Courts in Singapore have greatly improved in their interpretation of the ML and the IAA, not hesitating to look at the *travaux préparatoires*, sometimes at precedent from other Model Law countries rather than from England and implementing the ML as a uniform law.

The 2014 case of *PT First Media*[96] is the perfect consecration and the logical outcome of this new approach – when faced with a lacuna, a clear gap in the IAA, the Court of Appeal filled the gap, taking its inspiration from the ML and more specifically from article 36 of the ML, in effect almost implementing its very wording, notwithstanding the fact that Parliament specifically refused to adopt article 36 of the ML.

As mentioned above, article 19 IAA provides that Singapore-seated awards are enforceable but does not provide any ground authorizing a Court to refuse enforcement – there is no equivalent to article 36 of the ML.

In *PT First Media*, the Court of Appeal decided that the purpose of the IAA is the implementation of the ML and that even though Parliament did not adopt article 36 of the ML, in the spirit or philosophy of the ML the Courts should inspire themselves of the grounds found at article 36 ML, notwithstanding the fact that it is not in force in Singapore.

At para. 55 the Court stated:

> it is clear that the scope of the power to refuse enforcement in s 19 could no longer draw direct and complete inspiration from the English authorities once the IAA came into force. [. . .] The adoption of the Model Law was a game changer which necessitated an 'update' of the content of the power under s 19. In short, the construction of the power to refuse enforcement under s 19 now had to be consonant with the underlying philosophy of the Model Law on the enforcement of all awards generally and more specifically, domestic international awards.

---

[96] *PT First Media TBK* v. *Astro Nusantara International BV* [2014] 1 SLR 372.

And at para. 84:

> The content of the power to refuse enforcement under s 19 must be construed in accordance with the purpose of the IAA which, as we have stated, is to embrace the Model Law. Given that de-emphasising the seat of arbitration by maintaining the award debtor's 'choice of remedies' and alignment with the grounds under the New York Convention are the pervading themes under the enforcement regime of the Model Law, the most efficacious method of giving full effect to the Model Law philosophy would, in our view, be to recognise that the same *grounds* for resisting enforcement under Art. 36(1) are equally available to a party resisting enforcement under s 19 of the IAA.

Whereas more than a decade ago some Singapore judges were refusing to implement the spirit and philosophy of the ML even when Parliament had adopted its provisions, now we have a judgment of the Court of Appeal which implements the spirit and philosophy of the ML even though Parliament did not implement the relevant provision. The Court of Appeal is implementing the policy of Parliament – 'the Model Law philosophy' – rather than the wording of the Statute or the case law under the English Arbitration Act.

PT First Media is a watershed decision which not only changes the law in interpreting section 19 IAA but in fact seems radically to change the approach of the Court of Appeal in interpreting the ML and the IAA. The Singapore Court of Appeal seems completely to abandon its past, narrow and parochial approach to the interpretation of the ML and the IAA and endorses a purposive approach. In my view, this augurs well for the future implementation of the ML in Singapore.

PT First Media also confirms that a party has a choice of remedy at the seat of the arbitration: it may decide to contest the jurisdiction of the tribunal under 16(3) ML or to try to set aside the award on the one hand, or, on the other hand, it may decide to wait until the other party seeks enforcement and then resist enforcement – this choice of remedy is said to be a fundamental feature of the ML and the ML philosophy.

One can therefore conclude that, notwithstanding the fact that Singapore has not adopted articles 35 and 36 of the ML, as far as awards by a Singapore-seated tribunal are concerned, the effect of Singapore law is the same as the effect of articles 35 and 36 of the ML.

Recognition and Enforcement of Foreign Awards Governed by the New York Convention

As mentioned above, Singapore enforces foreign awards through the NYC as implemented by Part III of the IAA and does so by adopting international best practices – the Singapore Courts rarely refuse to enforce foreign awards – they interpret the concept of public policy, for example, very narrowly. Article 35 of the ML is similar in effect to the NYC and article 36 is even similar in wording to the NYC. Therefore, overall, the implementation of the NYC by the IAA achieves the same objectives as articles 35 and 36 of the ML as far as foreign awards are concerned.

Under the IAA, a foreign award can be enforced by action or simply with leave of the Court 'in the same manner as a judgment' as provided by section 19 IAA for the enforcement of awards by Singapore-seated tribunals.[97] The Rules of Court implements these recourses.[98]

As is the case under article 35(2) of the ML, and as provided by the NYC, the party seeking enforcement must produce: an original or certified copy of the award and of the arbitration agreement, and, when the award or agreement are not in English, a certified translation.[99]

As I have written elsewhere:[100]

> The IAA provides the very same limited grounds found in the NYC and the ML why a Court may refuse enforcement (incapacity, or other invalidity of the agreement, improper notice, inability to present one's case, lack or excess of jurisdiction, improper composition of tribunal or conduct of procedure, non-arbitrability in Singapore or the award is against the public policy of Singapore).[101]
>
> Whereas a Court may set aside an award from a tribunal seated in Singapore if it is 'induced or affected by fraud or corruption' or 'a breach of the rules of natural justice occurred in connection with the making of the award',[102] these additional grounds are not reasons to refuse enforcement of an award under Part III of the IAA for awards governed by the NYC.[103]

---

[97] Section 29(1) IAA. Section 29(2) provides for the recognition of awards as follows 'Any foreign award which is enforceable under subsection (1) shall be recognised as binding for all purposes upon the persons between whom it was made and may accordingly be relied upon by any of those parties by way of defence, set-off or otherwise in any legal proceedings in Singapore.'

[98] See Rule 69A of the Rules of Court on the procedure for the recourses under the IAA. Rule 69 plays a similar role under the *AA*.

[99] Section 30 IAA. This implements article IV of the New York Convention.

[100] Bell/Oxford, note 1 at [86]–[87].

[101] Section 31 IAA. These reasons are the same as those found at article 24 ML in the context of setting aside an award by a Singapore-seated tribunal.

[102] Section 24 IAA.

[103] It would be a violation of Singapore's obligations under the New York Convention to provide for additional reasons why a Court could refuse enforcement.

The Singapore Courts have an extremely good record at enforcing foreign awards and it is very rare that a Court would refuse enforcement. In fact, a Court has described the process as 'mechanistic'.[104]

There is one way, however, in which the enforcement of foreign awards under the NYC implemented by the IAA may be more restrictive than the enforcement of awards by Singapore-seated tribunals – the writing requirement for foreign awards is that of the NYC, which is more stringent than the writing requirement of section 2A IAA implementing parts of option 1 or article 7 ML 2006 which apply when an arbitration is seated in Singapore. This, however, remains in the vast majority of cases a theoretical problem as the vast majority of arbitration agreements are fully documented in writing.[105]

Finally, it should be noted that section 33(1) IAA, the last section in Part III, states: 'nothing in this Part shall affect the right of any person to enforce an arbitral award otherwise than as is provided for in this Part'. There therefore may be other ways to enforce foreign awards in Singapore.[106]

In summary, even though Singapore has not adopted articles 35 and 36 of the ML, in the end the result is almost exactly the same: almost all arbitral awards, whether domestic or foreign, can be enforced in Singapore and the list of grounds for refusing enforcement are as limited and exhaustive as they would be under article 36 of the ML. The difference is that the way to the identical result is much more convoluted in Singapore than under articles 35 and 36 of the ML.

Conclusion

The ML is now very well implemented in Singapore. It has not always been the case but nowadays the Courts do understand the ML well and have taken a very arbitration-friendly approach while maintaining proper Court supervision when needed. The Courts have even now taken an active role in interpreting the ML according to its purpose,

---

[104] *Aloe Vera of America, Inc.* v. *Asianic Food (S) Pte Ltd* [2006] 3 SLR(R) 174, [2006] SGHC 78 (High Ct) at [42].

[105] For a more complete and detailed analysis of this issue, see Bell/Oxford, note 1 at [91]–[98].

[106] For example, one could enforce an award under Singapore's Reciprocal Enforcement of Commonwealth Judgments Act, C. 264, rev. S. Sing. The Act is specifically mentioned at section 33(2) which makes clear that one may choose under which Act one wants to enforce. One could also enforce an award under the Arbitration (International Investment Disputes) Act, c. 11, rev. S. Sing, sections 4 and 5.

even going so far as interpreting the IAA and the AA in a manner consistent with the spirit and purpose of the ML.

Now that the interpretation and application of the ML is solidly established, there are a few things I suggest the legislator could undertake to consolidate the progress made thus far.

Consolidate the IAA and the ML into One Act

From the start, Singapore adopted the ML by saying it applies except when the IAA says otherwise. All these years the full English text of the ML 1985 has been a schedule to the IAA, and lawyers have had to figure out by reading the IAA which parts of the ML apply and which do not, and which parts of the ML apply but have been modified by the IAA. One needs to rely on lawyers who are familiar with Singapore's arbitration law to get a complete story. This is just too complicated.

Hong Kong's new Arbitration Ordinance[107] has consolidated its law into one piece of legislation which makes for very easy reading and provides greater legal certainty and clarity. The Ordinance follows the order of the ML and for each article of the ML tells us whether it applies verbatim or whether it does not apply. And if it does apply, it tells us, 'right there', what provision (an amendment of sort) replaces the ML provision. This makes for greater legal certainty and easier access to the law, especially for foreign parties.

Singapore should follow Hong Kong's example and consolidate the ML and the IAA in a similar fashion.

Also Consolidate the Arbitration Act into this New Unified Act

Increasingly the Arbitration Act is interpreted in a way that is consistent with the ML. So why not merge the two? Again, Hong Kong leads the way. Its new Ordinance applies to both international and domestic arbitrations. The few provisions from the former domestic regime which Hong Kong decided to keep for domestic arbitrations (for example, the possibility of an appeal on questions of law) were reduced to a few sections of the Ordinance which apply only to domestic arbitrations. This again simplifies the arbitration landscape.

---

[107] Arbitration Ordinance, Cap. 609 adopted in 2010 in force in 2011.

Adopt Article 2A(1) ML 2006

Even though the ML is now well interpreted, implemented and applied in Singapore, things could always be better. In particular, lawyers tend to refer to English cases when interpreting the ML even though England is not a ML jurisdiction. Maybe as a consequence of this the Singapore Courts rarely refer to cases and doctrine from other ML jurisdictions. The interpretation of the ML in Singapore needs to become much more international and what better way to encourage this than to remind the Courts and the Bar that '[i]n the interpretation of this Law, regard is to be had to its international origin and to the need to promote uniformity in its application and the observance of good faith' (article 2A(1) ML).

The implementation of the ML in Singapore is now a great success, and I hope that the proposed changes will be considered as ways of further improving the arbitration landscape in Singapore.

PART II

Jurisdictions That Have Not Adopted the
Model Law: Comparisons

9

People's Republic of China

Comparison between UN Model Law and Chinese Arbitration Law

GUO YU

Introduction

UNCITRAL Model Law on International Commercial Arbitration 2006, UN General Assembly Resolution 61/33 (4 December 2006) ('ML') is not adopted in mainland China.[1] However, UNCITRAL Model Law on International Commercial Arbitration 1985, UN General Assembly Resolution 40/72 (11 December 1985) ('ML 1985') was used as one of the references when the Arbitration Law of the People's Republic of China ('CAL') was drafted.[2] At present, China is considering amending the CAL, and the new development of the ML has been closely watched.

According to the legal theory of China, CAL must be read with the Civil Procedure Law of the People's Republic of China (CCPL).[3] International treaties are a source of law in China. If there is contradiction between Chinese domestic legislation and the international conventions ratified by China, the latter will prevail. The two most important international conventions ratified by China in the field of international commercial arbitration are the Convention on the Recognition and Enforcement of Foreign Arbitral Awards, New York, 10 June 1958, in force 7 June 1959, 330 UNTS 4739 ('NYC') and the Convention on the Settlement of Investment Disputes between States

Guo Yu is an associate professor and the Director of the Maritime Law Research Centre of the Law School, Beijing University. The author thanks the EW Barker Centre for Law & Business at the Faculty of Law of the National University of Singapore for financing her participation in the conference entitled, 'The UNCITRAL Model Law on International Commercial Arbitration in Asia', which led to this book.
[1] But the ML has been adopted by both Hong Kong SAR and Macao SAR of China.
[2] Promulgated on 31 August 1994, and effective from 1 September 1995. Amended in 2009 and 2017.
[3] Effective from 9 April 1991 and revised in 2007.

272   GUO YU

and Nationals of Other States, 1968. The judicial interpretations issued by the
Supreme People's Court are also an important part of the arbitration law of
China and can be referred to directly by the lower courts.[4]
There are more than 200 arbitration commissions in China. The China
International Economic and Trade Arbitration Commission (CIETAC)
and the China Maritime Arbitration Commission (CMAC) used to be
the only two arbitration commissions permitted to administer foreign-
related commercial arbitrations in China. But now all the arbitration
commissions may do so. Some local arbitration commissions have done
very well in foreign-related arbitrations, of which the most famous are the
Beijing Arbitration Commission (BAC) and the Shanghai International
Arbitration Center (SHIAC). All the arbitration commissions have their
own arbitration rules. Although these rules are not law, they are binding on
the parties and the institutions themselves as long as the rules are not
contrary to the law. Unlike the law, these arbitration rules usually reflect the
development and evolutionary trends of international commercial arbitration more rapidly. For example, both CIETAC and CIMC have revised
their Arbitration Rules to reflect the amendment of the ML1985 in 2006.[5]

Part I   General Provisions of the Model Law (Articles 1 to 6)

Article 1   Scope of Application

The ML applies to international commercial arbitration.
The CAL applies to both domestic and international arbitration.
Chapter 7 of the CAL is entitled 'Special provisions on foreign-related
arbitrations'. Foreign-related arbitrations are arbitrations of economic,
trade, transport and maritime disputes which involve foreign elements.[6]

---

[4] There are more than twenty judicial interpretations for the arbitration law, of which the
most important one is: The Interpretation of Issues Relating to Application of the
Arbitration Law of the People's Republic of China, promulgated by the Supreme People's
Court on 26 December 2005, effective from 8 September 2006. Adjusted in 2008.
[5] China International Economic and Trade Arbitration Commission Arbitration
Rules (2015), effective from 1 January 2015. China Maritime Arbitration Commission
Arbitration Rules (2015), effective from 1 January 2015.
[6] The 'foreign elements' include: (1) one or both parties are citizens of another country,
stateless individuals, or foreign entities or organizations; (2) the habitual residence of one
or both parties is located outside the territory of the People's Republic of China; (3) the
subject matter is located outside of China; (4) the facts that leads to the establishment,
change or termination of civil relationship occurs outside of China; (5) any other circumstance under which a case may be determined as a foreign-related civil case. See article 522
of Interpretation of the Supreme People's Court on the Application of the Civil Procedure
Law of the People's Republic of China, effective from 4 February 2015.

Normally, they should be arbitrations conducted by Chinese arbitration commissions. Arbitrations conducted by foreign arbitration commissions are called 'foreign arbitration' in China. There is no provision on foreign arbitration in the CAL, but there are provisions in the CCPL and some of the judicial interpretation of the Supreme People's Court. The conditions and procedures for the enforcement of these arbitrations are different.

It is still not clear whether the awards rendered within the territory of China by foreign arbitration institutions shall be regarded as 'domestic awards', 'foreign awards' or 'foreign-related awards' and how they will be enforced by Chinese courts.

The word 'commercial' does not appear in the CAL. It is stipulated in article 1 that the CAL is formulated in order to ensure that 'economic' disputes shall be impartially and promptly arbitrated, to protect the legitimate rights and interests of the relevant parties and to guarantee the healthy development of the socialist market economy. According to article 2 of the CAL, contractual disputes and other disputes over rights and interests in property between citizens, legal persons and other organizations that are equal subjects may be arbitrated. There is no official interpretation of the words 'other disputes over rights and interests in property'. There used to be disagreements on whether the words 'other disputes' cover tort disputes. In a judgment given in 1985, the Supreme People's Court denied the arbitrability of tort disputes.[7] However, in a series of subsequent judgments, the Supreme People's Court changed its position and gave an affirmative answer to this question. Nowadays it is generally accepted that the people's court will not exercise jurisdiction over a case if there is an effective arbitration agreement between the parties even if the cause of action is tort.

According to article 3 of the CAL, the following disputes may not be arbitrated:

(1) marital, adoption, guardianship, support and succession disputes;
(2) administrative disputes that shall be handled by administrative organs as prescribed by law.

The CAL does not apply to arbitration of labour disputes and arbitration of disputes over contracts for undertaking agricultural projects within agricultural collective economic organizations. According to article 77 of the CAL, these two kinds of arbitrations shall be stipulated separately.

---

[7] *China National Technical Import and Export Corporation* v. *Swiss Industrial Resources Company Inc.* [1985].

Article 2   Definitions and Rules of Interpretation

Article 2 of the ML defines 'arbitration' as any arbitration whether or not administered by a permanent arbitral institution. There is no special 'definition clause' in the CAL. However, article 16(2) of the CAL provides that a valid arbitration agreement must identify an 'arbitration commission', and essentially precludes 'ad hoc' or 'party-administered' arbitration in China. However, foreign-related arbitral awards made by ad hoc arbitrations conducted outside the territory of China will be recognized as valid awards and enforced by Chinese courts.

Article 3   Receipt of Written Communications

There is no provision on the receipt of written communications in the CAL. Normally, every arbitration commission has their own rules on these matters. Most arbitration rules do not give the parties the freedom to agree on how the fact and date of receipt of written communications in arbitral proceedings are to be determined but provide instead that these matters shall be decided by the arbitration commission or the arbitral tribunal.

The principle that the receipt of written communications in arbitral proceedings may be actual or constructive has been generally adopted in the arbitration rules of Chinese arbitration commissions. For example, the CIETAC Arbitration Rules provide that the communication shall be delivered to the addressed person directly, but if direct delivery is impossible, the arbitration correspondence can be delivered by any other means that can provide a record of the attempt at delivery, including but not limited to service by public notary, entrustment or retention.[8]

Article 4   Waiver of Right to Object

There is no provision on waiver in the CAL. But some articles deal with waiver indirectly. For example, article 20 of the CAL stipulates that 'a party's challenge of the validity of the arbitration agreement shall be raised prior to the arbitral tribunal's first hearing.' It implies that if one party fails to state his objection to the validity of the arbitration agreement prior to first hearing of the arbitral tribunal, the party shall be deemed to have waived his right to object. Another example is article 26. It is

---

[8] See article 8 of the CIETAC Arbitration Rules 2015.

stipulated in this article that if the parties have concluded an arbitration agreement and one party has instituted an action in a people's court without declaring the existence of the arbitration agreement and, after the people's court has accepted the case, the other party submits the arbitration agreement prior to the first hearing, the people's court shall dismiss the case unless the arbitration agreement is null and void. If, prior to the first hearing, the other party has not raised an objection to the people's court's acceptance of the case, he shall be deemed to have renounced the arbitration agreement and the people's court shall continue to try the case.

Article 5   Extent of Court Intervention

There is no provision in the CAL equivalent to article 5 of the ML which addresses the extent of court intervention. However, article 8 of the CAL provides that arbitrations shall be carried out independently according to law and shall be free from interference of administrative organs, social organizations or individuals.

Article 6   Court or other Authority for Certain Functions of Arbitration Assistance and Supervision

Article 6 of the ML requires each enacting state to specify the court to assist in the appointment of arbitrators or to set aside an arbitral award. According to the CAL, the authority to decide on the appointment of arbitrators is the chairman of the arbitration commission instead of the court,[9] and an application for setting aside an arbitral award shall be submitted to the intermediate people's court at the place where the arbitration commission is located.[10]

Part II   Arbitration Agreement (Articles 7 to 9)

Article 7   Definition and Form of Arbitration Agreement

Chapter III of the CAL, like part II of the ML, deals with 'arbitration agreement'.

The definition of 'arbitration agreement' in the CML is very close to that in the ML. Like what is provided in the ML, an arbitration agreement

---

[9] Article 31 and 32 CAL.   [10] Article 58 CAL.

under Chinese law can be in the form of an arbitration clause contained in a contract, or in the form of a separate agreement. It can be an agreement to submit an existing dispute or a future dispute to arbitration. It must be in writing.[11]

However, there are several differences.

The most important difference is that a valid arbitration agreement must designate an arbitration commission according to the CAL.[12] Although the CAL does not give a definition of 'arbitration commission', it has a whole chapter dealing with the establishment and legal status of arbitration commissions. In particular, it is provided in article 10 that arbitration commissions may be set up in some specific cities. The people's government in these cities shall organize relevant departments and the chambers of commerce to form the arbitration commission in a unified way. When an arbitration commission is set up, it shall register with the judicial and administrative departments of the relevant government. These provisions strongly suggest that an arbitration commission shall be a Chinese organization. This leads to the question whether foreign arbitration institutions can be qualified as 'arbitration commissions' within the meaning of the CAL. For a long time, it had been generally accepted that foreign arbitration institutions were not allowed to conduct arbitration within the territory of China. But in a judicial interpretation promulgated in March 2013, the Supreme People's Court confirmed the validity of an arbitration agreement which provides 'ICC Arbitration Court, place of jurisdiction shall be Shanghai'.[13] This is looked at as a milestone to open the arbitration market to the outside world. But a dispute without a foreign element cannot be submitted to a foreign arbitration commission, whether the place of arbitration is within or outside China. For example, an application to recognize and enforce an arbitral award made by the Korean Commercial Arbitration Court was refused by Beijing No. 2 intermediate court on the basis that no foreign element was involved in that case.[14]

Another difference is that 'writing' is not defined in the CAL, and there is no provision equivalent to article 7(2) of the ML. According to

---

[11] Article 16 CAL.   [12] *Ibid.*

[13] Reply of the Supreme People's Court Regarding the Dispute on the Validity of an Arbitration Agreement between Anhui Longlide Packing and Printing Co., Ltd and BP Agnati S.R.L., Min Si Ta Zi No. 13 [2013], made on 25 March 2013.

[14] No. 10670 Civil Law Order of Beijing No. 2 Intermediate Court, made on 20 January 2014.

article 11 of the Contract Law of China,[15] 'writing' includes any form capable of tangible representation of its transmitted documents, including telegrams, telexes, facsimiles, electronic data interchange and email. Some Chinese arbitration commissions define the term 'writing' in a very broad way in their arbitration rules. However, although an arbitration commission may adopt a liberal attitude to interpret the word 'writing', it cannot explicitly waive this requirement in its arbitration rules since this will contradict the provision of the CAL directly.

Although it is not stated in the law, it is generally accepted that a signature is not necessary for a valid arbitration agreement. It is not clear whether an arbitration agreement can be formed by conduct, such as the exchange of statements of claim and defence in which the existence of an agreement is alleged by one party and not denied by another. In one case, a party stated in a letter to the other party that he would apply to CIETAC for arbitration. The other party agreed to arbitrate in the reply but did not mention the arbitration commission. The Supreme People's Court refused to enforce the arbitration award on the basis that no valid arbitration agreement existed.[16]

The third difference is that there is no stipulation on reference to arbitration agreement in another contract in the CAL. However, it is generally accepted in China that reference in a contract to another written document containing an arbitration clause would constitute an arbitration agreement if it is such as to make that clause part of the contract. Chinese contract law remains applicable to determine the level of consent necessary for a party to become bound by an arbitration agreement allegedly made by reference. A good example is the validity of the arbitration clause in a bill of lading. If a charter party is incorporated into a bill of lading, and there is an arbitration clause in the charter party, the arbitration clause can be incorporated into the bill of lading validly and will have binding force to a third party bill of lading holder. However, the incorporation clause shall be very clear and must refer to the arbitration clause specifically. In one case in which the incorporation clause stipulated that 'the clauses, conditions and exclusions of the charter party are incorporated into the bill of lading' the Supreme

---

[15] Adopted on 15 March 1999, and effective from 1 October 1999.
[16] Reply of the Supreme People's Court Regarding the Application for Enforcement of CIETAC Arbitration Award No. 0256, Min Si Ta Zi No. 42 [2001], made on 6 January 2001.

People's Court decided that such a clause was not enough to incorporate the arbitration clause of the charter party into the bill of lading.[17] Unlike the ML, the CAL lists some circumstances that will make an arbitration agreement invalid, including: matters agreed upon for arbitration are beyond the scope of arbitration prescribed by law; an arbitration agreement concluded by persons without or with limited capacity for civil acts; one party forces the other party to sign an arbitration agreement by means of duress.[18] Some scholars have criticized these provisions on the invalidation of arbitration agreements as making the CAL one of the most unfriendly legislations toward arbitration agreements in the world.

Article 8   Arbitration Agreement and Substantive Claim before Court and Article 9 Arbitration Agreement and Interim Measures by Court

The provisions of article 8(1) of the ML can be found in article 5 and article 26 of the CAL, with some modifications.

Article 5 of the CAL provides that if the parties have concluded an arbitration agreement and one party institutes an action in a people's court, the people's court shall not accept the case unless the arbitration agreement is null and void. Unlike the ML, the CAL does not require the court to 'refer' the parties to arbitration.

Article 26 of the CAL further provides that if the parties have concluded an arbitration agreement and one party institutes an action in a people's court without mentioning the existence of the arbitration agreement the people's court shall dismiss the action if the other party submits the arbitration agreement before the first hearing of the case, unless the arbitration agreement is null and void. If the other party does not challenge the jurisdiction of the people's court before the first hearing of the case, the arbitration agreement will be considered as waived and the court proceeding will continue.

There is no provision in the CAL corresponding to article 8(2) and article 9 of the ML.

---

[17] Reply of the Supreme People's Court Regarding the Validity of Arbitration Clause in the Dispute Over Insurance Subrogation Claim under Contracts for Carriage of Goods by Sea in the Case of *China Ping An Insurance Company Dalian Branch* v. *COSCO Shipping Corporation Ltd and Guangzhou Ocean Shipping Corporation Ltd*, Min Si Ta Zi No. 49 [2006], made on 26 January 2007.

[18] Article 17 CAL.

Part III   Composition of Arbitral Tribunal (Articles 10 to 15)

Article 10   Number of Arbitrators

According to article 10 of the ML, the parties are free to determine the number of arbitrators and failing such determination the number of arbitrators shall be three. According to article 30 of the CAL, the number of arbitrators shall be either one or three, subject to the choice of the parties (article 31). However, unlike article 10(2) of the ML, the CAL does not state a default number of arbitrators if the parties do not agree on a number. For a three-arbitrator tribunal, a presiding arbitrator shall be appointed.

The CAL states, under article 13, that an arbitrator shall fulfil one of the following qualifications: (1) has eight years of arbitration experience; or (2) has practised as a lawyer for eight years; or (3) has served as a judge for eight years; or (4) is conducting legal research or engaging in legal educational and holds a senior professional title; or (5) has legal knowledge, and is working in the fields of economics or trade, and holds a senior professional title.

Article 11   Appointment of Arbitrators

Article 11(1) of the ML provides that no person shall be precluded by reason of his nationality from acting as an arbitrator, unless otherwise agreed by the parties. There is no corresponding provision in the CAL. But article 67 of the CAL provides that a foreign-related arbitration commission may appoint foreigners with professional knowledge in such fields as law, economics and trade and science and technology as arbitrators. And although only the appointment of foreign arbitrators by a foreign-related arbitration commission is mentioned it is widely accepted that foreign arbitrators can be appointed in domestic arbitrations. Both CITAC and CMAC have their lists of foreign arbitrators.

The ML provides in article 11(2) that the parties are free to agree on a procedure for appointing arbitrators. There is no similar provision in the CAL. Instead, article 31 of the CAL provides a specific method to nominate arbitrators. For a three-arbitrator tribunal, each party shall appoint an arbitrator or request the director of the arbitration commission to designate an arbitrator for that party, and the parties shall appoint the third arbitrator together or request the director of the arbitration commission to designate one for them. The third arbitrator shall be the presiding arbitrator.

While the ML provides for a thirty-day limit to appoint an arbitrator in an arbitration with three arbitrators, the CAL does not provide any time limit for appointment of an arbitrator. But it is provided in article 32 of the CAL that an arbitrator shall be appointed according to that article if the parties fail to agree on the method of formation of the arbitral tribunal or to select the arbitrators within the time limit specified in the arbitration rules of the arbitration commission.

If an arbitrator or arbitrators cannot be appointed in time, the appointment shall be made, upon request of a party, by the court or other authority specified in article 6 under the ML, while the appointment shall be made by the chairman of the arbitration commission under the CAL. The ML makes it clear that the decision of the court or other authority specified in article 6 cannot be appealed, but there is no similar provision in the CAL.

Article 12   Grounds for Challenge and Article 13 Challenge Procedure

There is no provision in the CAL that arbitrators shall disclose circumstances that may give rise to justifiable doubts as to their impartiality or independence when they are appointed (article 12 of the ML). But most of the arbitration commissions provide this duty in their arbitration rules. For example, both CIETAC and CMAC require an arbitrator nominated to sign a Declaration and disclose any facts or circumstances likely to give rise to justifiable doubts as to his impartiality or independence, and promptly disclose if such circumstances arise during the arbitral proceedings.[19]

It is provided in article 12(2) of the ML that an arbitrator 'may be challenged only if circumstances exist that give rise to justifiable doubts as to his impartiality or independence'. The grounds for the challenge of an arbitrator under the CAL are listed in article 34. Although the four circumstances listed in that article may cast doubt on the impartiality and independence of an arbitrator, the terms 'impartiality and independence' are not used.[20] At the same time, while the words 'only if' in article 12(2)

---

[19] See article 31 of CIETAC Arbitration Rules (2015) and article 35 of CMAC Arbitration Rules (2015).

[20] The circumstances listed in article 34 of CAL are as follows: the arbitrator 1. is a party or a close relative of a party or of a party's representative; 2. has a personal interest in the case; 3. has some other relationship with a party to the case or with a party's agent which could possibly affect the impartiality of the arbitration; 4. has met a party or his agent in private,

of the ML suggests that the grounds in that article is a necessary condition, article 34 of the CAL provides that 'if' one of the grounds listed in that article exists, an arbitrator 'must' withdraw from the arbitration and the parties have the right to apply for his withdrawal, and suggests that the grounds in that article is a sufficient condition.

Under the ML, the challenge must be brought 'fifteen days after becoming aware of the constitution of the arbitral tribunal or after becoming aware of any circumstance' giving rise to the challenge (article 13(2) ML). But article 35 of the CAL provides that the challenge must be brought before the first hearing or before the conclusion of the last hearing if reasons for the challenge only became known after the start of the first hearing.

Under the ML, the arbitral tribunal shall decide on the challenge of the arbitrator (13(2) ML). But under the CAL, the decision shall be made by the chairman of the arbitration commission. If the chairman is an arbitrator of the arbitral tribunal, the decision shall be made collectively by the arbitration commission (article 36 CAL). Under the ML, if a challenge of an arbitrator is not successful, the challenging party may request the court to make a decision, and the decision of the court shall be final and cannot be appealed (article 13(3) ML). Under the CAL, there is no corresponding provision.

While the parties are free to decide on the procedure for challenge under the ML, they have no such freedom under the CAL.

Article 14   Failure or Impossibility to Act

There is no rule in the CAL dealing with an arbitrator's impossibility or failure to act.

Article 15   Appointment of Substitute Arbitrator

Both the ML and the CAL allow a substitute arbitrator to be selected or appointed if an arbitrator cannot perform his duties due to his withdrawal or for other reasons. But there is an additional provision in the CAL. After a substitute arbitrator has been selected or appointed on account of an arbitrator's withdrawal, a party may request that the arbitration proceedings already carried out should be carried out anew.

accepted an invitation for dinner by a party or his representative or accepted gifts presented by any of them.

The decision as to whether to approve this or not shall be made by the arbitral tribunal. The arbitral tribunal may also make a decision on its own initiative.

In addition, there is a special penalty for arbitrators in the CAL. If an arbitrator meets a party or his agent in private, accepts an invitation for dinner by a party or his representative, or accepts gifts presented by any of them and the situation is serious, or if he has solicited or accepted bribes, practised favouritism and bent the law while arbitrating a case or making a ruling, he shall be liable for legal responsibilities according to the law and the arbitration commission shall remove his name from the panel.[21]

Part IV   Jurisdiction of Arbitral Tribunal (Article 16)

Article 16   Competence of Arbitral Tribunal to Rule on its Jurisdiction

Article 16(1) of the ML recognizes both the principle of *kompetenz-kompetenz/compétence-compétence* (an arbitral tribunal can rule on its own jurisdiction) and the principle of severability (an arbitration agreement is separate from the main contract). Unlike the ML, the CAL does not recognize the principle of *kompetenz-kompetenz/compétence-compétence*. In article 20 of the CAL, it is provided that if one party wishes to challenge the existence or validity of an arbitration agreement, he shall request the arbitration commission or the people's court to make a decision. If one party makes such a request to the arbitration commission and the other party makes a request to the people's court, the decision shall be made by the people's court.

The priority of the people's court in deciding the existence or validity of an arbitration agreement has been confirmed by the Supreme People's Court in several judicial interpretations. For example, in one of its judicial interpretations, the Supreme People's Court pointed out that if the parties disputed the validity of an arbitration agreement, and one party has submitted the matter to the arbitration commission while the other party has instituted an action in a court, if the arbitration commission has accepted this application and has made a decision, the court shall dismiss the case. However, if the arbitration commission has accepted this application but has not yet made a decision, the court

[21] See article 38 of the CAL.

shall accept the case and inform the arbitration commission to suspend the application.[22]

The judicial interpretation of the Supreme People's Court also provides that the validity of an arbitration agreement with a foreign element shall be decided according to the law agreed by the parties. If there is no such agreement but there is an agreement on the place of arbitration, the law of the place of arbitration will apply. Otherwise the law of the place of the court will apply.[23]

Some arbitration commissions in China have tried to remedy this situation through their own rules. For example, the Beijing Arbitration Commission provides in its rules that the challenge shall be decided by the arbitration commission and the arbitration commission can empower the arbitral tribunal to make the decision for it. This is an attempt to broaden the jurisdiction of the arbitral tribunal without contradicting directly the provisions of the CAL.[24]

The challenge of the jurisdiction of the arbitral tribunal shall be raised not later than the submission of the statement of defence under the ML, while the time to challenge is prior to the first hearing in China according to article 20 of the CAL. It is not provided in the CAL whether the decision on validity of the arbitration agreement can be appealed.

The Principle of Severability (Article 16)

Although the CAL does not adopt the principle of *kompetenz-kompetenz/compétence-compétence*, it does adopt the principle of severability. It is provided in article 19 of the CAL that arbitration agreements are deemed severable from the main contracts. Any modification, rescission, termination or invalidity of the main contract does not affect the validity of the arbitration agreement. This principle is also confirmed by article 57 of the Contract Law, which provides that the invalidity, rescission or termination of a contract does not affect the validity of independently existing clauses of the contract that concern the method of dispute resolution. An arbitration agreement will continue to be binding on the

---

[22] Reply of the Supreme People's Court Regarding Several Issues Relating to Validity of Arbitration Agreements, FaShi No.27 [1998], made on 26 October 1998.

[23] See article 16 of The Interpretation of Issues Relating to Application of the Arbitration Law of the People's Republic of China, promulgated by the Supreme People's Court on 26 December 2005, effective from 8 September 2006.

[24] See article 6 of Beijing Arbitration Commission Arbitration Rules (2015).

parties even if the main contract is terminated or suspended. This principle has also been stressed in legal practice. According to one judicial interpretation of the Supreme People's Court,[25] where a contract has not entered into force or has been cancelled after its formation, the principle of severability shall apply to the recognition of the validity of the arbitration agreement; where the parties concerned have reached an arbitration agreement at the conclusion of the contract, the non-formation of such contract shall not affect the validity of the arbitration agreement.

It is provided in article 16(2) of the ML that a party should not be estopped from invoking a lack of jurisdiction by the mere fact that it has participated in the appointment of an arbitrator. There is no similar provision in the CAL.

There is no mention that an arbitral tribunal may hear a challenge that it has exceeded its jurisdiction. Nor is there a principle that the arbitral tribunal has the discretion to rule on a plea that it has no jurisdiction either as a preliminary question or in an award on the merits.

It is not stated in the CAL whether the arbitral tribunal may continue with the arbitral proceeding if a court action on the tribunal's jurisdiction is pending. But both CIETAC and CMAC stipulate in their arbitration rules that the arbitration shall proceed notwithstanding an objection to the arbitration agreement and/or jurisdiction over the arbitration case.[26] Even if the arbitration is suspended because of a challenge of jurisdiction, if the challenge is dismissed by the court, the arbitral proceeding shall continue.

Part IV-A   Interim Measures and Preliminary Orders (Articles 17 to 17J)

Sub-Part I   Measures and Orders by the Tribunal (Articles 17 to 17G)

The words 'interim measures' and 'preliminary orders' have not been used in the CAL. While 'interim measures' under the ML is used in a much broader sense, the only recognized interim measures that can be used in arbitration in China are property preservation and evidence preservation.

---

[25] See article 10 of The Interpretation of Issues Relating to Application of the Arbitration Law of the People's Republic of China, promulgated by the Supreme People's Court on 26 December 2005, effective from 8 September 2006.

[26] See article 6 of CIETAC Arbitration Rules (2015) and article 6 of CMAC Arbitration Rules (2015).

According to the ML, both the court and the arbitral tribunal have power to give a preliminary order. In China, before 1982, the arbitration commission had the power to order a party to take interim measures. The CCPL enacted in 1982 changed this practice and provided that the arbitration commission shall submit the application to the court, and the court is the only authority that can give an order of interim measures. Accordingly, article 28 of the CAL provides that a party may apply for property preservation, and the arbitration commission shall submit the party's application to the people's court in accordance with the relevant provisions of CCPL. The arbitration commission has no power to order an interim measure of protection directly. And it must submit the party's application without review and without any condition. The legal theory supporting this is that the arbitration commission is a non-official organization and shall not have enforcement power.

It is suggested by some scholars that China should empower the arbitral tribunal to adopt interim measures and they believe that this can give the arbitral tribunal more control over the conduct of the arbitration and can save time and money. It is provided in the new CIETAC Arbitration Rules that unless otherwise agreed by the parties the arbitral tribunal has the power to order appropriate interim measures at the request of a party. Where the arbitral tribunal has not yet been formed, a party may apply for emergency relief pursuant to the CIETAC Emergency Arbitrator Procedures.[27] Similar provisions can be found in CMAC Arbitration Rules and China (Shanghai) Pilot Free Trade Zone (FTZ) Arbitration Rules.[28]

Sub-Part II   Recognition and Enforcement of Interim Measures (Articles 17H and 17I)

According to the relevant provisions of CAL and CCPL, the people's court is the only authority that can decide and enforce interim measures.

Since an arbitral tribunal does not have the power to give an interim measures order in China, if arbitration is conducted in China and the arbitral tribunal gives a preliminary order according to its arbitration rules or procedure rules chosen by the parties, the order cannot be enforced by Chinese courts. It is suggested that if interim measures need

---

[27] See article 77 of CIETAC Arbitration Rules (2015).
[28] See article 74 of CMAC Arbitration Rules (2015); article 22 of China (Shanghai) Pilot FTZ Arbitration Rules.

to be recognized and enforced in China, the arbitral tribunal shall not make an order to adopt such measures. If the interim measures shall be recognized and enforced in a foreign country and an arbitral tribunal is allowed to order interim measures in that country, then the arbitral tribunal can make such order.[29]

Sub-Part III   Court-Ordered Interim Measures (Article 17J)

Although the court is the only authority that can give an interim measures order, the parties cannot apply to the court to give such an order directly. The application must be first submitted to the arbitration commission and then transferred to the court by the arbitration commission. The court will decide to give an order 'if there is proof that irreparable loss will be caused if the interim measure is not adopted' (CCPL article 101). The court has the power to order the applicant to provide appropriate security (CCPL article 100). When the application is faulty, the applicant shall compensate the other party for the losses incurred from the adoption of interim measures (CCPL article 105).

Part V   Conduct of Arbitral Proceedings (Articles 18 to 27)

Article 18   Equal Treatment of Parties

Although there is no express provision in the CAL corresponding to Article 18 of the ML which provides the equal treatment of parties, the principle that the parties must be treated with equality can be inferred from several articles of the CAL. For example, article 1 of the CAL provides that 'this law is formulated with a view to ensuring fair and timely arbitration of disputes over economic matters, safeguarding the legitimate rights and interests of the disputing parties and guaranteeing the sound development of the socialist market economy.' Article 7 provides that 'arbitration shall be conducted on the basis of fact and in accordance with the law, and settle the disputes fairly and rationally.' Also, the principle that parties must be given a full opportunity of presenting their case can be inferred from several articles of the CAL. For example, article 39 of the CAL provides that a hearing shall be held unless the parties agreed otherwise. Article 41 provides that the

---

[29] Opinions on Judicial Review and Enforcement of Arbitration Cases under FTZ Arbitration Rules, promulgated by Shanghai No. 2 intermediate court on 4 May 2014.

arbitration commission shall notify both parties of the date of the hearing within the time prescribed in the arbitration rules. Article 47 provides that each party has a right to debate in the arbitration proceeding, and, at the end of the debate, the presiding arbitrator or the sole arbitrator shall solicit the final opinion of each party.

Article 19   Determination of Rules of Procedure

The principle that the parties are free to agree on the arbitral procedure is not adopted in the CAL. Nor is there a principle that, in the absence of the parties' agreement, the arbitral tribunal has discretion to decide on the arbitral procedure.

Article 20   Place of Arbitration

There is no provision on 'place of arbitration' in the CAL. But there are some provisions on 'place of the arbitration commission'. For example, it is provided in article 58 of the CAL that the application to set aside an arbitral award shall be applied to the intermediate people's court where the arbitration commission is located. Since ad hoc arbitration is not recognized in China, the place where the arbitration commission is located is normally the place of arbitration. However, since the foreign arbitration commissions are allowed to arbitrate in China now, a heated debate has been sparked on how to decide the place of arbitration in these arbitrations.

There is no provision on the free agreement of the place of arbitration in the CAL. But such freedom is recognized in practice. For example, it is provided in a judicial interpretation that in case the parties have not agreed on the law applicable to the arbitration agreement but have agreed the place of arbitration, the law of the place of arbitration will be applied to determine the validity of the arbitration agreement.[30] The parties are free to agree to meet at any place to conduct the arbitration regardless of the place of arbitration, and, in the absence of the parties' agreement, the arbitral tribunal may also elect to meet at places other than the place of arbitration.

---

[30] See article 16 of The Interpretation of Issues Relating to Application of the Arbitration Law of the People's Republic of China, promulgated by the Supreme People's Court on 26 December 2005, effective from 8 September 2006.

Article 21   Commencement of Arbitral Proceedings

Under the ML, the parties are free to agree on the point of time at which the arbitral proceedings commence, and, in the absence of agreement, the arbitration commences on the date on which a request for that dispute to be referred to arbitration is received by the respondent. Under the CAL, a party pursuing arbitration must formally submit to the arbitration commission a written application which is properly signed and/or stamped, containing the necessary particulars,[31] accompanied by the underlying arbitration agreement. Within five days from the receipt of the application, the arbitration commission will issue a Notice of Arbitration to the parties. The time of issue of the Notice of Arbitration is the official time at which an arbitration proceeding has started. But some Chinese arbitration commissions have different rules. For example, the new CIETAC Arbitration Rules stipulate that the arbitral proceedings shall commence on the day on which the Arbitration Court receives a request for arbitration.[32]

Article 22   Language

Under the ML, the parties are free to agree on the language(s) to be used in the arbitral proceedings. In the absence of parties' agreement, the arbitral tribunal is empowered to decide the language to be used in the arbitral proceedings. The documentary evidence needs to be translated into the language used in the arbitral proceedings only when so ordered by the arbitral tribunal.

There is no similar provision in the CAL. But some Chinese arbitration commissions have similar provisions in their arbitration rules. For example, according to CIETAC Arbitration Rules (2015), where the parties have agreed on the language of arbitration, their agreement shall prevail. In the absence of such agreement, the language of arbitration to be used in the proceedings shall be Chinese. CIETAC may also designate another language as the language of arbitration having regard to the

---

[31] According to article 23 of the CAL, the written application must have the following particulars: the name, sex, age, occupation, place of employment and address of each of the parties to the arbitration; the name and address of any legal representative or principal leading members; the arbitration claim and the facts and argument on which the claim is based; and evidence, together with the source of the evidence, and the names and addresses of all witnesses.

[32] See article 11 of CIETAC Arbitration Rules (2015).

circumstances of the case. The arbitral tribunal or the Arbitration Court may, if it considers it necessary, require the parties to submit a corresponding translation of their documents and evidence into Chinese or other languages.[33]

Article 23 Statements of Claim and Defence

Under the CAL, the claimant shall submit a written arbitration application (articles 21–23 CAL). After receiving the copy of the arbitration application, the respondent shall furnish a defence to the arbitration commission within the period prescribed in the arbitration rules (article 25 CAL). But the absence of a defence on the part of the respondent does not affect the arbitration process. The claimant may renounce or change the arbitration request. The respondent may acknowledge or rebut the arbitration request and has the right to submit a counter-request. There is no provision on the time limit to amendment or supplement.

Article 24 Hearings and Written Proceedings

Article 24 of the ML provides that unless otherwise agreed by the parties, the arbitral tribunal shall decide whether to hold a hearing or not. But, according to article 39 of the CAL, an arbitral tribunal must hold a hearing unless the parties have agreed that there would be no oral hearings. In that case, the arbitral tribunal may render an award in accordance with the arbitration application, the statement of defence and other documents.[34] The arbitral tribunal does not have the power to decide a written proceeding only, in the absence of the parties' agreement.

Under the CAL, the arbitration proceedings shall not be conducted openly. The parties can come to an agreement to conduct the arbitration openly, except for cases which involve state secrets.

Article 25 Default of a Party

Unlike article 25(3) of the ML which provides that the arbitral tribunal may continue to conduct the arbitration and make an award if either party fails to appear in the hearing or provide the evidence, article 42 of the CAL distinguishes between the failure of the claimant and the

---

[33] See article 81 of CIETAC Arbitration Rules (2015). [34] See article 39 of CAL.

failure of the respondent to appear in the hearing. If the claimant fails to appear before the arbitral tribunal without justified reasons after having been notified in writing or leaves the hearing prior to its conclusion without the permission of the tribunal, he may be deemed to have withdrawn his application for arbitration. If the respondent fails to appear before the arbitral tribunal without justified reasons after having been notified in writing or leaves the hearing prior to its conclusion without the permission of the tribunal, a default award may be made.[35]

Article 26   Expert Appointed by Arbitral Tribunal and Article 27
Court Assistance in Taking Evidence

According to article 27 of the ML, the arbitral tribunal or a party with the approval of the arbitral tribunal may request from a competent court assistance in taking evidence. The court may execute the request within its competence and according to its rules on taking evidence.

Article 43 of the CAL provides that parties shall offer evidence in support of their own arguments. The arbitral tribunal may, as it considers necessary, collect evidence on its own initiative. Article 46 of the CAL provides that if the evidence may be lost or hard to obtain in the future, the parties may apply for evidence preservation. The arbitration commission shall submit the application to the local people's court where the evidence is located. Article 45 provides that all the evidence shall be presented in the hearing and the parties can cross-examine each other.

The arbitration rules of some arbitration commissions allow parties more freedom and arbitral tribunal broader discretion with respect to the rule of evidence. For example, China (Shanghai) Pilot Free Trade Zone (FTZ) Arbitration Rules provide that where parties have agreed on rules relating to evidence the agreement between the parties shall prevail except where such agreement is inoperative. The tribunal can issue procedural directions and lists of questions, hold pre-hearing meetings and preliminary hearings, produce terms of reference, and make arrangements on exchange and/or examination of evidence. The tribunal can undertake investigations and collect evidence as well as consult with experts.[36]

---

[35] See article 42 of CAL.   [36] See article 44 and article 53 of FTZ Arbitration Rules.

Part VI Making of Award and Termination of Proceedings (Articles 28 to 33)

Article 28 Rules Applicable to Substance of Dispute

According to article 28 of the ML, arbitrators must decide the case in accordance with the rules of law chosen by the parties. If there is no such agreement, the arbitral tribunal will apply the rules of private international law to determine the applicable substantive law. Arbitrators shall make the award on the basis of the contractual agreement of the parties and with reference to the international practice.

According to article 7 of the CAL, disputes shall be fairly and reasonably settled by arbitration on the basis of facts and in accordance with the relevant provisions of law. There is no provision in the CAL on the choice of law problem. But there is a provision in the Contract Law of China that the parties are free to choose law by agreement to govern their contract and accordingly settle their contractual disputes under the chosen law.[37] There is no provision on whether the arbitral tribunal may decide the dispute *ex aequo et bono* or as *amiable compositeur*. Some arbitral commissions have tried to arbitrate *ex aequo et bono* in practice, but the legal effect is still not clear.[38]

Article 29 Decision-Making by Panel of Arbitrators

Both the ML and the CAL provide that the arbitral award shall be made by a majority. But CAL has further provisions addressing the issues of the minority opinion and the situation where a majority opinion cannot be attained. According to article 53 of the CAL, the arbitral award shall be made in accordance with the opinion of the majority of the arbitrators. The opinion of the minority of the arbitrators may be entered in the record. If the arbitral tribunal is unable to form a majority opinion, the arbitration award shall be made in accordance with the opinion of the presiding arbitrator. While under the ML, the presiding arbitrator can only decide the questions of procedures if so authorized by the parties or all members of the tribunal.

---

[37] See article 126 of the Contract Law of China.
[38] For example, there is a report that Tian Jin Arbitration Commission has tried to decide the construction disputes *ex aequo et bono*.

Article 30   Settlement

According to article 49 of CAL, after an application for arbitration has been made, the parties may settle their dispute on their own. If the parties have reached a settlement agreement, they may request the arbitral tribunal to make an arbitration award in accordance with the settlement agreement; alternatively, they may withdraw their application for arbitration. An arbitral award on agreed terms has the same status and effect as any other award on the merits of the case.

Article 31   Form and Contents of Award

According to article 54 of the CAL, an arbitration award shall specify the arbitration claim, the facts of the dispute, the reasons for the decision, the results of the award, the allocation of arbitration fees and the date of the award. If the parties agree that they do not wish the facts of the dispute and the reasons for the decision to be specified in the arbitration award, the same may be omitted. The arbitration award shall be signed by the arbitrators and receive the seal of the arbitration commission. An arbitrator with dissenting opinions as to the arbitration award may sign or not sign the award as he wishes. The dissenting opinions are neither required nor prohibited in the award. Each party of the arbitration shall be delivered a copy of the award properly signed and sealed.

Arbitral awards can be divided into two kinds: partial award and final award. In arbitration proceedings, if a part of the facts involved has already become clear, the arbitral tribunal may first make a partial award, that is, an award in respect of such part of the facts.[39] A partial award is also 'final' in the sense that it is binding as to the issues it deals with and cannot be changed. If an award resolves all the issues at stake, it is a final award. The arbitral tribunal is obliged to make a final award.

Article 32   Termination of Proceedings

Article 32 of the ML which deals with termination of proceedings, has not been adopted in the CAL. Under the CAL, the arbitral tribunal is not asked to make an order to terminate the arbitral proceedings. It is not clear whether the parties have a right to have the arbitral proceedings terminated as a result of their settlement during the proceedings. According to

[39] See article 55 of CAL.

article 42 of CAL, if the applicant for arbitration does not appear before the tribunal without good reasons or leaves the tribunal room during a hearing without the permission of the arbitral tribunal, such applicant shall be deemed as having withdrawn his application. It is not clearly stated in the law that the withdrawal of application will terminate the arbitral proceedings. But according to the arbitration rules of CIETAC and CMAC, the arbitral tribunal shall make the decision as to whether to dismiss a case if the claim and counterclaim have been withdrawn in their entirety.

There is no principle in the CAL that the arbitral proceedings shall be terminated if the continuation of the proceedings has become unnecessary or impossible. Nor is there the principle that the arbitrators would become *functus officio* only when the arbitral proceedings are terminated.

Article 33   Correction and Interpretation of Award; Additional Award

Article 56 of the CAL corresponds to article 33 of the ML. It provides that the parties may, within thirty days of the receipt of the award, request the arbitral tribunal to correct any typographical errors, calculation errors or matters which had been awarded but omitted in the award. The arbitral tribunal may do this correction on its own initiative, and there is no time limit. There is no provision in the CAL about the interpretation of the award. Nor is there any rule on additional awards.

Some arbitration commissions have made things clearer in their arbitration rules. For example, CMAC Arbitration Rules (2015) provides that the arbitral tribunal may, on its own initiative, make corrections in writing of any clerical, typographical or computational errors, or any errors of a similar nature contained in the award. Where any matter which should have been decided by the arbitral tribunal was omitted from the arbitration award, the arbitral tribunal may, on its own initiative or at the request of either party, make an additional award within a reasonable time after the award is made.

Part VII   Recourse against Award (Article 34)

Article 34   Application for Setting Aside as Exclusive Recourse against Arbitral Award

The provisions corresponding to article 34 of the ML are set forth in Chapter V of the CAL. There are also special provisions on the setting aside of foreign-related awards in article 70, Chapter VII of the CAL.

According to article 34(1) of the ML, an application for setting aside is the only recourse against an arbitral award. There is no similar provision in the CAL, although this is clear if article 9 and Chapter V of the CAL are read together.

Article 61 of the CAL corresponds to article 34(4) of the ML. Both articles permit the court to suspend the setting aside proceeding and remit the case to the arbitral tribunal for re-arbitration, but on different conditions. Under the ML, the court shall do so at the request of one party. Under the CAL, the court shall do so on its own initiative.

Grounds to Set Aside

The grounds for setting aside domestic arbitral awards and foreign-related arbitral awards are different under the CAL.

For domestic arbitral awards, the grounds are listed in article 58 as follows:

(1) there is no arbitration agreement;
(2) the matters decided in the award exceed the scope of the arbitration agreement or are beyond the arbitral authority of the arbitration commission;
(3) the formation of the arbitral tribunal or the arbitration procedure was not in conformity with statutory procedure;
(4) the evidence on which the award is based was forged;
(5) the other party has withheld evidence sufficiently to affect the impartiality of the arbitration;
(6) while arbitrating the case, the arbitrators committed embezzlement, accepted bribes, practiced graft or made an award that perverted the law.

The grounds listed above are not limited to procedural matters, just as is article 34(2) of the ML, but include grounds which concern or relate to the merits of the award.

In addition, the court shall rule *ex officio* to set aside a domestic award if the award is contrary to the social and public interest.

For foreign-related arbitral awards, the grounds are not listed in the CAL but in the CCPL. Article 70 of the CAL provides that a foreign-related arbitral award shall be set aside if one of the grounds listed in article 260(1) of the CCPL exists. These grounds are as follows:

(1) the parties have neither included an arbitration clause in their contract nor subsequently concluded a written arbitration agreement;

(2) the party against whom the enforcement is sought was not notified to appoint an arbitrator or to take part in the arbitration proceedings, or the party against whom the enforcement is sought was unable to state his opinions due to reasons for which he is not responsible;
(3) the formation of the arbitral tribunal or the arbitration procedure was not in conformity with the rules of arbitration; or
(4) matters decided in the award exceeded the scope of the arbitration agreement or were beyond the authority of the arbitration institution.

In addition, if the people's court determines that enforcement of the said award would be contrary to the social and public interests of the People's Republic of China, it shall rule to refuse enforcement.

Jurisdiction to Set Aside

Article 58 of the CAL provides that the application for setting aside an arbitral award shall be made to the intermediate people's court at the place where the arbitration commission is located.

This provision is widely criticized as 'outdated', since the place of arbitration commission was usually the same as the place of arbitration in the past, but today this is no longer the case. The common practice in today's world is to give jurisdiction to set aside an arbitral award to the court where the arbitral award is made. So, it is suggested that the proper court to hear an application to set aside an arbitral award shall be the intermediate people's court at the place where the arbitration is conducted.

Article 58 provides that the people's court shall set aside an award if the existence of one of the grounds listed in that article is confirmed by its collegiate bench upon examination and verification. The word 'shall' indicates that the court does not have the discretion to refuse to set aside an award if one of the grounds listed in article 58 exists. However, the court has the discretion to suspend a setting aside proceeding if it holds that the case may be re-arbitrated by the arbitral tribunal. In that case, the court shall inform the arbitral tribunal to re-arbitrate the case within a certain period of time. If the arbitral tribunal refuses to re-arbitrate, the court shall rule to resume the setting aside procedure.

Time Limit to Set Aside

Under the CAL, if a party applies for setting aside an award, his application shall be submitted within six months after receipt of the award.

This is twice as long as under the ML, which is three months. Under both the CAL and the ML, this starts after the time of receipt of the award. But there are exceptions to this time under the ML, and no such exception exists under the CAL.

According to the CAL, the people's court shall render its decision for setting aside the award or for rejection of the application within two months following receipt of the application for setting aside. There is no such provision in the ML.

Special Procedure to Set Aside a Foreign-Related Arbitral Award

The procedures for setting aside are also different for domestic awards and foreign or foreign-related awards. For setting aside a foreign or foreign-related award, a special prior reporting procedure shall be followed. That is, any people's court seeking to set aside a foreign or foreign-related award must first obtain approval from the superior people's court in the same jurisdiction. Any superior court that decides to uphold a lower court's decision to set aside the foreign or foreign-related award must, in turn, report its decision to the Supreme People's Court prior for finalizing the decision to set aside. This special procedure serves to avoid the negative impact of local protectionism and to safeguard the authority of arbitration. However, some criticisms have been made concerning this procedure. For example, it is not clear what the consequences are if a lower court fails to report its decision to set aside a foreign or foreign-related arbitral award. And the procedure can also cause problems regarding how to protect the interests of the respondent.

Part VIII   Recognition and Enforcement of Awards
(Articles 35 and 36)

Article 35   Recognition and Enforcement

Chapter VI of the CAL addresses the enforcement of arbitral awards. There are three articles in this chapter.

Article 62 provides that an arbitral award shall be executed by each party. If any party fails to perform his obligations under an award, the other party can apply to the court for enforcement, and the court shall enforce the award. Unlike article 35(1) of the ML, there is no specific requirement on the 'written' form of the application.

Article 36   Grounds for Refusing Recognition or Enforcement

Article 63 provides that if the party against whom an application for enforcement is made can prove the existence of one of the grounds listed in article 237(2) of the CCPL, the court shall not enforce the award. The grounds listed in article 237(2) of the CCPL are identical to those listed in article 58 of the CAL.

There is no special provision on the recognition and enforcement of foreign and foreign-related arbitral awards in the CAL. But the relevant provisions can be found in the CCPL. According to article 283 of the CCPL, if an award made by a foreign arbitral organ requires the recognition and enforcement by the people's court of the People's Republic of China, the party concerned shall directly apply to the intermediate people's court in the place where the party subjected to enforcement has his domicile or where his property is located. The people's court shall deal with the matter in accordance with the international treaties concluded or acceded to by the People's Republic of China or with the principle of reciprocity.

China is a contracting party to the NYC. When it acceded to the Convention, China made a reservation to NYC III. This means it will apply the Convention to the recognition and enforcement of awards made only in the territory of another contracting state. For recognition and enforcement of foreign or foreign-related awards made in the territory of another NYC contracting state, the grounds listed in the NYC will apply. For recognition and enforcement of other foreign or foreign-related awards, the principle of reciprocal treatment will apply.

Like article 36(2) of the ML, article 64 of the CAL provides that if one party applies for enforcement of an award, and the other party applies for setting aside, the court shall stop the enforcement until a decision has been made. But there is no provision on the authority of the court to order the other party to provide appropriate security in the CAL.

Special Procedure to Refuse a Foreign and Foreign-Related Award

As with the situation of setting aside, there is a special prior reporting procedure to refuse recognition and enforcement of foreign and foreign-related arbitral awards. In accordance with that procedure, any people's court seeking to refuse recognition and enforcement of a foreign or foreign-related award must first obtain approval from the superior people's court in the same jurisdiction, and the superior court must obtain approval from the Supreme People's Court if it decides to uphold the lower court's decision.

Document Requirements

There is no provision in the CAL corresponding to article 35(2) of the ML. However, to a foreign arbitral award made in the territory of another NYC contracting state, the provisions of the NYC will apply.[40] The applicant must therefore submit the following documents to the court: the application; the original arbitral award or its official copy; the original arbitration agreement or its official copy; and the legal grounds for application. If these documents are in foreign languages, the original documents shall be notarized in the country where the award was made, and a Chinese copy translated by a translation organization appointed by the court shall be submitted at the same time.

Conclusion

It is fair to say that the international commercial arbitration law in mainland China is very similar to the ML. However, it has some special features which need to be paid more attention by those who are not familiar with Chinese arbitration law and practice.

When considering international commercial arbitration in China, many people worry about the interference of the people's court. But the most important feature of Chinese arbitration law may not be the special authority of the people's court, but the special authority of arbitration commissions. According to the CAL, the arbitration commission has effective control of the whole process of arbitration. This can be seen from the requirement of a choice of a commission in arbitration agreements, the authority of the chairman of the arbitration commission in determining the validity of arbitration agreements and the role of the arbitration commission in the appointment of arbitrators. In fact, there is a whole chapter dealing with the legal status of arbitration commissions in CAL. The emphasis on commissions reflects their social and cultural backgrounds. Arbitration in China has long been regarded as a semi-judicial means to solve commercial disputes and concerns social fairness. Some degree of government control is needed. Contrary to the theory in

---

[40] See article IV of NYC.

many other countries that the independence of the arbitral tribunal is an assurance of the authority of arbitration, there is a general feeling in China that the official element will enhance the authority and reliability of arbitration, and the existence of the arbitration commission will make the arbitration look more official. However, the emphasis on the function of the arbitration commission has already caused some problems and there is a common worry that party autonomy may be damaged by this practice.

Amendment of the CAL is under consideration and in order to keep the law in line with international mainstream practice, some recommendations can be made. First, it is highly recommended that ad hoc or 'party-administered' arbitration should be allowed. Secondly, requirements for the validity of arbitration agreement, especially the requirement for written forms, should be relaxed. Thirdly, the arbitral tribunal should be empowered to make decisions on the challenges of an arbitrator or the jurisdiction of the arbitral tribunal. Fourthly, more details need to be clarified on procedural matters to guide the smooth conduct of arbitration. Fifthly, the stringent requirements on the formalities of evidence such as notarization and authentication should be removed.

In fact, some of the suggestions above have already been reflected in the arbitration rules of some leading Chinese arbitration commissions. These arbitration commissions have made great efforts to keep in line with international practice. Their efforts not only fill the vacuum left by the CAL, but also create a great opportunity to accumulate experience and may help to pave the way for evolution of the CAL. So, on an optimistic projection, in future, if amended, the CAL will be more in line with the ML.

10

Indonesia

Indonesian Arbitration Law and Practice in Light of the UNCITRAL Model Law

GATOT SOEMARTONO AND JOHN LUMBANTOBING

Introduction

On 29 August 1999, Indonesia enacted Law No. 30 of 1999 concerning Arbitration and Alternative Dispute Resolution ('New Arbitration Law' or 'Law').[1] The enactment was in line with the trend towards the liberalization of national arbitration laws which has taken place in almost all parts of the world. However, the New Arbitration Law does not adopt any version of the UNCITRAL Model Law on International Commercial

Gatot Soemartono holds a senior lectureship in law at Tarumanagara University (Untar) in Jakarta, Indonesia and serves as the Vice-Rector of the university. Email: gatots@fh.untar.ac.id. John Lumbantobing is an associate lecturer in international law and arbitration at the Faculty of Law, Universitas Katolik Parahyangan. Email: john.tobing@unpar.ac.id. The authors are immensely grateful to Professor Gary F. Bell of the National University of Singapore for his insightful comments and invaluable support throughout the preparation of this chapter. We also thank the EW Barker Centre for Law & Business at the Faculty of Law of the National University of Singapore for financing our participation in the conference 'The UNCITRAL Model Law on International Commercial Arbitration in Asia', which led to this book. Special thanks also go to our research assistants, Dimas Prasetyo and Pandhega Paramagama, for their help in reviewing and editing the translations, case law and citations. The usual caveats apply.
[1] Undang-Undang Nomor 30 Tahun 1999 tentang Arbitrase dan Alternatif Penyelesaian Sengketa (1999) State Gazette No. 138 [New Arbitration Law], with its Official Elucidation (1999) Supplement to the State Gazette No. 3872 of 1999 [Elucidation of the New Arbitration Law]. In Indonesia, an Act or legislation passed by parliament is always accompanied by a so-called 'elucidation', a document containing clarification or commentaries on the provisions of the Act. In one case regarding the New Arbitration Law, the Constitutional Court held that the Elucidation on art. 70 of the Law is unconstitutional, thus suggesting that the Elucidation itself is also legally binding. See Judgment of the Constitutional Court No. 15/PUU-XII/2014 (11 November 2014) ('Constitutional Court, Arbitration Law Case').

Arbitration 1985 with amendments as adopted in 2006 ('ML').[2] The ML also was generally not considered as a starting point in drafting the legislation, as the Official Elucidation to the New Arbitration Law does not mention the ML at all.

Previously, the law on arbitration in Indonesia was derived from the Dutch Civil Procedural Law ('Rv').[3] Even though the continuing applicability of the Rv after Indonesia's independence was often questioned, in practice the instrument continued to be referred to in Indonesian arbitration. Indeed, article 81 of the New Arbitration Law expressly revokes articles 615–651 of the Rv, indicating that at least this part of the Rv had in fact remained applicable up to that point. As the provisions of the Rv were no longer considered suitable for increasingly complex commercial disputes, the International Monetary Fund called on a reform of the Indonesian arbitration law during the Asian financial crisis in the late 1990s, making Indonesia 'a more investment-friendly environment'.[4] The New Arbitration Law is much more detailed than the ML, comprising 82 articles as opposed to 36 articles in the ML. The extensive scope suggests that the drafters may have intended to consolidate arbitration *law* and arbitration *rules* into a single framework.[5] Unfortunately, this brings certain adverse consequences on the flexibility of arbitration procedures in Indonesia, as will be elaborated below.

The ML is of particular importance since it has widely been used to investigate 'the role and the typical provisions of national laws on international arbitration'.[6] In that vein, this chapter examines certain aspects of the New Arbitration Law in conformity with the ML. Except

---

[2] UNCITRAL Model Law on International Commercial Arbitration 1985, UN General Assembly Resolution 40/72 (11 December 1985); UNCITRAL Model Law on International Commercial Arbitration 2006, UN General Assembly Resolution 61/33 (4 December 2006) ('ML').

[3] Reglement op de Burgerlijke Rechtsvordering (Staatsblad 1847:52).

[4] Komar Mulyana and Jan K. Schaefer, 'Indonesia's New Framework for International Arbitration: A Critical Assessment of the Law and its Application by the Courts' (2002) 17 *Mealey's International Arbitration Report* 39 at 40 ('Mulyana and Schaefer'). Among other shortcomings, the Rv did not provide for enforcement of foreign arbitral awards and lacked express limitation of court intervention. There were also other dated provisions such as the one barring women from acting as arbitrators.

[5] *Ibid.* For a concise explanation on the distinction between 'arbitration law' and 'arbitration rules', see also Simon Greenberg, Christopher Kee and Romesh Weeramantry, *International Commercial Arbitration, an Asia-Pacific Perspective* (Cambridge University Press, 2011) at 58–66 ('Greenberg, Kee and Weeramantry').

[6] John Collier and Vaughn Lowe, *The Settlement of Disputes in International Law: Institutions and Procedures* (Oxford University Press, 2000) at 53.

for the general provisions, the analysis goes through each article of the ML to find its corresponding provision(s) with the New Arbitration Law. The result is an evaluation of whether (or to what extent) the New Arbitration Law's main principles conform to (or deviate from) the ML. Identifying the characteristics of Indonesian arbitration law and practice and their suitability with the ML will assist the government in improving the arbitration system and in making feasible amendments. In practice, this will help both Indonesian and foreign parties (and their counsels) better understand the implementation of the New Arbitration Law with respect to international standards reflected in the ML.

Part I   General Provisions of the Model Law (Articles 1 to 6)

Scope of Application

It should first be noted that the New Arbitration Law does not employ the definition of 'international arbitration' as understood in the ML, which in principle refers to any arbitration with foreign elements.[7] The New Arbitration Law instead distinguishes between 'domestic' and 'international' arbitration, in which the latter is defined as any arbitration where the award is rendered outside of Indonesia.[8] Hence the notion of 'international arbitration' under the New Arbitration Law is effectively equivalent to 'foreign arbitration' or 'foreign award' under the ML. Any subsequent reference to 'international arbitration' in this chapter should be understood in that regard.

However, some uncertainty may remain because the New Arbitration Law does not provide any definition of 'domestic award'. While 'international award' is defined as any arbitral award rendered in a foreign country, the logical inference is that 'domestic award' would be those rendered within Indonesia. Nevertheless, certain court practices have deviated from that logic. For example, in *Pertamina* v. *Lirik*,[9] the Supreme Court affirmed the district court decision holding that an award rendered in Jakarta under the ICC Rules is an international award. Those courts reasoned that the ICC is a foreign arbitration institution based in Paris and that the currency in the contract and the language used in

---

[7] See ML art. 1(3).   [8] See New Arbitration Law art. 1(9).
[9] *PT Pertamina EP and PT Pertamina (Persero)* v. *PT Lirik Petroleum*, Supreme Court, Judgment No. 904 K/Pdt.Sus/2009 (9 June 2010) ('*Pertamina* v. *Lirik*'). See also the district court judgment, Central Jakarta District Court, Judgment No. 01/Pembatalan Arbitrase/2009/PN.Jkt.Pst. (3 September 2009).

arbitration are all foreign. This holding cannot be correct as the courts departed from the express definition of 'international arbitral award' in the New Arbitration Law. The decision also illustrates the courts' lack of understanding of some basic concepts on arbitration, such as the role of arbitration rules and arbitral institutions.

As to its scope of application, the New Arbitration Law does not contain any express provision as regards international or domestic arbitration other than in the context of recognition and enforcement of arbitral awards. Given that international awards are only expressly referred to in the provisions on enforcement of awards, the common view is that the rest of the New Arbitration Law does not apply to international arbitration.[10] This is in line with article 1(2) of the ML, which applies the territorial principle whereby the putative arbitration Act only applies to arbitrations having its seat in that state's territory.

Waiver of the Right to Object

Unlike article 4 of the ML, the New Arbitration Law does not address the issue whereby a party is deemed to have waived his right to object if he knows of non-compliance but instead proceeds with the arbitration without any objection. However, two relevant cases are worth noting.

First, in *Manunggal Engineering* v. *BANI*,[11] the Supreme Court upheld a district court judgment that rejected an application to set aside an award issued by BANI (the Indonesian National Arbitration Board). The applicant argued that the appointment of one arbitrator by BANI had not complied with the terms of the arbitration agreement as it was made without prior consultation with the party. But the court considered that the parties had acquiesced to the appointment during the proceedings.

---

[10] This view appeared to be supported by the Supreme Court in one of its *Karaha Bodas* decisions. See Judgment No. 01/Banding/Wasit.Int/2002 (8 March 2004) at 42 ('*Pertamina* v. *Karaha Bodas*, Supreme Court Appeal'). The Court stated that 'with regards to international arbitration, Law No. 30 of 1999 only governs them in articles 65–69 [...]'; thus, the Court rejecting the argument that art. 70 of the New Arbitration Law governing annulment of awards may be applied to international awards. Kindly note that throughout this chapter translations from Indonesian to English are by the authors unless otherwise stated.

[11] *PT Manunggal Engineering* v. *Badan Arbitrase Nasional Indonesia (BANI)*, Supreme Court, Judgment No. 770 K/Pdt.Sus/2011 (19 March 2012).

Yet the Supreme Court appeared to take a different approach in *Royal Industries Indonesia,*[12] where the court upheld a district court judgment setting aside an award rendered by BAKTI (Indonesian Futures Trading Arbitration Board) on the basis that the respondent in the arbitration was not a party to the arbitration agreement. This was despite the fact that the respondent had declared its submission to the arbitration proceedings and had fully participated throughout. The court further emphasized that parties to the arbitration shall be those in the written arbitration agreement. It is possible though to read this case rather as the court's reaffirmation of the requirement for a written arbitration agreement which cannot be overcome by the parties' waiver. Thus, waiver of the right to object may be upheld depending on the context and nature of the right(s) at issue.

Court Intervention

In line with article 5 of the ML providing that the court shall not intervene in an arbitration proceeding 'except where so provided in this Law', article 11(2) of the New Arbitration Law also bars district courts from making any intervention. The provision states that district courts shall refuse to settle, and shall not intervene in, any dispute subject to an arbitration agreement, except for 'certain cases as stated in this Act'. Notwithstanding this, some district courts still entertained cases subject to an arbitration agreement.[13]

In another class of cases, the courts intervened in the conduct of arbitral proceedings. In the notorious *Himpurna* dispute,[14] the Indonesian state-owned oil company Pertamina initiated proceedings at the

[12] *PT Royal Industries Indonesia and Badan Arbitrase Perdagangan Berjangka Indonesia (BAKTI)* v. *PT Identrust Security International and PT Bursa Komoditi dan Derivatif Indonesia,* Supreme Court, Judgment No. 367 K/Pdt.Sus-Arbt/2013 (26 August 2013) ('*Royal Industries*').
[13] See discussion on the cases *Tempo* v. *Roche* and *PLN* v. *Paiton.*
[14] See *Himpurna California Energy Ltd* v. *PT Perusahaan Listrik Negara (Persero),* Final Award of 4 May 1999, reprinted in (2000) 25 *Yearbook Commercial Arbitration* 13 ('*Himpurna,* Arbitration'); *Perusahaan Pertambangan Minyak dan Gas Bumi Negara* v. *Himpurna California Energy Ltd, PT Perusahaan Listrik Negara dan Menteri Keuangan Republik Indonesia,* Central Jakarta District Court, Judgment No. 272/Pdt.G/1999/ PN.Jkt.Pst. See also *Perusahaan Pertambangan Minyak dan Gas Bumi Negara* v. *Patuha Power Ltd, PT Perusahaan Listrik Negara dan Menteri Keuangan Republik Indonesia,* Central Jakarta District Court, Judgment No. 271/Pdt.G/1999/PN.Jkt.Pst [both district court decisions referred together as *Himpurna,* District Court].

Central Jakarta District Court, requesting an injunction to suspend an ongoing UNCITRAL arbitration case. Pertamina submitted that as a party to the relevant agreement it was not enjoined in the arbitration proceedings. The court issued the injunction despite an applicable arbitration agreement between all the relevant parties in the dispute and the absence of any provision in the New Arbitration Law giving the court the authority to issue such injunction. Meanwhile, in *Pura Barutama* v. *PERURI*,[15] the Kudus District Court annulled a BANI award and appointed a new panel to hear the case in Kudus. This was despite the fact that the agreement provided for arbitration in Jakarta and that the appointment of a new panel shall follow the same procedures as the original panel.

Part II   Arbitration Agreement (Articles 7 to 9)

Article 7   Definition and Form of Arbitration Agreement

Article 1(1) of the New Arbitration Law refers to an arbitration agreement as one 'entered into in writing'. Like the ML, the Law recognizes arbitration agreements both in the form of a *compromis* or *clause compromissoire*, stating in article 1(3) that 'arbitration agreement shall mean a written agreement in the form of an arbitration clause entered into by the parties before a dispute arises, or a separate arbitration agreement entered into by the parties after a dispute arises'.[16] It should be noted that the ML currently provides two options in article 7 governing arbitration agreement, of which option I requires a written agreement. The term 'in writing' in that provision refers to the content of the consent to arbitrate that is recorded in any form, and not the process – even if the consent is made orally.[17] Meanwhile, option II does not even impose any formal requirement. This goes into the question of how to satisfy the writing requirements.

---

[15] *PT Pura Barutama* v. *Perusahaan Umum Percetakan Uang Negara Republik Indonesia (PERURI)*, Kudus District Court, Judgment No. 30/Pdt.P/2002/PN.Kds (2 July 2003). See summary of the case in Karen Mills, 'Enforcement of Arbitral Awards in Indonesia & Other Issues of Judicial Involvement in Arbitration', www.karimsyah.com/imagescontent/Art/20050923090933.pdf at 20–22 ('Mills') (accessed 11 April 2015).

[16] New Arbitration Law art. 1(3).

[17] UNCITRAL, *2012 Digest of Case Law on the Model Law on International Commercial Arbitration* (2012) at 25 ('UNCITRAL, *Digest of Cases* ').

Compared to the ML, the New Arbitration Law is rather inconsistent in this regard. On the one hand, article 1(3), quoted above, shows that the Law only leaves room for consent in the form of a proper, written agreement. This is reinforced by the wording of articles 4(2) and 9(1), both of which require the agreement to be 'signed by the parties'. On the other hand, article 4(3) of the Law appears to follow article 7(3) option I of the ML and envisages that consent to arbitrate may be given 'in the form of exchange of letters', hence the provision requiring that to that end 'the sending of telex, telegram, fax, email or in any other forms of communication be acknowledged with a receipt by the parties'.

Amidst this confusion, it has been observed above that in *Royal Industries* the Supreme Court set aside a BAKTI award because the respondent in the arbitration was not party to the arbitration agreement relied upon by the claimant, even though the respondent had declared its submission to the arbitration proceedings and had fully participated throughout.[18] This decision may lend further support to the argument that Indonesian law ultimately only recognizes a written arbitration agreement signed by all the relevant parties. In other words, Indonesian law does not recognize oral arbitration agreement, even if such agreement has been properly recorded in some other written forms.

Article 8   Arbitration Agreement and Substantive Claim before Court

Article 8(1) of the ML states that 'A court before which an action is brought in a matter which is the subject of an arbitration agreement shall, if a party so requests not later than when submitting his first statement on the substance of the dispute, refer the parties to arbitration unless it finds that the agreement is null and void, inoperative or incapable of being performed.' Meanwhile, under article 11(2) of the New Arbitration Law, district courts shall refuse to adjudicate, or to intervene, in any dispute where there has been an applicable arbitration agreement, except for particular instances provided in the New Arbitration Law. Other provisions in the Law also add strength to the rule stipulated here.[19]

---

[18] See note 12.
[19] See New Arbitration Law art. 3, 'The District Court shall have no jurisdiction to hear disputes of parties bound by an arbitration agreement.'; art. 11(1), 'The existence of a written agreement shall exclude the parties' right to submit their disputes or different opinion contained in the agreement to the District Court.'

INDONESIA 307

However, it can also be seen that article 11(2) of the New Arbitration Law does not fully adopt the rules contained in the corresponding ML provision. First, while the ML requires the court to refer the parties to arbitration, the emphasis in article 11(2) is the obligation of the court to refrain from adjudicating without requiring referral to arbitration. Second, the New Arbitration Law does not require any request by a party for the court to declare itself without jurisdiction; in fact, the court is under an obligation to so declare *proprio motu*. This follows the general rule of the Indonesian civil procedural law as stated in article 132 of Rv, providing that civil courts shall on their own initiative declare themselves to be without subject matter jurisdiction (*ratione materiae*), if that is indeed the case, despite no jurisdictional objection or challenge. The Supreme Court has affirmed that such obligation applies and must be observed by courts when facing an arbitration clause.[20] Finally, with regards to timing, unlike the ML, the New Arbitration Law does not foreclose the opportunity for a party to make a jurisdictional objection after its submission on the merits. In line with the rule of Indonesian civil procedural law, an objection on subject matter jurisdiction may be raised at any time prior to the issuance of the judgment.[21]

Despite those minor differences with the ML, the fundamental similarity remains that the courts must not entertain any claim which has been subject to an arbitration agreement. Nevertheless, in several instances, Indonesian courts still admit claims brought by one of the parties bound by an arbitration agreement[22] – sometimes even though the arbitration has been commenced or completed.[23]

---

[20] See Judgment No. 317 K/Pdt/1984 (9 May 1984), cited in Yahya Harahap, *Hukum Acara Perdata* (Jakarta: Sinar Grafika, 2005) at 421 ('Harahap').

[21] *Het Herziene Indonesisch Reglement* (Staatsblad 1941:44), Article 134 ('HIR Civil Procedural Code'). As with Rv, HIR is a vestige of Dutch colonial law where many of its provisions are still in use today as sources of Indonesian civil procedural law.

[22] See, among others, *PT Perusahaan Dagang Tempo* v. *PT Roche Indonesia*, South Jakarta District Court, Interlocutory Decision No. 454/Pdt.G/1999/PN.Jkt.Sel (25 January 2000) ('*Tempo* v. *Roche*'); *PT Perusahaan Listrik Negara (Persero)* v. *PT Paiton Energy*, Central Jakarta District Court, Interlocutory Decision No. 517/Pdt.G/1999/PN.Jkt.Pst (13 December 1999) ('*PLN* v. *Paiton*'); and the *Bankers Trust* v. *Mayora* dispute, a thorough discussion of which can be found in Tony Budidjaja, *Public Policy as Grounds for Refusal of Recognition and Enforcement of Foreign Arbitral Awards in Indonesia* (Tatanusa, 2002) at 85–95 ('Budidjaja'). Mr Budidjaja's firm represented Bankers Trust in the Indonesian court proceedings.

[23] One notorious case in this regard is the *ED & F Man (Sugar)* cases. *Yani Haryanto* v. *ED. & F. Man (Sugar) Ltd*, Central Jakarta District Court, Judgment No. 499/Pdt/G/1988/PN. Jkt.Pst (29 June 1989); *ED. & F. Man (Sugar) Ltd* v. *Yani Haryanto*, Jakarta Appellate

The *Tempo* v. *Roche* case[24] illustrates a typical method whereby a plaintiff seeks to bypass an arbitration agreement by asserting that the claim is one of tort and therefore outside the scope of the arbitration agreement. In that case, Tempo sought damages because of Roche's unilateral termination of the distribution agreement between the parties. In accepting jurisdiction, the court asserted that the main dispute between the parties was not linked to the pertinent distribution agreement, which had to be resolved by the BANI. Instead, the main dispute essentially concerned a tort action arising out of Roche's unilateral termination of the distribution agreement. Therefore, the court held that the dispute shall not be settled through arbitration, which was a more competent and familiar forum dealing only with technical business issues. This comment regarding arbitration being the forum to resolve technical rather than legal issues appears to stem from the court's lack of understanding of the concept of arbitration in general. It is reasonable to say that this view, pronounced in the early days of the New Arbitration Law, has now largely been abandoned.

Court practices have since shown encouraging development, whereby a tort claim is not simply taken at face value. One example is the following passage from a judgment concerning a termination of contract by the Central Jakarta District Court:

> Considering that even though the Plaintiff has made a tort claim [...] in our opinion the purported tort in fact arose from the termination of the contract by the Respondent which has been subjected to settlement by arbitration under the arbitration clause in the contract [...] We must declare ourselves to be without absolute jurisdiction to examine and adjudge this case.[25]

While not every case may have the same result, one hopes the above passage reflects a more general trend in which Indonesian courts have a much better understanding on the restraint that they need to exercise in dealing with disputes already subject to arbitration agreement.

Court, Judgment No. 486/Pdt/1989/PT.DKI rendered on 14 October 1989; and *ED. & F. Man (Sugar) Ltd* v. *Yani Haryanto*, Supreme Court, Judgment No. 1205 K/Pdt/1990 (4 December 1991). While these cases admittedly occurred long before the enactment of the New Arbitration Law, they nevertheless set the precedence followed in later cases such as *Bankers Trust* v. *Mayora*.

[24] *Tempo* v. *Roche*, note 22.

[25] *PT Digital Fiducia Indonesia* v. *Hendrisman Rahim*, Central Jakarta District Court, Interlocutory Decision No. 106/Pdt.G/2013/PN.Jkt.Pst (19 September 2013) at 43.

Article 9   Arbitration Agreement and Interim Measures by Court

The New Arbitration Law does not address this issue of court-ordered interim relief in aid of arbitration. This may result in a serious gap. Without a clear provision that provides the district courts with such authority, this would leave the parties without an effective mechanism to obtain such relief, especially where there is still much uncertainty on the enforcement of interim measures issued by arbitral panel themselves. See further discussion on 'Interim Measures and Preliminary Orders' below.[26]

Part III   Composition of Arbitral Tribunal (Articles 10 to 15)

It is often said that 'an arbitration is only as good as the arbitrator'.[27] The expression demonstrates the importance of the arbitrator's role in making the arbitration process a success. Even more important in this regard is the fact that one of the foremost benefits in choosing to submit to arbitration is the right of the parties to choose the arbitrator(s). The New Arbitration Law seems to acknowledge this and commences by affirming the autonomy of the parties in appointing the arbitrators.

Article 10   Number of Arbitrators

Article 10 of the ML states that, should the parties fail to determine the number of arbitrators, the arbitral tribunal consists of three arbitrators.[28] Meanwhile, the New Arbitration Law provides that it is the district court that shall intervene if the parties fail to agree on the number of arbitrators. Article 13(1) of the Law states, 'The President of the District Court shall be authorized to appoint the arbitrator or arbitral tribunal if the parties are not able to reach an agreement on the selection of arbitrator(s) or there are no terms having been set concerning the appointment of arbitrator(s).'[29] Nevertheless, the New Arbitration Law allows disputing parties to choose freely the number of arbitrators. Otherwise, the claimant may propose the number of arbitrators in his request for arbitration, provided that it is an odd number.[30]

[26] See Part IV A.
[27] See Stephen Bond, *The Experience of the ICC in the Confirmation/Appointment Stage of an Arbitration*, in *The Arbitral Process and the Independence of Arbitrators* (ICC Publishing, 1991) at 8.
[28] See ML art. 10(1)(2). See also ML art. 11(3)(a).   [29] New Arbitration Law art. 13(1).
[30] New Arbitration Law art. 8(2)(f).

Article 11   Appointment of Arbitrators

Similar to the ML,[31] the New Arbitration Law also makes no restrictions on the appointment of foreign arbitrators. But the Law is silent on the parties' rights to place further conditions such as language spoken and nationality. Instead, the New Arbitration Law imposes two broad classes of restrictions. The first one concerns those already holding offices in the judiciary. The Law provides that judges, prosecutors, clerks of courts and other court officials are not eligible for appointment as arbitrator.[32] A more peculiar difference with the ML is the New Arbitration Law's elaborate qualifications of arbitrators, which effectively excludes a sizeable number of lawyers and practitioners. For example, the Law states that those appointed as arbitrators shall meet certain conditions, such as being competent to perform legal acts, being at least thirty-five years of age and having fifteen years of experience in particular fields.[33] The rationale for such strict requirements has been questioned. Unfortunately, the Elucidation comes without further explanation on this particular issue. Such requirements will prevent younger lawyers or practitioners from being appointed as arbitrators, a situation which discourages arbitration as a viable method of dispute settlement for small or medium-sized claims – not to mention an entry barrier for young arbitrators. Those conditions also run counter to the current trend in international arbitration.[34]

Furthermore, unlike article 11(3)(a) of the ML that refers the appointment of the arbitrator to the court if one of the parties fails to appoint,[35] the New Arbitration Law states that if within thirty days after notification for arbitration is received by the respondent 'one of the parties fails to appoint an arbitrator, the arbitrator appointed by the other party shall act as sole arbitrator and his/her award shall be binding upon both parties'.[36] This unusual provision seems intended to establish the most efficient process to avoid a delay – which may have been created on purpose by one of the disputing parties. Yet this strict doctrine may compromise the fair balance between the objectives of an efficient appointment procedure and impartiality on the part of the sole arbitrator.

---

[31] See ML art. 11.   [32] New Arbitration Law art. 12(2).
[33] New Arbitration Law art. 12(1).
[34] See Matthieu de Boisseson, 'Introductory Note', in Emmanuel Gaillard (ed.), *Towards a Uniform International Arbitration Law?* (Juris Publishing, 2008) at 125–26.
[35] ML art. 11(3)(a).   [36] New Arbitration Law art. 15(3) (emphasis added).

Article 12   Grounds for Challenge

Article 12 of the ML discusses grounds for challenging arbitrators, providing that an arbitrator 'shall disclose any circumstances likely to give rise to justifiable doubts as to his impartiality or independence'[37] and that '[a]n arbitrator may be challenged only if circumstances exist that give rise to justifiable doubts as to his impartiality or independence.'[38] The New Arbitration Law also provides the same grounds involving 'independence and impartiality'.[39] To safeguard against the risk of any challenge, article 18 of the Law stipulates that a prospective arbitrator asked by one of the parties shall disclose any matter which may influence his/her independence or result in partiality. Reflecting the notion of independence and impartiality, the New Arbitration Law offers further, more detailed, grounds for challenging an arbitrator. These include whether the challenged arbitrator has family, financial or business links with either of the parties or their counsel.[40]

Article 13   Challenge Procedure

Article 13 of the ML stipulates that parties are free to agree on a procedure for challenging an arbitrator. Failing such agreement, a party who intends to challenge an arbitrator shall send within fifteen days a written statement of the reasons for the challenge to the arbitral tribunal that shall decide on the challenge. If such a challenge is not successful, the challenging party may within thirty days request the court to decide on the challenge, which decision shall be subject to no appeal.

The New Arbitration Law provides different procedures for challenging an arbitrator. For an arbitrator appointed by the president of the district court, an application for recusal shall be submitted to the district court concerned.[41] Should a party intend to challenge a member of an arbitral tribunal, an application for the challenge shall be sent to the arbitral tribunal concerned.[42] An application for challenging a sole arbitrator shall be addressed to the arbitrator in question.[43] However, the method of challenging an arbitrator in practice appears to deviate from the Law because nowadays any challenge is normally resolved by an

---

[37] ML art. 12(1).   [38] ML art. 12(2).   [39] New Arbitration Law art. 22(1).
[40] New Arbitration Law art. 22(2).   [41] New Arbitration Law art. 23(1).
[42] New Arbitration Law art. 23(3).   [43] New Arbitration Law art. 23(2).

authority at the relevant arbitral institution rather than by the challenged arbitrator himself pursuant to the applicable arbitration rule.

As regards the procedure in the New Arbitration law, if a challenge is accepted by the other party, the arbitrator concerned must resign and a substitute arbitrator shall be appointed.[44] If a challenge is not successful because it is not accepted by the other party and the arbitrator concerned also declines to resign, the challenging party may request the president of the district court to decide on the challenge, subject to no appeal.[45] Unfortunately, unlike article 13 of the ML, there is no deadline for making the appeal and for the president of the district court to render a decision. This may lead to uncertainty and frustration since: (1) it is not clear whether the arbitral tribunal, including the challenged arbitrator, is allowed to continue the proceedings and make an award while such a request is pending; and (2) in practice the courts cannot be relied upon to deal with challenges against arbitrators.

This problem is illustrated in *Berdikari Insurance* v. *Kaltim Daya Mandiri*,[46] where a party had submitted a challenge against the arbitrator to the relevant district court in the middle of the arbitration proceedings. However, the court gave no response before the award was issued in the arbitration and annulment proceedings were subsequently brought. It is possible that the courts' poor handling came as a result of the absence of any specific mechanism or guidance in administering challenges against arbitrators. Without a clear and detailed standard operating procedure – usually issued by the Supreme Court – the district court would most likely take no action.

Article 14   Failure or Impossibility to Act

In addition to 'challenging' an arbitrator, the New Arbitration Law also provides reasons for 'discharging' an arbitrator, although without a clear distinction between the two. This is quite unusual and may result in confusion. The Law stipulates that an arbitrator may be discharged if the arbitrator has been biased and demonstrated disgraceful conduct that must be legally proven.[47] Neither the provision nor the Elucidation

---

[44] New Arbitration Law art. 24(6).   [45] New Arbitration Law art. 25(1).

[46] *PT Berdikari Insurance* v. *Majelis Arbitrase Ad-Hoc and PT Kaltim Daya Mandiri*, Central Jakarta District Court, Judgment No. 02/P/PembatalanArbitrase/2008/PN.Jkt. Pst (22 September 2008).

[47] New Arbitration Law art. 26(2).

defines what constitutes 'disgraceful conduct' or the standard for such conduct. It is also vague about the authorized party that can dismiss an arbitrator, whether the arbitral tribunal or the court. Furthermore, the provision is silent on the procedural arrangements – whether the parties to a dispute shall request a dismissal or the court or arbitral tribunal may take action on its own motion. This is different from article 14 of the ML, where these issues are clearly governed.

Article 15   Appointment of Substitute Arbitrator

Article 15 of the ML provides that a substitute arbitrator shall be appointed according to the rules applicable to the appointment of the arbitrator being replaced. Article 75(1) of the New Arbitration Law stipulates that the parties shall appoint a substitute arbitrator if an original arbitrator passes away, or a demand for his recusal or dismissal is granted. If within thirty days the parties are unable to reach an agreement on the appointment of a new arbitrator, any party may request the president of the district court to make the appointment.[48] Two issues arise out of these provisions: (1) it is not clear whether the court president's appointment is subject to appeal, and (2) a substitute arbitrator may not necessarily be appointed in accordance with the same applicable rules as the arbitrator being replaced. The second issue is particularly unsettling because it may result in one party unduly losing the opportunity to nominate a replacement arbitrator in the event that that party appointed the original arbitrator.

It is interesting to note, however, that other provisions in the New Arbitration Law contradict the wording of article 75 and are more faithful to the principle reflected in the ML. Article 25(2) of the Law provides that in the event a challenge reaches the president of the district court and the president finds the challenge well founded, a substitute arbitrator is appointed in accordance with the procedures applicable for appointing the arbitrator being replaced. Meanwhile, article 26(3) of the Law provides the same in the event that an arbitrator passes away, becomes incapable or resigns. While these provisions are in line with the rule of the ML, court practice is not always consistent. One example is *Pura Barutama* v. *PERURI*, already discussed above.[49]

---

[48] New Arbitration Law art. 75(2).   [49] See note 15 and the elaboration in the text.

Part IV   Jurisdiction of Arbitral Tribunal (Article 16)

Article 16 of the ML deals with the competence of an arbitral tribunal to rule on its own jurisdiction. There are two important elements embodied in this provision. First, the arbitral tribunal can rule on its own jurisdiction (*kompetenz-kompetenz/compétence-compétence*). For instance, the arbitral tribunal can address a party's questions about the validity of the arbitration agreement, the dispute beyond the scope of the arbitration agreement or the non-arbitrability of the subject matter. Secondly, an arbitration clause is separate from and independent of the rest of the contract, which contains the commercial transaction by the parties: the separability principle.

This provision also strengthens a position that prevents courts from interfering and leaves the arbitral tribunal to rule upon its own jurisdiction. The arbitrator's *kompetenz-kompetenz/compétence-compétence* is therefore 'the procedural instrument of the principle of separability, allowing him to decide himself on the validity of the main agreement'.[50] Here both the *kompetenz-kompetenz/compétence-compétence* and separability are based on 'the intention of the parties to submit all disputes to arbitration, beginning with the issue of jurisdiction and as a result to have a single procedure'.[51] This argument is reinforced by incorporating wording in an arbitration clause which refers all disputes in relation to a contract to arbitration, including the existence and validity of the contract itself.

Unfortunately, the New Arbitration Law does not contain a provision that affirms the *kompetenz-kompetenz/compétence-compétence* principle. The closest provision dealing with the arbitrators' authority is article 4, which only states that if the parties have agreed in advance to resolve their future disputes through arbitration, the arbitrators shall have the authority to decide the parties' rights and obligations.[52] On plain reading, that provision deals with the authority of the arbitrator or tribunal to make decisions on the merit, not jurisdiction. The omission of the *kompetenz-kompetenz/compétence-compétence* principle in the New Arbitration Law is unfortunate since it means that disputes regarding an arbitrator's jurisdiction are likely to end up in Indonesian

---

[50] See Jean-François Poudret and Sébastien Besson (translated by Stephen V. Berti and Annette Ponti), *Comparative Law of International Arbitration* (Thomson, Sweet & Maxwell, 2007) at 134.
[51] *Ibid.*   [52] See New Arbitration Law art. 4.

courts. This is a serious impediment for international commercial arbitration in Indonesia.[53]

Nonetheless, unlike the previous Rv arbitration law, there is a significant improvement in the New Arbitration Law in that it expressly recognizes the principle of separability. Article 10 of the Law states 'an arbitration agreement shall not become null or void because of: [...] (f) the cancellation of the main contract; [...] and (h) the expiration or invalidity of the main contract.' This provision clearly indicates that an arbitration clause is separable from the main contract of which it is part.

Despite the recognition of the separability principle, in *PLN v. Paiton*, the Central Jakarta District Court disregarded the arbitration agreement between PLN, a state-owned electricity company as plaintiff, and Paiton, an independent power producer as defendant.[54] This case took place as PLN sought a court ruling to nullify a power purchase agreement (PPA) with Paiton. PLN argued that the PPA was contrary to laws, morality and public order, and hence was null and void. According to PLN, the court had jurisdiction to hear the dispute since the arbitration clause – as part of the PPA – was also null and void. Paiton challenged the court jurisdiction on the basis of the arbitration clause in the PPA which provides for arbitration, including to resolve disputes on the validity of the PPA itself. The court noted this challenge, but in its legal analysis the court merely held that the existence of an arbitration clause as the basis of Paiton's challenge was 'inappropriate' and hence unjustified. Unfortunately, the court did not elaborate what constitutes inappropriateness. The parties were then ordered to continue the court proceedings.[55]

It is painfully clear that the court has completely ignored the separability principle. However, apart from the apparent lack of understanding and discipline in applying the Law, it is also possible to attribute this situation to the fact that the New Arbitration Law does not expressly recognize the principle of *kompetenz-kompetenz/compétence-compétence*. On the other hand, again another possibility is that this practice merely reflects the early days of the New Arbitration Law, with courts

---

[53] Gatot Soemartono, 'Persoalan Pilihan-pilihan Pengadilan, Hukum, dan Arbitrase dalam Penyelesaian Sengketa Bisnis Internasional' (2002) 9 *Jurnal Ilmiah Era Hukum* 2 at 15–25.

[54] See *PLN v. Paiton*, note 22.

[55] *Ibid.* Note that the case was subsequently settled out of court. See also similar disregard of the principle of severability in *Man v. Yani Haryanto* cases, note 23, and elaboration in the main text.

nowadays gaining a better understanding of the rules and principles that must be applied when dealing with an arbitration-related case. One exemplary episode is the consideration of the Central Jakarta District Court in the *Digital Fiducia* case as quoted earlier.[56]

Part IV-A   Interim Measures and Preliminary Orders
(Articles 17 to 17J)

Sub-Part I   Measures and Orders by the Tribunal (Articles 17 to 17G)

Sub-Part II   Recognition and Enforcement of Interim Measures (Articles 17H and 17I)

Sub-Part III   Court-Ordered Interim Measures (Article 17J)

Article 17 of the ML deals with the power of an arbitral tribunal to order interim measures. Based on the provision, an arbitral tribunal may grant interim measures at the request of a party at any time prior to the issuance of the award by which the dispute is finally decided.

The New Arbitration Law has only one provision dealing with interim measures. Article 32(1) of the Law states: 'The arbitral tribunal, at the request of one of the parties, may render a provisional award or other interim awards to regulate the order of proceedings including granting the attachment of assets, ordering the deposit of goods to a third party or the sale of perishable goods.' The first thing to note is that the scope of the measure – which mainly concerns measures related to assets – is far more limited than the scope provided in the ML. In particular, there is no provision expressly allowing tribunals to issue injunctions or to order measures related to the preservation of evidence. Again, this may be attributed to Indonesia's civil law traditions, where the power of courts to take interim measures is similarly limited to conservatory attachment and the like.[57] Furthermore, the New Arbitration Law does not provide for court-ordered interim measures. Thus, the parties do not have recourse to Indonesian courts in order to obtain such measures.

The next issue regarding interim measures under the New Arbitration Law is their enforcement. It is clear from the wording of article 32(1) of

---

[56] See note 25 and passage quoted in the text.
[57] See Harahap, note 20 at 339–67. See also Alexander Bruns, 'Provisional Measures in European Civil Procedure Laws: Preservation of Variety or Need for Harmonisation', in R. Stürner and M. Kawano (eds.), *Comparative Studies on Enforcement and Provisional Measures* (Mohr Siebeck, 2011) at 183.

the Law that an order for provisional measures will take the form of a provisional or interim award. However, no procedures to enforce these measures are currently in place. This situation would raise serious doubt as to the effectiveness of the interim measures ordered by the arbitrator or arbitral tribunal. So far as we are aware, there have not been any court judgments involving interim measures issued by arbitral tribunals. However, one case is worth noting for its potential relevance. In *Astro v. Lippo*, the Central Jakarta District Court issued a *non-exequatur* against a SIAC award.[58] The court held that the award, being a partial award, was not enforceable because it is not a final award.[59] The Supreme Court subsequently upheld the district court's *non-exequatur*.[60] Irrespective of its possible error in understanding the nature of a partial award,[61] the court's attitude in this case may cast some light on how Indonesian courts would probably approach the issue of enforcement of interim measures. If courts indeed refuse to enforce interim measures ordered by arbitral tribunals, that arguably would go against the purpose – if not the wording – of article 32(1) of the New Arbitration Law itself.

Part V Conduct of Arbitral Proceedings (Articles 18 to 27)

Article 18 Equal Treatment of Parties

The principle of parties' equality is affirmed in both the ML and the New Arbitration Law. However, each instrument has different formulations in its wordings. Article 18 of the ML provides for equal treatment for the parties and each party 'shall be given a full opportunity of presenting his case' (emphasis added). There is little reason to believe that the word 'full' should be applied literally, especially at the expense of effective and efficient proceedings. The emphasis rather is on the opportunity to present the case – irrespective of whether a party has actually presented

---

[58] *Astro Nusantara International BV, et al.* v. *PT Ayunda Primamitra, et al.*, Writ of the President of the Central Jakarta District Court No. 05/Pdt.ARB.INT/2009 (28 October 2009) ('*Astro*, Non-exequatur').

[59] In the sense of being a final award rendered to solve any and all remaining issues in the dispute.

[60] *Astro Nusantara International BV, et al.* v. *PT Ayunda Primamitra, et al.*, Supreme Court, Judgment No. 01 K/Pdt.Sus/2010 (24 February 2010) ('*Astro*, Supreme Court Judgment No. 1').

[61] The Court may have misunderstood, thinking that the partial award did not deal with the merit of the case.

every single point that it can or plans to make.[62] Therefore many arbitration rules instead provide for the parties' reasonable opportunity to present their case, avoiding reference to the word 'full'.[63] Regardless of the precise degree, in any event, the principle remains that the parties have the right to present their case. Such right encompasses the entitlement to be notified of any hearings and other steps in the proceedings, the right to answer the opposing parties' assertions and the right to present evidences and witnesses.[64]

In contrast to the ML, the corresponding provision of the New Arbitration Law does not address the parties' right to a full opportunity to present their case. Article 21(1) of the Law only states: 'The disputing parties have equal right and opportunity in presenting their respective opinion.' The first thing to note is that the provision only refers to equal treatment regarding the parties' opinion ('*pendapat*' in Indonesian), thus is narrower than the express wording of the ML. The provision does speak of the parties' equal opportunity, but that does not necessarily explain the degree of such opportunity – whether reasonable, full or otherwise. In this respect, the rules of Indonesian arbitral bodies are clearer, providing for the parties' 'fair and reasonable opportunity' to present their case.[65]

Broadly speaking, the New Arbitration Law does contain provisions that reflect such a principle. There is no provision which expressly establishes a general right of the parties to present evidence. However, there are other provisions dealing with evidence (e.g., provision on translation of evidence[66] and the last opportunity to present evidence following the hearing),[67] thus in practice the presentation of evidence has been treated as a matter of right. The New Arbitration Law also

---

[62] See *Dadras International* v. *Islamic Republic of Iran* (1995) 31 Iran-US CTR 127 at 144; see also Alan Redfern, Martin Hunter, Nigel Blackaby and Constantine Partasides (eds.), *Law and Practice of International Commercial Arbitration*, 4th edn (Sweet & Maxwell, 2004) at para. 6-07.

[63] See, e.g., UNCITRAL Rules art. 17(1); HKIAC Rules art. 13.1; ICC Rules arts. 15(2) and 22.

[64] Greenberg, Kee and Weeramantry, note 5 at 313.

[65] See BANI Rules art. 13(3): 'Subject to these Rules and applicable law, the Arbitral Tribunal may conduct the arbitration in any such manner as it considers appropriate, provided that the parties are treated with equality and that at any stage of the proceedings each party is given a fair and equal opportunity of presenting its case.'; BAPMI Rules art. 14(3): 'The Arbitrator shall provide equal and fair opportunities to each Party to be heard their information, and present evidence.' BAPMI stands for *Badan Arbitrase Pasar Modal Indonesia*, the Indonesian Capital Market Arbitration Board.

[66] See New Arbitration Law art. 35.   [67] See New Arbitration Law art. 46(2).

provides that the parties may ask that witnesses, including expert witnesses, be called and examined.[68] Finally, a few provisions deal with notice of submissions to the opposing party and of hearings.[69] Therefore, arguably, the fundamental elements are already in place.

Article 19   Determination of Rules of Procedure

Arbitration is conducted according to the arbitration law at the seat of arbitration (*lex arbitri*). As reflected in article 19(1) of the ML, the *lex arbitri* typically allows the parties to agree on the procedures to conduct the arbitration. The freedom embodied in that provision is supplemented by paragraph (2), which affords similar freedom to the arbitral tribunal failing the parties' agreement. This autonomy is of special importance in international cases because it allows the parties to select or tailor the rules according to their specific wishes and needs, unimpeded by traditional and possibly conflicting domestic concepts.[70] Article 31(1) of the New Arbitration Law adopts the same principle, stating: 'The parties in an express and written agreement are free to determine the arbitration procedures to be used in the examination of the dispute as long as it is not contrary to the provisions of this law.'

Based on its wording, the provision in Article 31(1) above is essentially no different from the ML, which also subjects the parties' freedom to any mandatory provisions. However, while ML preserves such freedom in making most procedural determinations, the same cannot be said of the New Arbitration Law. For example, article 31(2) already requires the arbitral tribunal to apply the provisions of the New Arbitration Law failing the parties' agreement on the procedures of arbitration – hence no discretion on the part of the tribunal. More importantly, unlike the ML, many procedural points in the New Arbitration Law appear to be governed by mandatory provisions, which leave no room for the party's agreement or for the tribunal's freedom to

---

[68] New Arbitration Law art. 49(1).
[69] See New Arbitration Law arts. 8(1), 39, 40, 41 and 44(1).
[70] UNCITRAL, Explanatory Note by the UNCITRAL secretariat on the 1985 Model Law on International Commercial Arbitration as amended in 2006, para. 35 ('UNCITRAL, Explanatory Note').

conduct the arbitration as they see fit.[71] Examples abound in the discussion on other provisions concerning procedures in this chapter.

This issue has been somewhat settled in the context of institutional arbitration, in which the institution's arbitration rules trump the procedural provisions in the Law. Article 34(2) of the New Arbitration Law states that 'The settlement of dispute through arbitration institution [...] shall be done pursuant to the rules and procedures of the chosen institution, unless otherwise determined by the parties.' This position was reaffirmed in the *TPI* dispute, where the South Jakarta District Court affirmed the primacy of the procedure to challenge the arbitrators under the BANI Rules over the procedure under the New Arbitration Law.[72] As a result, the court declined to adjudge on the challenge against one of the arbitrators brought by the Plaintiff. Nevertheless, this judgment did not deal with the issue of ad hoc arbitration. Therefore, questions remain on whether the New Arbitration Law does afford the parties procedural autonomy in ad hoc arbitrations.

Article 20   Place of Arbitration

The provisions of the New Arbitration Law in this respect are fully consonant with the principles reflected in the ML. Article 37(1) of the Law provides that the place of arbitration is determined by the tribunal unless the place has been agreed by the parties themselves. The second paragraph of the provision allows the tribunal to hear witnesses or hold meetings outside the place of arbitration.

The only known court practice of relevance on this matter is unfortunately unsettling. Thoughts instantly turn to the *Himpurna* case, mentioned above[73] – an UNCITRAL arbitration where the tribunal relocated the hearings from Jakarta as the seat of arbitration to The Hague.[74] Most of the uproar was not directed at the relocation itself but at the court order issued by the Central Jakarta District Court restraining further arbitral proceedings until the court can hear a related case brought by Pertamina – one of the parties in the pertinent contract but left out by the

---

[71] Mulyana and Schaefer, note 4 at 57.
[72] *Mohamad Jarman v. Badan Arbitrase Nasional Indonesia (BANI), PT Berkah Karya Bersama, et al.*, South Jakarta District Court, Judgment No. 533/Pdt.G.Arb/2014/PN. Jkt.Sel. (28 October 2014).
[73] See Part I, 'Court Intervention', and the *Himpurna* cases, note 14.
[74] See *Himpurna*, Arbitration, note 14.

claimant in the arbitration claim.[75] However, this court order concerned the suspension of arbitration in general pending the conclusion of court proceedings commenced by Pertamina, and not because the hearings were moved to The Hague – although admittedly those hearings fell within the scope of the court order. Hence such court order should not automatically be viewed as an injunction against arbitration hearings outside of Indonesia as the arbitral seat.

Article 21   Commencement of Arbitral Proceedings

The determination of the date at which arbitral proceedings are deemed to begin can be very important. This can make a difference for the purposes of time limits that may have been imposed by a statute of limitations or by the parties' own contract.[76] The New Arbitration Law does not address this point, unlike article 21 of the ML, which is to the effect that the arbitral proceedings commence on the date on which 'a request for that dispute to be referred to arbitration is received by the respondent'. If pressed for an answer, under the New Arbitration Law the commencement probably is deemed to occur on the date when the tribunal is constituted. This is because the New Arbitration Law provides that the examination of the dispute must be concluded within 180 days from that date,[77] thus suggesting that the constitution of the tribunal is the logical starting benchmark to determine the timeline of arbitral proceedings.

---

[75] See *Himpurna*, District Court, note 14. See summary of the facts leading to the injunction in Stephen Schwebel, *Justice in International Law: Further Selected Writings* (Cambridge University Press, 2011) at 212–19 ('Schwebel'). For the other view in favour of the injunction against the hearings at The Hague, see Mills, note 15 at 22–27. This fascinating saga was peppered with allegations of 'kidnapping' and forcible return of the Indonesian arbitrator. See the first-hand account of the arbitrator in Priyatna Abdurasyid, 'They Said I Was Going to be Kidnapped' (2003) 18(6) *Mealey's International Arbitration Report* 29. There was also an issue of the truncated tribunal resulting from the absence of the Indonesian arbitrator. For an analysis on the power of the truncated tribunal in the *Himpurna* arbitration, see, among others, Schwebel, *Justice in International Law*; Julian Lew, Loukas Mistelis and Stefan Kröll, *Comparative International Commercial Arbitration* (Kluwer Law International 2003) at 324–25.

[76] Margaret Moses, *The Principles and Practices of International Commercial Arbitration*, 2nd edn (Cambridge University Press, 2012) at 158 ('Moses').

[77] New Arbitration Law art. 48(1). Meanwhile, BANI Rules art. 6(1) provides that 'The arbitral procedure commences with the registration and filing [of] the petition for arbitration.'

Article 22   Language

Article 22(1) of the ML essentially provides that the parties are free to agree on the language(s) to be used in the arbitral proceedings. Failing such agreement, the arbitral tribunal shall make the determination. The parties' freedom to choose the language of the arbitration is likewise recognized in the New Arbitration Law, but the Law leaves the tribunal with no discretion in the event that the parties have not made any choice. Article 28 of the Law stipulates that the language to be used in all arbitration proceedings is Indonesian (*Bahasa Indonesia*) unless, with the approval of the arbitrator or arbitral tribunal, the parties choose another language. The Law also provides the arbitrators with the power to order the translation of evidence into their determined languages.[78]

Article 23   Statements of Claim and Defence

This is a particular ML provision where almost none of its underlying principles are adopted by the New Arbitration Law, except for the very basic principle that parties must submit a statement of claim and defence. Article 38 of the New Arbitration Law stipulates that within the period of time determined by the tribunal the claimant shall submit a statement of claim to the tribunal comprising the following: the full name and residence or domicile of the parties and a brief description of the dispute accompanied with evidence and clear contents of the claim. Hence, unlike the ML, the New Arbitration Law does not provide the parties with the liberty to agree on the amendment or supplement of their statements of claim or defence.

Article 47(2) of the New Arbitration Law provides that the claimant may not amend its statement of claim after the respondent has submitted the statement of defence, save with the respondent's consent and the amendments concerning only facts (not the legal basis of the claim). For this reason, the parties and the tribunal are not free to tailor the limits of the amendment. Such restrictions, however, concern the statement of claim and do not apply to the statement of defence.

The New Arbitration Law does not stipulate the requirements for the content of the statement of defence. However, article 39 requires the respondent to submit its statement of defence at the latest within fourteen days after the respondent receives notice of the statement of claim.

[78] New Arbitration Law art. 35.

This is considerably shorter than the thirty days given for the respondent in BANI Rules and other arbitration rules affording longer time limits,[79] not to mention that the parties or tribunal no longer have the freedom to determine the appropriate time limit to submit the statement of defence. Of even more serious concern, however, is that this may put the respondent in an unfavourable situation compared to the claimant because the New Arbitration Law does not impose a similar time limit for the statement of claim – such time limit being fixed by the tribunal.[80] Subject to any unique circumstances in a given case, it is probably advisable for the tribunal to also fix the time limit of fourteen days for the submission of the statement of claim in order to maintain the equality of the parties.[81]

Article 24   Hearings and Written Proceedings

Article 36 of the New Arbitration Law stipulates that examination of the dispute in arbitration shall be held in writing, but oral hearings may be held with the approval of the parties or if they are deemed necessary by the tribunal. This stipulation largely reflects the same principle as the one adopted in article 24 of the ML, although a few issues remain. The New Arbitration Law is unclear as to the effect of any agreement by the parties to preclude oral hearings on the tribunal's power to hold such hearings, which power is expressly preserved in article 36 of the Law. The New Arbitration Law also does not expressly adopt the fundamental right of a party to oral hearings. Finally, as regards notice of hearings, the New Arbitration Law – by requiring a fourteen-day notice for hearings[82] – is more specific than the ML, which only requires 'sufficient' notice.

Article 25   Default of a Party

The consequences of an absence of one or all parties in arbitration are dealt with in articles 43–45 of the New Arbitration Law. If the claimant

---

[79] See BANI Rules art. 8(2) and (3). See also, e.g. UNCITRAL Rules art. 25 (allowing at most forty-five days); ICC Rules art. 5(1) (allowing thirty days).

[80] New Arbitration Law art. 38(1).

[81] The practice as reflected in BANI Rules and BAPMI Rules may actually render this point moot because those rules appear to make no distinction between notice of arbitration (termed 'petition for arbitration' in both rules) and the statement of claim. Both rules provide that the petition of arbitration shall contain the statement of claim. See BANI Rules art. 16(1); BAPMI Rules arts. 1(1)(j) and 6(2)(a).

[82] New Arbitration Law arts. 40(2) and 41.

does not appear before the arbitration tribunal even though it has been duly summoned, the claim shall fall and the tribunal's mandate will end.[83] If it is the respondent who does not appear before the arbitration tribunal, even though it has been duly summoned, there will be a second summons for the respondent.[84] If the respondent still does not appear without any valid reason, the proceedings will continue *ex parte* with the tribunal granting the entire claims except if the claims are unfounded or are contrary to law.[85] Here there is a slight difference with the ML, particularly in the event where the respondent is in default. The New Arbitration Law appears to adopt a presumption that the claims are to be granted, while no such presumption exists in the ML.

Article 26   Expert Appointed by Arbitral Tribunal

Article 26 of the ML provides that the arbitral tribunal may appoint experts to report on specific issues and may require a party to give the expert any relevant information or to produce any relevant documents, goods or other property for his inspection. In addition, 'if a party so requests or if the arbitral tribunal considers it necessary', the expert must participate in a hearing where the parties have the opportunity to examine the expert.

Article 49 of the New Arbitration Law provides that, upon the order of the arbitrator or arbitral tribunal or at the request of the parties, one or more witnesses or expert witnesses may be summoned to give testimony. The costs of the summonses and travel expenses of the witnesses or expert witnesses shall be borne by the party that requests the testimony. Before giving the testimony, witnesses or expert witnesses shall take an oath. The Law also provides for the assistance of expert witnesses to give a written report.[86] Hence the New Arbitration Law has largely adopted the same principles as the ML in this particular area. The only difference is that the New Arbitration Law does not confer the parties with the right to exclude by agreement the power of the tribunal with regards to expert witnesses.

Article 27   Court Assistance in Taking Evidence

The New Arbitration Law does not contemplate any court assistance in taking evidence – for instance, by ordering non-parties to provide

---

[83] New Arbitration Law art. 43.   [84] New Arbitration Law art. 44(1).
[85] New Arbitration Law art. 44(2).   [86] New Arbitration Law art. 50.

evidence or compelling the parties in the arbitration to comply with evidentiary orders made by the tribunal.[87] More generally, Indonesian civil procedural law holds the principle that the parties manage to procure and present their own evidence while the judges are not active (e.g., by requesting the parties to submit certain evidence).[88] There are certain exceptions to this principle, such as the power of the court to call a witness at the request of one party if the witness has been unwilling to appear in court.[89] However, this power would be applicable only in cases adjudicated by the court itself and does not extend to court assistance to arbitral proceedings.

Part VI   Making of Award and Termination of Proceedings (Articles 28 to 33)

Article 28   Rules Applicable to Substance of Dispute

With regards to the law applicable to the substance of the dispute, the New Arbitration Law adopts the principle that the parties are free to choose the governing law. Article 56(2) of the Law states: 'The parties have the right to determine the choice of law which will be applicable to the settlement of dispute which may arise or have arisen between the parties.'

However, unlike the ML, the New Arbitration Law does not confer the power to the tribunal to determine the applicable law failing the parties' agreement. Neither the main provision nor the Elucidation contemplates any application of conflict of laws rules. The Elucidation only states that where the parties do not determine otherwise, the applicable law would be the law of the place of arbitration. This would in effect mean that Indonesian law automatically applies whenever the parties do not specify any other laws in their agreement. Under such circumstances it might still be possible for a tribunal to apply *renvoi* by way of Indonesian conflict of laws rules. Nevertheless, we are not aware of any reported cases in that regard. Interestingly, the Elucidation also states that the parties are given the freedom to determine the law that will be applied in the arbitration 'process'.

A few issues arise from the broad overview above. First, by referring to arbitral 'process', the Elucidation conflates the concept of applicable law

---

[87] See ML art. 27.   [88] See, *inter alia*, Harahap, note 20 at 499–500.
[89] HIR Civil Procedural Code, note 21 art. 139.

governing the procedures and the one governing the substance of dispute. It makes a sweeping reference to arbitral 'process', while the main provision actually concerns the applicable substantive law. In this respect, the drafters of the Elucidation did not appear to comprehend fully – or at least consistently subscribe to – the idea of multiple laws being applicable for different aspects in a given dispute. It is an idea that should be familiar to most arbitration academics and practitioners and will not be discussed at length here.[90] Of course, it is possible that this is just a minor oversight, especially considering that the New Arbitration Law does have separate provision on the parties' choice for procedural rules (see earlier under 'Determination of Rules of Procedure').

In any case, a better guidance may be drawn from a passage in the Supreme Court review judgment in *Pertamina* v. *Karaha Bodas*, where the court stated: '[W]ith regards to the law or procedures for setting aside the Arbitral Award, it is subject to the procedural law of the State where the Arbitral Award is rendered, different from the substantive law applied by the Arbitrator, where the parties can choose which State's law to be applied.'[91] This passage arguably does not specifically concern the distinction between the procedural law and substantive law in arbitration proceedings, but it does draw on the distinction between the more general *lex arbitri* and the applicable substantive law.

Second, the New Arbitration Law severely restricts the tribunal's autonomy in determining the applicable substantive law failing the parties' agreement. This adds to the discussion on the restrictive nature of the New Arbitration Law in the context of procedural law.[92] There is even an indication that the understanding of the parties' freedom to choose the applicable substantive law, as pronounced by the Supreme Court above, may not be fully shared by other court panels.

In *PT Comarindo* v. *Yemen Airways*, the pertinent agreement between the parties contains a clause with a heading that reads 'arbitration' but the content of which actually deals with the governing law of the contract – referring to Yemeni law. The Supreme Court considered that there is in fact no arbitration clause in the contract, hence the BANI award in

---

[90] See Moses, note 76, Chapter 4; Greenberg, Kee and Weeramantry, note 5, chapters 2–3. For an explanation in the context of investor–state arbitration, see Zachary Douglas, *The International Law of Investment Claims* (Cambridge University Press, 2009), chap. 2.

[91] *Perusahaan Pertambangan Minyak dan Gas Bumi Negara (Pertamina)* v. *Karaha Bodas Company LLC and PT PLN (Persero)*, Supreme Court, Judgment No. 444 PK/Pdt/2007 (9 September 2008) at 44 [*Pertamina Karaha Bodas*, Supreme Court Review].

[92] See Part V.

that case must be set aside because the tribunal lacks jurisdiction. However, in commenting on the so-called 'arbitration clause', the court stated: 'from the wording it is clear that the settlement of dispute arising from the agreements must be resolved according to the law of the Republic of Yemen, and therefore BANI Surabaya branch has no competence to settle the dispute between the Applicant and the Respondent'.[93] The court appears to imply that disputes governed by a foreign law cannot be settled through an Indonesian arbitration. Arguably, the court's ruling rests primarily on the fact that there is no actual arbitration clause to begin with. It is also possible that this is just a case of loose drafting, the court having intended to convey a different message. Nevertheless, the passage calls into question the soundness of an Indonesian court's understanding of applicable laws in arbitration.

One final point concerns the power of tribunals to decide *ex aequo et bono* or as *amiable compositeur*. The Elucidation of article 56(1) clarifies that this power can only be exercised if so authorized by the parties. The provision in BAPMI Rules reflects the general practice that the authorization is 'sufficiently proved by the request of the Parties in the Petition for Arbitration, written submission documents or Conclusion stating, "we request an award in justice and fairness"'.[94] In this regard, Indonesian arbitration law and practice are consonant with the principles in the ML.

Article 29   Decision-Making by Panel of Arbitrators

Article 29 of the ML reflects the principle that the tribunal decides by majority, except the questions of procedures where the presiding arbitrator may decide 'if so authorized by the parties or all members of the tribunal'. The New Arbitration Law does not have any provisions which specifically address the issue of decision-making by a tribunal, although there is a hint of the majority principle since the Law provides for a dissenting opinion in the event of disagreement amongst the tribunal.[95] A clearer expression of the majority principle is instead found in the arbitration rules of major domestic arbitral bodies.[96]

---

[93] *PT Comarindo Express Tama Tour & Travel* v. *Yemen Airways*, Supreme Court, Judgment No. 03/Arb.Btl/2005 (17 May 2005) at 21 ('*PT Comarindo* v. *Yemen Airways*').
[94] BAPMI Rules art. 34(4).   [95] See New Arbitration Law art. 54(1)(g).
[96] See BANI Rules art. 27; BAPMI Rules art. 35(3). Even though BAPMI Rules provides for decision by consensus, failing which the decision is by majority, the principle remains that consensus is not an absolute requirement and a majority decision is sufficient.

Article 30   Settlement

The New Arbitration Law requires the tribunal first to endeavour to achieve settlement for the parties.[97] If settlement is reached, the tribunal shall make a final and binding deed of settlement and order the parties to comply with the terms of the settlement.[98] These reflect a similar obligation incumbent upon judges in a civil case who must first refer the parties to mediation in the first court hearing.[99] If mediation results in settlement, the parties may ask the judge to make a deed of settlement recording the terms of settlement and ordering the parties to comply with those terms.[100] The deed of settlement is virtually a consent award, to borrow from arbitration parlance.

Here the New Arbitration Law only provides for a mechanism of tribunal-endorsed settlement, leaving unaddressed the question of settlement effort not initiated by the arbitral tribunal but nevertheless successful in the midst of arbitration proceedings. Compared to article 30 of the ML governing settlement, the different mechanism envisaged by the New Arbitration law is one of the reasons that the Law does not deal with details such as the parties' right to have the arbitration proceedings terminated and the possibility of the tribunals' right to refuse issuing a consent award because of certain circumstances such as alleged fraud.[101] Nevertheless, these differences with the ML do not necessarily mean that Indonesian arbitration practice precludes parallel settlement effort or the adoption of such settlement into a consent award. On this note, BANI Rules contemplate a settlement process 'with assistance of an independent third-party mediator or facilitator'[102] and under BAPMI Rules the parties are entitled to propose settlement 'at every stage of examination'.[103] These provisions may help accommodating circumstances not contemplated by the New Arbitration Law while still achieving the final outcome of terminating the proceedings – with or without a consent award.

---

[97] New Arbitration Law art. 45(1).   [98] New Arbitration Law art. 45(2).

[99] Supreme Court Regulation No. 1 of 2016 regarding Mediation Procedures at Court (2016) State Gazette No. 175 art. 4(1).

[100] *Ibid.* art. 27(4). If the parties do not wish for a deed of settlement from the judge, they must ensure that the settlement agreement contains a clause for revocation of the lawsuit or an express statement that the dispute is resolved. See Article 27(5) of the Supreme Court Regulation.

[101] See ML art. 30(1) and UNCITRAL, *Digest of Cases*, note 17 at 125 and cases cited therein.

[102] BANI Rules art. 20(1).   [103] BAPMI Rules art. 27(6).

Article 31   Form and Contents of Award

The requirements for a valid arbitral award in the New Arbitration Law are set out in article 54(1), namely: (1) the heading of 'FOR THE SAKE OF JUSTICE BASED ON BELIEF IN THE ALMIGHTY GOD';[104] (2) details of the parties and the arbitrators; (3) a brief description of the dispute; (4) each party's arguments; (5) the considerations and conclusions of the tribunal; (6) the dissenting opinion (if any); (7) the dispositive section of the award; (8) the place and date of the award; and (9) the signature(s) of the arbitrators. Furthermore, the award must state the timeline by which the award must be satisfied by the parties.[105] The absence of a signature by one of the arbitrators because of the arbitrator's illness or demise would not render the award invalid, but the explanation for such absence must be made in the award.[106] These are more detailed than the requirements in the ML, but the basic principles concerning the form and content of awards are largely similar. Some of the slight variations on the principle will be considered below.

The first variation concerns the award's reasons and dissenting opinion. While the ML allows the parties to agree on dispensing with reasons,[107] the New Arbitration Law makes it mandatory. Nevertheless, this is not controversial, as 'it is now a nearly universal principle that international arbitral awards must set forth the reasons for the tribunal's decision'.[108] The New Arbitration Law also requires a dissenting opinion where there is disagreement between members of the tribunal, while the ML neither requires nor prohibits dissenting opinions.[109]

The second variation concerns the place of the award. In the ML, the award is deemed to be made at the place of arbitration, while the New Arbitration Law makes no such presumption. In this vein the Law leaves a gap that does not account for the modern practice of making an award that does not necessarily coincide with one factual event where the arbitrators are all gathered in one place and sign the award.[110] In fact, there are reasons to infer that such a factual situation is exactly the kind

---

[104] In Indonesian language: *'DEMI KEADILAN BERDASARKAN KETUHANAN YANG MAHA ESA'*.
[105] New Arbitration Law art. 54(4).   [106] New Arbitration Law art. 54(2) and (3).
[107] ML art. 31(2).
[108] Gary Born, *International Commercial Arbitration* (Aspen Publishers, 2009) at 2450–51.
[109] UNCITRAL, *Explanatory Note*, note 70, para. 43.
[110] See UNCITRAL, *Explanatory Note*, note 70, para. 42; Greenberg, Kee and Weeramantry, note 5 at 338.

envisaged by the New Arbitration Law, given other provisions, such as article 57, which requires the award to be 'read out' within thirty days of the conclusion of the examination, and article 55, which provides for the determination of the day of a hearing to read out the award. Those provisions in effect mean that there must be a hearing where the tribunal reads through the entire award in the presence of the parties.

As for an additional requirement on the award's hearing: that follows the same requirement as for ordinary court judgments.[111] This again shows the New Arbitration Law's close adherence to the laws and practice applicable to ordinary courts.

Article 32   Termination of Proceedings

The New Arbitration Law does not address the termination of proceedings as such. The closest that the Law comes to governing this issue is by providing grounds for the termination of the arbitrator's mandate, namely: (1) an award has been rendered; (2) the time period as stipulated in the arbitration agreement including the agreed time extension has lapsed; or (3) the appointment of the arbitrator is revoked by agreement of the parties. The issue remains whether the third ground applies for only a single arbitrator or for the tribunal as a whole. It is perfectly possible that the appointment of one of the arbitrators is revoked while the other members of the tribunal remain. If that ground only affects the mandate of the individual arbitrator, then we obviously cannot equate this provision with article 32 of the ML.

Article 33   Correction and Interpretation of Award;
Additional Award

Article 58 of the New Arbitration Law provides that a party may request the tribunal to make correction on an administrative error or to add or reduce the orders in the award. The Elucidation of this provision defines an 'administrative error' as typographical ones which do not affect the substance of the award, while the request for addition or reduction refers to a situation where a party objects to the award because of, among others matters: (1) the award grants something not requested by the opposing party (*ultra petita*); (2) the award does not

---

[111] See Elucidation of the New Arbitration Law, General Part at para. 12.

make a ruling on something requested by the party in the proceedings; and (3) the award contains contradictory rulings. Therefore, the request for amendment appears only to deal with the dispositive section of the award.

As such, article 58 and its Elucidation are much less detailed than the corresponding provision in the ML.[112] Most notably, the New Arbitration Law does not contemplate any possibility for clarification of an award. On the other hand, the possibility of a party asking the tribunal substantively to amend the award is not contemplated by the ML where 'an arbitral tribunal is not empowered [. . .] to correct errors of judgment, whether of law or of fact'.[113] Instead, the closest that the ML deals with similar defects is by treating those defects as a ground to vacate or to resist enforcement of the award.[114] The same situation may also occur in Indonesia.

In *PT Tringgading* v. *ConocoPhillips*,[115] one party made an application to set aside an arbitral award based on grounds such as inconsistent rulings without first exhausting the procedure under article 58. No party in the setting aside proceedings ever raised any arguments that involved the power and ability of the tribunal to itself correct the award; the court did not consider this either. It is submitted here that in a case such as this, the court could have considered to require the plaintiff to exhaust its right to request for award correction from the tribunal before bringing a claim to set aside the award to the district court – otherwise the application to set aside would be held inadmissible. This is admittedly a problematic situation because on the one hand the provision of article 58 of the New Arbitration Law should not be made otiose, while on the other hand there is indeed a thirty-day limitation period on the application to set aside an arbitral award.[116] Hence a party wishing to set aside an award will probably prefer to make a setting aside application straight away just to be safe.

---

[112] See ML art. 33.

[113] UNCITRAL, *Digest of Cases*, note 17 at 132 and cases cited therein.

[114] See ML arts. 34(2)(a)(iii) and 36(1)(a)(iii). See also Convention on the Recognition and Enforcement of Foreign Arbitral Awards, New York, 10 June 1958, in force 7 June 1959, 330 UNTS 4739 ('NYC') art. V(1)(c).

[115] *PT Tringgading Agung Pratama* v. *ConocoPhillips (Grissik), Ltd*, South Jakarta District Court, Judgment No. 593/Pdt.G.ARB/203/PN.Jkt.Sel. (9 December 2013) ('*Tringgading* v. *ConocoPhillips*').

[116] New Arbitration Law art. 71.

Part VII   Recourse against Award (Article 34)

It is a universally recognized principle that arbitral awards are final and binding on the parties. The New Arbitration Law adopts this principle, stating at article 60 that 'arbitral awards are final and have a permanent legal force and bind the parties'. Nevertheless, in general, there are exceptions to the principle of finality: (1) where appeals are permitted by the *lex arbitri* or the arbitration rules; (2) where an award is set aside by the court at the seat of arbitration; and (3) where an application for enforcement of an award is refused by the court at the place of enforcement.

The New Arbitration Law does not contemplate any appeals against arbitral awards, leaving only the annulment of awards and the refusal of enforcement. However, in some annulment cases, Indonesian courts effectively act as an appellate court by unduly scrutinizing the substantive considerations of the award. This section will deal with issues on setting aside awards. Issues regarding enforcement of awards will be dealt with in the next section.

Overview of the Provisions

The New Arbitration Law contemplates the application to set aside as the only means for 'attacking' an arbitral award. The requirements are governed in article 70, which states:

> The parties may submit an application for nullification of an arbitral award if such award is alleged to contain the following: (a) Letters or documents submitted in the proceedings are, after the award is rendered, acknowledged to be false or declared to be forgeries; (b) After the award has been rendered documents are found which are decisive in nature and which were deliberately concealed by the opposing party or (c) The award is rendered as a result of fraud committed by one of the parties in the proceedings.

The application to set aside the award must be submitted to the district court where the award is registered at the latest thirty days from the day of the award's registration.[117] The district court's decision is subject to appeal directly to the Supreme Court.[118]

---

[117] New Arbitration Law art. 71.   [118] New Arbitration Law art. 72(4).

Grounds to Set Aside Awards

On its express wording, the grounds under article 70 of the New Arbitration Law are markedly narrower than the provision of the ML enumerating the grounds for setting aside arbitral awards.[119] On the other hand, those grounds are quite novel and not commonly found in other jurisdictions. It is also curious that fundamental grounds such as party incapacity, due process violations, excess of jurisdiction, irregularity of arbitral tribunal composition and the like do not feature in this provision.[120] Also missing is the ubiquitous ground of public policy.[121]

In fact, the origin of the three grounds under article 70 can be traced to article 643 of the old Rv, which provided ten grounds to set aside an award, including the three grounds maintained by the New Arbitration Law.[122] The reason that the New Arbitration Law left out the other seven grounds in Rv is quite unclear until now.[123] What is certain is that the three grounds are unique in that they concern criminal conduct, but that still does not explain why the other grounds must be discarded. This is even more perplexing considering that some – if not most – of those other grounds would normally be acceptable in most jurisdictions.

However, the door remains open for more expansive grounds to set aside arbitral awards in Indonesia. Budidjaja has commented that article 70 only provides the grounds that a party may invoke in its application, hence that provision does not necessarily restrict the court

---

[119] See ML art. 34(2) which, in turn, is taken from NYC art. V setting forth the grounds for refusing recognition and enforcement of foreign awards.

[120] Greenberg, Kee and Weeramantry, note 5 at 424.

[121] Noah Rubins, 'The Enforcement and Annulment of International Arbitration Awards in Indonesia' (2005) 20 *American University International Law Review* 359 at 371 ('Rubins').

[122] The other seven grounds in the Rv which are left out in the New Arbitration Law are: (1) the award exceeds the scope of the arbitration agreement, (2) the award is based on an invalid arbitration agreement, (3) the award is rendered by an arbitrator who is not authorized to do so without the presence of the other arbitrators, (4) the award contains an order in its dispositive section which has not been requested or grants more than requested, (5) the award contains contradictory rulings, (6) the arbitrators have been negligent in failing to decide one or more prayers requested by the parties and (7) the arbitrators have violated mandatory procedural law, the violation of which may result in annulment.

[123] Constitutional Court, *Arbitration Law Case*, note 1 at 20 (Expert Opinion of Professor Satya Arinanto).

in setting aside an award based on other grounds.[124] However, it is the Elucidation of the New Arbitration Law which provides the decisive authority, stating that the grounds for setting aside arbitral awards are, 'among others', the three grounds as listed in article 70.[125] Numerous court decisions have since seized on that wording and held that the grounds stipulated in article 70 of the New Arbitration Law are not exhaustive.[126] Other grounds which so far have been employed by Indonesian courts to set aside arbitral awards include, among others: (1) the arbitral tribunal having no jurisdiction, in one case because there was no arbitration agreement,[127] while in another because one of the parties was not party to the arbitration agreement;[128] (2) violation of public order, in one case because of grave prejudice to the economy of the Indonesian state,[129] while in another for violation of civil procedural law by the tribunal;[130] (3) defect in the appointment of the arbitral tribunal;[131] and (4) disregard or violation by the arbitral tribunal of Indonesian law as the law governing the substance of the dispute.[132]

---

[124] Tony Budidjaja, 'Pembatalan Putusan Arbitrase di Indonesia', www.hukumonline.com/berita/baca/hol13217/pembatalan-putusan-arbitrasedi-indonesia, paras. 2–3 (accessed 15 April 2015).

[125] See Elucidation of the New Arbitration Law, General Part, para. 18.

[126] Admittedly there are also other court decisions which still hold that the requirements under art. 70 are exhaustive. See, among others, *PT Padjadjaran Indah Prima* v. *PT Pembangunan Perumahan (Persero)*, Supreme Court, Judgment No. 729 K/Pdt.Sus/2008 (30 March 2009); *Kepala Dinas Pekerjaan Umum Provinsi Riau* v. *BANI, et al.*, Supreme Court, Judgment No. 709 K/Pdt.Sus/2011 (24 January 2012); *PT Hutama Karya (Persero) Wilayah I* v. *PT Bersaudara Simalungun Energi*, Supreme Court, Judgment No. 146 K/Pdt.Sus/2012 (23 May 2012); *PT Sumi Asih* v. *Vinmar Overseas Ltd and The American Arbitration Association (AAA)*, Supreme Court, Judgment No. 268 K/Pdt.Sus/2012 (25 May 2012) at 38–39 ('*PT Sumi Asih* v. *Vinmar* ').

[127] See *PT Comarindo* v. *Yemen Airways*, note 93, discussed at Part VI.

[128] *Royal Industries*, note 12.

[129] *Perusahaan Pertambangan Minyak dan Gas Bumi Negara (Pertamina)* v. *Karaha Bodas Company LLC and PT PLN (Persero)*, Central Jakarta District Court, Judgment No. 86/Pdt.G/2002/PN.Jkt.Pst. (27 August 2002) ('*Pertamina* v. *Karaha Bodas*, District Court') (but this district court judgment has since been overturned by two Supreme Court judgments: *Pertamina* v. *Karaha Bodas*, Supreme Court Appeal, note 10 and *Pertamina* v. *Karaha Bodas*, Supreme Court Review, note 91; see also *Pertamina* v. *Lirik*, note 9 at 98 (Judge Rhengena Purba, dissenting opinion).

[130] *Tringgading* v. *ConocoPhillips*, note 115. But this district court judgment has since been overturned by the Supreme Court in its judgment No. 220 B/Pdt.Sus-Arbt/2014 (11 June 2014).

[131] *Pertamina* v. *Karaha Bodas*, District Court, note 129.   [132] *Ibid.*

It should be noted that many of the district court judgments setting aside arbitral awards, including some of the above, were later over-turned by the Supreme Court.[133] For instance, in *Pertamina* v. *Karaha Bodas*, the Supreme Court twice decided to overturn the district court judgment based on jurisdictional ground because the disputed award was a Swiss UNCITRAL award.[134] Meanwhile, in *PT Tringgading* v. *ConocoPhillips*, the Supreme Court overturned the district court decision to set aside a BANI award for lack of evidence.[135] Nevertheless these district court judgments, even though devoid of legal force, may still serve as illustrations of the practice of Indonesian courts on this matter.

One related issue concerns the possibility of setting aside an award on grounds related to the merits. That would in effect turn the court into an appellate court. As stated earlier, the New Arbitration Law does not contemplate any appeal. One of the consequences would be that the court deciding on setting aside an award may only scrutinize the juris-diction of the tribunal as well as procedural or formal aspects of the award, not its substance or the merits. However, certain court judgments in annulment proceedings have done exactly that while ostensibly relying on grounds provided in article 70.

In *PT Natrustparadigma* v. *Deutz*, the district court set aside a BANI award because the award had been made based on fraud committed by one of the parties in the proceedings.[136] Interestingly, the supposed fraud in the court's view was that Deutz had mischaracterized the nature of the issue in the dispute concerning an engine as 'decreasing engine performance' whereas it was in fact a defect in the machine's

---

[133] See notes 129–30.   [134] See note 129.

[135] See note 130, Supreme Court, at 131. Originally, the Elucidation of art. 70 requires that the grounds to set aside an award must be satisfied by a (prior) court judgment as proof of the forgery or deception, thus constituting an additional evidentiary requirement for setting aside an arbitral award. However, that requirement has been struck down as unconstitutional by the Indonesian Constitutional Court and therefore would not be considered here. See Constitutional Court, *Arbitration Law Case*, note 1 at 73–75. The *Tringgading* case occurred before the Constitutional Court case, hence the outcome in the Supreme Court's judgment.

[136] *PT Natrustparadigma Listrik Mandiri* v. *Deutz Asia Pacific Pte Ltd*, East Jakarta District Court, Judgment No. 151/Pdt.G/2012/PN.Jkt.Tim (27 February 2013) ('*Natrustpara-digma*, District Court'). Thankfully this decision was overturned on appeal at the Supreme Court. See *Badan Arbitrase Nasional Indonesia (BANI) and Deutz Asia Pacific, Pte Ltd* v. *PT Natrustparadigma Listrik Mandiri*, Supreme Court, Judgment No. 602 K/Pdt.Sus-Arb/2013 (9 January 2014).

design – such mischaracterization by Deutz having been followed and adopted by the tribunal in the award.[137] The District Court tried to justify its second-guessing the tribunal's appreciation of the fact, saying that it had not re-examined the substance of the award; it simply considered whether the allegation of fraud was true.[138] Nevertheless, the outcome in effect is a re-examination of the merits of the award.

In *Pertamina* v. *Karaha Bodas*, the district court judgment is also an example of the court setting aside an award by looking into the tribunal's consideration of the substance. In the view of the court, the arbitral tribunal had disregarded or incorrectly interpreted Indonesian law on force majeure by defining the circumstances constituting force majeure too narrowly, thus excluding non-performance due to government regulation.[139] These judgments, which resemble an appeal, have the unfortunate consequences of opening the door for setting aside arbitral awards based on grounds related to the merits of the award.

The overview above leads to the conclusion that the Indonesian arbitration regime may recognize wide-ranging grounds for setting aside arbitral awards. It is tempting to say that the courts' jurisprudence has opened a floodgate with no ascertainable end, as presently there is virtually no clear limit to the grounds which can be invoked. Such limit remains to be established by a case in which the court expressly rejects a particular, permissible ground. To the best of our knowledge, no such decision has so far been reported or discovered. At this point, there may be a good chance that Indonesian courts would also accept the grounds for setting aside as provided in the ML as well as those provided in the Rv. Beyond that, it is up to the creativity of the plaintiff in the setting aside proceedings to persuade the court of whatever grounds that they can come up with. Sadly, for Indonesia, with a judiciary vulnerable to outside influence and notorious for being generally hostile to international arbitration, this may pose a danger since 'eliminating legitimate and precisely-tailored grounds for annulment may tempt judges to take the law into their own hands'.[140]

---

[137] *Natrustparadigma*, District Court, at 87.   [138] *Ibid.*, at 85.
[139] *Pertamina* v. *Karaha Bodas*, District Court, note 129 at 109–10.
[140] Rubins, note 121 at 398.

Jurisdiction to Set Aside Awards

The principle that an arbitral award normally can only be annulled at the seat of arbitration is universally recognized including in the ML.[141] Nevertheless, in the first few years after the enactment of the New Arbitration Law, it was somewhat uncertain whether Indonesian arbitration law also recognized such a principle. This was because articles 70–72 of the New Arbitration Law, which govern the setting aside proceedings, do not expressly distinguish between domestic and foreign awards. This period of uncertainty culminated in the infamous district court judgment in *Pertamina* v. *Karaha Bodas*. There, Pertamina brought an application to the Central Jakarta District Court to set aside an UNCITRAL award rendered in Switzerland.[142] Given the lacunae in the New Arbitration Law, the court referred to article V(1)(e) of the 1958 New York Convention ('NYC') which refers to an annulment of arbitral award by 'a competent authority of the country in which, or under the law of which, that award was made'.[143] The court considered that it had the competence to set aside the Swiss award because the pertinent contracts between the parties were all governed by Indonesian law.[144] The court did not specifically analyse or clarify whether Indonesian law is also the law governing the arbitration or whether Indonesian law merely governs the substance of the dispute. There were arguments made for either Indonesian law or Swiss law as the law governing the procedures of the arbitration.[145] In any case, the main conclusion from this judgment is that an Indonesian court asserted jurisdiction to set aside a foreign arbitral award.

---

[141] See ML art. 34(2).

[142] Pertamina also requested the court to refuse the enforcement of the Swiss award in the same application, thus conflating the nullification application with the one concerning enforcement. For a discussion on this particular confusion by the court, see Rubins, note 121 at 385–87. But see subsequent court decisions which clearly distinguish between the proceedings to set aside an award and the one to enforce an award, *PT Direct Vision and PT Ayunda Prima Mitra* v. *Astro Nusantara Holdings BV, et al.*, Central Jakarta District Court, Judgment No. 300/Pdt.G/2010/PN.Jkt.Pst (5 May 2011) ('*Astro*, District Court Judgment No. 300').

[143] NYC, note 114.   [144] See note 129, District Court Judgment at 101.

[145] See Rubins, note 121 at 391–92, arguing for Swiss law; but see Sam Luttrell, 'The Enforcement of Foreign Arbitral Awards in Indonesia: A Comment of Karaha Bodas Company LLC v. Perusahaan Pertambangan Minyak dan Gas Bumi Negara' (2008) 74 *Arbitration* 101 at 105–06, laying out arguments for Indonesian law. As a side note, expert opinions were given by Professor van den Berg and Judge Stephen Schwebel to the effect that Indonesian law is the law governing the arbitration.

But the tide started to turn towards clarity in the appeal proceedings before the Supreme Court. There, the court started its reasoning with a restatement of the proposition that the New Arbitration Law mainly governs domestic arbitration, while international arbitral awards are only subject to those provisions governing the requirements and procedures for recognition and enforcement of such awards.[146] Therefore the court concluded that the district court does not have jurisdiction to set aside an international arbitral award. Afterwards, the Supreme Court also circulated an official guidance for all district courts expressly stating: 'The object of the application to set aside is for domestic arbitral award, and as long as the application satisfies the requirements pursuant to the provisions of Arts 70–72 of Law No. 30 of 1999.'[147]

Nevertheless, Pertamina still made one final attempt to have the appeal judgment reversed by a second Supreme Court panel. This was to no avail, as the Supreme Court again affirmed the exclusive jurisdiction of the Swiss court to set aside the award, stating: 'the appeals court did not commit a manifest error because the "country of origin" must be defined as the country where the Award is rendered i.e. Switzerland. Besides, with regards to the law or procedures for setting aside the Arbitral Award, it is subject to the procedural law of the State where the Award is rendered.'[148] Subsequent court decisions have since followed this stance, including judgments by both the Supreme Court[149] and the district court.[150]

---

[146] See *Pertamina v. Karaha Bodas*, Supreme Court Appeal, note 10.

[147] Supreme Court, *Pedoman Pelaksanaan Tugas dan Administrasi Pengadilan* (2007) at 178.

[148] *Pertamina v. Karaha Bodas*, Supreme Court Review, note 91 at 33–34.

[149] See, among others, *PT Bungo Raya Nusantara v. PT Jambi Resources Ltd (d/h PT Basmal Utama Internasional*, Supreme Court, Judgment No. 64 K/Pdt.Sus/2010 (26 April 2010) at 42–43; *Harvey Nichols and Company Ltd v. PT Hamparan Nusantara and PT Mitra Adiperkasa Tbk.*, Supreme Court, Judgment No. 631 K/Pdt.Sus/2012 (27 December 2012) at 36. See also decisions holding that an application to set aside a foreign award is inadmissible simply because the provision of art. 70 of the New Arbitration Law only applies to domestic awards: *PT Global Mediacom Tbk v. KT Corporation*, Supreme Court, Judgment No. 212 K/Pdt.Sus-Arbitrase/2013 (15 August 2013) at 33.

[150] See, among others, *Astro*, District Court Judgment No. 300, note 142; *PT Daya Mandiri Resources Indonesia and PT Dayaindo Resources Internasional Tbk. v. SUEK AG*, Central Jakarta District Court, Judgment No 117/Pdt.G/Arb/2012/PN.Jkt.Pst (24 October 2012) at 28–29; *PT Sumber Subur Mas, et al. v. Transpac Capital Pte Ltd and Transpac Industrial Holdings Ltd*, Central Jakarta District Court, Judgment No. 494/Pdt.Arb/ 2011/PN.Jkt.Pst (10 January 2013) at 45–48.

Admittedly, there are still a few decisions that seemingly sidestep the issue of jurisdiction, rejecting an application to set aside foreign arbitral awards because the requirements of article 70 of the New Arbitration Law are not satisfied.[151] These judgments might give the impression of inconsistencies in court practices.[152] Nevertheless, virtually no court decisions post-Karaha Bodas saga expressly asserted jurisdiction to set aside a foreign arbitral award.

Miscellaneous Issues on Setting Aside Awards

To round up the discussion on setting aside arbitral awards, the New Arbitration Law does not adopt the principle that courts have the discretion to refuse to set aside an award even if there is a ground to do so. So far, the practice of courts also shows that courts never made further enquiries beyond establishing that the ground for setting aside the award had been satisfied.

Furthermore, the New Arbitration Law does not adopt the principle that courts have the power to suspend a setting aside proceeding at the request of a party and remit the case to the arbitral tribunal to cure a remediable defect. The court may rectify this omission by interpreting the New Arbitration Law in such a way that a party applying for setting aside an award is required to exhaust the procedure under article 58 of the New Arbitration Law to the extent that the defect which gives rise to the application for setting aside can be rectified through such procedure. This particular issue has been discussed above in the section concerning the correction of an award.[153]

Part VIII   Recognition and Enforcement of Awards
(Articles 35 to 36)

Article 35   Recognition and Enforcement

Unlike article 35(1) of the ML, which does not discriminate on matters of award enforcement on the basis of origin, the New Arbitration Law

---

[151] See *PT Sumi Asih* v. *Vinmar*, note 126 at 38–39; *PT Raga Perkasa Ekaguna* v. *Menck Gmbh*, cited in Timur Sukirno and Reno Hirdarisvita, 'Indonesia', in *Baker & McKenzie International Arbitration Yearbook: 2010-2011* (2011) at 54–55 ('Sukirno & Hirdarisvita').

[152] Sukirno & Hirdarisvita, at 54.

[153] See Article 33 Correction and Interpretation of Award; Additional Award.

distinguishes the requirements and procedures for enforcing domestic and foreign awards:

(i) Domestic awards can be enforced through the district court where the award is registered[154] by submitting an application for the execution of the award to the president of the district court. In order to issue the writ of execution, the president must be satisfied that the award is based on a valid arbitration agreement, that the dispute is arbitrable under Indonesian law, and that the award is not contrary to public morals and public order.[155] Arguably, they form very limited grounds to refuse execution of a domestic award. The president's decision is final and not subject to any appeal.[156] After a writ of execution is issued, the award will be executed in the same manner as an ordinary court judgment.[157]

These procedures look simple and straightforward enough. The fact that no recourse is available against any enforcement of the district court decision may explain the virtual absence of any court judgment in the context of enforcement of domestic arbitral awards. That leaves the annulment proceedings as the only option for an award-debtor to resist the enforcement of the award. The other alternative would be to subsequently submit an objection against a particular execution or seizure of assets by the court,[158] but this is a process governed by civil procedural law applicable to ordinary court judgments and thus does not need to be specifically discussed within the ambit of arbitration law.

(ii) Foreign awards can be enforced through the Central Jakarta District Court, which has the exclusive jurisdiction on this matter.[159] The award must first be registered at the Court,[160] after which an

---

[154] New Arbitration Law art. 59(1) provides that an arbitral award must be registered by the arbitrators at the district court in the respondent's domicile within thirty days since the day the award is issued. Failure to so register would render the award unenforceable. See New Arbitration Law art. 59(4).

[155] New Arbitration Law art. 62(2), with reference to New Arbitration Law arts. 4 and 5 concerning arbitration agreement and arbitrability.

[156] New Arbitration Law art. 62(3).   [157] New Arbitration Law art. 64.

[158] Mills, note 15 at 4.

[159] New Arbitration Law art. 65. The exception is if the Indonesian state itself is a party in the foreign arbitration, in which case the enforcement decree is issued by the Supreme Court. New Arbitration Law art. 66(e).

[160] As with domestic awards, foreign awards must be registered by the arbitrators. However, court practices with regards to foreign awards have deviated from the express wording of art. 59. First, the Supreme Court has sensibly held that the thirty-day deadline to register

application for a writ of enforcement or *exequatur* can be submitted. There are a few requirements for enforceability of foreign awards which will be discussed in detail below. A decision by the President of the Central Jakarta District Court to issue an *exequatur* is final and not subject to any appeal, while a decision to refuse enforcement or *non-exequatur* is subject to cassation directly to the Supreme Court.[161]

As noted earlier, there is virtually no court judgment concerning the enforcement of domestic awards. The process for registering and obtaining a writ of execution for such awards normally goes smoothly.[162] The New Arbitration Law sets out the requirements for an enforceable foreign arbitral award in article 66, namely: (a) the award must be rendered in a country bound by a treaty concerning recognition and enforcement of foreign arbitral awards with Indonesia – the reciprocity requirement; (b) the award must fall within the scope of commercial law under Indonesian law – the arbitrability requirement; and (c) the award must not be contrary to public order.[163] Article 67(2) then sets out the documents that the applicant must submit, namely: (a) the original copy or certified true copy of the award and its Indonesian translation; (b) the original copy or certified true copy of the arbitration agreement and its

---

an award does not apply to foreign awards (see *Pertamina v. Lirik*, note 9 at 96). This in effect means that a foreign award can be registered whenever – most likely once an application to enforce in Indonesia is imminent, either because the award-debtor is an Indonesian entity or because it has assets in Indonesia. Second, the court has not always insisted on the arbitrators (or their proxy) registering the award. There have been instances where the court accepted the registration of a foreign award by one party itself without any power of attorney from the arbitrators. For instances of registration by the winning party, see *Balmac International Inc. v. Firma Sinar Nusantara* and *Noble Americas Corp. v. PT Wahana Adhireka Wiraswasta* (reference to both instances in Timur Sukirno and Reno Hirdarisvita, 'Indonesia', in *Baker & McKenzie International Arbitration Yearbook: 2011–2012* (2012) at 258). Interestingly, Pertamina registered an award as the losing party in the arbitration against Karaha Bodas (see *Perusahaan Pertambangan Minyak dan Gas Bumi Negara (Pertamina)*, Central Jakarta District Court, Deed of Award Registration No. 01/Arb.Int/2002/PN. Jkt. Pst. (8 March 2000). Karaha Bodas never intended to enforce the UNCITRAL Swiss award in Indonesia. Hence Pertamina registered the award instead with the sole purpose of enabling itself to subsequently submit an application to set aside the award.

[161] New Arbitration Law art. 68(1) and (2).   [162] Mills, note 15.
[163] There are two other requirements under art. 66, but they are procedural: (i) there must be an *exequatur* before the award can be enforceable, and (ii) award involving the Indonesian state as a party must obtain an *exequatur* from the Supreme Court, not the district court.

Indonesian translation; and (c) declaration from the Indonesian diplomatic representative at the place the award is rendered certifying that both Indonesia and that country is bound by a treaty concerning recognition and enforcement of foreign arbitral awards.

Two observations can be made from the overview of the requirements above. First, the New Arbitration Law appears to start from a position that arbitral awards are not enforceable. This is true even for domestic awards, and more apparent in the provisions concerning foreign awards. Despite recognizing that arbitral awards are final and binding upon the parties,[164] the grounds set out in article 62(2) on domestic awards and in article 66 on foreign awards are 'grounds for enforcement'. This is different from the way the corresponding provisions are constructed in the ML, where an award is enforceable unless there exists any ground to refuse enforcement.[165] Ideally, 'The role of national courts is trimmed back to an almost administrative function of ordering the award to be enforced.'[166] However, this is not the case in the New Arbitration Law, looking at how the provisions on award enforcement are constructed.

Second, the New Arbitration Law clearly does not adopt the principle that any arbitral award can be enforced regardless of the place of origin. Indonesia made a declaration when ratifying NYC requiring reciprocity in recognizing and enforcing foreign awards as well as requiring that a foreign award falls within what Indonesian law considers as matters of commercial law.[167] The reciprocity declaration explains the requirement to supply a certificate from an Indonesian diplomatic representative at the place of arbitration. While such a declaration is permissible under NYC,[168] the requirement to provide a certificate from an Indonesian diplomatic representative can be considered to be more onerous than the ones provided in the Convention itself. This may potentially constitute a breach of article III of NYC.[169]

---

[164] New Arbitration Law art. 60. See also the Elucidation on art. 62(4).

[165] See UNCITRAL, *Digest of Cases*, note 17 at 168.

[166] Greenberg, Kee and Weeramantry, note 5 at 443.

[167] See Annex of the Presidential Decree No. 34 of 1981 regarding the Ratification of the 'Convention on the Recognition and Enforcement of Arbitral Awards' (1981) State Gazette No. 400.

[168] See NYC, note 114, art. I(3).

[169] The question of whether there is a breach of art. III of NYC would hinge on whether the requirement to provide the embassy certificate is 'substantially' more onerous than the ones provided in the convention. On the one hand, the process of obtaining an embassy or consular certificate may not be too much of a hassle in terms of effort, time and expenses. However, in some situations this requirement may indeed become

Article 36   Grounds for Refusing Recognition or Enforcement

The New Arbitration Law does not contain any separate provision which specifically enumerates the grounds to refuse enforcement of foreign awards. Logically, the requirements for enforcing foreign awards under article 66 also serve as grounds to refuse enforcement if any of those requirements are not satisfied. Hence the New Arbitration Law provides fewer grounds to refuse enforcement than NYC. However, as is the case with annulment of awards, Indonesian courts have not restricted themselves only to grounds expressly set out in the New Arbitration Law. There are a few ways that courts may venture into using more expansive grounds.

First, the court directly refers to NYC and utilizes one of the grounds provided in article V of the Convention. This occurred in the *Pertamina v. Karaha Bodas* district court judgment, where the court held that the UNCITRAL award issued in Switzerland was unenforceable after citing articles V(1)(d) and (e) as well as article V(2)(b) of NYC.[170] It is unclear, however, in what way the court applied those grounds. After citing the provisions, the court went on to consider that the award prejudiced the economic interest of the Indonesian state, that the arbitral tribunal disregarded Indonesian law, and that the composition of the arbitral tribunal was in violation of the parties' agreement.[171] The court did not specify which provision of NYC served as the basis for each of those considerations. This judgment is suspect because it conflated the idea of refusing enforcement and setting aside an award in a single court proceeding – not to mention that it was subsequently twice overturned by the Supreme Court. However, the point remains that the court purportedly considered the enforceability of a foreign award based on the provisions of NYC as such instead of the New Arbitration Law.

Second, the courts simply come up with a novel ground without any particular basis. In one of the *Astro* cases, the Central Jakarta District Court refused to enforce a SIAC partial award because the court did not

substantially burdensome. The most obvious example is if the foreign award is rendered in a country that has ratified the Convention but with which Indonesia does not have diplomatic relations (e.g., Israel). In a more extreme example where the Indonesian government itself is the award-debtor, the government may simply have the consular office at the seat of arbitration withholding issuance of the certificate to prevent enforcement in Indonesia.

[170] *Pertamina v. Karaha Bodas*, District Court, note 129 at 102–03.   [171] *Ibid.*, at 103–11.

344 GATOT SOEMARTONO AND JOHN LUMBANTOBING

consider the award to be final.[172] This bizarre consideration appeared to stem from an obvious lack of understanding regarding the nature of partial award. But as far as novel grounds are concerned, it is possible that the absence of any express enumeration of grounds for refusal of enforcement in the New Arbitration Law have freed up the court to rely on any consideration that it deems appropriate.

Another example of such unusual grounds is the existence of parallel court proceedings related to the dispute. In *Bankers Trust* v. *Mayora* the court refused to issue an *exequatur* because of an ongoing tort claim in another district court brought by the respondents in arbitration.[173] For obvious reasons, the use of parallel proceedings as a ground to refuse enforcement has been blasted, not least because it opens the door for award-debtors to defeat enforcement of an award simply by bringing a suit in Indonesian courts.[174] Even if the suit is eventually defeated, chances are it would have taken years until the case reached the Supreme Court for a final judgment – greatly reducing the value of the award.

Third, the courts come up with a novel ground while ostensibly relying on one of the grounds provided in the New Arbitration Law or NYC. The problem mainly arises with the way the courts interpret and apply existing concepts such as 'public policy' or 'public order' and 'arbitrability', coupled with a lack of awareness of the interactions between various concepts and rules in the context of arbitration.

The Supreme Court judgment in the *Astro* case serves as a good illustration. There, the Supreme Court upheld the *non-exequatur* issued by the district court because: (1) the order in the SIAC award for the respondents to discontinue parallel claims in Indonesian courts is a violation of Indonesia's sovereignty and thus contrary to public order; and (2) such order also does not fall within the ambit of commercial law because it concerns court procedures.[175] This is a confused reasoning because the order in the award was only directed at the respondents, not at Indonesian courts. Furthermore, with the existence of an arbitration agreement, Indonesian courts are no longer with jurisdiction to adjudicate the disputes in question. The New Arbitration Law itself expressly recognizes such a principle.[176] Therefore, it is hard to see why the

---

[172] See *Astro*, Non-exequatur, note 58. This *non-exequatur* was upheld by the Supreme Court in the cassation stage, *Astro*, Supreme Court Judgment No. 1, note 60.
[173] See Budidjaja, note 22.   [174] See Budidjaja, note 22 at 93.
[175] See *Astro*, Supreme Court Judgment No. 1, note 60 at 37.
[176] See New Arbitration Law art. 11 and elaboration at 4–5, 7–9.

injunction in the SIAC award was considered as contrary to public order and why the Supreme Court turned to the issue of arbitrability by holding that the SIAC award is not within the ambit of commercial law.[177]

It has been widely commented that Indonesian courts take a very expansive view of what constitutes 'public order' or 'public policy'.[178] It is not the place here to discuss in detail the conformity of such view with the common understanding of that concept. But, again, the point here is that such curious interpretation and application of the concept by Indonesian courts has given rise to peculiar grounds for refusing enforcement of foreign arbitral awards.

To conclude the discussion on the grounds for refusal, at first sight the New Arbitration Law provides fewer grounds than the ML (which, in turn, mirrors the grounds provided in NYC). However, the whole picture, taking into account court practices, becomes more complicated. The courts have relied directly on the grounds provided in article V of NYC. In other cases, the courts have come up with yet other grounds, including by way of interpreting or applying concepts such as public order expansively.

Miscellaneous Issues on Recognition and Enforcement of Awards

The New Arbitration Law does not adopt the principle that courts have the discretion to recognize and enforce arbitral awards notwithstanding any ground to refuse recognition and enforcement. The New Arbitration Law also does not contemplate any adjournment of enforcement proceedings when there is a concurrent proceeding in other domestic or foreign courts to set aside the award.

---

[177] To be fair, it is possible that the source of the court's confusion is the discrepancy between the wording of art. 4 of the New Arbitration Law governing arbitrability (stating that 'Disputes which can be settled through arbitration are those in the area of commercial law') and the wording of art. 66(b) governing enforcement of foreign awards (requiring that 'The international arbitral award [...] is within the ambit of commercial law').

[178] See generally, Budidjaja, note 22; Tineke Tuegeh Longdong, Asas Ketertiban Umum Dan Konvensi New York 1958 (Citra Aditya Bakti, 1998); Tin Zuraida, Prinsip Eksekusi Putusan Arbitrase Internasional di Indonesia (Wastu Lanas Grafika, 2009), chap. 3; Fifi Junita, 'Judicial Review of International Arbitral Awards on the Public Policy Exception in Indonesia' (2012) 29(4) Journal of International Arbitration 405.

Conclusion

Indonesia is not an ML country, and the ML does not appear to have been considered as a source material in the drafting of the New Arbitration Law. However, the Law in general does share some of the ML's basic principles, such as the principles of severability, equality of the parties and the final and binding nature of arbitral awards. It is subject to an open debate to suggest whether the New Arbitration Law contains a greater number of similar or different principles compared with the ML. If there is any rate of comparison, this cannot be based on an exact number of either the similarities or differences since the quantity is also subject to the appreciation of the effect of a given similarity or difference. For example, there are only a few fundamental principles in the ML left out in the New Arbitration Law, but those principles tend to be the ones that have far-reaching consequences at the heart of the arbitration system, such as the principle of *kompetenz-kompetenz/compétence-compétence.*

The *kompetenz-kompetenz/compétence-compétence* principle forms the very foundation of the autonomy of arbitration to settle disputes outside of the ordinary court system. Without a clear reflection of *kompetenz-kompetenz/compétence-compétence* in the New Arbitration Law it becomes clear that in some cases Indonesian courts have assumed jurisdiction to take up a claim which actually is subject to an arbitration clause. The other principle is party autonomy with regards to the procedures governing arbitration. There are several inconsistent provisions in the New Arbitration Law in this regard. On the one hand, there are a few provisions that in principle recognize the freedom of the parties and the discretion of arbitrators. On the other hand, some other provisions regarding the conduct of arbitration appear to be mandatory. This might be a theoretical issue, however, as practices show that arbitrations in Indonesia are often conducted in accordance with specific arbitration rules such as BANI Rules, or UNCITRAL or ICC Rules, each of which has stipulations deviating from the New Arbitration Law in certain aspects.

After all, Indonesian arbitration law and practice have been marked with numerous peculiarities and inconsistencies, both on a normative level and in their implementation. Even though many aspects of the New Arbitration Law have largely adopted the same principles as the ML, the interpretation and application of those principles by Indonesian courts have often been inconsistent. Strong understanding and leadership by the Supreme Court is required to improve the situation and rein in recalcitrant district courts. This is evidenced, for instance, by the development of the jurisprudence regarding the exclusive jurisdiction of the court at the seat of arbitration to set aside foreign awards, where the Supreme Court acted decisively in the cassation of the *Karaha Bodas* case and issued official guidance to district courts on that matter. We hope the Supreme Court can follow that footstep in other arbitration issues. In other words, in addition to the urgent need for improvement on the provision of the New Arbitration Law, its effective implementation would always require a reliable judiciary.

11

Taiwan

Comparative Analysis of the Arbitration Law of Taiwan and the UNCITRAL Model Law

CHANG-FA LO

Introduction

The current arbitration legislation of Taiwan is the 'Arbitration Law' ('the Law'), which was enacted in 1998 to replace the 'Commercial Arbitration Act' of 1961. When the Arbitration Law was drafted, foreign legislation, such as those of the United Kingdom, the USA, Germany and Japan, as well as the UNCITRAL Model Law on International Commercial Arbitration of 1985 ('ML 1985') were taken into important consideration. However, the ML 1985 was not directly adopted and transplanted as the text of the current Arbitration Law. The Arbitration Law includes some key elements of the ML 1985, together with other elements introduced from other countries. The Arbitration Law has not been subject to major changes since its enactment in 1998. Hence the amended provisions in the UNCITRAL Model Law on International Commercial Arbitration 2006 ('ML') have not been introduced into or reflected in the current legislation.

Having explained the above background, it is fair to say that although Taiwan is not one of the UNCITRAL Model Law jurisdictions, the main features of the ML 1985 had been considered and introduced into Taiwan's Arbitration Law of 1998. But the new provisions in the ML are yet to be incorporated into its Arbitration Law.

Chang-fa Lo has been Justice of the Constitutional Court since October 2011. The author thanks the EW Barker Centre for Law & Business at the Faculty of Law of the National University of Singapore for financing his participation in the conference entitled, 'The UNCITRAL Model Law on International Commercial Arbitration in Asia', which led to this book.

Part I General Provisions of the Model Law (Articles 1 to 6)

Article 1 Scope of Application

The Arbitration Law of Taiwan does not distinguish domestic and international arbitration cases for the purpose of applying the procedures provided in the Law. Thus, the Arbitration Law can be applied to both domestic and international arbitration cases. For international arbitration cases, as long as the disputing parties decide to have their arbitration conducted under the Arbitration Law or decide to choose Taiwan as the seat of their international arbitration cases, the Law will apply.

There is no definition of an 'international arbitration' in the Arbitration Law. But Article 47 defines a foreign arbitral award. It provides in paragraph 1 that 'A foreign arbitral award is an arbitral award which is issued outside the territory of the Republic of China or issued pursuant to a foreign law within the territory of the Republic of China.'[1] The term 'foreign law' here should be understood as a foreign arbitration law. It does not refer to a foreign substantive law which governs the contractual relations between the disputing parties.

Under this provision, there are two criteria to decide the 'nationality' of an arbitral award, namely the seat of arbitration and the arbitration law governing the arbitral proceedings. An arbitral award will be treated as a foreign arbitral award if the seat of arbitration is not within the jurisdiction of Taiwan or if the applied arbitration rules are foreign ones.

Although it is not explicitly provided in the Law, the foreign law which governs the arbitral proceedings should include a foreign arbitration legislation, the arbitration rules of a foreign or international arbitration institution, and a set of international arbitration rules (such as UNCITRAL Arbitration Rules).

There is no distinction in the coverage and application of the Arbitration Law between the handling of a commercial dispute and the handling of any other civil matter. Both commercial and other civil arbitration disputes are covered by the Arbitration Law. As long as a specific dispute, either current or future, is specified in the arbitration agreement and the issue can be freely disposed of by the parties, it can be subject to the Law. Article 1, paragraph 1, of the Arbitration Law provides that: 'Parties to a dispute arising at present or in the future may enter into an arbitration

---

[1] The translation of the Arbitration Law from Chinese into English is made available by the Ministry of Justice, at http://law.moj.gov.tw/Eng/LawClass/LawAll.aspx?PCode=I0020001.

agreement designating a single arbitrator or an odd number of arbitrators to constitute an arbitral tribunal to determine the dispute.'

But concerning the nature of a dispute, the Law requires that the matter must be freely disposable by the disputing parties. Article 1, paragraph 2 provides: 'The dispute referred to in the preceding paragraph is limited to those which may be settled in accordance with the law.' There are some types of civil matters which cannot be freely disposed of by the disputing parties. For instance, issues concerning marriage and custody and those which are subject to mandatory substantive rules cannot be freely disposed of by the parties.

Article 2   Definitions and Rules of Interpretation

There is no definition for the term 'arbitration' in the Law. Article 1 of the Arbitration Law states: 'Parties to a dispute arising at present or in the future may enter into an arbitration agreement designating a single arbitrator or an odd number of arbitrators to constitute an arbitral tribunal to determine the dispute.' It does not require that an arbitration case must always be administered or conducted by an arbitration institution. Hence the Law can accommodate institutional and ad hoc arbitration. But it must also be noted that ad hoc arbitration is not common in Taiwan. Sometimes the courts have misunderstanding that the Arbitration Law only recognizes an institutional arbitration.

There are no provisions in the Arbitration Law similar to ML article 2(d), (e) and (f) concerning the interpretation of certain phrases provided in the ML. This is basically because of the fact that the Arbitration Law was not enacted through adopting the ML and hence there is no issue concerning the interpretation of the ML provisions.

Article 2A   International Origin and General Principles

There is no explicit provision in the Arbitration Law requiring uniformity and good faith in the application of the ML. Since the Arbitration Law is not directly transplanted from the ML, the uniformity and good faith application of the ML is not quite relevant in the context of the Arbitration Law. Having said this, it must be noted that the Arbitration Law provisions are interpreted by arbitrators more in line with international practices. But the courts tend to interpret the Arbitration Law purely as a domestic law and to consider this Law being of not much difference from other domestic laws. International practices are not systematically taken into account by the court when the Law is interpreted.

Article 3 Receipt of Written Communications

There is no explicit provision in the Law governing receipt of written communication. If the communication is between the parties concerning their contractual relations, it is governed by the Civil Code, Article 95, which provides in part that: 'An expression of intent *inter absentes* becomes effective at the moment when the notification of the expression reaches such other party.' If the communication is about the arbitration proceeding, the Code of Civil Procedure (CCP) applies. Article 19 of the Arbitration Law provides that: 'In the absence of an agreement on the procedural rules governing the arbitration, the arbitral tribunal shall apply this Law. Where this Law is silent, the arbitral tribunal may adopt the Code of Civil Procedure *mutatis mutandis* or other rules of procedure which it deems proper.' Under CCP Article 124, service of process can be effectuated by an execution officer or post office. CCP Article 136 further provides: 'Service shall be effectuated in the domicile or residence, office or place of business of the person to be served; but service may also be effectuated at the place where the person to be served is found.' 'In cases where the place to which the service should be effectuated under the preceding paragraph is unknown or where service cannot be effectuated therein, service may be effectuated at the employment place of the person to be served.' 'The same shall apply to cases where the person to be served has notified the court that service may be effectuated at his/her employment place.'[2]

Article 4 Waiver of Right to Object

Parties have the right and discretion to decide whether to exercise or to waive an objection to procedural issues. A waiver can be exercised explicitly or impliedly. Article 22 of the Arbitration Law states: 'An objection raised by a party as to the scope of authority of the arbitral tribunal shall be determined by the arbitral tribunal. However, a party may not object if it has submitted the statement of defense regarding the subject matter of the dispute.'

---

[2] The translation of the Code of Civil Procedure is made available by the Ministry of Justice, at http://law.moj.gov.tw/Eng/LawClass/LawAll.aspx?PCode=B0010001.

Concerning the objection to other procedural issues, Article 29 of the Arbitration Law, which is quite similar to ML article 4, provides:

> A party who knows or may know that the arbitral proceedings have derogated from the provisions of this Law or has not complied with the requirements under the arbitration agreement yet proceeds with the arbitration without objecting to such non-compliance shall be deemed to have waived the right to object.
>
> Any objection raised shall be considered by the arbitral tribunal and the decisions made with respect thereto shall not be subject to appeal.
>
> An objection shall not suspend the arbitral proceedings.

Article 5   Extent of Court Intervention

In principle, courts do not have power to intervene in an arbitration proceeding under the Arbitration Law. There are limited exceptions to this principle provided in the Arbitration Law. Here are some examples: Article 9, paragraphs 2 and 3, of the Arbitrational Law read:

> If the arbitrators fail to agree on a chair within thirty days of their appointment, the final appointment shall be made by a court upon the application of any party.
>
> Where an arbitration is to be conducted by a sole arbitrator and the parties fail to agree on an arbitrator within thirty days upon the receipt of the written request to appoint by any party, the appointment shall be made by a court pursuant to the application of any party.

Article 12 of the Arbitration Law states:

> Where the arbitrator has not been appointed within the time period specified in the first paragraph of the preceding Article, the requesting party may apply to an arbitration institution or the court to make the appointment.
>
> Where the arbitrator has not been appointed within the time period specified in the second paragraph of the preceding Article, the requesting party may apply to the court to make the appointment.

Article 13, paragraphs 1 and 3 to 5, of the Arbitration Law provide:

> An arbitrator appointed in an arbitration agreement may be replaced if such arbitrator becomes unable to perform as a result of death or any other cause, or refuses to conduct the arbitration, or delays the performance of arbitration. In the event that the parties fail to agree upon a replacement, either party may apply to an arbitration institution or the court to appoint the replacement.
>
> [...]

When the party receiving the request to appoint a replacement fails to do so within the time period specified in the preceding paragraph of this Article, the requesting party may apply to an arbitration institution or the court to make the appointment.

Should any one of the circumstances mentioned in paragraph 1 of this Article occur in respect of an arbitrator or arbitrators appointed by an arbitration institution or by the court, such arbitration institution or the court may appoint a replacement or replacements upon an application by any party or by its own volition.

Should any one of the circumstances mentioned in paragraph 1 of this Article occur in respect of the chair of an arbitral tribunal, the court may appoint a replacement upon an application by any party or by its own volition.

Article 17, paragraphs 3 and 6, of the Arbitration Law provide:

Where a party wishes to challenge a decision made hereunder by the arbitral tribunal, such party shall apply for a judicial ruling within fourteen days of receiving notice of the arbitral decision.

An application to withdraw a sole arbitrator shall be submitted to the court for determination.

Article 28 of the Arbitration Law provides:

The arbitral tribunal, if necessary, may request assistance from a court or other agencies in the conduct of the arbitral proceedings.

A requested court may exercise its investigative powers in the same manner and to the same extent as permitted in a legal action.

Article 6   Court or other Authority for Certain Functions of Arbitration Assistance and Supervision

The functions referred to in Articles 11(3), 11(4), 13(3), 14, 16(3) and 34(2) ML are sometimes performed by an arbitral institution and a court collaboratively, and sometimes by a court alone in Taiwan.

For instance, Article 13, paragraphs 1 and 3, of the Arbitration Law state:

An arbitrator appointed in an arbitration agreement may be replaced if such arbitrator becomes unable to perform as a result of death or any other cause, or refuses to conduct the arbitration, or delays the performance of arbitration. In the event that the parties fail to agree upon a replacement, either party may apply to an arbitration institution or the court to appoint the replacement.

When the party receiving the request to appoint a replacement fails to do so within the time period specified in the preceding paragraph of this

Article, the requesting party may apply to an arbitration institution or the court to make the appointment.

For instance, Article 17, paragraphs 1 and 3, of the Arbitration Law provide:

A party intending to request for the withdrawal of an arbitrator shall do so within fourteen days of knowing the cause [for withdrawal]. Such party shall submit a written application stating the reasons for the withdrawal to the arbitral tribunal. The arbitral tribunal shall make a decision within ten days upon receipt of such application, unless the parties have agreed otherwise.

Where a party wishes to challenge a decision made hereunder by the arbitral tribunal, such party shall apply for a judicial ruling within fourteen days of receiving notice of the arbitral decision.

Part II   Arbitration Agreement (Articles 7 to 9)

Article 7   Definition and Form of Arbitration Agreement

There is no definition of the term 'arbitration agreement' in the Arbitration Law. But the meaning of arbitration agreement under the Law can be inferred from some provisions, especially Article 1, paragraph 1, of the Arbitration Law, which provides that: 'Parties to a dispute arising at present or in the future may enter into an arbitration agreement designating a single arbitrator or an odd number of arbitrators to constitute an arbitral tribunal to determine the dispute.' The interpretation of Article 1 of the Arbitration Law would lead to the same definition of 'arbitration agreement' as provided in ML article 7, which defines arbitration as 'an agreement by the parties to submit to Arbitration all or certain disputes which have arisen or which may arise between them in respect of a defined legal relationship, whether contractual or not' and which may be 'in the form of an arbitration clause in a contract or in the form of a separate agreement.'

In principle, if the disputing parties decide to rely on arbitration, they must have a valid arbitration agreement. However, there are some exceptions to this general rule of arbitration being based on a valid arbitration agreement in Taiwan. For instance, the Law Governing the Settlement of Labour Disputes provides in paragraph 2 of Article 24 that in case the competent authority considers that the situation of a labour dispute is serious and needs to be submitted for arbitration, it may decide on its own initiative to submit the dispute for arbitration and notify the disputing parties. Also, paragraph 1 of Article 166 of the Securities Transaction Law provides that the disputes between a securities dealer and the stock exchange as well as those between different securities dealers shall be settled through arbitration with or without an arbitration agreement between the parties. Also, Article 85-1, paragraph 2, of the Government Procurement Law of Taiwan has a mandatory arbitration provision for construction contracts. It provides in essence that in the event where the government procurement entity and the supplier fail to reach an agreement over the dispute in relation to the performance of the government procurement contract in question, and if mediation conducted by the Complaint Review Board for Government Procurement is unsuccessful due to the procuring entity not agreeing to the proposal or resolution suggested in a mediation proceeding, and if the dispute arises from a construction contract, the supplier may submit its dispute to arbitration. The procuring entity may not object to the arbitration filed by the supplier based on the fact that there is no arbitration agreement between the parties.

The common feature of these provisions is that arbitration agreement between the disputing parties is not needed for the purpose of submitting a dispute in certain fields to arbitration, as long as the provided requirements are met.

In terms of the form of arbitration agreement, paragraph 3 of Article 1 of the Arbitration Law states that the arbitration agreement shall be in writing. The term 'in writing' is defined in a broad way. It is provided in paragraph 4 of Article 1 that written documents, documentary instruments, correspondence, facsimiles, telegrams or any other similar types of communications between the parties evidencing prima facie arbitration agreement shall be deemed to have established an arbitration agreement. The term 'any other similar types of communications' can be very broad. In essence, if the communication is capable of leaving traceable evidence, it should have met the requirement of being 'in writing'. For instance, an email correspondence should be one of such types of communication.

It must be noted that the parties to an arbitration agreement may include a pre-arbitration proceeding to be performed or completed before an arbitration proceeding can be initiated. The widely accepted view is that if such pre-arbitration proceeding has not been performed and completed, the arbitration can be refused. However, if the pre-arbitration proceeding is to require the parties to try to settle their dispute first, but if the initiating party believes that it is not possible to settle the dispute, an arbitration proceeding directly initiated by this party without first trying to settle their dispute should still be accepted.

Article 8   Arbitration Agreement and Substantive Claim before Court

Under the Arbitration Law, a court cannot 'refer' the parties to arbitration. The court can only suspend the court proceeding and order the plaintiff to submit their dispute to arbitration. This is different from the provisions in ML Article 8. Article 4 of the Arbitration Law provides in this respect that:

> In the event that one of the parties to an arbitration agreement commences a legal action contrary to the arbitration agreement, the court may, upon application by the adverse party, suspend the legal action and order the plaintiff to submit to arbitration within a specified time, unless the defendant proceeds to respond to the legal action.
>
> If a plaintiff fails to submit to arbitration within the specified time period prescribed in the preceding paragraph, the court shall dismiss the legal action.
>
> After the suspension mentioned in the first paragraph of this Article, the legal action shall be deemed to have been withdrawn at the time an arbitral award is made.

Article 9   Arbitration Agreement and Interim Measures by Court

Parties have the right to request from a court an interim measure of protection under the Arbitration Law. But after a measure is granted by the court, the requesting party will have to proceed with arbitration in accordance with the request by the other party. The adopting of an interim measure by the court is governed by the CCP.

In this regard, Article 39 provides the following:

> If a party to an arbitration agreement applies to the court for a provisional seizure or disposition in accordance with the conservation provisions of the Code of Civil Procedure prior to submitting to arbitration, the court at the request of the respondent shall order the applicant to submit to arbitration by a certain time period. However, in the event that the applicant may also proceed by legal action in accordance with the law, the court may order the parties concerned to proceed with legal action.
>
> Upon the failure of the applicant seeking provisional relief in the preceding paragraph to submit to arbitration or proceed with legal action by the aforementioned time period, the court may, pursuant to a petition by the respondent, invalidate the order for provisional seizure or disposition.

Part III   Composition of Arbitral Tribunal (Articles 10 to 15)

Article 10   Number of Arbitrators

There is no requirement concerning the number of arbitrators under the Arbitration Law. The Arbitration Law allows the parties to an arbitration agreement to decide the number of arbitrators to resolve their dispute. Thus, it is possible for the parties to rely on the sole arbitrator to decide their case under certain conditions. Article 36 of the Arbitration Law indicates the situation where the arbitration tribunal is composed of a single arbitrator: 'Any dispute that shall be settled pursuant to the summary proceeding prescribed in the Code of Civil Procedure may be submitted to an arbitration institution upon the agreement of the parties for it to appoint a sole arbitrator to conduct the arbitration pursuant to the procedural rules for expedited arbitration stipulated by the arbitration institution.' CCP Article 427 provides the situations for the application of summary proceedings:

> A summary proceeding as provided in this Chapter shall apply to actions with regard to proprietary rights where the price or claim's value of claim is not more than NTD 500,000.
> A summary proceeding shall apply to the following actions irrespective of the price or value of the claim:
>
> 1. Actions arising from disputes over a fixed-term lease of a building or other object of work, or from a fixed-term lender-borrower relationship;
> 2. Actions between an employer and an employee arising from an employment contract with an employment term of less than one year;
> 3. Actions between a guest and the owner of a hotel or the owner of a food and beverage store, or a carrier arising from food/ accommodation, freight costs or deposit of baggage or money/property;
> 4. Actions arising from the protection of possessions;
> 5. Actions arising from the fixing of the boundaries or the demarcation of a real property;
> 6. Actions arising from claims in a negotiable instrument;
> 7. Actions arising from claims in a cooperative association;
> 8. Actions arising from claims in interest, bonus, rent, alimony, retirement/severance payment, or other periodical payments;
> 9. Actions arising from the lease of personal property or a lender-borrower relationship with respect to the use of personal property;
> 10. Actions arising from the guarantee for the claims provided in the first to the third subparagraphs inclusive and the sixth to the ninth subparagraphs inclusive.

In addition to the above situation, parties can always mutually decide the number of their arbitrators in a case. But, normally, there are almost always three arbitrators forming an arbitral tribunal to decide a case. It is rare in Taiwan that an arbitral tribunal consists of a single arbitrator.

Article 9, paragraph 1 of the Arbitration Law provides: 'Where in the absence of an appointment of an arbitrator or a method of appointment in an arbitration agreement, each party shall appoint an arbitrator for itself. The appointed arbitrators shall then jointly designate a third arbitrator to be the chair and the arbitral tribunal shall notify the parties, in writing, of the final appointment.' This indicates that the arbitration agreement can decide not only the number of arbitrators, but also the ways of appointing the arbitrators and the chair of an arbitral tribunal.

Article 11   Appointment of Arbitrators

Parties to an arbitration agreement may appoint their arbitrator(s) in their arbitration agreement in order to form an arbitral tribunal. If they fail to appoint the arbitrator(s) in their agreement or fail to specify the method of appointing the arbitrator(s), each party will be asked to appoint one arbitrator, who shall in turn, jointly with the arbitrator appointed by the other party, appoint a third arbitrator as the chairman of the arbitral tribunal. If the arbitrators fail to decide jointly on the chairman for the arbitral tribunal within thirty days of their appointments, either party may file an application asking the court to choose the chairman of the arbitral tribunal. If the arbitration agreement provides that there shall be a sole arbitrator to conduct arbitration proceedings, the parties can decide the appointment of the arbitrator by agreement. In the event that both parties are not able to come to an agreement on the appointment of the arbitrator, each party has the right to file an application asking the court to appoint the arbitrator. This must be accomplished within thirty days of one party having received a written request from the other party about the appointment. If the parties have chosen an arbitration institution to handle their case, then the arbitration institution, rather than the courts, shall appoint the chairman or the sole arbitrator for the arbitral tribunal (Article 9 of the Law).

After one of the parties has appointed an arbitrator, that party may request in writing that the other party appoints its arbitrator within fourteen days from the receipt of the request. In cases where an arbitrator is to be appointed by an arbitration institution, a party may request that the institution appoints the arbitrator within a time period of fourteen days. In cases where the party who has received the written request fails to appoint an arbitrator within the prescribed time period, the party who made the request can file an application to request the arbitration institution or the court to make such appointment. If the arbitration institution, after receiving the written request, fails to appoint an arbitrator, the requesting party can file an application to request the court to make such an appointment (Articles 11 and 12 of the Arbitration Law).

Article 12   Grounds for Challenge

It is important that the arbitrators possess the expected expertise and that the arbitration procedure and the award are carried out and made in an impartial manner. Thus, if there is a factor that may affect impartiality, the arbitrator is expected to disqualify himself and to withdraw from handling the case. Otherwise, the parties may request the arbitrator to withdraw. The situations under the Arbitration Law allowing a party to request an arbitrator to withdraw himself are as follows: (1) not having acquired the qualification agreed upon by the parties; (2) being in one of the situations listed in the second paragraph of Article 15, which requires disclosure (paragraph 1 of Article 16 of the Arbitration Law). However, a party may not apply to disqualify an arbitrator whom it appointed unless the cause for the withdrawal arose after the appointment or the cause is only known after the appointment (paragraph 2 of Article 16 of Arbitration Law).

Article 13   Challenge Procedure

Other procedures about the challenge of an arbitrator are provided in Article 17 of the Arbitration Law, which states:

> A party intending to request for the withdrawal of an arbitrator shall do so within fourteen days of knowing the cause [for withdrawal]. Such party shall submit a written application stating the reasons for the withdrawal to the arbitral tribunal. The arbitral tribunal shall make a decision within ten days upon receipt of such application, unless the parties have agreed otherwise.
>
> In the event that the arbitral tribunal has not yet been constituted, the time period for [requesting] a withdrawal mentioned in the preceding paragraph shall commence from the date that the arbitral tribunal is constituted.
>
> Where a party wishes to challenge a decision made hereunder by the arbitral tribunal, such party shall apply for a judicial ruling within fourteen days of receiving notice of the arbitral decision.

A party shall not challenge the ruling reached by the court mentioned in the preceding paragraph of this Article.

An arbitrator shall withdraw in the event that both parties request the withdrawal.

An application to withdraw a sole arbitrator shall be submitted to the court for determination.

If an arbitrator has decided to disqualify himself and to withdraw from the case or if the arbitral tribunal or the court has decided that an arbitrator has to withdraw, a new arbitrator would have to be appointed. The procedure of appointing a new arbitrator is provided in Article 13 of the Arbitration Law, which reads:

An arbitrator appointed in an arbitration agreement may be replaced if such arbitrator becomes unable to perform as a result of death or any other cause, or refuses to conduct the arbitration, or delays the performance of arbitration. In the event that the parties fail to agree upon a replacement, either party may apply to an arbitration institution or the court to appoint the replacement.

So long as an arbitrator appointed by one party becomes unable to perform as a result of any of the circumstances mentioned in the preceding paragraph of this Article, the other party may request the former party to appoint a replacement within fourteen days after receipt of the request. However, the chair appointed pursuant to paragraph 1 of Article 9 shall not be affected [by the appointment of the replacement].

When the party receiving the request to appoint a replacement fails to do so within the time period specified in the preceding paragraph of this Article, the requesting party may apply to an arbitration institution or the court to make the appointment.

Should any one of the circumstances mentioned in paragraph 1 of this Article occur in respect of an arbitrator or arbitrators appointed by an arbitration institution or by the court, such arbitration institution or the court may appoint a replacement or replacements upon an application by any party or by its own volition.

Should any one of the circumstances mentioned in paragraph 1 of this Article occur in respect of the chair of an arbitral tribunal, the court may appoint a replacement upon an application by any party or by its own volition.

Article 14   Failure or Impossibility to Act

It is possible that an appointed arbitrator may become unable to perform his duties. In such a situation, he must be replaced. The procedure of replacing an arbitrator is provided in Article 13, paragraph 1 of the Arbitration Law, which states: 'An arbitrator appointed in an arbitration agreement may be replaced if such arbitrator becomes unable to perform as a result of death or any other cause, or refuses to conduct the arbitration, or delays the performance of arbitration. In the event that the parties fail to agree upon a replacement, either party may apply to an arbitration institution or the court to appoint the replacement.'

Article 15   Appointment of Substitute Arbitrator

In addition to Article 13, paragraph 1 of the Arbitration Law mentioned above, paragraphs 2 to 5 further deal with the appointment of a new arbitrator to replace an original arbitrator who is not able to perform his job. These paragraphs provide the following:

> So long as an arbitrator appointed by one party becomes unable to perform as a result of any of the circumstances mentioned in the preceding paragraph of this Article, the other party may request the former party to appoint a replacement within fourteen days after receipt of the request. However, the chair appointed pursuant to paragraph 1 of Article 9 shall not be affected [by the appointment of the replacement].
>
> When the party receiving the request to appoint a replacement fails to do so within the time period specified in the preceding paragraph of this Article, the requesting party may apply to an arbitration institution or the court to make the appointment.
>
> Should any one of the circumstances mentioned in paragraph 1 of this Article occur in respect of an arbitrator or arbitrators appointed by an arbitration institution or by the court, such arbitration institution or the court may appoint a replacement or replacements upon an application by any party or by its own volition.
>
> Should any one of the circumstances mentioned in paragraph 1 of this Article occur in respect of the chair of an arbitral tribunal, the court may appoint a replacement upon an application by any party or by its own volition.

Part IV   Jurisdiction of Arbitral Tribunal (Article 16)

Article 16   Competence of Arbitral Tribunal to Rule on its Jurisdiction

Article 22 of the Arbitration Law adopts *kompetenz-kompetenz/compétence-compétence* doctrine to allow the arbitral tribunal to decide its own jurisdiction. It provides that an objection raised by a party as to the scope of authority of the arbitral tribunal shall be determined by the arbitral tribunal. In other words, an arbitral tribunal is authorized to decide the issues about its own jurisdiction, including challenges to its jurisdiction.

Part IV-A   Interim Measures and Preliminary Orders
(Articles 17 to 17J)

Sub-Part I   Measures and Orders by the Tribunal (Articles 17 to 17G)

Article 17   Power of Arbitral Tribunal to Order Interim Measures

There is no explicit power provided in the Arbitration Law being granted to the arbitral tribunal to order interim measures, either to maintain or restore the status quo pending determination of the dispute, to take action that would prevent, or refrain from taking action, to provide a means of preserving assets out of which a subsequent award may be satisfied, or to preserve evidence that may be relevant and material to the resolution of the dispute.

However, the Arbitration Rules of the Chinese Arbitration Association issued by the CAA provide in Article 36 the following:

> At the request of either party, the arbitral tribunal may take any interim measures as agreed by the parties in respect of the subject-matter of the dispute for purposes of the conservation of the perishable goods or providing immediate protection, such as ordering the sale or their deposit with a third person of the goods or other interim measures as the tribunal considers appropriate.
>
> In the circumstances specified in the preceding paragraph, where there is an arbitration agreement covering the interim measures, the arbitral tribunal may make a record of the settlement on agreed terms and may order the requesting party to make advance payment on the costs for such measures.

It must be noted that if an interim measure is to be enforced by the court there must be a basis in the legislation. There has not been a court case to decide whether an 'arbitral award' ordering an interim measure can be enforced. Due to the provision of Article 39, there is a possibility that the court might consider that such award is not enforceable because the order must be issued by a court. From this perspective, an arbitral tribunal's power to order an interim measure of protection is still limited. Basically, an arbitral tribunal does not have the power to issue a temporary order to attach the asset of a party. The complaining party would have to file an application with the court to obtain a temporary injunctive order to secure future enforcement against the respondent. A party may apply for such temporary relief with the court before or after its submission to the arbitration. If the temporary relief is applied before the submission to the arbitration, the party may be required by the court to submit to arbitration within a specified time period. Paragraph 1 of Article 39 of the Arbitration Law provides in part that 'If a party to an arbitration agreement applies to the court for a provisional seizure or disposition in accordance with the conservation provisions of the Code of Civil Procedure prior to submitting to arbitration, the court at the request of the respondent shall order the applicant to submit to arbitration by a certain time period.'

If the arbitral tribunal considers it necessary, it could ask the court or other government agencies to assist. Article 28 of the Arbitration Law reads: 'The arbitral tribunal, if necessary, may request assistance from a court or other agencies in the conduct of the arbitral proceedings.' 'A requested court may exercise its investigative powers in the same manner and to the same extent as permitted in a legal action.'

Article 17A Conditions for Granting Interim Measures Under the Arbitration Law, there is no power granted to the arbitral tribunal to order interim measures. But if it is an interim order issued by a court, there are also some conditions to be met. CCP Article 368, paragraph 1 provides: 'Where it is likely that evidence may be destroyed or its use in court may be difficult, or with the consent of the opposing party, the party may move the court for perpetuation of such evidence; where necessary, the party who has legal interests in ascertaining the status quo of a matter or object may move for expert testimony, inspection or perpetuation of documentary evidence.'

CCP Article 522, paragraph 1 further provides: 'A creditor may apply for provisional attachment with regard to monetary claims or claims exchangeable for monetary claims for purposes of securing the satisfaction of a compulsory execution.' CCP Article 523, paragraph 1 states: 'No provisional attachment is to be granted unless there is a showing of the impossibility or extreme difficulty to satisfy the claim by compulsory execution in the future.'

Article 17B Applications for Preliminary Orders and Conditions for Granting Preliminary Orders Again, there is no power granted to the arbitral tribunal to order interim measures under the Arbitration Law. But if it is a court which orders an interim measure, the other party will not be notified and will not be provided with information prior to the issuance of such measure. This is to ensure that the order can be effectively and successfully enforced.

Article 17C Specific Regime for Preliminary Orders There is no power granted to the arbitral tribunal to order interim measures. But if it is a court-issued order, the other party will receive the information after the measure is carried out. This is to balance the protection of the alleged debtor so that he will be able to pursue possible remedies after the implementation of the interim measure.

Article 17D Modification, Suspension, Termination Under the Arbitration Law, there is no power granted to the arbitral tribunal to order interim measures. But if it is a court-issued order, the measure can be modified or revoked by the applying party.

Article 17E Provision of Security Since there is no power granted to the arbitral tribunal to order interim measures under the Arbitration Law, the rule concerning the provision of appropriate security is not relevant in the context of the Law. But it must be noted that when a court is to issue such order, appropriate security is always required.

Article 17F Disclosure Since there is no power granted to the arbitral tribunal to order interim measures under the Arbitration Law, the disclosure issue is not relevant to the Law. But if it is a court which is to order an interim measure, it would also require the applicant to provide prima facie evidence to show the need of such measure.

Article 17G Costs and Damages There is no power granted to the arbitral tribunal to order interim measures under the Arbitration Law. But if it is a court which issues a preliminary order and if the arbitral tribunal ultimately determines that the requesting party does not have the alleged substantive rights, the requesting party shall be liable for any costs and damages caused by the order.

Sub-Part II Recognition and Enforcement of Interim Measures (Articles 17H and 17I)

Article 17H Recognition and Enforcement There is no power granted to the arbitral tribunal to order interim measures under the Arbitration Law. So, if the court encounters an application to recognize and enforce such 'arbitral award', it is possible that there will not be recognition and enforcement of it. But there has not been a previous court decision on this issue.

TAIWAN   365

Article 17I   Grounds   for   Refusing   Recognition   or   Enforcement
There is no power granted to the arbitral tribunal to order interim
measures under the Arbitration Law. So, the rules concerning grounds
for refusing recognition or enforcement of an arbitral award to order
interim measures are not relevant.

Sub-Part III   Court-Ordered Interim Measures (Article 17J)

As mentioned earlier, Article 39 of the Arbitration Law explicitly
recognizes the court's power to order interim measures. Paragraph
1 of Article 39 states: 'If a party to an arbitration agreement applies to
the court for a provisional seizure or disposition in accordance with the
conservation provisions of the Code of Civil Procedure prior to submitting to arbitration, the court at the request of the respondent shall
order the applicant to submit to arbitration by a certain time period.
However, in the event that the applicant may also proceed by legal
action in accordance with the law, the court may order the parties
concerned to proceed with legal action.'

Part V   Conduct of Arbitral Proceedings (Articles 18 to 27)

Article 18   Equal Treatment of Parties

There is no explicit provision specifying that the parties shall be treated
with equality. But it is implied in Article 23, paragraph 1, of the
Arbitration Law, which requires the arbitral tribunal to 'ensure that
each party has a full opportunity to present its case and the arbitral
tribunal shall conduct the necessary investigations of the claims by the
parties.'

Article 19   Determination of Rules of Procedure

The parties are allowed mutually to decide the procedural rules for their
case. However, the parties may fail to come to an agreement on such
procedural rules governing the arbitration. In such situations, the procedures provided for in the Arbitration Law will apply. In the absence of
any provision in the Arbitration Law, the Code of Civil Procedure may be
applied, *mutatis mutandis*, to the arbitration proceedings. The arbitral
tribunal may also apply any other rules it deems appropriate (Article 19
of the Arbitration Law).

In order to ensure proper fact-finding procedures and legal opinions, the arbitral tribunal is required to provide full opportunities to the parties to present their cases. It is also required to conduct the necessary investigation of the allegations presented by the parties. Unless otherwise agreed upon by both parties, the arbitration proceedings shall not be carried out in open court (Article 23 of the Arbitration Law).

Article 20   Place of Arbitration

The parties may decide the place and venue for conducting their arbitration. In cases where the parties cannot come to an agreement on the place or venue of arbitration, it is to be decided by the arbitral tribunal (Articles 20 and 21 of the Arbitration Law).

Article 21   Commencement of Arbitral Proceedings

Unless otherwise agreed by both parties, the arbitral proceedings for a dispute shall commence on the date specified on the written notice of arbitration received by the respondent party (Article 18, paragraph 2 of the Arbitration Law).

Article 22   Language

Under Article 25 of the Arbitration Law, parties to a dispute with an international character may designate a language or languages to be used to conduct the arbitral proceedings. However, the arbitral tribunal or a party may request that any documents relating to the arbitration are accompanied with a translation in another language. Also, interpreters shall be provided under the direction of the arbitral tribunal in the event that a party or an arbitrator is not familiar with Mandarin.

Article 23   Statements of Claim and Defence

There is no explicit provision in the Arbitration Law governing the period of time agreed upon by the parties or determined by the arbitral tribunal concerning the claimant's statement of the facts supporting its claim, the points at issue and the relief or remedy sought, and the respondent's statement of its defence in respect of these particulars. In practice, when a claimant submits its dispute for arbitration, it is expected to provide the facts supporting its claim, the points at issue and the relief or remedy sought. After the tribunal is established, the parties will be informed of the first meeting. The respondent is then expected to submit its defence in respect of these aspects.

Article 24   Hearings and Written Proceedings

Article 23 of the Arbitration Law states: 'The arbitral tribunal shall ensure that each party has a full opportunity to present its case and the arbitral tribunal shall conduct the necessary investigations of the claims by the parties.' This implies that there must be an oral hearing for the parties to present their evidence and arguments. Of course, the disputing parties can mutually agree on their proceedings. If they decide not to conduct an oral hearing, it is acceptable under the Arbitration Law.

Article 25   Default of a Party

There is no direct provision in the Arbitration Law concerning default of a party. Article 19 of the Arbitration Law states: 'In the absence of an agreement on the procedural rules governing the arbitration, the arbitral tribunal shall apply this Law. Where this Law is silent, the arbitral tribunal may adopt the Code of Civil Procedure *mutatis mutandis* or other rules of procedure which it deems proper.' Hence, the arbitral tribunal can rely on the CCP to decide the default situation.

CCP Article 385 provides the default situation:

Where one of the parties fails to appear at the oral-argument session, the court may, on the appearing party's motion, enter a default judgment based on the appearing party's arguments; where the party who fails to appear is summoned and fails to appear again, the court may also on its own initiative enter a default judgment based on the appearing party's arguments.

The provision of the preceding paragraph shall also apply to cases where the claims must be adjudicated jointly with regard to all co-parties and one of the co-parties appears in the oral-argument session.

In entering a judgment provided in the preceding paragraph, the court shall take into consideration any argument made, evidence-taking conducted, or the preparatory pleading submitted by the party who fails to appear; if necessary, the evidence stated by the party who fails to appear shall also be taken.

CCP Article 386 provides:

> In case of any of the following, the court shall deny the motion provided in the preceding article by a ruling and postpone the oral-argument session: (1) Where the party who fails to appear has not been legally summoned within a reasonable period of time; (2) Where there is reason to believe that the failure of a party to appear is due to force majeure or other justifiable reasons; (3) Where the appearing party cannot provide necessary proof for the matters which the court shall investigate on its own initiative; (4) Where the statements, facts or evidence presented by the appearing party have not been notified to the opposing party within a reasonable period of time.

CCP Article 387 provides that where a party refuses to present any argument in the oral-argument session, such refusal shall be deemed a failure to appear.

Article 26   Expert Appointed by Arbitral Tribunal

Under Article 26 of the Arbitration Law, the arbitral tribunal may summon witnesses or expert witnesses to appear for questioning but may not compel any witness to enter any undertaking. In the event that a witness fails to appear without sufficient reason, the arbitral tribunal may apply for a court order compelling the witness to appear.

Article 27   Court Assistance in Taking Evidence

If the arbitral tribunal considers it necessary, it can ask the court or other government agencies to assist in taking evidence. Article 28 of the Arbitration Law reads: 'The arbitral tribunal, if necessary, may request assistance from a court or other agencies in the conduct of the arbitral proceedings.' 'A requested court may exercise its investigative powers in the same manner and to the same extent as permitted in a legal action.'

Part VI   Making of Award and Termination of Proceedings (Articles 28 to 33)

Article 28   Rules Applicable to Substance of Dispute

For international arbitration cases, there is no explicit provision in the Arbitration Law to decide the applicable law. The arbitral tribunals will have to apply the Act Governing the Choice of Law in Civil Matters Involving Foreign Elements (AGCL) to decide applicable law for a dispute involving foreign elements. According to Article 20 of the AGCL, the applicable law regarding the formation and effect of a juridical act which results in a relationship of obligation is determined by the intention of the parties. Where there is no express intention of the parties or their express intention is void under the applicable law determined by them, the formation and effect of the juridical act are governed by the law which is most closely connected with the juridical act.

Article 29   Decision-Making by Panel of Arbitrators

Article 32, paragraphs 2 and 3 of the Arbitration Law deal with the decision-making of arbitral awards: 'If there is more than one arbitrator, the arbitral award shall be determined by a majority vote.' 'When calculating an amount in dispute and none of the opinions of the arbitrators prevail, the highest figure in an opinion shall be averaged with the second highest figure in another opinion and so forth, until a majority consensus is obtained.' But the Law does not include an explicit provision on decision-making of other matters. The majority rule should be applicable for such other matters too.

Article 30   Settlement

Article 44 of the Arbitration Law allows the arbitral tribunal to record the settlement agreement of the parties and to conclude the case. It provides:

> Parties to an arbitration may settle their dispute prior to the issuance of an arbitral award. If the parties reach a settlement [prior to the conclusion of the arbitration], the arbitrator shall record the terms of settlement in a settlement agreement.
>
> A settlement agreement under the preceding paragraph has the same force and effect as that of an arbitral award. However, the terms of the settlement agreement may be enforced only after the court has granted an application by a party for enforcement and issued an enforcement order.

It is also possible for the arbitral tribunal to incorporate the contents of a settlement agreement in an arbitral award, the form of which needs to be made in line with the required form for ordinary arbitral awards under the Law if it is to be enforced.

Article 31   Form and Contents of Award

According to paragraph 2 of Article 33 of the Arbitration Law, an arbitral award shall contain the following items: (1) Names and residence or domicile of the individual parties. For a party that is a corporate entity or another type of organization or institution, then its name(s), administrative office(s), principal office(s) or business office(s) [address]; (2) Names and domiciles or residences of the statutory agents or representatives, if any, of the parties; (3) Names, nationalities and residences or domiciles of the interpreters, if any; (4) The main text of the decision; (5) The relevant facts and reasons for the arbitral award, unless the parties have agreed that no reasons shall be stated; and (6) The date and place of the arbitral award. It is apparent from this provision that an arbitral award must be made in writing.

The original copy of the award shall be signed by the arbitrator(s) who deliberated on the award. If an arbitrator refuses to or cannot sign the award for any reason, the arbitrator(s) who do sign the award shall state the reason for the missing signature(s) (paragraph 3 of Article 33).

Article 32   Termination of Proceedings

Although there is no explicit provision stating this, the arbitral proceedings are terminated by the final award. Parties may also agree on the termination of the proceedings.

Concerning a claimant's withdrawal of their claim, there is no direct provision in the Arbitration Law. Article 19 of the Arbitration Law states that where this Law is silent the arbitral tribunal may adopt the CCP *mutatis mutandis* or other rules of procedure which it deems proper. Under Article 262 of the CCP, the plaintiff may, before the judgment becomes final and binding, voluntarily dismiss the action in whole or in part, and except where the defendant has proceeded orally on the merits such dismissal shall be subject to his/her consent.

The Arbitration Law has a very unique time limit provision in paragraph 1 of Article 21: 'The arbitral tribunal shall render an arbitral award within six months [of commencement of the arbitration]. However, the arbitral tribunal may extend [the decision period] an additional three months if the circumstances so require.' Paragraph 3 of the same article further provides the effect of exceeding the time limit to render an award: 'If an arbitral award has not been rendered by the arbitral tribunal within the above-mentioned time period, either party may, unless compelled to arbitrate, refer the dispute to the court or proceed with a previously initiated legal action. The arbitral proceedings shall be deemed terminated thereafter.'

*Article 33   Correction and Interpretation of Award;
Additional Award*

Article 35 of the Arbitration Law provides that: 'The arbitral tribunal may correct, on its own initiative or upon request, any clerical, computational or typographic errors or any other similar obvious mistakes in the award and shall provide written notification of this correction to the parties as well as the court. The foregoing is likewise applicable to any discrepancy between a certified copy of the arbitral award and the original version thereof.' Under the Arbitration Law, there is no power vested to the original arbitral tribunal to issue an interpretation of award or to issue an additional award.

Part VII   Recourse against Award (Article 34)

*Article 34   Application for Setting Aside as Exclusive Recourse
against Arbitral Award*

The Arbitration Law specifically recognizes an arbitration award to have the same effect for both parties as a final judgment of the court and to be enforceable when a party has obtained an enforcement order from the court. However, if both parties agree that a court enforcement order is unnecessary in order to enforce the award and if the following circumstances are met, then the award may be enforced without a court order: (1) The subject matter is payment of certain specified amounts of money, fungible things or securities; (2) The subject matter is the delivery of identified movable property (Article 37 of the Arbitration Law).

In cases when there is a significant defect in the procedure or in the award, it might not be appropriate for the court to grant an enforcement order. Thus, the Arbitration Law requires the court to reject the application for an enforcement order in any of the following situations: (1) The arbitration award is not made in respect to the subject matter of the arbitration agreement, or the award has exceeded the scope of the arbitration agreement; this is provided, however, that the remaining parts not having such problems shall still be legally binding if separable; (2) The arbitration award fails to include the reasons required, unless they have later been supplemented by the arbitral tribunal; (3) The arbitration award orders a party to carry out an act prohibited by law (Article 38 of the Arbitration Law).

Article 40 of the Arbitration Law further provides that:

> A party may apply to a court to set aside the arbitral award in any of the following circumstances: (1) The existence of any circumstances stated in Article 38; (2) The arbitration agreement is nullified, invalid or has yet to come into effect or has become invalid prior to the conclusion of the arbitral proceedings; (3) The arbitral tribunal fails to give any party an opportunity to present its case prior to the conclusion of the arbitral proceedings, or if any party is not lawfully represented in the arbitral proceedings; (4) The composition of the arbitral tribunal or the arbitral proceedings is contrary to the arbitration agreement or the law; (5) An arbitrator fails to fulfil the duty of disclosure prescribed in paragraph 2 of Article 15 herein and appears to be partial or has been requested to withdraw but continues to participate, provided that the request for withdrawal has not been dismissed by the court; (6) An arbitrator violates any duty in the entrusted arbitration and such violation carries criminal liability; (7) A party or any representative has committed a criminal offense in relation to the arbitration; (8) If any evidence or content of any translation upon which the arbitration award relies, has been forged or fraudulently altered or contains any other misrepresentations; (9) If a judgment of a criminal or civil matter, or an administrative ruling upon which the arbitration award relies, has been reversed or materially altered by a subsequent judgment or administrative ruling.

Article 41, paragraph 2 of the Arbitration Law provides the time limit for setting aside an arbitral award:

> An application to set aside an arbitral award shall be submitted to the court within the thirty-day statutory period after the arbitral award has been issued or delivered. However, if any cause mentioned in items 6 to 9 of the first paragraph of the preceding Article exists and if sufficient reasons are offered that the failure of a party to apply to the court to set aside an award before the limitation period does not arise from any fault of such party, then the thirty-day statutory period commences to run from the time when the party becomes aware of the cause for revocation. In any event, the application to set aside an arbitral award shall be barred after five years have elapsed from the date on which the arbitral award was issued.

Part VIII   Recognition and Enforcement of Awards
(Articles 35 to 36)

Article 35   Recognition and Enforcement

As mentioned earlier, arbitral awards are recognized and enforced by the court. But if an award is a foreign one, it will be recognized and enforced only when there is no ground for refusing recognition and enforcement and after a court order to recognize such an award has been obtained. The Arbitration Law lists two situations where arbitration awards will be considered as foreign ones. The first is where arbitration awards were made outside the territories of Taiwan. The second is where the awards were made in accordance with the procedures provided for under a foreign law, notwithstanding that the awards might be made within the territories of Taiwan (Article 47 of the Arbitration Law).

Article 36   Grounds for Refusing Recognition or Enforcement

The Arbitration Law treats foreign awards and domestic ones somewhat differently. Foreign arbitration awards will become enforceable only after a court order to recognize such an award has been obtained. In cases where there is any one of the following situations, the court will have to reject the application to recognize a foreign arbitration award: (1) The recognition or enforcement of the arbitration award is contrary to the public order or good morals of Taiwan; (2) The subject dispute is not arbitrable under the laws of Taiwan (Paragraph 1 of Article 49 of the Arbitration Law).

Taiwan is not a party to the New York Convention (NYC); hence the NYC does not apply to Taiwan. The Arbitration Law adopts the 'reciprocity' principle in the recognition of foreign arbitral awards. Thus, the court may reject the application to recognize a foreign award if the country where the arbitration was carried out, or the country whose arbitration laws and regulations were applied in the award, does not recognize Taiwan's arbitration awards (Paragraph 2 of Article 49 of the Arbitration Law).

The Law further provides that upon the request of the respondent, made within twenty days from the receipt of notification, the court shall reject applications to recognize a foreign arbitration award, in any one of the following situations: (1) The arbitration agreement is not legally effective due to the fact that a party is incapable of concluding the agreement in accordance with the applicable law; (2) The arbitration agreement is null and void in accordance with the governing law agreed upon by both parties. In cases where there is no law agreed upon by both parties, it is null and void in accordance with the law of the place of arbitration; (3) One of the parties did not receive proper notification in regard to the appointment of arbitrators or to the arbitration proceedings, or there is any other situation where due process has not been observed in the arbitration proceedings; (4) The arbitration award is not made with respect to the subject matter of the arbitration agreement or the award has exceeded the scope of the arbitration agreement; this is provided, however, that the remaining parts not having such a problem shall still be legally binding awards if separable; (5) The establishment of the arbitral tribunal or the arbitration proceeding is in violation of the arbitration agreement or, if there is no agreement in this regard, the law of the place of arbitration; (6) The arbitral award has not become effective as to the parties or it has been invalidated or its effect has been suspended (Article 50 of the Arbitration Law).

Conclusion

It could be said that the Arbitration Law in Taiwan is quite similar to the ML 1985 in the majority of their rules, although the provisions of the ML 1985 had to be adjusted into the legal system of Taiwan. But it is clear that the amendments to the ML adopted in 2006, especially those provisions governing interim measures, are not reflected in the Arbitration Law.

Also, since the Arbitration Law is not directly adopted from the ML, there is no such provision or interpretation rule to require the court to interpret the Law in a way to respect its international origin and to promote international uniformity in its application.

There is definitely an urgent need to introduce the 2006 amendments in the ML into the Arbitration Law. An equally important issue is the way of introducing the ML. As explained above, it is the legislative practice to adopt the 'elements' in the ML 1985 into the Arbitration Law. The result has been that there are various provisions in the Arbitration Law which are different from the ML 1986. In order to make the domestic legislation more compatible with the ML and international practice, the legislative body will have to adopt fully the text of the ML and to transform it directly into the legal system of Taiwan so as to make Taiwan a jurisdiction which adopts the ML.

12

Vietnam

The Vietnamese Law on Commercial Arbitration 2010 Compared to the UNCITRAL Model Law on International Commercial Arbitration 2006

DANG XUAN HOP

Introduction

As a young developing economy in South East Asia competing for international trade and investment, Vietnam has been trying to bring its domestic legal framework closer and closer to international standards, including its law on arbitration. While the first piece of arbitration legislation of Vietnam dates back to 1994,[1] it was not until 2003 when the Ordinance on Commercial Arbitration 2003 (OCA) was issued that Vietnam's arbitration legislation started to reflect international standards. After five years of implementing the OCA, the Vietnamese legislature considered it necessary to enhance its arbitration legal framework even further. A drafting committee was then set up in 2008 to draft a law on commercial arbitration. Two years of hard work at different levels of the government and legislature eventually resulted in the enactment by the Vietnamese National Assembly of the Law on Commercial Arbitration, 2010 (LCA).

The LCA has a number of improvements compared to its predecessor, the OCA. The drafting committee of the LCA reviewed the provisions of the OCA, the strengths and problems it had revealed in the preceding five years of practice and examined at length the arbitration laws of

Dang Xuan Hop is a full time arbitrator based in Hanoi, Vietnam. He has been a Visiting Senior Fellow at the Law Faculty, National University of Singapore and a Senior Fellow at the Law Faculty, University of Melbourne. The author thanks the EW Barker Centre for Law & Business at the Faculty of Law of the National University of Singapore for financing his participation in the conference entitled, 'The UNCITRAL Model Law on International Commercial Arbitration in Asia', which led to this book.
[1] Decree 114/CP 1994 on commercial arbitration.

developed jurisdictions such as England or Singapore and, of course, the UNCITRAL Model Law on International Commercial Arbitration 2006, UN General Assembly Resolution 61/33 (4 December 2006) ('ML'). Many provisions in these laws, considered by the drafting committee as representing international standards, were considered, adopted or adapted and incorporated into the LCA. At the same time, other provisions were considered and eventually not adopted for one reason or another. As a result, there remain certain gaps between the LCA and the ML at the moment and Vietnam is therefore not regarded as an ML jurisdiction. In this chapter, the author attempts to identify some key differences between the LCA and the ML, to explain and analyse them to arrive at a conclusion regarding whether such differences should be reconsidered for incorporation into the LCA when it is next amended or re-enacted. The analysis will follow the order of the provisions as they appear in the ML.

Part I   General Provisions of the Model Law (Articles 1 to 6)

The ML and the LCA are different in one important aspect: the ML only applies to international commercial arbitrations[2] while the LCA, like its predecessor the OCA, applies to both domestic and international arbitrations (seated in Vietnam). Being such a generic law, most of the provisions in the LCA apply equally to both domestic and international arbitrations, except for a small number of provisions specifically designed for disputes with 'foreign elements' (i.e., those involving foreign parties or assets located in foreign countries) or Vietnamese businesses with foreign ownership.[3] This position is consistent with the practice of Vietnam of having one uniform law governing both domestic and international activities such as the Law on Investment, 2005 applying to both domestic and foreign investments and the Law on Enterprises, 2005 applying to both domestic and foreign-owned companies.

---

[2] ML art. 1.
[3] For example, in case of disputes involving foreign elements or foreign-owned businesses, art. 10 allows the parties to choose or, in the absence of a choice by the parties, the tribunal to determine the language of arbitration. For domestic disputes, the language of arbitration must be the Vietnamese language. Under art. 14, while Vietnamese law must be used as the substantive law to resolve domestic disputes, for disputes with foreign elements, the tribunal shall apply the law chosen by the parties or, in the absence of a choice by the parties, the law that the tribunal considers the most appropriate.

For this reason, the LCA does not have provisions equal to those found in the first Part of the ML, in particular article 2A, regarding the international nature or origin of the ML. The jurisprudence and literature stemming from the international nature of the ML therefore will hardly be relevant in the context of the LCA, except where the dispute is one with foreign elements or perhaps with foreign-owned businesses. For the most part, the LCA will be viewed as a domestic piece of legislation, subject to ordinary rules of statutory interpretation under Vietnamese domestic law.

Apart from that, there are a lot of similarities between the ML and the LCA in terms of general provisions. In terms of scope, the LCA aims to permit and regulate arbitration of a wide range of disputes including disputes arising from commercial activities, disputes involving at least one party conducting commercial activities, and disputes specifically stated by law to be arbitrable. In short, the LCA, like the ML, aims to regulate 'commercial arbitration'. The concept of commercial activities is not defined in the LCA itself but is defined in the Commercial Law, 2005 as including all activities 'conducted for a profit making purpose'. This was considered by the drafting committee a fairly wide concept, sufficient to cover most ordinary commercial activities from which a dispute may practically arise and needs to be arbitrated in Vietnam. The drafting committee did not consider it necessary to incorporate a definition of 'commercial' as in the ML, lest it may create confusion with the concept of 'commercial activities' already defined in the Commercial Law, 2005. There is in theory a risk that a future law may alter this concept of 'commercial activities' in a way prejudicial to the current wide scope of the LCA. However, this risk, practically, is not high, as it is generally believed that later laws will be even more liberal on these matters.

There are other similarities between the general provisions in Part I of the ML and the position under the LCA. Both will yield to international treaties to the extent of any conflict. This is stated in article 1(1) of the ML and, for the LCA, is stated in article 82 of the Law on Promulgation of Normative Legal Instruments, 2008.[4] Like the ML, the LCA gives the parties a fairly high degree of freedom to agree to determine certain matters in the arbitral process and this implicitly includes the right to authorize a third party to make such determination. For example, where

[4] Article 82 sets out the general principle under Vietnamese law that international treaties prevail over domestic law.

the parties have agreed to conduct arbitration at an arbitration institution, the rules of that institution will be taken as part of the agreement
of the parties.[5] Under both the ML and the LCA, receipt of documents is
effective upon actual or constructive receipt (to mailing address on
record).[6] Regarding waiver of the right to object, both the ML and the
LCA contemplate that failure to object may be deemed to be a waiver of
the right to object. A slight difference is that article 13 of the LCA refers
to failure to object within the time limits prescribed by the LCA
while article 4 of the ML also refers more generally to undue delay which
is a broader, albeit more uncertain, concept. As article 6 of the ML
contemplates that the relevant court with supervisory jurisdiction over
arbitration should be specified, article 7 of the LCA first leaves it to the
parties to agree to determine the court with supervisory jurisdiction. In
the absence of such agreement, article 7 of the LCA specifies certain
courts with jurisdiction over certain matters. For example, the court of
the place where the defendant resides has jurisdiction for appointing
arbitrators. The court in the place of arbitration has jurisdiction over the
challenge of arbitrators and the court in the place where the award is
rendered has the jurisdiction over the setting aside of the award.

A key difference is that the LCA has no provision equivalent to article 5
of the ML which provides that no court shall intervene in arbitration
except where so provided in this Law. In other words, the ML's position
is that the arbitration law is a *lex specialis* which will prevail over other
laws in matters relating to arbitration. However, this concept of *lex
specialis* is not yet generally recognized in the Vietnamese legal system
and the general principle is simply that later laws will prevail over earlier
laws at the same level. Therefore, if a law issued by the Vietnamese
National Assembly after the LCA provides differently from the LCA,
such later law shall prevail. The concept of *lex specialis* has been recognized in some cases in Vietnam[7] but has not become a universal principle
in the Vietnamese legal system. Therefore, it is open to the Vietnamese
legislature to pass a later law to override provisions in the LCA. For
example, the recently re-enacted Civil Procedures Code, 2016 contains
certain provisions on exclusive jurisdiction of Vietnamese courts which

---

[5] Article 2(d) & (e) of the ML and art. 12 on notice; arts. 40 and 41 on establishment of
tribunals; arts. 63 on time limits in the LCA.
[6] Article 3 of the ML and art. 12 of the LCA.
[7] For example, the Law on Enterprises 2005 prescribes general provisions on corporate
governance and goes on to say that specialized laws shall prevail (art. 3.2).

may have the effect of narrowing the wide concept of arbitrability currently recognized under the LCA. Another law may give the courts the power to intervene in arbitral proceedings in some special contexts such as land or other matters of public interest. With these fundamental principles still in place, it is impossible to make the LCA a *lex specialis* in the way that the ML contemplates.

In conclusion, it seems that the general provisions in the ML and the LCA are mostly similar. The differences are justified or appropriate in the Vietnamese context and there seems to be no need to amend the LCA any further in this regard.

Part II   Arbitration Agreement (Articles 7 to 9)

The ML and the LCA contain fairly similar provisions regarding the requirements for an arbitration agreement in that an arbitration agreement has to be in writing and writing can be in documentary or electronic form. The slight difference is that article 7 of the ML refers in more detail to electronic and data messages as constituting forms of writing, while article 16 of the LCA only refers to emails and then defers to other laws to prescribe what are permissible forms of 'writing'.[8] Once again, it seems that the drafting committee did not consider it wise to interfere with the definitions of electronic messages and data which are already regulated under the Law on Electronic Commerce, 2014. This is the reason why the LCA did not refer to electronic forms of writing in more detail. Article 16 of the LCA, as article 7 of the ML, also provides that reference to another document or exchange of claims and defence with an arbitration agreement alleged and not denied are examples of arbitration agreements in writing.

Another similarity is that article 6 of the LCA and article 8 of the ML both provide that a court has to decline jurisdiction where a valid arbitration agreement exists, except where the arbitration is found to be invalid or incapable of being performed. Article 48.2 of the LCA, similar to article 9 of the ML, provides that the application for interim relief from a court does not invalidate or waive the existence of an arbitration agreement. In addition, article 19 of the LCA provides for the separability of the arbitration agreement from the main contract, which is similar to the principle laid down in article 16(1) of the ML.

---

[8] This may include the Law on Electronic Commerce or the Law on Electronic Signatures.

There are some additional provisions in the LCA which one does not find in the ML. For example, article 18 provides for grounds on which an arbitration agreement can be found to be invalid, including where the dispute is not arbitrable, lack of capacity of the party, the arbitration agreement not being in the correct form, a party entering into the agreement under duress or fraud or the arbitration agreement violating a legal prohibition. This provision was created to give some clarity on this issue which had often arisen in practice and over which the OCA had created some unnecessary and undesirable confusion.[9] Article 17 gives consumers the right to go to court, if they wish to, notwithstanding the presence of an arbitration agreement in a standard form contract which they have entered into.

In conclusion, the provisions of the LCA and the ML on this aspect are rather similar, although they are not worded in identical terms. Some differences can be justified by the specific Vietnamese circumstances and therefore no amendments seem to be required to bring the LCA closer to the ML.

Part III   Composition of Arbitral Tribunal (Articles 10 to 15)

This is a part where the LCA has some differences compared to the ML.

Both the LCA and the ML start with similar provisions on general matters. For example, both article 39 of the LCA and article 10 of the ML state that the parties are free to agree on the number of arbitrators, and failing such agreement the default position will be a three-member tribunal. Consistent with article 11(1) of the ML, which states that no person shall be precluded by his nationality from acting as an arbitrator unless otherwise agreed by the parties, the LCA no longer requires that arbitrators must be Vietnamese nationals, which used to be the position in the OCA.[10] Both the ML[11] and the LCA[12] give full autonomy to the parties in agreeing on the procedures for the appointment of arbitrators. Failing such agreement, both the ML and the LCA provide fairly similar default mechanisms for the appointment of arbitrators by the parties, arbitral institution and finally the court. Articles 40 and 41 of the LCA

---

[9] For example, under the OCA, not specifying or putting the wrong name of the arbitration centre in the arbitration clause may be a reason for holding the arbitration agreement invalid.
[10] Article 12(1).   [11] Article 11(2).
[12] Article 40 and 41 both start with 'Unless otherwise agreed by the parties . . .'

are more prescriptive than article 11 of the ML in providing for time limits and procedural steps in the arbitrator appointment process, but generally the position is rather similar to the position in article 11 of the ML. While articles 40 and 41 of the LCA do not specifically state that the appointment by the arbitral institution or the court is final, as does article 11(5) of the ML, this seems to be the intent as the LCA does not provide for any appeal procedures in respect of such decisions.

Under article 11(4) of the ML, in the case of an institutional arbitration, if the parties fail to appoint arbitrators and then the arbitral institution itself also fails to make the appointment, the court will be the final appointing authority. This position is not provided for in the LCA. Article 40 stops at requiring the arbitral institution to make the appointment and does not go on to say who will make the appointment if the arbitral institution fails to do so. It is recommended that this aspect of article 11(4) of the ML should be adopted in the LCA.

Article 11(5) of the ML provides some guidance to arbitral institutions and courts in making appointments by requiring them to have due regard to any qualifications required of arbitrators as agreed by the parties and any considerations likely to secure independent and impartial arbitrators. Article 11(5) also suggests that in appointing a sole arbitrator or third arbitrator one should consider the advisability of appointing someone of a nationality different from those of the parties. The LCA does not provide such guidance. Although, in practice, arbitral institutions and courts, acting reasonably, should have due regard to those matters in any event, it would be desirable to have such guidance clearly stated in the LCA, given the early stage of development of arbitration in Vietnam.

Another difference between the LCA and the ML relates to disclosure and challenge of arbitrators. Article 12 of the ML requires an arbitrator to disclose circumstances likely to give rise to justifiable doubts as to his impartiality or independence and, if such circumstances exist, the arbitrator may be challenged. On the other hand, article 42.2 of the LCA requires arbitrators to disclose the circumstances which may affect their independence and impartiality. Article 42.1 provides that an arbitrator may be challenged where he or she is a related person, a representative of a party or has an interest in the dispute or where there is clear evidence showing that he is not impartial and objective. It remains to be seen how the thresholds of 'may affect' and 'clear evidence' will be applied in practice, but they seem in theory different from the test of 'justifiable doubts' in the ML. Depending on how Vietnamese courts apply this in practice, it could make it more difficult or easier to challenge arbitrators under the LCA.

Article 12(2) of the ML allows parties to challenge an arbitrator where he does not possess the qualifications as agreed by the parties. However, the LCA has no such provision and it would be better to have this clearly stated in the LCA. In addition, the LCA has no provision equal to article 12(2) of the ML which allows a party to challenge its own arbitrator only for reasons of which it becomes aware after the appointment has been made. This should be added to the LCA to ensure that a party does not challenge its own arbitrator for reasons it already knew before making the appointment.

Under article 13(1) of the ML, parties are free to agree on the procedures for challenging arbitrators. There is no such provision in the LCA. Instead, the LCA has some brief prescriptive provisions providing that the challenge of an arbitrator shall be determined by either the remaining members of the tribunal, the arbitral institution (where the tribunal has not been constituted) or the court (in case of ad hoc arbitrations), and such decisions of the arbitral tribunal, the arbitral institution or the court shall be final. The drafting committee of the LCA must have considered it more user-friendly for the LCA to spell out these provisions, rather than leaving it to the parties to agree. In any event, for institutional arbitrations, the challenge procedures are provided for in the rules of the institution. Therefore, there seems to be no practical need for the LCA to have an equivalent article 13(1) of the ML.

Finally, article 14 of the ML allows the parties to agree to or seek a court order for the withdrawal or termination of an arbitrator's mandate where he is unable to perform *de jure* or *de facto* or fails to perform without undue delay. On the other hand, the LCA does not provide for this and merely states that where an arbitrator cannot continue because of force majeure or objective reasons, a substitute arbitrator will be appointed. However, the LCA does not provide for how a controversy over this issue will be resolved. It is recommended that a position similar to article 14 of the ML should be adopted in the LCA so that the court or the arbitral institution can make a final decision on the termination of the mandate of an arbitrator who cannot continue. In addition, in this context, the LCA should also adopt article 14(2) of the ML to the effect that a withdrawal by an arbitrator, either voluntary or as agreed by the parties, does not imply the existence of a ground for challenge.

In conclusion, the composition of the arbitral tribunal is a part where it would be desirable for the LCA to adopt some additional positions from the ML, as stated above. That would facilitate the constitution of tribunals and its operations in the process.

Part IV Jurisdiction of Arbitral Tribunal (Article 16)

The ML and the LCA contain substantially the same position on this aspect, although the relevant provisions in the LCA are found in various articles, rather than mostly contained in one place as in article 16 of the ML.

Both the ML[13] and the LCA[14] empower an arbitral tribunal to decide on its own jurisdiction (and the validity of the arbitration agreement) and the LCA even requires an arbitral tribunal to conduct this exercise prior to hearing the merits of the dispute. The independence of the arbitration agreement from the main contract is recognized in both the LCA[15] and the ML.[16] As with the ML, the LCA requires a jurisdictional challenge to be made in the statement of defence and no later than that.[17] The LCA has no express provision, as does the ML,[18] that the jurisdictional challenge can be ruled on separately from or as part of the final award, but the practice in Vietnam has been that the jurisdictional decision is often made separately in order to allow the parties to file a challenge in the court on this issue if they wish to do so. The time limit for such a challenge under the LCA is five working days from the receipt of the tribunal's decision, whereas it is thirty days in the ML. Under article 44 of the LCA, the relevant court will decide such challenge within fifteen working days and this decision shall be final. Pending the court's decision, under both the ML[19] and the LCA,[20] the tribunal can continue the arbitral proceeding. In addition, article 16.2 of the ML allows the parties to raise a challenge where the tribunal exceeds its jurisdiction and this is also addressed in article 43.2 of the LCA.[21]

So, overall, the positions under the LCA and the ML are rather similar on this aspect and there is no need to make any significant addition to the LCA to bring it closer to the ML. It may be useful to add that article 43 of the LCA provides for some peculiar situations which have often arisen in practice in Vietnam. For example, under article 43.3, where the arbitral institution chosen by the parties no longer exists, the parties need to agree on a substitute institution, failing which the matter needs to be brought to the court. Under article 43.5, where the arbitration agreement does not specify an arbitration institution, the parties need to agree on

---

[13] Article 16(1). [14] Article 43.1. [15] Article 19. [16] Article 16(1).
[17] Article 35.4. [18] Article 16(3). [19] Article 16(3). [20] Article 44.5.
[21] Article 16(2) of the ML requires the parties to raise this challenge as soon as the matter arises but allows the tribunal to admit a later challenge where the tribunal considers the delay justified. The LCA does not provide for such details.

DANG XUAN HOP

the specific arbitration institution, failing which the claimant has the right to choose the arbitration institution.

Part IV-A   Interim Measures and Preliminary Orders (Articles 17 to 17J)

Sub-Part I   Measures and Orders by the Tribunal (Articles 17 to 17G)

This is a part where the ML and the LCA are similar as much as they are different. First, both the LCA[22] and the ML[23] empower arbitral tribunals to order certain forms of interim relief, including maintenance of the status quo, taking actions or refraining from taking actions prejudicial to the proceeding and seizure/preservation of assets. However, a difference is that the LCA[24] allows a tribunal to make temporary payment orders, which is not stipulated in the ML, and the ML[25] allows a tribunal to order preservation of evidence, which is not stipulated in the LCA.

The conditions for granting interim relief are also different between the LCA and the ML. Under article 50.2 of the LCA, the applicant for interim relief needs to produce evidence showing the <u>necessity</u> of the relief sought. This requirement is rather vague, compared to article 17A(1) of the ML, which requires the applicant to satisfy the tribunal that harm not adequately reparable by damages will probably occcur if the interim relief is not ordered and there is a reasonable possibility of success for the applicant on merit. Under the LCA, it remains rather unclear how the general requirement of 'necessity' of the relief will be interpreted and applied by Vietnamese courts and tribunals. This may be open to different interpretations, and it may be desirable to adopt the position set out in article 17A(1) of the ML as clearer guidance on this issue.

Both the ML[26] and the LCA[27] allow the tribunal, upon the application of a party, to modify or terminate an interim relief that has been ordered, although article 51 of the LCA provides for the procedures in some more detail. However, a difference is that article 17D of the ML allows the tribunal itself to modify or terminate the relief in exceptional circumstances and with prior notice to the parties but this is not provided in the LCA. It is suggested that this aspect of article 17D of the ML be reflected

---

[22] Article 49.   [23] Article 17.   [24] Article 49.2(dd).   [25] Article 17(2)(d).
[26] Article 17D.   [27] Article 51.

into the LCA in order to broaden the powers of tribunals on this matter to facilitate the arbitral process.

Regarding provision of security, both the LCA[28] and the ML[29] allow the tribunal to require the applicant to provide security for the relief sought. The LCA[30] and the ML[31] are also similar in providing that if subsequently the tribunal finds that the relief sought should not have been ordered the applicant shall be liable for damage caused to any party. However, the LCA has no equivalent provision to article 17F of the ML, which requires the applicant to disclose to the tribunal all the circumstances that may be relevant to the application for the relief and allows the tribunal to require the parties to disclose any material change in circumstances. It is suggested that this article 17F of the ML be incorporated into the LCA so that the tribunal may be fully informed in considering the issue of the relief or its modification.

Finally, it is noteworthy that the LCA has no provisions on preliminary orders as contemplated by Article 17B and C of the ML. This subject matter was not even considered by the drafting committee at the time of drafting and, in the practical circumstances of Vietnam, this was not considered necessary.

Sub-Part II   Recognition and Enforcement of Interim Measures (Articles 17H to 17I)

Since the LCA only regulates arbitrations seated in Vietnam, the LCA does not, unlike the ML, address interim relief orders issued by tribunals seated in other countries. This is the first difference between the LCA and the ML in this part. Apart from that, both the LCA[32] and the ML[33] recognize that interim relief orders made by tribunals may be enforced in the court (under the ML) or by the civil judgment enforcement agency (under the LCA).

Under article 17H(2) of the ML, where an interim relief is modified, suspended or terminated, the party seeking enforcement of such relief must inform the court. Article 51.4 of the LCA provides for a similar obligation to inform the civil judgment enforcement agency, but only where the interim relief is terminated. It is suggested that this notification obligation also applies where the relief is modified or suspended.

---

[28] Article 49.4.   [29] Article 17E.   [30] Article 52.   [31] Article 17G.
[32] Article 50.5.   [33] Article 17H(1).

Finally, article 17H(3) of the ML allows the court to require security before ordering enforcement of the relief. This article is not present in the LCA for the reason that interim relief orders are not enforced through the court, but through the enforcement agencies (which do not have the power to require security). Similarly, the LCA does not contain any provision similar to article 17I regarding the grounds for a court to refuse enforcement of interim orders. In theory, at least, the interm relief orders made by tribunals should be directly enforceable by the enforcement agencies.

Sub-Part III   Court-Ordered Interim Measures (Article 17J)

Both the LCA[34] and the ML[35] provide that courts have jurisdiction to issue interim relief orders in the context of arbitral proceedings as they do in court proceedings. Article 53 of the LCA also goes on to say that where the same relief has been sought from an arbitral tribunal, the court must decline the request, except where the relief is beyond the jurisdiction of the tribunal.

Part V   Conduct of Arbitral Proceedings (Articles 18 to 27)

This is another part in which the LCA shares some similarities with the ML, but they also have a number of divergences.

Most importantly, the LCA contains no provision equivalent to article 18 of the ML which requires that the parties must be treated equally and that they must be given full opportunity to present their case. This is a rather fundamental shortcoming in the LCA and it is strongly recommended that this point from the ML be incorporated into the LCA. While, in practice, tribunals should try to ensure that the parties are treated equally and they have full opportunities to present their case, it is important that this requirement be expressly stated in the law as the primary guidance.

In addition, the LCA also contains no provision equivalent to article 19 of the ML, which states that the parties are free to determine the procedures to be followed by the tribunal in conducting the proceeding and in the absence of agreement of the parties the tribunal may determine such procedures as it deems fit, including matters of evidence.

---

[34] Article 53.   [35] Article 17J.

On the contrary, the LCA is rather prescriptive in setting out procedural aspects of arbitral proceedings for tribunals and parties to follow, although it is noted that the LCA gives tribunals pretty broad powers in how to conduct proceedings. For example, articles 45 to 47 set out the tribunal's powers regarding fact finding, collecting evidence, summoning witnesses and calling for expert evidence, if necessary. Article 45 allows the tribunal to meet with the parties or third parties (in the presence of the parties) to verify facts. Article 46 allows the tribunal to call for evidence, including expert evidence, or seek the assistance from the courts in collecting evidence. Article 47 empowers the tribunal to summon witnesses and if they do not appear to ask the court to issue orders requiring the witnesses to appear. All these provisions are rather similar to the position in articles 26 and 27 of the ML. The only major difference is that the LCA does not require, as does article 26(2) of the ML, that the expert witness attend the hearing upon the request of a party in order to be cross examined. It seems that the drafting committee of the LCA did not consider this provision necessary because the tribunal has the power to summon a witness upon the request of a party in any event.

On the place of arbitration, article 11 of the LCA provides for the same position as article 20 of the ML in that the parties are free to agree on the place of arbitration, failing such agreement, the tribunal shall decide. In addition, the tribunal may also decide to meet at any place that it finds appropriate.

On the date for commencement of the arbitral proceeding, there is a slight difference between the ML and the LCA. Unless the parties agree otherwise, under article 21 of the ML, the arbitral proceeding commences when the notice of arbitration is received by the respondent. Under the LCA, this is only true in respect of ad hoc arbitrations. In respect of institutional arbitration, article 31 of the LCA provides that the arbitral proceeding commences when the arbitral institution receives the notice of arbitration. The drafting committee of the LCA must have considered that the arbitral institution should promptly forward the notice of arbitration to the respondent and, therefore, more certainty would be achieved by referring to the date the institution receives the notice. However, it is suggested that this may not be fair to the respondent when there is a gap between the receipt by the institution and receipt by the respondent of the notice of arbitration. Therefore, for consistency, it would seem desirable that the LCA adopt the position in the ML that the proceeding only commences when the respondent receives the notice of arbitration.

On the issue of language of arbitration, article 22 of the ML allows the parties to agree on the language, failing which agreement, the tribunal shall decide. Article 10 of the LCA provides for the same position with respect to disputes with foreign elements or foreign-owned businesses.[36] Regarding the pleadings, article 23(1) of the ML allows the parties, following the notice of arbitration and response thereto, to agree on the timing for submission of statement of claim and defence. Under the LCA, the notice of arbitration is also the statement of claim, which means that the claimant has to submit the full case at the start of the arbitral proceeding. Article 35 of the LCA gives the respondent thirty days to provide the statement of defence and this period may be extended by the arbitral centre. Under article 37 of the LCA, pleadings may be amended during the course of proceeding and the tribunal may disallow such amendments if the tribunal finds that this is abused to delay or thwart the proceeding or exceed the jurisdiction of the tribunal. This is essentially similar to article 23(2) of the ML.

Regarding the hearing, while article 24(1) of the ML allows the tribunal to decide the case only on the basis of written documents unless the parties agree otherwise, article 54 of the LCA implicitly requires that an oral hearing must take place and, unless otherwise agreed by the parties or provided in the rules of the arbitral institution, a thirty-day notice must be given to the parties. The intent behind this mandatory requirement in the LCA may have been to give the parties full opportunities to present their case. However, this rigid requirement makes it inefficient in cases where a documents-only arbitration would be the most efficient method. It is strongly recommended that this provision in the ML be reflected in the LCA to allow the tribunal to decide the cases based on documents only if that is appropriate and the parties do not request otherwise.

Apart from that, the remaining provisions of the LCA on this part are similar to the ML, or only differ in insignificant respects. Both the ML[37] and the LCA[38] provide that all communications supplied by one party to the tribunal must be sent to the other party. On the issue of default of appearance, there are some insignificant differences between the LCA and the ML. Article 25(a) of the ML provides that if the claimant fails to provide the statement of claim, the tribunal shall terminate the

---

[36] For purely domestic disputes, the language of arbitration has to be the Vietnamese language.
[37] Article 24(3).   [38] Article 12.1.

proceeding. There is no equivalent in the LCA simply because, under the LCA, a statement of claim is contained in the notice of arbitration. Both article 35.5 of the LCA and article 25(b) of the ML provide that where the respondent fails to submit the statement of defence, the proceeding shall continue. Article 25(b) of the ML, however, goes on to say that such failure by the respondent shall not be treated as admission of the claimant's allegations, but this is often the practical position in any event. Where the claimant fails to appear at the hearing without cause, under article 56.1 of the LCA, it shall be deemed to have withdrawn its statement of claim and so the proceeding shall be terminated. On the other hand, if the respondent fails to appear without cause, the proceeding shall continue. This is rather different from the position under article 25(c) of the ML, which provides that where any party fails to appear, the tribunal may still continue the proceeding based on the documents and evidence available before it.

Part VI Making of Award and Termination of Proceedings (Articles 28 to 33)

In this part, the LCA and the ML are rather similar in most respects.

Regarding substantive applicable law, article 14 of the LCA requires the tribunal to apply Vietnamese law for domestic disputes. In disputes involving foreign elements, the tribunal shall apply the law chosen by the parties or, if not chosen by the parties, the law the tribunal considers the most appropriate. International practices may be applied where the chosen law is silent provided they do not contradict fundamental principles of Vietnamese law.

Compared to article 28 of the ML, the LCA is similar in that it requires the tribunal to respect the parties' choice of law. In the absence of the parties' choice, the LCA takes a rather direct approach in allowing the tribunal to apply the law it considers most appropriate, while article 28(2) of the ML requires the tribunal to refer to applicable conflict of laws rules to determine the applicable law. However, in the Vietnamese context, this difference in approach may not result in a real difference in outcome in any event, since most tribunals are rather unsophisticated in choice of law exercises and would simply apply the legal system with the most real connection with the transaction anyway. Finally, the LCA does not allow parties to direct tribunals to decide cases as *amiable compositeur*, which is possible under article 28(3) of the ML, and the LCA allows the tribunal to apply trade usages or international practices only where the chosen law is silent and such application does not contradict fundamental principles of Vietnamese law. In this respect, article 28 of the ML gives the parties more freedom than the LCA. However, given the level of development of arbitration in Vietnam, it seems that the LCA has struck a right balance between the parties' freedom and the need to ensure quality and certainty of arbitration in general, given the uncertainty in how tribunals may operate as *amiable compositeur* and apply trade usages and international practices.

Regarding decision-making by the tribunal, both the LCA and the ML provide that decisions shall be made by majority. However, under article 60.2 of the LCA, where no majority is reached, the view of the presiding arbitrator shall prevail. On the other hand, article 29 of the ML allows the presiding arbitrator to make only procedural decisions and only when so authorized by the parties or all members of the tribunal. The LCA therefore gives more weight to the view of the presiding arbitrator than the ML. For efficiency, this seems a more practical approach.

On the issue of settlement, both the ML[39] and LCA[40] provide that the parties can settle any time during the arbitral proceeding, and if so, the tribunal can issue an award to record the terms of the settlement. A difference between the LCA and the ML is that articles 8 and 58 of the LCA both contemplate that the parties can request the arbitral tribunal to mediate the dispute. This is not contemplated in the ML, presumably on the basis that one should not arbitrate a dispute after having been the mediator. In fact, this point is also recognized in article 42.1(d) of the LCA, which does not allow one to be an arbitrator if he or she has been the mediator in the case before the arbitral proceeding is started. Since there is little difference between being a mediator before and after the start of the arbitral proceeding, it is suggested that a mediator should not also act as the arbitrator and therefore, articles 8 and 58 of the LCA should be amended to not allow tribunals to mediate the dispute. Mediation should be handled by different individuals, in order to ensure the independence and impartiality of the arbitrators.

Regarding the form and content of the award, the LCA[41] and the ML[42] are similar in that they both require that the award has to be in writing, stating the date and place of the arbitration, the reasons for the decision

---

[39] Article 30.   [40] Articles 9, 38 and 58.   [41] Article 61.   [42] Article 31.

(unless waived by the parties) and signed by at least the majority of the arbitrators, with explanations for any omitted signatures. However, the LCA is more prescriptive than the ML and article 61 of the LCA provides for more details of the award such as names and addresses of the parties, the tribunal members, summary of the dispute, decision, time limit for executing the decision and cost allocation. Importantly, article 61.3 of the LCA requires that the award must be issued within thirty days from the date of the final hearing whereas no time limit is prescribed in the ML. The intent behind this relatively short time limit in the LCA is to make the arbitration process more time efficient. This indeed puts significant pressure on the tribunal to issue the award within such a short period of time and where this is practically not possible or where further submissions are required tribunals will need to hold an additional hearing. However, in practice, this has not created too much difficulty and tribunals are often able to produce the award within the thirty-day time limit, given most arbitration cases in Vietnam are not yet too complex.

The LCA expressly stipulates in article 61.5 that the award is final and effective from the date of issue. Both the LCA and the ML require that the parties be provided with copies of the award, immediately in the case of the LCA. Neither the LCA nor the ML requires or prohibits dissenting opinions.

On termination of proceedings, both the LCA and the ML provide that the arbitral proceeding terminates when the parties agree or where the claimant withdraws its claim, unless the respondent wishes to continue. In this case the ML,[43] but not the LCA, requires that the tribunal must recognize a legitimate interest for the respondent to obtain a final settlement of the dispute. It is recommended that this requirement in the ML be incorporated into the LCA so that the tribunal has the discretion to consider whether the proceeding should continue once the claimant has withdrawn.

In this part, there are some other differences between the LCA and the ML but most of them do not require any amendment to the LCA. For example, the LCA states that the arbitral proceeding terminates where the claimant ceases to exist without a successor or where the court has found that the tribunal has no jurisdiction or the arbitration agreement is not valid. This is not stated in the ML, but seems to be the practical

[43] Article 32(2)(a).

position in any event. The ML, on the other hand, provides more generally that the proceeding terminates where the tribunal finds that the continuation of the proceeding has for any reason become unnecessary or impossible. This gives broad discretion to the tribunal, which seemed rather unclear to the drafting committee of the LCA and hence it was not adopted. The ML states explicitly in article 32(3) that the mandate of the tribunal terminates upon the termination of the proceeding, except with respect to correction, rectification under article 33 or elimination of grounds for setting aside as allowed by the court under article 34(4). Article 32(1) of the ML also states that the arbitral proceeding comes to an end upon the issue of the final award. This is not expressly stated in the LCA, but is implicitly the position in any event.

On the issue of correction, interpretation of the award and additional awards, the LCA and the ML provide for essentially the same position. They both allow each party, within thirty days from the time of receipt of the award, to request the tribunal to correct typographical, calculation or similar errors or issue an interpretation on a specific point in the award. The tribunal, if it considers the request justified, must issue such correction or interpretation within thirty days. The tribunal may also issue a correction or interpretation on its own initiative within thirty days from the date of the award. In addition, within thirty days from the date of receipt of the award, a party may also request the tribunal to issue an additional award on a point raised in the proceeding but omitted from the award. If the tribunal considers the request justified, it must issue an additional award within sixty days under the ML or within forty-five days under the LCA. These time limits can also be extended by the tribunal. Article 33(5) of the ML goes on to clarify that the provisions on correction and interpretation of an award also apply to an additional award. This is not explicitly stated in the LCA but should practically be the position in any event.

Finally, the LCA has provisions for registration of ad hoc awards to facilitate their enforceability. This is a useful provision which is not present in the ML.

Part VII   Recourse against Award (Article 34)

On this important issue, the LCA is largely similar to the ML, but there are also some differences, especially on the grounds for setting aside an award.

Both the ML and the LCA provide that arbitral awards can be set aside by the courts upon certain grounds, including: (i) the arbitration agreement does not exist or is not valid; (ii) the composition of the tribunal or the arbitral procedure is not in accordance with the agreement of the parties or not in accordance with the law; (iii) the dispute is not within the jurisdiction of the tribunal wholly or partly.

However, some other grounds for setting aside awards are stated in the LCA but not in the ML, and vice versa. First, the ML refers to the ground of lack of capacity of a party,[44] but this is not expressly included in article 68.2 of the LCA, presumably on the ground that this is part of the ground involving invalidity of the arbitration agreement.[45] Secondly, the ML refers to the ground of the party not being given proper notice of the appointment of the arbitrator or the arbitral proceeding or otherwise unable to present its case. The LCA is completely silent on this ground and there is no obvious reason for this omission. Thirdly, the ML refers to the ground that the subject matter is not capable of settlement by arbitration. The LCA does not refer to this, but presumably this is included within the ground of invalidity of the arbitration agreement already. Fourthly, the LCA refers to the grounds of the tribunal basing its decision on false evidence supplied by a party. This ground is completely absent from the ML, as it seems too close to a review of the merit of the dispute, which has been done by the tribunal. It is suggested that the grounds for setting aside awards in the LCA be amended to be in line with the ML, i.e., the ground of a party not being given proper notice of the appointment of the arbitrator or the arbitral proceeding or otherwise unable to present its case should be added and the ground of false evidence should be removed. In addition, the LCA provides for another ground for setting aside the award which is where the tribunal members receive money or other material interests from a party affecting the impartiality of the arbitral award. This is not referred to in the ML, but was considered necessary as a safeguard in the Vietnamese practical circumstances.

Finally, the ML refers to the last ground for setting aside as the award being in conflict with the public policy of the state,[46] whereas the LCA refers to this ground as the award contradicting the fundamental principles of the laws of Vietnam.[47] The concept of public policy does not exist in Vietnamese law but at least some of the fundamental

---

[44] Article 34(2)(a)(i).   [45] Article 18.2.   [46] Article 34.2(b)(ii).
[47] Article 68.2(dd).

principles of Vietnamese law, although not entirely clear, are referred to in the Vietnamese Civil Code. As far as the drafting of the LCA is concerned, there is no need to use the exact literal phrase 'public policy'. The important thing is whether courts will construe the 'fundamental principles of Vietnamese law' in a way supportive of arbitration or not.

In terms of the procedures for applying for the awards to be set aside, the LCA is rather more prescriptive compared to the ML. Under the ML,[48] a party has three months from the receipt of the award to apply for it to be set aside, while, under the LCA, the time limit is only thirty days,[49] although the LCA also contemplates that delay due to force majeure reasons will not count towards this time limit. Article 70 of the LCA prescribes the required content of the application for setting aside of awards, as well as support documents to go with it (including original or certified copies of awards and arbitration agreements, together with Vietnamese translations, if required). Within seven working days after receiving the application, the court must appoint a three-judge panel which shall have thirty days to hold the hearing to dispose of the case.[50] The hearing shall continue even if one of the parties fails to appear, except that where the applicant itself fails to appear or leaves the proceeding without cause or leave of the court, the court will terminate the proceeding. The court will make its decision by majority and will base its decision only on the grounds in article 68 and will not review the merit of the dispute which has been decided by the tribunal. The decision of the court is final. If the award is set aside, the parties can only recommence the arbitration proceeding if they agree; otherwise, they need to bring a court action. Article 71.9 also makes it clear that the duration of time for the arbitral proceeding and the setting aside proceeding will not count towards the limitation period for the action. All such provisions in the LCA are either largely in line with the ML or were added to cater for the peculiar circumstances of Vietnam at the time.

Both the ML and the LCA contemplate that the court may suspend the setting aside proceedings to give the tribunal the opportunity to rectify any procedural irregularities to remove the ground for setting aside the award. The LCA again is more prescriptive than the ML in providing that

---

[48] Article 34(3).   [49] Article 69.1.   [50] Article 71.

the court may only suspend the setting aside proceedings for no more than sixty days and the tribunal has to inform the court of the procedural rectification and the court will resume the setting aside proceeding if no procedural rectification takes place.

Part VIII   Recognition and Enforcement of Awards
(Articles 35 to 36)

The LCA only addresses domestic awards made under the LCA and does not address the enforcement of foreign arbitral awards. Under article 66 of the LCA, a party may submit the award to the judgment enforcement agency for enforcement without the need to go through the court system. This is a strong feature of the LCA which makes an arbitral award equally effective as a court judgment.

The ML on the other hand provides that all arbitral awards can be enforceable through the court system, irrespective of the country in which it was made. An original of the award has to be submitted to the relevant court (together with translation if the court so requires).[51] The court has to enforce the award except where it can refuse enforcement on one of the grounds stipulated in article 36, including lack of capacity of the parties, invalidity of the arbitration agreement, no proper notice of arbitral appointment or proceeding, tribunal having no jurisdiction, composition of the tribunal or arbitral proceeding not in accordance with the agreement of the parties or the law, award not having become binding or having been set aside in the place of issue, subject matter not capable of settlement by arbitration or enforcement of the award being contrary to the public policy of the state.

The issue of recognition and enforcement of foreign arbitral awards in Vietnam is not addressed in the LCA but in the Civil Procedures Code (CPC), which contain detailed provisions on the recognition and enforcement of foreign arbitral awards in Vietnam. It sets out the grounds for refusing recognition and enforcement which are in very similar terms to article 36 of the ML, except that the reference to 'public policy' is replaced with 'fundamental principles of Vietnamese law', as mentioned above. Apart from that, this part in the CPC sets out lengthy provisions on the process and required documentation for recognition and enforcement of arbitral awards through the Ministry

---

[51] Article 35.

Table 12.1 *Model Law provisions that might be considered when the LCA is next amended*

No.	Part	Article	Content
1	III	11(4)	Court is the final appointing authority if the arbitration institution does not appoint arbitrators.
2	III	11(5)	Courts and authorities to have due regard to certain factors in making appointments.
3	III	12	Justifiable doubts as the basis for challenging arbitrators.
4	III	12(2)	Challenging arbitrator on the ground of not having qualification as agreed by parties; a party to challenge its own arbitrator only on the grounds it becomes aware of after the appointment is made.
5	III	14	Court to resolve controversy over arbitrators not continuing *de jure* or *de facto*; arbitrators withdrawing not considered admission of a ground for challenge.
6	IV	17A(1)	Applicant for interim relief to show irreparable harm and reasonable possibility of success on merit.
7	IV	17D	Tribunal to modify interim relief on its own initiative.
8	IV	17H(2)	Court/enforcement agency to be informed where interim relief is modified or suspended.
9	V	18	Parties to be treated equally and be given full opportunity to present their case.
10	V	19	Parties to be able to agree on procedures.
11	V	21	Proceeding to commence upon receipt of notice by respondent (even in institutional proceedings).
12	V	24(1)	Tribunals may decide on the basis of documents only without a hearing.
13	VI		Mediators not acting as arbitrators in the same case.
14	VI	32(2)(a)	Where claimant withdraws and respondent wishes to continue, tribunal has discretion whether to continue.
15	VII	34	Award can be set aside on the ground of no proper notice to parties, but not on ground of false evidence.

of Justice and then Vietnamese courts, with the Supreme Court being the final court of appeal in this matter. In general, the practice of enforcement of foreign arbitral awards in Vietam has varied, with some cases in which the Supreme Court has taken a wide construction of 'fundamental principles of Vietnam', making it difficult for foreign arbitral awards to be enforced.[52]

Conclusion

The above analysis shows that the LCA is largely consistent with the positions or spirit of the ML. For a small number of differences, some are already explicable in the peculiar context of Vietnam while others may be more difficult to justify and so it is submitted that when the LCA is next amended, the ML provisions in Table 12.1 should be considered to be adopted.

The arbitration legislation and profession in Vietnam are still relatively young and there have not been many court cases dealing with some relevant topics. However, if the legislation could be brought closer to the ML, it could be open to Vietnamese courts to interpret the LCA with reference to the philosophy, history and rationale of the provisions in the ML. That would bring the Vietnamese legal framework on arbitration closer to international standards, contributing to the development of the legal system and the economy of Vietnam as a whole.

---

[52] *Tyco Services Singapore Pty Ltd* v. *Leighton Contractors (VN) Ltd* Decision No. 2/PTDS dated 21 January 2003 of the Appellate Court in Ho Chi Minh City, to be found in Do Van Dai and Tran Hoang Hai, *Collection of Vietnamese Courts' Judgments and Decisions on Commercial Arbitration* [In Vietnamese: *Tuyển tập các bản án, quyết định của Tòa án Việt Nam về trọng tài thương mại, NXB Lao Động*] (Vietnam, Labour Publishing House, 2010), 244–52.

Appendix

UNCITRAL Model Law on International Commercial Arbitration

2006 version, with old 1985 version of amended articles reproduced where they used to stand (in bold, in square brackets and indented)

Reprinted with the kind permission of the UNCITRAL Secretariat

(United Nations documents A/40/17, annex I and A/61/17, annex I)
(As adopted by the United Nations Commission on International Trade Law on 21 June 1985, and as amended by the United Nations Commission on International Trade Law on 7 July 2006)

Chapter I   General Provisions

Article 1   Scope of Application[1]

(1) This Law applies to international commercial[2] arbitration, subject to any agreement in force between this State and any other State or States.
(2) The provisions of this Law, except articles 8, 9, 17H, 17I, 17J, 35 and 36, apply only if the place of arbitration is in the territory of this State.

> *(Article 1(2) has been amended by the Commission at its thirty-ninth session, in 2006)*
> [**1985 version of Article 1(2):**]
> [**(2) The provisions of this Law, except articles 8, 9, 35 and 36, apply only if the place of arbitration is in the territory of this State.**]

---

[1] Article headings are for reference purposes only and are not to be used for purposes of interpretation.
[2] The term 'commercial' should be given a wide interpretation so as to cover matters arising from all relationships of a commercial nature, whether contractual or not. Relationships of a commercial nature include, but are not limited to, the following transactions: any trade transaction for the supply or exchange of goods or services; distribution agreement; commercial representation or agency; factoring; leasing; construction of works; consulting; engineering; licensing; investment; financing; banking; insurance; exploitation agreement or concession; joint venture and other forms of industrial or business cooperation; carriage of goods or passengers by air, sea, rail or road.

(3) An arbitration is international if:

(a) the parties to an arbitration agreement have, at the time of the conclusion of that agreement, their places of business in different States; or

(b) one of the following places is situated outside the State in which the parties have their places of business:

(i) the place of arbitration if determined in, or pursuant to, the arbitration agreement;

(ii) any place where a substantial part of the obligations of the commercial relationship is to be performed or the place with which the subject-matter of the dispute is most closely connected; or

(c) the parties have expressly agreed that the subject matter of the arbitration agreement relates to more than one country.

(4) For the purposes of paragraph (3) of this article:

(a) if a party has more than one place of business, the place of business is that which has the closest relationship to the arbitration agreement;

(b) if a party does not have a place of business, reference is to be made to his habitual residence.

(5) This Law shall not affect any other law of this State by virtue of which certain disputes may not be submitted to arbitration or may be submitted to arbitration only according to provisions other than those of this Law.

Article 2 Definitions and Rules of Interpretation

For the purposes of this Law:

(a) 'arbitration' means any arbitration whether or not administered by a permanent arbitral institution;

(b) 'arbitral tribunal' means a sole arbitrator or a panel of arbitrators;

(c) 'court' means a body or organ of the judicial system of a State;

(d) where a provision of this Law, except article 28, leaves the parties free to determine a certain issue, such freedom includes the right of the parties to authorize a third party, including an institution, to make that determination;

(e) where a provision of this Law refers to the fact that the parties have agreed or that they may agree or in any other way refers to an agreement of the parties, such agreement includes any arbitration rules referred to in that agreement;

(f) where a provision of this Law, other than in articles 25(a) and 32(2)(a), refers to a claim, it also applies to a counter-claim, and where it refers to a defence, it also applies to a defence to such counter-claim.

Article 2A   International Origin and General Principles

(As adopted by the Commission at its thirty-ninth session, in 2006)

(1) In the interpretation of this Law, regard is to be had to its international origin and to the need to promote uniformity in its application and the observance of good faith.

(2) Questions concerning matters governed by this Law which are not expressly settled in it are to be settled in conformity with the general principles on which this Law is based.

Article 3   Receipt of Written Communications

(1) Unless otherwise agreed by the parties:
  (a) any written communication is deemed to have been received if it is delivered to the addressee personally or if it is delivered at his place of business, habitual residence or mailing address; if none of these can be found after making a reasonable inquiry, a written communication is deemed to have been received if it is sent to the addressee's last-known place of business, habitual residence or mailing address by registered letter or any other means which provides a record of the attempt to deliver it;
  (b) the communication is deemed to have been received on the day it is so delivered.

(2) The provisions of this article do not apply to communications in court proceedings.

Article 4   Waiver of Right to Object

A party who knows that any provision of this Law from which the parties may derogate or any requirement under the arbitration agreement has not been complied with and yet proceeds with the arbitration without stating his objection to such non-compliance without undue delay or, if a time-limit is provided therefor, within such period of time, shall be deemed to have waived his right to object.

Article 5   Extent of Court Intervention

In matters governed by this Law, no court shall intervene except where so provided in this Law.

Article 6   Court or Other Authority for Certain Functions of Arbitration Assistance and Supervision

The functions referred to in articles 11(3), 11(4), 13(3), 14, 16(3) and 34(2) shall be performed by [Each State enacting this model law specifies the court, courts or, where referred to therein, other authority competent to perform these functions.]

Chapter II   Arbitration Agreement

Option I

Article 7   Definition and Form of Arbitration Agreement

(As adopted by the Commission at its thirty-ninth session, in 2006)

(1) 'Arbitration agreement' is an agreement by the parties to submit to arbitration all or certain disputes which have arisen or which may arise between them in respect of a defined legal relationship, whether contractual or not. An arbitration agreement may be in the form of an arbitration clause in a contract or in the form of a separate agreement.

(2) The arbitration agreement shall be in writing.

(3) An arbitration agreement is in writing if its content is recorded in any form, whether or not the arbitration agreement or contract has been concluded orally, by conduct, or by other means.

(4) The requirement that an arbitration agreement be in writing is met by an electronic communication if the information contained therein is accessible so as to be useable for subsequent reference; 'electronic communication' means any communication that the parties make by means of data messages; 'data message' means information generated, sent, received or stored by electronic, magnetic, optical or similar means, including, but not limited to, electronic data interchange (EDI), electronic mail, telegram, telex or telecopy.

(5) Furthermore, an arbitration agreement is in writing if it is contained in an exchange of statements of claim and defence in which the existence of an agreement is alleged by one party and not denied by the other.

(6) The reference in a contract to any document containing an arbitration clause constitutes an arbitration agreement in writing, provided that the reference is such as to make that clause part of the contract.

Option II

Article 7   Definition of Arbitration Agreement

(As adopted by the Commission at its thirty-ninth session, in 2006)
    'Arbitration agreement' is an agreement by the parties to submit to arbitration all or certain disputes which have arisen or which may arise between them in respect of a defined legal relationship, whether contractual or not.

[1985 version of Article 7:]

[*Article 7. Definition and form of arbitration agreement*]

[(1) 'Arbitration agreement' is an agreement by the parties to submit to arbitration all or certain disputes which have arisen or which may arise between them in respect of a defined legal relationship, whether contractual or not. An arbitration agreement may be in the form of an arbitration clause in a contract or in the form of a separate agreement.]

[(2) The arbitration agreement shall be in writing. An agreement is in writing if it is contained in a document signed by the parties or in an exchange of letters, telex, telegrams or other means of telecommunication which provide a record of the agreement, or in an exchange of statements of claim and defence in which the existence of an agreement is alleged by one party and not denied by another. The reference in a contract to a document containing an arbitration clause constitutes an arbitration agreement provided that the contract is in writing and the reference is such as to make that clause part of the contract.]

Article 8   Arbitration Agreement and Substantive Claim before Court

(1) A court before which an action is brought in a matter which is the subject of an arbitration agreement shall, if a party so requests not later than when submitting his first statement on the substance of the dispute, refer the parties to arbitration unless it finds that the agreement is null and void, inoperative or incapable of being performed.

(2) Where an action referred to in paragraph (1) of this article has been brought, arbitral proceedings may nevertheless be commenced or continued, and an award may be made, while the issue is pending before the court.

Article 9   Arbitration Agreement and Interim Measures by Court

It is not incompatible with an arbitration agreement for a party to request, before or during arbitral proceedings, from a court an interim measure of protection and for a court to grant such measure.

Chapter III   Composition of Arbitral Tribunal

Article 10   Number of Arbitrators

(1) The parties are free to determine the number of arbitrators.

(2) Failing such determination, the number of arbitrators shall be three.

Article 11   Appointment of Arbitrators

(1) No person shall be precluded by reason of his nationality from acting as an arbitrator, unless otherwise agreed by the parties.

(2) The parties are free to agree on a procedure of appointing the arbitrator or arbitrators, subject to the provisions of paragraphs (4) and (5) of this article.

(3) Failing such agreement,

(a) in an arbitration with three arbitrators, each party shall appoint one arbitrator, and the two arbitrators thus appointed shall appoint the third arbitrator; if a party fails to appoint the arbitrator within thirty days of receipt of a request to do so from the other party, or if the two arbitrators fail to agree on the third arbitrator within thirty days of their appointment, the appointment shall be made, upon request of a party, by the court or other authority specified in article 6;

(b) in an arbitration with a sole arbitrator, if the parties are unable to agree on the arbitrator, he shall be appointed, upon request of a party, by the court or other authority specified in article 6.

(4) Where, under an appointment procedure agreed upon by the parties,

(a) a party fails to act as required under such procedure, or

(b) the parties, or two arbitrators, are unable to reach an agreement expected of them under such procedure, or

(c) a third party, including an institution, fails to perform any function entrusted to it under such procedure, any party may request the court or other authority specified in article 6 to take the necessary measure, unless the agreement on the appointment procedure provides other means for securing the appointment.

(5) A decision on a matter entrusted by paragraph (3) or (4) of this article to the court or other authority specified in article 6 shall be subject to no appeal. The court or other authority, in appointing an arbitrator, shall have due regard to any qualifications required of the arbitrator by the agreement of the parties and to such considerations as are likely to secure the appointment of an independent and impartial arbitrator and, in the case of a sole or third arbitrator, shall take into account as well the advisability of appointing an arbitrator of a nationality other than those of the parties.

Article 12   Grounds for Challenge

(1) When a person is approached in connection with his possible appointment as an arbitrator, he shall disclose any circumstances likely to give rise to justifiable doubts as to his impartiality or independence. An arbitrator,

from the time of his appointment and throughout the arbitral proceedings, shall without delay disclose any such circumstances to the parties unless they have already been informed of them by him.

(2) An arbitrator may be challenged only if circumstances exist that give rise to justifiable doubts as to his impartiality or independence, or if he does not possess qualifications agreed to by the parties. A party may challenge an arbitrator appointed by him, or in whose appointment he has participated, only for reasons of which he becomes aware after the appointment has been made.

Article 13   Challenge Procedure

(1) The parties are free to agree on a procedure for challenging an arbitrator, subject to the provisions of paragraph (3) of this article.

(2) Failing such agreement, a party who intends to challenge an arbitrator shall, within fifteen days after becoming aware of the constitution of the arbitral tribunal or after becoming aware of any circumstance referred to in article 12(2), send a written statement of the reasons for the challenge to the arbitral tribunal. Unless the challenged arbitrator withdraws from his office or the other party agrees to the challenge, the arbitral tribunal shall decide on the challenge.

(3) If a challenge under any procedure agreed upon by the parties or under the procedure of paragraph (2) of this article is not successful, the challenging party may request, within thirty days after having received notice of the decision rejecting the challenge, the court or other authority specified in article 6 to decide on the challenge, which decision shall be subject to no appeal; while such a request is pending, the arbitral tribunal, including the challenged arbitrator, may continue the arbitral proceedings and make an award.

Article 14   Failure or Impossibility to Act

(1) If an arbitrator becomes *de jure* or *de facto* unable to perform his functions or for other reasons fails to act without undue delay, his mandate terminates if he withdraws from his office or if the parties agree on the termination. Otherwise, if a controversy remains concerning any of these grounds, any party may request the court or other authority specified in article 6 to decide on the termination of the mandate, which decision shall be subject to no appeal.

(2) If, under this article or article 13(2), an arbitrator withdraws from his office or a party agrees to the termination of the mandate of an arbitrator,

this does not imply acceptance of the validity of any ground referred to in this article or article 12(2).

Article 15   Appointment of Substitute Arbitrator

Where the mandate of an arbitrator terminates under article 13 or 14 or because of his withdrawal from office for any other reason or because of the revocation of his mandate by agreement of the parties or in any other case of termination of his mandate, a substitute arbitrator shall be appointed according to the rules that were applicable to the appointment of the arbitrator being replaced.

Chapter IV   Jurisdiction of Arbitral Tribunal

Article 16   Competence of Arbitral Tribunal to Rule on its Jurisdiction

(1) The arbitral tribunal may rule on its own jurisdiction, including any objections with respect to the existence or validity of the arbitration agreement. For that purpose, an arbitration clause which forms part of a contract shall be treated as an agreement independent of the other terms of the contract. A decision by the arbitral tribunal that the contract is null and void shall not entail *ipso jure* the invalidity of the arbitration clause.

(2) A plea that the arbitral tribunal does not have jurisdiction shall be raised not later than the submission of the statement of defence. A party is not precluded from raising such a plea by the fact that he has appointed, or participated in the appointment of, an arbitrator. A plea that the arbitral tribunal is exceeding the scope of its authority shall be raised as soon as the matter alleged to be beyond the scope of its authority is raised during the arbitral proceedings. The arbitral tribunal may, in either case, admit a later plea if it considers the delay justified.

(3) The arbitral tribunal may rule on a plea referred to in paragraph (2) of this article either as a preliminary question or in an award on the merits. If the arbitral tribunal rules as a preliminary question that it has jurisdiction, any party may request, within thirty days after having received notice of that ruling, the court specified in article 6 to decide the matter, which decision shall be subject to no appeal; while such a request is pending, the arbitral tribunal may continue the arbitral proceedings and make an award.

> [1985 version of Article 17:]
> [*Article 17. Power of arbitral tribunal to order interim measures*]
> [Unless otherwise agreed by the parties, the arbitral tribunal may, at the request of a party, order any party to take such interim measure of protection as the arbitral tribunal may consider necessary in respect of the subject-matter of the dispute. The arbitral tribunal

may require any party to provide appropriate security in connection
with such measure.]

Chapter IVA   Interim Measures and Preliminary Orders

(As adopted by the Commission at its thirty-ninth session, in 2006)

Section 1   Interim Measures

Article 17   Power of Arbitral Tribunal to Order Interim Measures

(1) Unless otherwise agreed by the parties, the arbitral tribunal may, at the
request of a party, grant interim measures.
(2) An interim measure is any temporary measure, whether in the form of an
award or in another form, by which, at any time prior to the issuance of
the award by which the dispute is finally decided, the arbitral tribunal
orders a party to:
  (a) Maintain or restore the status quo pending determination of the
  dispute;
  (b) Take action that would prevent, or refrain from taking action that is
  likely to cause, current or imminent harm or prejudice to the arbitral
  process itself;
  (c) Provide a means of preserving assets out of which a subsequent award
  may be satisfied; or
  (d) Preserve evidence that may be relevant and material to the resolution
  of the dispute.

Article 17A   Conditions for Granting Interim Measures

(1) The party requesting an interim measure under article 17(2)(a), (b) and (c)
shall satisfy the arbitral tribunal that:
  (a) Harm not adequately reparable by an award of damages is likely to
  result if the measure is not ordered, and such harm substantially
  outweighs the harm that is likely to result to the party against whom
  the measure is directed if the measure is granted; and
  (b) There is a reasonable possibility that the requesting party will succeed
  on the merits of the claim. The determination on this possibility shall
  not affect the discretion of the arbitral tribunal in making any subsequent determination.

(2) With regard to a request for an interim measure under article 17(2)(d), the requirements in paragraphs (1)(a) and (b) of this article shall apply only to the extent the arbitral tribunal considers appropriate.

Section 2   Preliminary Orders

Article 17B   Applications for Preliminary Orders and Conditions for Granting Preliminary Orders

(1) Unless otherwise agreed by the parties, a party may, without notice to any other party, make a request for an interim measure together with an application for a preliminary order directing a party not to frustrate the purpose of the interim measure requested.

(2) The arbitral tribunal may grant a preliminary order provided it considers that prior disclosure of the request for the interim measure to the party against whom it is directed risks frustrating the purpose of the measure.

(3) The conditions defined under article 17A apply to any preliminary order, provided that the harm to be assessed under article 17A(1)(a), is the harm likely to result from the order being granted or not.

Article 17C   Specific Regime for Preliminary Orders

(1) Immediately after the arbitral tribunal has made a determination in respect of an application for a preliminary order, the arbitral tribunal shall give notice to all parties of the request for the interim measure, the application for the preliminary order, the preliminary order, if any, and all other communications, including by indicating the content of any oral communication, between any party and the arbitral tribunal in relation thereto.

(2) At the same time, the arbitral tribunal shall give an opportunity to any party against whom a preliminary order is directed to present its case at the earliest practicable time.

(3) The arbitral tribunal shall decide promptly on any objection to the preliminary order.

(4) A preliminary order shall expire after twenty days from the date on which it was issued by the arbitral tribunal. However, the arbitral tribunal may issue an interim measure adopting or modifying the preliminary order, after the party against whom the preliminary order is directed has been given notice and an opportunity to present its case.

(5) A preliminary order shall be binding on the parties but shall not be subject to enforcement by a court. Such a preliminary order does not constitute an award.

*Section 3   Provisions Applicable to Interim Measures
and Preliminary Orders*

Article 17D   *Modification, Suspension, Termination*

The arbitral tribunal may modify, suspend or terminate an interim measure or
a preliminary order it has granted, upon application of any party or, in
exceptional circumstances and upon prior notice to the parties, on the arbitral
tribunal's own initiative.

Article 17E   Provision of Security

(1) The arbitral tribunal may require the party requesting an interim measure
to provide appropriate security in connection with the measure.

(2) The arbitral tribunal shall require the party applying for a preliminary
order to provide security in connection with the order unless the arbitral
tribunal considers it inappropriate or unnecessary to do so.

Article 17F   Disclosure

(1) The arbitral tribunal may require any party promptly to disclose any
material change in the circumstances on the basis of which the measure
was requested or granted.

(2) The party applying for a preliminary order shall disclose to the arbitral
tribunal all circumstances that are likely to be relevant to the arbitral
tribunal's determination whether to grant or maintain the order, and such
obligation shall continue until the party against whom the order has been
requested has had an opportunity to present its case. Thereafter, paragraph (1) of this article shall apply.

Article 17G   Costs and Damages

The party requesting an interim measure or applying for a preliminary order
shall be liable for any costs and damages caused by the measure or the order to
any party if the arbitral tribunal later determines that, in the circumstances,
the measure or the order should not have been granted. The arbitral tribunal
may award such costs and damages at any point during the proceedings.

Section 4   Recognition and Enforcement of Interim Measures

Article 17H   Recognition and Enforcement

(1) An interim measure issued by an arbitral tribunal shall be recognized as
binding and, unless otherwise provided by the arbitral tribunal, enforced
upon application to the competent court, irrespective of the country in
which it was issued, subject to the provisions of article 17I.

(2) The party who is seeking or has obtained recognition or enforcement of an interim measure shall promptly inform the court of any termination, suspension or modification of that interim measure.

(3) The court of the State where recognition or enforcement is sought may, if it considers it proper, order the requesting party to provide appropriate security if the arbitral tribunal has not already made a determination with respect to security or where such a decision is necessary to protect the rights of third parties.

Article 17I Grounds for Refusing Recognition or Enforcement[3]

(1) Recognition or enforcement of an interim measure may be refused only:

(a) At the request of the party against whom it is invoked if the court is satisfied that:

(i) Such refusal is warranted on the grounds set forth in article 36(1) (a)(i), (ii), (iii) or (iv); or

(ii) The arbitral tribunal's decision with respect to the provision of security in connection with the interim measure issued by the arbitral tribunal has not been complied with; or

(iii) The interim measure has been terminated or suspended by the arbitral tribunal or, where so empowered, by the court of the State in which the arbitration takes place or under the law of which that interim measure was granted; or

(b) If the court finds that:

(i) The interim measure is incompatible with the powers conferred upon the court unless the court decides to reformulate the interim measure to the extent necessary to adapt it to its own powers and procedures for the purposes of enforcing that interim measure and without modifying its substance; or

(ii) Any of the grounds set forth in article 36(1)(b)(i) or (ii), apply to the recognition and enforcement of the interim measure.

(2) Any determination made by the court on any ground in paragraph (1) of this article shall be effective only for the purposes of the application to recognize and enforce the interim measure. The court where recognition or enforcement is sought shall not, in making that determination, undertake a review of the substance of the interim measure.

---

[3] The conditions set forth in article 17I are intended to limit the number of circumstances in which the court may refuse to enforce an interim measure. It would not be contrary to the level of harmonization sought to be achieved by these model provisions if a State were to adopt fewer circumstances in which enforcement may be refused.

Section 5   Court-Ordered Interim Measures

Article 17J   Court-Ordered Interim Measures

A court shall have the same power of issuing an interim measure in relation to arbitration proceedings, irrespective of whether their place is in the territory of this State, as it has in relation to proceedings in courts. The court shall exercise such power in accordance with its own procedures in consideration of the specific features of international arbitration.

Chapter V   Conduct of Arbitral Proceedings

Article 18   Equal Treatment of Parties

The parties shall be treated with equality and each party shall be given a full opportunity of presenting his case.

Article 19   Determination of Rules of Procedure

(1) Subject to the provisions of this Law, the parties are free to agree on the procedure to be followed by the arbitral tribunal in conducting the proceedings.
(2) Failing such agreement, the arbitral tribunal may, subject to the provisions of this Law, conduct the arbitration in such manner as it considers appropriate. The power conferred upon the arbitral tribunal includes the power to determine the admissibility, relevance, materiality and weight of any evidence.

Article 20   Place of Arbitration

(1) The parties are free to agree on the place of arbitration. Failing such agreement, the place of arbitration shall be determined by the arbitral tribunal having regard to the circumstances of the case, including the convenience of the parties.
(2) Notwithstanding the provisions of paragraph (1) of this article, the arbitral tribunal may, unless otherwise agreed by the parties, meet at any place it considers appropriate for consultation among its members, for hearing witnesses, experts or the parties, or for inspection of goods, other property or documents.

Article 21   Commencement of Arbitral Proceedings

Unless otherwise agreed by the parties, the arbitral proceedings in respect of a particular dispute commence on the date on which a request for that dispute to be referred to arbitration is received by the respondent.

Article 22   Language

(1) The parties are free to agree on the language or languages to be used in the arbitral proceedings. Failing such agreement, the arbitral tribunal shall determine the language or languages to be used in the proceedings. This agreement or determination, unless otherwise specified therein, shall apply to any written statement by a party, any hearing and any award, decision or other communication by the arbitral tribunal.

(2) The arbitral tribunal may order that any documentary evidence shall be accompanied by a translation into the language or languages agreed upon by the parties or determined by the arbitral tribunal.

Article 23   Statements of Claim and Defence

(1) Within the period of time agreed by the parties or determined by the arbitral tribunal, the claimant shall state the facts supporting his claim, the points at issue and the relief or remedy sought, and the respondent shall state his defence in respect of these particulars, unless the parties have otherwise agreed as to the required elements of such statements. The parties may submit with their statements all documents they consider to be relevant or may add a reference to the documents or other evidence they will submit.

(2) Unless otherwise agreed by the parties, either party may amend or supplement his claim or defence during the course of the arbitral proceedings, unless the arbitral tribunal considers it inappropriate to allow such amendment having regard to the delay in making it.

Article 24   Hearings and Written Proceedings

(1) Subject to any contrary agreement by the parties, the arbitral tribunal shall decide whether to hold oral hearings for the presentation of evidence or for oral argument, or whether the proceedings shall be conducted on the basis of documents and other materials. However, unless the parties have agreed that no hearings shall be held, the arbitral tribunal shall hold such hearings at an appropriate stage of the proceedings, if so requested by a party.

(2) The parties shall be given sufficient advance notice of any hearing and of any meeting of the arbitral tribunal for the purposes of inspection of goods, other property or documents.

(3) All statements, documents or other information supplied to the arbitral tribunal by one party shall be communicated to the other party. Also any

expert report or evidentiary document on which the arbitral tribunal may rely in making its decision shall be communicated to the parties.

Article 25   Default of a Party

Unless otherwise agreed by the parties, if, without showing sufficient cause,

(a) the claimant fails to communicate his statement of claim in accordance with article 23(1), the arbitral tribunal shall terminate the proceedings;
(b) the respondent fails to communicate his statement of defence in accordance with article 23(1), the arbitral tribunal shall continue the proceedings without treating such failure in itself as an admission of the claimant's allegations;
(c) any party fails to appear at a hearing or to produce documentary evidence, the arbitral tribunal may continue the proceedings and make the award on the evidence before it.

Article 26   Expert Appointed by Arbitral Tribunal

(1) Unless otherwise agreed by the parties, the arbitral tribunal
   (a) may appoint one or more experts to report to it on specific issues to be determined by the arbitral tribunal;
   (b) may require a party to give the expert any relevant information or to produce, or to provide access to, any relevant documents, goods or other property for his inspection.
(2) Unless otherwise agreed by the parties, if a party so requests or if the arbitral tribunal considers it necessary, the expert shall, after delivery of his written or oral report, participate in a hearing where the parties have the opportunity to put questions to him and to present expert witnesses in order to testify on the points at issue.

Article 27   Court Assistance in Taking Evidence

The arbitral tribunal or a party with the approval of the arbitral tribunal may request from a competent court of this State assistance in taking evidence.

   The court may execute the request within its competence and according to its rules on taking evidence.

Chapter VI   Making of Award and Termination of Proceedings

Article 28   Rules Applicable to Substance of Dispute

(1) The arbitral tribunal shall decide the dispute in accordance with such rules of law as are chosen by the parties as applicable to the substance of the

dispute. Any designation of the law or legal system of a given State shall be construed, unless otherwise expressed, as directly referring to the substantive law of that State and not to its conflict of laws rules.

(2) Failing any designation by the parties, the arbitral tribunal shall apply the law determined by the conflict of laws rules which it considers applicable.

(3) The arbitral tribunal shall decide *ex aequo et bono* or as *amiable compositeur* only if the parties have expressly authorized it to do so.

(4) In all cases, the arbitral tribunal shall decide in accordance with the terms of the contract and shall take into account the usages of the trade applicable to the transaction.

Article 29   Decision-Making by Panel of Arbitrators

In arbitral proceedings with more than one arbitrator, any decision of the arbitral tribunal shall be made, unless otherwise agreed by the parties, by a majority of all its members. However, questions of procedure may be decided by a presiding arbitrator, if so authorized by the parties or all members of the arbitral tribunal.

Article 30   Settlement

(1) If, during arbitral proceedings, the parties settle the dispute, the arbitral tribunal shall terminate the proceedings and, if requested by the parties and not objected to by the arbitral tribunal, record the settlement in the form of an arbitral award on agreed terms.

(2) An award on agreed terms shall be made in accordance with the provisions of article 31 and shall state that it is an award. Such an award has the same status and effect as any other award on the merits of the case.

Article 31   Form and Contents of Award

(1) The award shall be made in writing and shall be signed by the arbitrator or arbitrators. In arbitral proceedings with more than one arbitrator, the signatures of the majority of all members of the arbitral tribunal shall suffice, provided that the reason for any omitted signature is stated.

(2) The award shall state the reasons upon which it is based, unless the parties have agreed that no reasons are to be given or the award is an award on agreed terms under article 30.

(3) The award shall state its date and the place of arbitration as determined in accordance with article 20(1). The award shall be deemed to have been made at that place.

(4) After the award is made, a copy signed by the arbitrators in accordance with paragraph (1) of this article shall be delivered to each party.

Article 32   Termination of Proceedings

(1) The arbitral proceedings are terminated by the final award or by an order of the arbitral tribunal in accordance with paragraph (2) of this article.
(2) The arbitral tribunal shall issue an order for the termination of the arbitral proceedings when:
   (a) the claimant withdraws his claim, unless the respondent objects thereto and the arbitral tribunal recognizes a legitimate interest on his part in obtaining a final settlement of the dispute;
   (b) the parties agree on the termination of the proceedings;
   (c) the arbitral tribunal finds that the continuation of the proceedings has for any other reason become unnecessary or impossible.
(3) The mandate of the arbitral tribunal terminates with the termination of the arbitral proceedings, subject to the provisions of articles 33 and 34(4).

Article 33   Correction and Interpretation of Award; Additional Award

(1) Within thirty days of receipt of the award, unless another period of time has been agreed upon by the parties:
   (a) a party, with notice to the other party, may request the arbitral tribunal to correct in the award any errors in computation, any clerical or typographical errors or any errors of similar nature;
   (b) if so agreed by the parties, a party, with notice to the other party, may request the arbitral tribunal to give an interpretation of a specific point or part of the award.

If the arbitral tribunal considers the request to be justified, it shall make the correction or give the interpretation within thirty days of receipt of the request. The interpretation shall form part of the award.

(2) The arbitral tribunal may correct any error of the type referred to in paragraph (1)(a) of this article on its own initiative within thirty days of the date of the award.
(3) Unless otherwise agreed by the parties, a party, with notice to the other party, may request, within thirty days of receipt of the award, the arbitral tribunal to make an additional award as to claims presented in the arbitral proceedings but omitted from the award. If the arbitral tribunal considers the request to be justified, it shall make the additional award within sixty days.

(4) The arbitral tribunal may extend, if necessary, the period of time within which it shall make a correction, interpretation or an additional award under paragraph (1) or (3) of this article.

(5) The provisions of article 31 shall apply to a correction or interpretation of the award or to an additional award.

Chapter VII   Recourse against Award

Article 34   Application for Setting Aside as Exclusive Recourse against Arbitral Award

(1) Recourse to a court against an arbitral award may be made only by an application for setting aside in accordance with paragraphs (2) and (3) of this article.

(2) An arbitral award may be set aside by the court specified in article 6 only if:

    (a) the party making the application furnishes proof that:

        (i) a party to the arbitration agreement referred to in article 7 was under some incapacity; or the said agreement is not valid under the law to which the parties have subjected it or, failing any indication thereon, under the law of this State; or

        (ii) the party making the application was not given proper notice of the appointment of an arbitrator or of the arbitral proceedings or was otherwise unable to present his case; or

        (iii) the award deals with a dispute not contemplated by or not falling within the terms of the submission to arbitration, or contains decisions on matters beyond the scope of the submission to arbitration, provided that, if the decisions on matters submitted to arbitration can be separated from those not so submitted, only that part of the award which contains decisions on matters not submitted to arbitration may be set aside; or

        (iv) the composition of the arbitral tribunal or the arbitral procedure was not in accordance with the agreement of the parties, unless such agreement was in conflict with a provision of this Law from which the parties cannot derogate, or, failing such agreement, was not in accordance with this Law; or

    (b) the court finds that:

        (i) the subject-matter of the dispute is not capable of settlement by arbitration under the law of this State; or

        (ii) the award is in conflict with the public policy of this State.

(3) An application for setting aside may not be made after three months have elapsed from the date on which the party making that application had received the award or, if a request had been made under article 33, from the date on which that request had been disposed of by the arbitral tribunal.

(4) The court, when asked to set aside an award, may, where appropriate and so requested by a party, suspend the setting aside proceedings for a period of time determined by it in order to give the arbitral tribunal an opportunity to resume the arbitral proceedings or to take such other action as in the arbitral tribunal's opinion will eliminate the grounds for setting aside.

Chapter VIII   Recognition and Enforcement of Awards

Article 35   Recognition and Enforcement

(1) An arbitral award, irrespective of the country in which it was made, shall be recognized as binding and, upon application in writing to the competent court, shall be enforced subject to the provisions of this article and of article 36.

(2) The party relying on an award or applying for its enforcement shall supply the original award or a copy thereof. If the award is not made in an official language of this State, the court may request the party to supply a translation thereof into such language.[4]

> (Article 35(2) has been amended by the Commission at its thirty-ninth session, in 2006)
>
> [1985 version of Article 35(2):]
>
> [(2) The party relying on an award or applying for its enforcement shall supply the duly authenticated original award or a duly certified copy thereof, and the original arbitration agreement referred to in article 7 or a duly certified copy thereof. If the award or agreement is not made in an official language of this State, the party shall supply a duly certified translation thereof into such language.***]
>
> [***The conditions set forth in this paragraph are intended to set maximum standards. It would, thus, not be contrary to the harmonization to be achieved by the Model Law if a State retained even less onerous conditions.]

---

[4] The conditions set forth in this paragraph are intended to set maximum standards. It would, thus, not be contrary to the harmonization to be achieved by the model law if a State retained even less onerous conditions.

Article 36   Grounds for Refusing Recognition or Enforcement

(1) Recognition or enforcement of an arbitral award, irrespective of the country in which it was made, may be refused only:

   (a) at the request of the party against whom it is invoked, if that party furnishes to the competent court where recognition or enforcement is sought proof that:

   (i)   a party to the arbitration agreement referred to in article 7 was under some incapacity; or the said agreement is not valid under the law to which the parties have subjected it or, failing any indication thereon, under the law of the country where the award was made; or

   (ii) the party against whom the award is invoked was not given proper notice of the appointment of an arbitrator or of the arbitral proceedings or was otherwise unable to present his case; or

   (iii) the award deals with a dispute not contemplated by or not falling within the terms of the submission to arbitration, or it contains decisions on matters beyond the scope of the submission to arbitration, provided that, if the decisions on matters submitted to arbitration can be separated from those not so submitted, that part of the award which contains decisions on matters submitted to arbitration may be recognized and enforced; or

   (iv) the composition of the arbitral tribunal or the arbitral procedure was not in accordance with the agreement of the parties or, failing such agreement, was not in accordance with the law of the country where the arbitration took place; or

   (v)   the award has not yet become binding on the parties or has been set aside or suspended by a court of the country in which, or under the law of which, that award was made; or

   (b) if the court finds that:

   (i)   the subject-matter of the dispute is not capable of settlement by arbitration under the law of this State; or

   (ii) the recognition or enforcement of the award would be contrary to the public policy of this State.

(2) If an application for setting aside or suspension of an award has been made to a court referred to in paragraph (1)*(a)*(v) of this article, the court where recognition or enforcement is sought may, if it considers it proper, adjourn its decision and may also, on the application of the party claiming recognition or enforcement of the award, order the other party to provide appropriate security.

INDEX